The Shadow Warriors of
NAKANO

Other History Titles from Brassey's

Eisenhower: Soldier-Statesman of the American Century by Douglas
  Kinnard

Mitchell's Legacy: Case Studies in Strategic Bombing edited by R.
  Cargill Hall

*Their War for Korea: American, Asian, and European Combatants and
  Civilians, 1945–53* by Allan R. Millett

The Shadow Warriors of
NAKANO

A History of the Imperial Japanese Army's
Elite Intelligence School

STEPHEN C. MERCADO

Brassey's, Inc.
Washington, D.C.

Library of Congress Cataloging-in-Publication Data

Mercado, Stephen C.
  The shadow warriors of Nakano : a history of the Imperial Japanese Army's elite intelligence school / Stephen C. Mercado.
    p. cm.
  Includes bibliographical references and index.
  ISBN 1-57488-443-3 (cloth : alk. paper)
    1. Nakano Gakkō (Japan)--History. 2. World War, 1939-1945--Military intelligence--Japan.
  3. Military intelligence--Japan--History--20th century.   I. Title.
  D810.S7M43 2002
  940.54'88752--dc21

                                                            2002008094

Map by Jay Karamales

Printed in the United States of America on acid-free paper that meets the American National Standards Institute Z39-48 Standard.

Brassey's, Inc.
22841 Quicksilver Drive
Dulles, Virginia 20166

First Edition

10 9 8 7 6 5 4 3 2 1

To the memory of
my grandfather, Ramon C. Mercado,
who inspired and encouraged me
to study Japanese.

Contents

Preface

On 2 September 1945, the Second World War came to an end in Asia as Japanese delegates signed the articles of surrender in the presence of Gen. Douglas MacArthur and other representatives of the victorious United Nations. Marking the surrender ceremony, held on board the mighty battleship *Missouri*, hundreds of American warplanes roared past in a display calculated to impress on the Japanese their utter defeat. Tokyo's ambitions to extend the Japanese empire over all of Asia had turned to ashes.

Japan's crushing defeat seemingly opened the way for the European members of the alliance to restore their own Asian empires. While the United States had promised before the war to grant independence to the Philippines, Washington's European allies intended to resume their rule in Asia. After all, Europe's Great Powers had dominated Asia for more than four centuries. In the years since the Portuguese maritime explorer Vasco da Gama had reached India in 1498, Europeans had conquered or informally controlled nearly all of Asia. Only Japan had succeeded in escaping Western subjugation, building its own empire, and joining the imperial club. Gambling on Hitler's early victories in the Second World War, Japan's leaders had gone to war to dispossess Great Britain, Holland, France, and the United States of their Asian colonies. In the First World War, Tokyo had joined the winning side, sharing with London the Pacific island territories of a defeated imperial Germany. In the Second World War, however, Tokyo had backed the wrong horse. Worse than a crime, to borrow the phrase of a French statesman, Japan had committed a blunder. The fateful choice had taken the Japanese down the path of destruction.

In going down to defeat, however, imperial Japan ended centuries of European rule over Asia. The Japanese military had uncorked the genie of Asian nationalism during the war. Asians had seen the colo-

nial forces of the West swept away by an Asian power. Some nationalists who emerged as leaders in postwar Asia first experienced power
during the war in cooperation with the Japanese. They would lead their
awakened peoples against a return to colonial servitude. Throughout
Asia, the war had fanned the embers of nationalism into unquenchable
fires. The British, Dutch, and French all failed in the years after the
war to rebuild their shattered colonies. The British, having kept their
grip on their great Indian empire during the war, quit the subcontinent in 1947 in the face of implacable demands for independence.
Burma, lost to the Japanese in 1942, chose independence from Great
Britain in 1947. The Netherlands recognized Indonesia's independence in 1949 after failing to reconquer the archipelago. France's
ambitions to reclaim by force of arms its empire in Indochina died in
the defeat at Dienbienphu in 1954.

In time, Tokyo recovered from the war to assert once again its
influence as a major power in Asia. With sovereignty restored in 1952,
Japan won in Asia through trade and aid a position of influence that
today far outstrips that of any of the region's former European masters. Japan long ago lost its wartime empire, but Japanese influence
throughout Asia is now paramount in industry, commerce, and technology. Even in military affairs, the area most strewn with political
land mines, Tokyo is strengthening its presence through participation
in United Nations peacekeeping operations and other international
activities.

Within the Japanese Army, whose victories drove the Western
powers from Southeast Asia at the war's onset, were men who fought
in the shadows as intelligence officers and commandos. They were the
shadow warriors in the Empire of the Rising Sun. Many fell in battle
against U.S. and British forces during the war. Others perished after
the war in Soviet captivity. Some survived to serve alongside American intelligence officers in the shadows of the Cold War against the
Soviet Union. Still others labored to rebuild Japan, regain lost territories, and reclaim Japanese history.

In 1937, the Imperial Japanese Army was already waging an
undeclared war against China while preparing to fight the Soviet
Union. Short on trained men for intelligence missions, the Army
ordered some of its best minds to create an institution for training
men in intelligence gathering and covert action. The following year, a
select band of nineteen reservists began a year of secret training. At

the same time, military authorities also established a research institute outside the capital to support covert operations. By the time the Nakano School, so called for its location in Tokyo's Nakano Ward, disbanded at the war's end in the summer of 1945, dozens of the Japanese Army's top intelligence experts had trained more than twenty-five hundred men. In addition, more than a thousand others had labored in the associated Noborito Research Institute to develop the covert devices and special weapons required by operatives of the Nakano School.

Those men applied their talents to countless missions throughout the world, gathering intelligence from South America to the South Pacific. Some carried out covert operations to undermine European colonial rule in India and Southeast Asia. Others spent the war years along the border of the Soviet Union, keeping watch for signs of a Soviet invasion. In Manchukuo, Japan's puppet empire in northeast China, they tracked down communist guerrillas. Still others waged commando raids in New Guinea, the Philippines, and Okinawa. In the Japanese home islands, the Nakano School's men guarded against domestic opposition to the war and prepared the population to serve as guerrilla auxiliaries in a final showdown.

Even after America's atomic bombs and Soviet entry into the conflict in August 1945 compelled Japan to surrender, the war continued for many of the shadow warriors. Some of the unfortunates taken by the Red Army in Manchuria at the war's end later perished as prisoners in the Soviet Union's vast gulag archipelago. Caught in the Soviet intelligence dragnet in 1945, Japan's last surviving intelligence officers would leave Soviet captivity for Japan only in 1956. The Nakano School's veterans also came to the attention of American intelligence, which was soon seeking to enlist their services in the emerging Cold War. Throughout the Occupation and the Korean War, a number of Japanese military intelligence veterans worked for the U.S. Army.

Once Japan regained her sovereignty, some men continued to apply their talents in postwar Japanese military and police intelligence. Some helped to rebuild ties with Japan's wartime partners. In Burma, for example, "old boys" of the Nakano School helped cement Japan's relations in the 1960s with Ne Win, the Burmese leader who had joined a covert Japanese program before the war. Others labored to recover lost territory, playing prominent roles in the successful campaign to recover Okinawa from the United States and the continuing efforts to pry Japan's lost Northern Territories from Russia. Last, the Nakano School's veterans over the years insisted that the Allied verdict of criminal Japanese aggression in the Second World War was a case of vindictive victor's justice. Certain old boys, with connections to prominent members of Japan's ruling political party and the mass media, worked to sway the public in Japan's debate over the nature of the Second World War. Their view by now has largely eclipsed the verdict, still widely held overseas and by liberals within the country, that Japan had committed a criminal act by waging war.

Despite their wartime exploits and postwar activities, the names of these men have remained largely in the shadows. Only one is widely known outside Japan: Lt. Onoda Hiroo, who made headlines around the world when he emerged alive from the jungles of the Philippines in 1974. While countless articles and books on the Nakano School have appeared over the years in Japan, almost nothing has surfaced elsewhere. It is a striking omission in intelligence history for the Japanese equivalent of America's Office of Strategic Services (OSS) or Great Britain's Special Operations Executive (SOE).

One goal in writing this book has been to bring to light the story of the Nakano School. No less than the men of the OSS or SOE, those of the Nakano School served their country in war and peace. Their story deserves a telling. Another objective is to give readers in the United States and elsewhere a better appreciation for Japanese intelligence. Given both Japan's status as one of the great powers of the twentieth century and the nation's formidable talent for intelligence, the history of Japanese intelligence deserves greater attention. I would be pleased if this book should make some contribution toward fostering such an appreciation.

In closing, I would like to express my appreciation to those who contributed to this endeavor. Chalmers Johnson, Theodore Cook, Bruce Cumings, Carter Eckert, Frank Gibney, and Michiko Wilson offered early encouragement. Edward Drea, Michael Haverstock, Edward Lincoln, Andrew Oros, Richard Samuels, James Slutman, and Nathan White took the time to comment on various chapters. James Zobel guided me through the MacArthur Memorial's archives. In Japan, the late Suetsugu Ichiro, through his assistant Baba Megumi, contacted old comrades from the Nakano School, who sent photographs. Onoda Hiroo, with his wife, Machie, generously offered photographs and critiques of certain manuscript passages. Mary

Sunaga found numerous newspaper articles of interest. To my wife, Rie, I owe much for her corresponding with those in Japan who contributed to this book and for encouraging me from start to finish. Richard Valcourt, my agent, found a publisher for me. Donald McKeon, Donald Jacobs, and other talented staff at Brassey's took the manuscript and turned it into a book. To all those who helped, I am most grateful.

A Note on Sources, Spelling, and Names

I have written this book based largely on Japanese publications, with American archival materials and other sources playing a supplementary role. Memoirs published by veterans of the Nakano School have proven invaluable. Several memoirs offer details found nowhere else. It was my good fortune to find those insider accounts, as well as many other sources, at the National Diet Library in Tokyo. In numerous trips to the city's many fine bookstores over the years, I also came across several valuable books related to the Nakano School and the Imperial Japanese Army.

Searches in the United States also yielded many valuable sources of information. In Washington, D.C., I found much useful archival material at the Library of Congress, the National Archives, the U.S. Army Center of Military History, and the University of Maryland. In Norfolk, Virginia, the MacArthur Memorial's archives proved valuable for its holdings on the Occupation period.

A word is in order regarding dates and military ranks. Times and dates are those of Japan, the protagonist in this story. Hence, I describe Japan as launching its attacks on Pearl Harbor and British Malaya on 8 December (7 December in the United States) 1941. Military ranks are those held by the individuals at the time, not necessarily the highest ranks in their careers.

A brief explanation is also necessary regarding Asian names. Japanese, Chinese, and Korean names appear as they are written in Japan, China, and the Korean peninsula, with the given name following the surname. The spelling of Asian personal and geographic names is a headache, for such names have been rendered in a bewildering number of ways in the West over the years. There is also the issue of geographic names. Cities, provinces, and regions today often have different spellings or, in some cases, entirely different names. My approach here has been to follow certain conventions. I have retained

xvi   A NOTE ON SOURCES, SPELLING, AND NAMES

the older names for places whose names have changed since the Second World War. Hence, for example, I use the name Mukden for the Chinese city known today as Shenyang. I have also used the Wade-Giles system of spelling Chinese geographic and personal names, rather than the pinyin system used by the People's Republic of China today. Wade-Giles, still used by the Republic of China on Taiwan today, was the standard system during the time this story unrolls in China. Korean names are rendered according to a simplified version of the conventional McCune-Reischauer system.

Introduction

The old Japanese veteran waved to the young Filipino children lining his path one spring day in 1996. Onoda Hiroo wore a suit. Around his neck hung a garland of flowers. He had worn a makeshift uniform and carried a rifle embossed with the Japanese Army's imperial chrysanthemum in his previous appearance on the island of Lubang. On that occasion, in March 1974, Onoda had emerged from the jungle to terminate his mission in the Philippines. The media wrote in terms of surrender, but that term was, in Onoda's view, inappropriate. He had not so much surrendered as left the jungle after receiving orders to end his wartime mission. Nearly thirty years earlier, in December 1944, Lieutenant Onoda had flown into Manila in a Japanese military aircraft, fresh from his training in guerrilla warfare at the Nakano School's Futamata Branch. The flight was the first part of a journey that would lead to his assignment on the island of Lubang, in West Mindoro Province.

On 21 May 1996, he traveled to Lubang via Manila. More than fifty years ago, he had flown into the Philippines as a soldier. Now he flew to Lubang as a guest, courtesy of the Philippine Air Force. On that small island, which lies southwest of the main island of Luzon, he laid flowers at a Japanese peace monument erected some years earlier at the spot where a Philippine patrol had shot to death a comrade of his in 1972. Following his visit, Onoda attended that night a reception hosted by the province's governor, Josephine Ramirez Sato. Two days later, the man who had remained in the jungle for nearly thirty years spoke before a local gathering of boy scouts and girl scouts on the importance of nature and of the nature camp for youths he was running in Japan. Once back in Manila, Onoda visited an air force museum, where he saw his old rifle and other military equipment on display in a glass case. He also paid a courtesy call to President Fidel Ramos at Malacanang Palace. In 1974, after emerging from the jungle, he had visited President Ferdinand Marcos before returning to Japan.[1]

Onoda's return to the Philippines, another moment in the public spotlight for Japan's most famous soldier, pointed in a quiet way to the spirit of the Nakano School. The visit showed the determination of leading "old boys" from the school to honor the memory of their fallen comrades without apology. Whatever the verdict of the victors, Japanese soldiers had fought and died for their country in the Second World War. Suetsugu Ichiro, Onoda's classmate from Futamata Branch, had arranged the visit in memory of all who had died during his thirty-year mission.[2]

For Suetsugu and the other organizers, Onoda's return to Lubang was an act of homage, not contrition. Onoda during his week in the Philippines brushed aside questions from reporters on the alleged killing of a number of Filipinos and the theft of property by him and soldiers under his command. He asserted that he had acted as a soldier executing his mission. As for the peace monument, erected where one of Onoda's comrades had fallen in a gun battle, former Prime Minister Fukuda Takeo and other influential Japanese conservatives had arranged to have it built in 1981.

Following his visit to the monument, Onoda presented the local mayor with ten thousand dollars in scholarship money. On the other hand, he ignored the demands of local protesters demanding compensation for his alleged acts against their relatives. In so doing, Onoda and his surviving comrades were acting in line with Tokyo's postwar policy regarding wartime compensation. The Japanese position has long been that Japan settled all accounts through the San Francisco Peace Treaty of 1952 and several bilateral agreements with Asian nations. Onoda, like his government, was prepared to show generosity as a gesture of goodwill. Bowing to various claimants and offering them compensation, however, was another matter.

Onoda's visit to Lubang also showed the importance Asian nations attach to relations with Japan. Philippine dignitaries rolled out the red carpet for these Japanese veterans with access to the corridors of power in Tokyo. In the autumn of 1995, Governor Sato, whose Japanese husband had years ago joined a search party that combed Lubang for Onoda, had led a group to Japan to invite him to pay a return visit. As a token of their esteem, they made him an honorary citizen of Lubang. In Manila, Juan Ponce Enrile and other members of the nation's elite gathered to welcome him. For the Philippines, Japan has long been a vital source of foreign investment and assistance. The ties between Manila and Tokyo, and those between veterans of the Nakano School and Japanese leaders, accounted for the treatment accorded Onoda in 1974 and 1996. How else would one explain the gracious treatment accorded a former Japanese lieutenant by two Philippine presidents and other politicians? Japan, having lost so much in the war, had recovered much in the peace. Among those who had worked to restore Japan's prominent position in Asia were old boys of the Nakano School. In war and peace, Japan's shadow warriors had exercised a considerable influence.

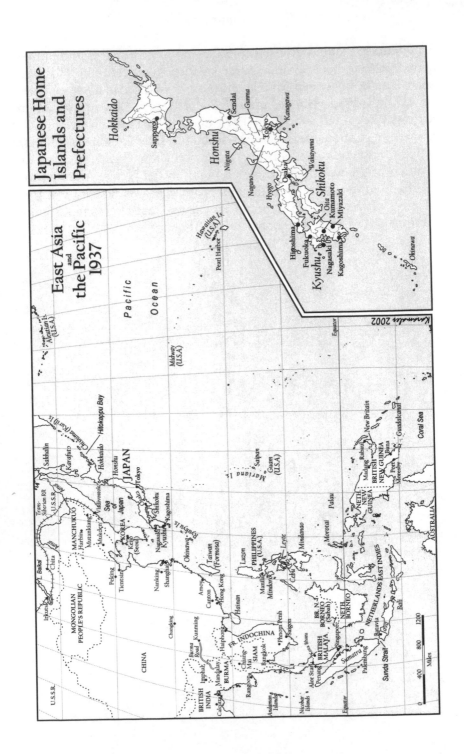

Japanese Home Islands and Prefectures

Hokkaido

Honshu

Sapporo
Sendai
Niigata
Nagano
Tokyo
Gunma
Kanagawa
Hyogo
Osaka
Wakayama
Shikoku
Higashima
Fukuoka
Oita
Kumamoto
Nagasaki
Kagoshima
Miyazaki
Kyushu
Okinawa

East Asia
and
the Pacific
1937

Pacific

Ocean

Hawaiian Is.
(U.S.A.)
Pearl Harbor

Midway
(U.S.A.)

Equator

Kaminski 2002

U.S.S.R.

L. Baikal

Irkutsk

Chita

Aleutian Is.
(U.S.A.)

Trans-
Siberian RR

MONGOLIAN
PEOPLE'S REPUBLIC

Harbin

MANCHUKUO

Mukden
Mutankiang

Peking
Tientsin

Chungking

CHINA

Nanking
Shanghai

Amoy

Canton

Hong Kong

Hainan

Sakhalin
Karafuto

Chishima (Kurile) Is.

Hitokappu Bay

Hokkaido
Honshu
JAPAN
Tokyo

Vladivostok

Sea
of
Japan

KOREA
Keijo
(Seoul)

Shikoku

Nagasaki
Kyushu
Kagoshima

Ryukyu Is.

Okinawa

Taiwan
(Formosa)

Saipan

Mariana Is.

Guam
(U.S.A.)

BRITISH
INDIA

Calcutta

Imphal

Mandalay

BURMA

Rangoon

Chiang
Mai

SIAM

Bangkok

Andaman
Islands

Nicobar
Islands

Kunming

Burma
Road

Haiphong

FR. INDOCHINA

Phnom Penh

Saigon

Alor Star

Penang

BRITISH
MALAYA

Singapore

Sumatra

Palembang

Sunda Strait

Batavia

Equator

Luzon

Manila
Mindoro

PHILIPPINES
(U.S.A.)

Cebu

Leyte

Mindanao

BR. N.
BORNEO
(Sabah)

NETH.
BORNEO

NETHERLANDS EAST INDIES

Bali

Morotai

Palau

Rabaul

Madang

BRITISH
NEW GUINEA

NETH.
NEW
GUINEA

New Britain

Buna

Port
Moresby

Guadalcanal

Coral Sea

AUSTRALIA

0   400   800   1200
Miles

1

PLANNING THE
NAKANO SCHOOL

The Japanese Army had made impressive advances in a few decades. On the heels of the Imperial Restoration of 1868 came the elimination of the samurai class in 1871 and the introduction of conscription two years later. The fledgling national army soon thereafter defeated a rebellious samurai force in a brief civil war as a prelude to greater challenges overseas. Japan's generals led their men to victories on the continent, defeating China in 1895 and Russia in 1905. The Japanese Army also saw action on the Allied side in the First World War and the Siberian Intervention that followed. In 1931, officers of the Kwantung Army in Manchuria seized control of that vast area to protect past gains and prepare a base for the inevitable war to come with the Soviet Union. In six decades, the Japanese Army had grown from its samurai roots to become one of the world's great land forces.

Military intelligence had also matured. The years of *metsuke* and *ninja*, the spies and operatives of feudal Japan, gave way to military attachés reporting to the several sections of Second Bureau, the intelligence nerve center of the Army General Staff (AGS). A number of officers, working in the shadows, had done much to contribute to the military's victories. Colonel Akashi Motojiro, military attaché in Moscow on the eve of the Russo-Japanese War, had directed a campaign of subversion in Europe during the conflict. His network of anti-Russian revolutionaries included one V.I. Lenin, whose Bolsheviks would later bring down imperial Russia.[1] Another intelligence officer, Colonel Doihara Kenji, fluent in Chinese and a master of intrigue, played a major role in the Kwantung Army's seizure of Manchuria. He had contributed in part by spiriting the last emperor of China from Tientsin into Manchuria, opening the way for the Japanese Army to establish the puppet empire of Manchukuo.

Enhanced Intelligence for a New Era

For all the efforts of Doihara and other Army officers who built Manchukuo and dominated northern China, the Japanese position in China seemed under greater threat than ever. For all the local warlords and government officials under Japanese influence, Tokyo was at a loss for how to deal with the rising forces of Chinese nationalism. Generalissimo Chiang Kai-shek from his base in southern China was moving to take control of all China. The Japanese, however, had no intention of abandoning the territory, assets, and privileges accumulated since 1895.

Tokyo would need more muscle both in the field and behind the scenes to handle the growing Chinese threat. The Japanese Army put more resources into intelligence while shifting the entire military into high gear. Shooting between Japanese and Chinese troops near the Marco Polo Bridge in July 1937 soon grew into general fighting, Chiang refusing to bow before Japanese pressure. In September, the Army moved the Military Academy from its cramped quarters in Tokyo to a more spacious campus at Sobudai in nearby Kanagawa Prefecture to train the many more officers required to lead its growing forces. In November, Tokyo activated Imperial General Headquarters (IGHQ) to prosecute the war in China.

The month before, the Army had elevated the status of its covert operations programs by establishing Eighth Section in AGS Second Bureau. With the soldiers bogging down in the vastness of China, the new section was chiefly concerned with developing operations to subvert Chinese resistance. The new section's first chief was Col. Kagesa Sadaaki, an exceptional officer. A native of Hiroshima Prefecture, Col. Kagesa had taken top honors at the General Staff College on his way to becoming one of the Army's top China experts. A steady gaze behind glasses and a prominent forehead enhanced by thinning hair gave him an appearance of forbidding intellect. His superiors had recognized his abilities by sending him to attend lectures on law and political science at Tokyo Imperial University, a mark of distinction given to only a handful of officers.

Prior to heading Eighth Section, Kagesa had run Second Bureau's China Section. In a section better known for hatching plots with Chinese warlords than for rigorously analyzing the shifting kaleidoscope of forces vying for power, Kagesa impressed others with an outstanding intellect. One fellow officer later wrote that "Kagesa alone was different" from the "men of action" in China Section. He was also blunt in speaking his mind, telling his subordinates, "I've come here to educate you numbskulls in China Section." It was Kagesa who induced Wang Ching-wei, a prominent Nationalist leader and rival of Chiang, to break with his party and lead the collaborationist regime installed in March 1940 at Nanking. Kagesa later served as military advisor to Wang's regime.[2]

Developing Technology

The Army, while paying greater attention to subversion, also acted to build a solid technical base for its covert programs. In November 1937, the Army procured land at Noborito, Kanagawa Prefecture, for one of its research laboratories. Known by the name of its location as the Noborito Research Institute, formally called the Army Ninth Technical Research Institute, it was the sole Army technical facility directly under the authority of Second Bureau's Eighth Section.

Within the common wooden buildings clustered on the site, Army technicians would develop the equipment to support the military intelligence activities. Noborito's diligent staff developed various tools of the trade, including secret inks, cameras hidden in cigarette lighters, and explosives disguised as canned food and coal. While the other technical laboratories were conducting research to develop weapons for the front lines, Noborito was shaping the tools for the military's war in the shadows.[3] In total warfare, frontal attacks are insufficient. Blowing up boilers with explosive coal, stealing secrets, and assassinating leaders weakened the enemy from behind. Covert action would help to erase any notion of a sanctuary to the rear of the fighting. During the Second World War, Japanese commandos would use the laboratory's incendiary explosives in raids against Australian and American soldiers in New Guinea. By 1945, the Noborito's ranks would grow to nearly a thousand people.[4]

Planning the Nakano School

In addition to quelling Chinese challenges, the Japanese faced grow-ing problems on the Soviet front. Japanese intelligence officers had been confronting a sealed border in Siberia since 1934. Army plan-ners were grappling with the daunting challenge of subduing the vast-ness that was China without lowering their guard against the Soviet Union. Within Japan, they needed to detect and counter foreign intel-ligence officers and agents.

The Japanese turned to new methods and formations to overcome these challenges. The Army instituted a military courier system in 1934, with the military officers serving as couriers noting the intelli-gence visible from their windows as they rode the Trans-Siberian Rail-way between the Soviet Far East and Moscow.[5] With travel otherwise impossible across Stalinist Russia, riding the train was one of the few ways for officers to gather intelligence. In Manchukuo, the Kwantung Army established a military intelligence unit of White Russians, the Asano Unit, in July 1937. In the event of war, the Russians would scout, raid, and gather intelligence.[6]

In Tokyo, the Army enhanced its counterintelligence (CI) capabil-ities by establishing the Yama (Mountain) Agency. Lt. Col. Akigusa Shun and Maj. Fukumoto Kameji—both experienced in military intel-ligence—were at the center of the planning for the shadowy organiza-tion. Named the Military Administration Bureau Annex, a suitably bland designation to cover its true nature, the Yama Agency began its CI operations in the spring of 1937. Almost no published information has surfaced on the Yama Agency, but its members reportedly engaged in such standard CI activities as detecting illegal radio trans-missions, running agent networks, picking locks, and intercepting the mail. Akigusa served briefly as its first chief before passing the baton in December that year to Lt. Col. Utsunomiya Naokata.[7]

In December 1937, soon after setting up IGHQ and Eighth Sec-tion, the Army established a training facility for covert operations. The Military Administration Bureau began by forming a preparatory com-mittee. Col. Tanaka Shinichi, chief of IGHQ's Army Affairs Section, selected three excellent officers to do the preliminary spadework. They were Lt. Col. Akigusa Shun, recently transferred from his post as chief of Second Bureau's Fifth Section (Soviet Union); Maj. Fuku-moto Kameji, chief of the Special Higher Police (*Tokko*) section of the

Tokyo Kempeitai; and Lt. Col. Iwakuro Hideo, a senior staff officer at the Military Affairs Section. All three officers were well versed in intelligence and political affairs. Earlier that year, the first two had worked under Maj. Gen. Anami Korechika, head of the Military Affairs Bureau, to set up the Yama Agency.[8]

Akigusa Shun, one of the Army's leading Soviet experts, was a natural choice to establish the training center. With a pair of round glasses framing intelligent eyes, longish hair, and a gentle demeanor, Akigusa more resembled a professor or executive than a soldier. For a man whose career was steeped in intelligence work, this was appropriate. He had graduated in 1914 from the Military Academy in the Twenty-Sixth Class, where he studied Russian. Akigusa then served in the Siberian Intervention as an interpreter attached to the Third Division. In Vladivostok and elsewhere, he honed his language skills and area knowledge in work for the Army's Signal Security Agency (SSA). The Army later sent him to the Tokyo School of Foreign Languages in 1926 for another year of training in Russian.[9]

After the language training, he went to Harbin for one year. On his return to Tokyo, he worked on Soviet intelligence in Second Bureau. Ordered back to Harbin in 1933, he served in the Harbin SSA as deputy to Maj. Gen. Komatsubara Michitaro. For nearly four years at the SSA, Akigusa worked on Soviet operations. He worked in particular on organizing the White Russian community. Long familiar with Russians and one of a few Japanese officers who could converse with them at ease in their language, Akigusa organized Manchukuo's disparate White Russian groups into the Bureau of Russian Émigré Affairs, an umbrella organization under Kwantung Army control. His Russian collaborators included Konstanin Rodzaevsky and other members of the Russian Fascist Party.[10] Akigusa also proved resourceful when faced with the Soviet's sealing of the Siberian border. Among his responses was the development of the Harbin SSA's program of document exploitation to mine Soviet publications for useful information. From battlefield orders to daily newspapers and science journals, foreign documents can yield a wealth of intelligence to discerning language officers. When opportunities to recruit agents or interrogate defectors are few, and borders are sealed, document exploitation shines.[11]

Complimenting Akigusa's experience in foreign intelligence was Fukumoto Kameji, a veteran in the field of counterintelligence. Fukumoto, a native of Hiroshima Prefecture, graduated as a Kempeitai (military police) officer from the Military Academy's Twenty-ninth Class in 1917. He also attended a political science course at Tokyo Imperial University, one of a handful of officers in the Army's elite program at Japan's leading university. Later in his career, following his role in establishing the Nakano School, Fukumoto would continue to rise in the ranks of the military police. After appointment in 1940 as the Nakano School's assistant commandant, he would go to China in 1944 to take command of the Kempeitai in Hankow. Near the war's end, Fukumoto would return to Japan for his new assignment in July 1945 as Kempeitai commander for the Sixth Area Army.

Iwakuro Hideo, the third member of the committee, was one of the Army's most gifted strategic thinkers and political operators. Clean shaven, with his hair cropped close and piercing eyes framed by glasses, his intelligence and ambition seemed visible. Iwakuro, like Fukumoto a native of Hiroshima, had graduated with the Thirtieth Class of the Military Academy in 1918. A promising young infantry officer, he gained entry to the elite General Staff College, where he emerged as one of the top students in his class upon graduation in 1926. In his early career, Iwakuro gained administrative experience as a staff officer of the Kwantung Army, Army General Staff, and War Ministry. He was assigned in 1936 to the Military Administration Bureau, where he advocated a more systematic and professional approach to intelligence.[12] In the area of technical support to intelligence, Iwakuro played a role in the creation of the Noborito Research Institute.[13]

Over many years, the Army had never developed a systematic training program for intelligence gathering and subversion. Officers without much experience or training often conducted covert operations in a haphazard manner. In addition, the Army depended on the Amur River Society, other nationalist groups, and overseas Japanese for support. Iwakuro himself had been supporting a non-official training school for pan-Asian activists run by the nationalist Okawa Shumei. A leading scholar of Islam who had seen much of the continent as an executive with the South Manchuria Railway Company, Okawa was one of the better resources whose expertise Iwakuro could tap, but he preferred seeing the Army put intelligence on a sounder footing.[14]

In Iwakuro's view, the Army had too often in the past taken a swashbuckling, irregular approach to operations that ultimately harmed Japan's national interest. Iwakuro explained in a postwar interview how little lasting advantage Japan gained from such ill-considered operations as the Japanese assassination of Korea's Queen Min in 1895. As Iwakuro saw the problem, the Army needed to build a solid foundation for covert action by training "true specialists."[15] So convinced, he submitted in 1936 to his superiors in the War Ministry a memo, "Making Intelligence and Clandestine Affairs Scientific." His call for a more "rational" and "scientific" basis for military intelligence had its effect. In autumn 1937, Iwakuro received assignment as a senior staff officer to the office in Second Bureau elevated in October to Eighth Section (Covert Operations).[16]

Working together, Akigusa, Fukumoto, and Iwakuro prepared to launch the Army's first facility to train intelligence officers. Its name, the Training Center for Rear Duties Personnel, blandly suggested some sort of logistics and was devised to conceal its true function. Using War Ministry funds, the officers procured temporary classrooms in the annex building of the Patriotic Women's Association in the Kudan section of Tokyo, near the Army Officers' Club and Yasukuni Shrine. Hung on the wall at the entrance was the sign "War Ministry Annex." Officers drawn from the War Ministry and AGS served as instructors.

In August 1938, Akigusa took command of the new center, with Fukumoto as his deputy. Akigusa was a fitting officer for the school. He was unconventional for a Japanese Army officer. He abstained from alcohol and enjoyed coffee, when military men drank a good deal of alcohol and most Japanese favored green tea for their caffeine. In his zeal to put the fledgling school on the right track, he reportedly pawned some of his own possessions to supplement the meager official funds. His thinking ran counter to the strong currents of nativism in the Army. Comfortable with the finer points of occidental culture, Akigusa would take his students dining at the imposing Imperial Hotel, a monumental landmark designed by Frank Lloyd Wright, to hone their Western table etiquette. Thinking regular Army officers generally too "stiff-necked" for intelligence work, Akigusa looked to reservists for the school's First Class.[17]

The First Class was a collection of elite students. Recruiters started with a field of six hundred candidates, winnowing it to sixty. Those few received summonses to the Army Officers' Club for discreet examinations. In the end, only eighteen reservists passed the test, a rigorous Kempeitai background investigation, and the course to graduate a year later as members of the First Class.[18] In an army that slighted intelligence in its focus on operations and drilled its recruits in absolute obedience and rote learning, these first students doubtless were different. Yanagawa Motoshige, who secretly landed in Australia during the war to survey the northern beaches, found his classmates to be elite "intellectuals." He further credited his education with instilling in him an elite sense of esprit de corps, the Nakano spirit. Kato Masao recalled that students from Tokyo Imperial University, the apex of Japanese education, were the most numerous members of his class of 150. Students from Takushoku University, strong in international affairs, as well as such other elite schools as Waseda and Keio, were also well represented.[19]

Within the walls of the Nakano School, accomplished athletes rubbed shoulders with stellar students. Narazaki Masahiko was already a swordsman of great promise when he first passed through the front gate. Born in Kyushu's Saga Prefecture in 1922, he had begun from the age of eleven to study kendo, the martial art of the Japanese sword. After years spent practicing his forms and sparring against other athletes, he entered in 1941 a prominent kendo school to master the art. Army officials not long afterwards recruited the budding sword master into the Nakano School.[20]

The Army from the start had great expectations for its new school. Key backers included lieutenant generals Sawada Shigeru and Anami Korechika, respectively the army vice chief of staff and deputy war minister.[21] Lt. Gen. Imamura Hitoshi, head of the Military Administration Bureau, invited the entire First Class to dine with him at the Officers' Club at the start of their training in 1938. Imamura, a veteran of Anglo-American affairs who would later lead the invasion of the Philippines in 1941, spoke to them of his past intelligence duties in Britain and India. In October 1938, Lt. Gen. Tojo Hideki, then Vice-Minister of War, paid a visit to those first few students. He returned in late 1940 as War Minister to attend a following class's graduation ceremony.[22]

Akigusa's sophistication and commitment to intelligence had brought him to the position of the new center's director, but the plotting of a subordinate soon unseated him. Maj. Ito Samata was an ardent nationalist. In an earlier age, he would have been one of the insurgents battling under the slogan of "Revere the Emperor, expel the barbarians." Ito had come to Tokyo from duty in Manchukuo to take charge of education at the center.[23] A native of Yamaguchi Prefecture who graduated with the Thirty-seventh Class from the Military Academy, he had been a classmate of several young officers executed for staging a failed coup d'etat in the February 26 Incident of 1936. Ito's fiery character had saved his life. Before his classmates had led their troops into the streets of Tokyo that snowy day, Army authorities had already identified him in advance as a dangerous element and transferred him from Tokyo to Manchukuo.

Akigusa represented the rational current in modern military intelligence. He had expressed the view, when the currents of imperial fanaticism were surging, that the supposedly divine Emperor Hirohito was a man like any other. Ito, on the other hand, was a man of the nativist martial tradition. He was known to his students at the training center as a modern Yoshida Shoin, a fellow patriot of Yamaguchi Prefecture revered as a martyr of the Meiji Restoration. An accomplished swordsman, Ito was rumored to have cut down eighty-one spies and guerrillas in Manchukuo. One could say that his swashbuckling approach was what such officers as Akigusa and Iwakuro were working to overcome in military intelligence. Ito, who had personally opposed the center's creation, had apparently taken his position there through the intervention of his patron, Lt. Gen. Ushiroku Jun, chief of the Military Affairs Bureau and one of the most vocal proponents of expanding the war in China.

Ito's actions brought about Akigusa's removal early in 1940. The intemperate major hatched a plot to raid the British Consulate in Kobe, convinced that Great Britain was manipulating Japan's war in China to its advantage. He had planned with a number of the students to seize the consulate, force his captives to confess to British misdeeds, and make public his findings. He thus hoped to fan nationalist emotions against Great Britain and those internationalist Japanese politicians and businessmen he viewed as their lackeys. But Ito's plot failed when a former student on assignment in the Kobe area, possibly serving in the Yama Agency, detected it. The Kempeitai, alerted to the plot, took Ito into custody at a Kobe hotel on 4 January 1940 and rounded up his student followers the next day at a nearby Shinto shrine. The Army avoided bringing attention to its new covert training center by compelling Ito to go quietly on the reserve list. The two students involved with him were quietly sent on overseas assignments. Akigusa, who had been promoted to full colonel the previous year, took responsibility for his subordinate's action by accepting a transfer. In March 1940, the Army assigned him to Berlin as chief of the Hoshi (Star) Agency under cover as an official of the Manchukuo Legation.[24]

Training in Nakano: Suits and Disguises

Akigusa's successor was Maj. Gen. Kitajima Takumi, a native of Kyushu's Saga Prefecture. Kitajima had graduated in the Military Academy's Twenty-fifth Class in 1913 and the General Staff College's Thirty-seventh Class in 1925. His previous assignments had included a stint as instructor at the General Staff College. During his tenure, the school's administration changed hands. In August 1940, a year after the school's move to Army land in Nakano Ward, AGS took over responsibility for the school's administration from the War Ministry. The Training Center for Rear Duties Personnel was now known as the Army Nakano School.[25]

In April 1939, the faculty and students had moved from the Patriotic Women's Association annex in Kudan to Nakano Ward, in the northwest area of Tokyo. A sign bearing the inscription "Army Communications Research Institute" appeared one day at the main gate. The buildings within the compound, one or two stories high, built of wood, topped with roof tiles, were unexceptional. Formerly the site of a military telegraph unit, the compound sprouted telegraph poles. The school's appearance suggested some sort of communications facility. Accordingly, the school was designated the Army Communications Research Institute.[26] The compound seemed common enough. What was uncommon was the appearance of the young men who passed through the gate. In and out of the compound strolled Japanese who seemed not at all the military type. At a time of increasing regimentation in Japanese society, with drab nationalist garb and shaved heads for men increasingly common, they sported fashionable haircuts and dressed in suits. Enduring the silent stares of passersby and the rebukes of policemen became part of their experience.

As striking as their appearance was their education, based on the theory of total war. The experience of the First World War, with both sides mobilizing their civilian populations, industries, and technology for war, gave rise in Germany and elsewhere to the theory of total war. In war, nations would now have to develop their resources in every respect. Military planners would thus have to take into account everything from industrial policy to education. Training officers and securing weapons would no longer suffice. Many Japanese officers embraced the writings of Gen. Erich von Ludendorff and other military theorists who were propounding this way of thinking.[27]

Total war, among its demands, called for a new way of intelligence. Simple tactical intelligence, such as counting the number of enemy troops or ships, was no longer sufficient. Intelligence increasingly required an understanding of politics and religion. While much of the Japanese Army viewed such broad strategic intelligence with suspicion, the Military Administration Bureau included men who grasped its importance. Kimura Takechiyo, one of the students of the Nakano School, remembered that his instruction included the lessons of both the contemporary German theorist Ludendorff and the ancient Chinese strategist Sun Tzu. Kimura learned at the Nakano School that a military assault with weapons blazing should be the last resort against an enemy. An approach based on religion and other elements of intelligence operations, broadly understood, came first. Knowing one's enemy, one could use that knowledge covertly to foment religious strife, aggravate class conflict, or sap economic strength.[28] Sakai Kiyoshi, another student, heard from his instructors that a single spy was more valuable than a division of soldiers.[29]

In their temporary rooms in Kudan, then within the walled compound at Nakano, the school's first students learned the arts of covert action. The school's administrators scrambled to put together a curriculum for which the Japanese Army had no precedent. For their model, the Nakano School's administrators turned to Col. Akashi Motojiro, using as a text his secret report on his subversive activities during the Russo-Japanese War. The students found him an inspiration. The valedictorian at the graduation ceremony in late 1940, with War Minister Tojo Hideki attending, spoke of his wartime exploits. Akashi served as a model not only for his successes but also for the lack of glory a shadow warrior should expect. While the generals and frontline officers paraded as heroes in Tokyo at the end of the Russo-Japanese War, Akashi returned to Tokyo without fanfare.[30] In the same way, the Nakano School's shadow warriors were to execute their missions without expecting public honors.

The several dozen school military officers lecturing at the school included many of the Army's intelligence experts. Fukumoto lectured on ideology. Iwakuro taught intelligence theory. Maj. Fujiwara Iwaichi of Second Bureau's Eighth Section spoke to the students on propaganda. Lt. Col. Yano Muraji, who would later join Gen. Douglas MacArthur's Japanese auxiliary staff during the Occupation, lectured on the United States.[31] Officers on duty at the War Ministry and Army General Staff visited Nakano to brief the students on such topics as Hitler's invasion of Poland, the political situation in the United States, and the war in China. The students also studied Lawrence of Arabia's exploits among the Arabs against the Ottoman Empire in the First World War, pondered the implications of India's caste system for British rule, and took notes on the role of intelligence in administering occupied territory.

General education included ideology, psychology, aviation, marine navigation, and pharmacology. Foreign studies covered the Soviet Union, Western Europe, the United States, Southeast Asia, and China. Students also studied Russian, Chinese, English, Malay, or another language as preparation for overseas missions. They took special courses in covert action, propaganda, economic subversion, CI, secret weapons, and codes. They also learned to photograph documents surreptitiously, don disguises, and crack safes. For such unconventional courses, the Army recruited even career criminals to fill out their teaching ranks.[32] Interestingly, training at the Nakano School resembled that through which America's Office of Strategic Services (OSS) put its officers at Camp X in Canada and training sites in the United States. Let us call it a case of parallel evolution in the history of intelligence.

Kato Masao, who entered the Nakano School after graduating from Waseda University, learned the various skills of the shadow warrior. Outside the compound, he learned such skills as how to pass through streams to evade military dogs. He and his classmates also practiced assessing, infiltrating, and demolishing targets. In one exercise, instructors ordered Kato and his classmates in November 1944 to conduct a mock nocturnal raid against the air defense school at Mikatagahara, Shizuoka Prefecture. After several days of scouting the area and putting together a plan, the students stealthily approached the school late one night. If the team ran into a patrol, the exercise would end in failure. Creeping past the barracks and other buildings,

Kato made his way to the airfield. Reaching the control room of the main building, he left behind in large characters a message in chalk that he had infiltrated the heart of the compound.[33]

Yanagawa Motoshige was another of those promising young soldiers who went through the Nakano School's special training. In the autumn of 1939, while with the Second Division, he had received an order to report to the War Ministry. There he accepted the challenge of becoming a covert warrior who would, if need be, lay down his life without glory or recognition for the empire. At the Nakano School, Yanagawa received the pseudonym Yanai Mamoru. For the entire year he trained there, he went by that name; each of the twenty-six members of his section lived and trained together without knowing the true identity of his comrades. Yanagawa never did learn, apart from the few with whom he worked later, the true names of those he knew at the Nakano School.

Issued a serge black suit, Yanagawa shed his military uniform and grew his hair to civilian length. In the school compound, he studied the tricks of the intelligence trade. He practiced the art of disguise. A false beard, some fake teeth, and a pair of glasses could transform a man's appearance. He also learned the basics of code breaking and encryption. Then there were the techniques of secret communications, such as how to use invisible ink. His instructors also introduced him to such tools as a camera attached to a man's waistband and operated by a vest button, and a camera disguised as a cigarette lighter. There was even an 8-mm camera hidden in a briefcase. But gathering intelligence was not the whole game. The Nakano School also taught Yanagawa how to handle explosives, incendiaries, and time bombs. For a quieter means of assault that promised results no less lethal, the school taught Yanagawa how to handle bacteria. Some microbes released from an instrument resembling a fountain pen into an occupied town's well could incapacitate or kill the enemy.

Yanagawa's training also included practice in a variety of military arts that, if mastered, would make him a formidable operative. He trained in operating automobiles, aircraft, and tanks. He rode horses and swam laps. He also practiced the time-honed Japanese martial arts of judo, karate, and kendo. The young man in the black serge suit had seen and learned a great deal in little more than a year. His teachers had also drilled into him the lessons of sacrifice underpinning "spiritual education" at the school. The result, for Yanagawa and others, was a sense that they were elite defenders of the empire. Indeed, as he later wrote, he and others emerged with a sense of "Nakano-ism." Theirs was the covert way of the warrior.[34]

Indeed, the Nakano School's administrators worked to mold students who were both patriotic and professional. Spiritual education was a major influence. Immediately inside the front gate, to the right, stood the Nanko Shrine. It was not by chance that the school's administrators had placed in so prominent position a shrine of Kusunoki Masashige, a general of the fourteenth century who had died in battle in the service of his emperor. Instructors also raised as another moral example Yoshida Shoin, the samurai executed in the last years of Tokugawa rule for hotly demanding that Japan change to meet the Western threat.[35] The view was that a competent officer, well trained in the technical aspects of his craft, should still be a Japanese patriot. Kuwahara Takeshi described aspects of the spiritual education that he and his classmates received. Each morning, students would bow in reverence in the direction of the Yasukuni Shrine. Every evening, they would show their respect by bowing towards the Imperial Palace. While serious, however, the students were not monks. Following their evening ritual, the students would often head for the bright lights of Ginza or some other pleasure district.[36]

At the same time, the Nakano School demanded flexibility and initiative, qualities contrary to the spirit of unquestioningly executing orders that instructors drilled into the officers and men elsewhere in the Army. Nakano's teachers had the trainees grow their hair long, dress in suits, and abandon the stiff military bearing that marked men as regular officers in and out of uniform. Students once taken to task in prior military training for executing a poor salute or some other lapse in etiquette now had to resist the urge to salute their superiors or betray other signs of military bearing. Contrary to rote learning and set answers found elsewhere, the Nakano School encouraged debate and unconventional solutions. Only those committed need stay the course, for the school's administrators allowed students to return to their units on request. No other military institution resembled it.

Graduating Under Darkening War Clouds

The Nakano School's first students graduated in the summer of 1939, a time of peril and promise for the Japanese Empire. Japanese and

Soviet forces in May had clashed on the border of Manchukuo and Outer Mongolia, which some Japanese officers had welcomed as a chance to test the strength and resolve of the Red Army. The fighting, which by July had escalated to the level of a small war, would end in crushing defeat for Japan's Kwantung Army by year's end. As the Nakano School's First Class worked at various postgraduate assignments in Japan as final preparation for overseas assignments, Germany invaded Poland in September. Great Britain and France, whose leaders had vacillated in the face of previous provocations, finally declared war in response to Hitler's latest aggression. The Second World War had begun in Europe.

In Asia, Japan suffered a diplomatic reversal when Hitler betrayed the spirit of Berlin's Anti-Comintern Pact with Tokyo by signing in August a nonaggression pact with Moscow while Soviet tanks were overrunning Japanese positions at Nomonhan. As the First World War had afforded Japan the occasion to divest imperial Germany of her Asian colonies, however, so the latest war in Europe temptingly offered Japan the chance to seize the Asian possessions of the other Western powers. On Taiwan, Japan's colonial outpost off the south China coast, Imperial General Headquarters established in December 1940 the Taiwan Army Research Department to gather the intelligence needed to fight in Southeast Asia. Germany seemed about to conquer Europe, so why not drive the colonial garrisons of England, France, and Holland from Asia? As the leading light of Asia, in Tokyo's view, what reason did Japan have to honor the territorial integrity of Europe's colonies in her own backyard?

In June 1941, Hitler invaded the Soviet Union. His early successes against Stalin encouraged the Japanese to think that the Russian Far East could be their prize as well. How far could they go? The Soviet Maritime Province? Lake Baikal? All the way west to the Urals separating European Russia from its Asian lands? If the chance arose, and Hitler conquered European Russia, why leave Siberia in Stalin's hands? The Russians had taken the region by force from the Chinese and various local peoples over the past hundred years. What moral claim had they to the vast expanse of Asian territory? Would not a Russia with borders pushed back to the European heartland put an end to the Russian menace that had loomed over the Japanese archipelago since the nineteenth century? Such was the thinking in Tokyo.

Japanese leaders felt pressure to act on the changing world situation before they missed their opportunity. The war would give Japan the opportunity to reverse a century of Western encroachment in Asia. In the Opium War (1840–1842), Great Britain had humbled China, taken Hong Kong, and flooded China with opium and industrial goods. Czarist Russia had negotiated away from China vast territories to the north of Manchuria. France had wrested from Chinese control the traditional vassal nations of Vietnam, Laos, and Cambodia. Germany had seized the Chinese port of Kiaochow and acquired a number of islands in the South Pacific. Even the United States had built an Asian empire, snatching the Philippines from a moribund Spanish Empire. The Japanese had little respect for the West's ill-gotten gains. Takaoka Daisuke, an expert on South Asia and a legislator of Japan's Imperial Diet, opined that the West's Asian colonies stemmed from an "age of piracy" following Marco Polo's published account of his Asian travels in the thirteenth century.[37]

The competition for colonial possessions had brought nearly all of Africa and Asia under European rule. Japan's rulers had decided to make Asia their own. As the Western journalist John Gunther noted in his sweeping work *Inside Asia*, published at the end of the 1930s: "Japan was late to the imperialist feast, and perhaps her methods were more brusque, more brutal and direct. *But in essence Japan did nothing that the other powers had not done.* No European hands were clean." [italics in the original][38]

Lieutenant Inomata Goes North

Lt. Inomata Jinya, a member of the Nakano School's inaugural class, joined Fifth Section (Soviet Union) of Second Bureau at the end of his training in 1939. A native of Fukushima Prefecture, Inomata had the steady temperament for which Japanese from the Tohoku region in northeast Japan are known.[39] While in Fifth Section, he gained experience and gathered intelligence on the Soviet Union while riding the Trans-Siberian Railroad as a courier between Japan and Europe. He then received an assignment to Manchukuo. Inomata joined the Kwantung Army Headquarters Intelligence Section (KAHIS) at Harbin, working under Lt. Col. Shiraki Suenari. He then became the first chief of the Kwantung Army's First Field Intelligence Unit. He concurrently headed the Special Communications Unit. The second unit's purpose was to serve as a dedicated intelligence conduit between KAHIS and its field units; communicate with agents in the Soviet Union; carry out guerrilla training; and conduct communications research and development. Inomata had also been senior officer of the KAHIS Fourth Section when he took charge of the communications unit.

While serving in Manchukuo, Inomata suffered from an intelligence reversal that hit the Kwantung Army a number of times over the years. Inomata was leading a number of operatives he had trained to the Soviet border for a covert infiltration when headquarters called them back. The Kwantung Army had intercepted a Soviet communication that indicated that the Soviets had learned of Inomata's mission and knew that he was en route to the border. A later investigation determined that White Russians working for the Japanese had betrayed the mission.[40] The Kwantung Army's problem with White Russians and other collaborators in Manchukuo was due in part to aggressive Soviet efforts to penetrate Russian expatriate communities, including those in Manchukuo from which the Kwantung Army drew many of its agents. Part of the problem, however, stemmed from the arrogance and insensitivity with which some Japanese treated subject races in Manchukuo. Such treatment earned the Kwantung Army numerous betrayals by White Russians in its service, including those who would betray Japanese intelligence officers to the Soviet Union after the Red Army overran Manchuria in the final days of the Second World War.[41]

Lieutenant Kimura Goes to Latin America

While Inomata and other graduates of the Nakano School were operating against the Soviets, some were working against the U.S. target in the Western Hemisphere. The Army, concerned above all with preparing for war with the Soviet Union and ending the fighting in China, still had to watch the United States. As Russian expansion to the east had led to competition with Japanese ambitions on the Asian continent, so American expansion to the west had been a source of conflicts with Japan.

The United States, seizing vast territories in the Mexican War of 1846–48, had expanded across North America to the shores of the Pacific Ocean. In 1853, Commodore Matthew Perry led a fleet of warships to press the Japanese for trade. The United States then acquired territories in the Pacific. In what for Washington was a "splendid little war," the United States seized the Philippines from Spain in 1898. Only three years after Japan had taken Taiwan from China, Japanese leaders found the American empire had expanded to their backyard. That same year, the United States established a formal protectorate over Hawaii. In 1903, after Colombia's refusal to permit the United States to build a canal across its isthmus of Panama, President Theodore Roosevelt encouraged a revolt in that Colombian province that led to the separation of Panama and permission from the new republic to begin constructing a canal.

The Panama Canal greatly reduced the sailing time for American warships and troops from the Atlantic to the Pacific, thereby posing a maritime threat to Japan. The canal was an American military threat by sea, as the Trans-Siberian Railroad constituted a Russian military threat by land. The American challenge grew in the first decades of the twentieth century. The two powers had kept their relations on an even keel in the early decades of the competition in Asia. In the Taft-Katsura Agreement of July 1905, Washington had recognized Japan's hegemony on the Korean peninsula in exchange for Tokyo accepting American rule over the Philippines. In November 1917, the two nations had sought common ground in the Lansing-Ishii Agreement, by which Washington recognized Tokyo's "special relations" on the continent arising from Japan's "geographical propinquity." In return, Tokyo pledged to honor the "open door" in China, meaning an equal opportunity for all the great powers to exploit commercial opportunities there.

Nevertheless, Japan's relations with the United States grew increasingly strained. President Theodore Roosevelt had welcomed Japan's victory over Russia in 1905 as a check on Moscow's expansion in Asia. But Washington eyed with suspicion Japan's dominant military presence among the Allies during the Siberian Intervention. The United States later simply refused to recognize Manchukuo, then opposed Japan's undeclared war against China. This course of events moved military planning. Following the Washington Conference of 1921, the Japanese Army had added the United States to its list of hypothetical enemies and drafted plans for an invasion of the Philippines.[42] By the time the Nakano School's First Class graduated in 1939, war against the United States had become a distinct possibility.

Lt. Kimura Takechiyo, a fellow member with Inomata of the First

Class, drew as his intelligence target the United States. Kimura, a native of Shikoku, had graduated in 1937 from the pinnacle of Japanese education, the elite Tokyo Imperial University Law Faculty. He briefly became a cadet at the Military Academy before entering the Training Center for Rear Duties Personnel.[43] His training finished, Kimura joined Second Bureau's Covert Operations Section.[44] Kimura, along with another classmate, then went under cover as a clerk to the military attaché office of the Japanese legation in Mexico City.[45] At the attaché office, Kimura worked under the attaché, Col. Nishi Yoshiaki. Nishi, who had lectured at the Nakano School on the United States, would later direct "Tokyo Rose" and other Japanese-American radio announcers in his work on radio propaganda as chief of the Covert Operations Section.[46]

Kimura's main target in gathering intelligence, according to different sources, was either Central America or Mexico.[47] If Central America were the target, then the Panama Canal would have been the main object of his efforts. Since a classmate, Lt. Makizawa Yoshio, was working on the Panama Canal target from Colombia, however, it seems reasonable to assume that Mexico was Kimura's focus.[48] Of likely interest to Japanese intelligence was determining who in Mexico were sufficiently hostile to the United States or sufficiently opportunistic to work as Japanese agents. As Colonel Akashi had worked with Finns and Poles in the Russo-Japanese War, so Lt. Kimura could have been working to make Mexico a base for covert action against the United States. Another concern was that, in the event of war, Japan's extensive intelligence operations inside the United States, directed from the Japanese Embassy in Washington and operating from the various consulates and semiofficial organs, would be closed. Any operatives who remained in place would have difficulty passing intelligence from American soil. Mexico and Canada, on the borders, were obvious candidates for wartime intelligence bases.

In any event, Kimura had to curtail his assignment when Japan attacked Pearl Harbor, an act applauded by many people in Latin America who resented the American colossus to the north. In Colombia, for example, Lieutenant Makizawa was greeted on the streets with cheers after people there heard of the attack on the Hawaiian naval base.[49] Despite the short period spent on the ground, Kimura had reportedly done well. The details, regrettably, remain obscure.[50] In any event, Kimura was one of five intelligence officers from the

Nakano School repatriated from the Western Hemisphere in 1942, when the Allies and Axis exchanged diplomats and other noncombatants at Lourenço Marques in Portuguese East Africa. Kimura and the others arrived at Singapore, renamed Shonan (Japanese for the "Shining South") following its capture by the Japanese earlier in the year, on 9 August 1942 before reaching Japan on 20 August.

Lieutenant Abe in India

Germany's war in Europe gave Japan an opportunity to seek advantage in Asia. In the First World War, Japan had taken Germany's island territories in the South Pacific. With the stakes much higher this time, the Japanese Army was gathering intelligence on Great Britain's colonies while preparing to strike south. Lt. Abe Naoyoshi, a reservist and former student of the humanities at Rissho University, had graduated in the Nakano School's First Class. He was going to carry out his mission in India.[51]

The scholarly Abe before leaving the Nakano School had requested India as his top choice for a first overseas assignment. His pick, bypassing such obvious choices for a Japanese intelligence officer as Manchukuo or China, was inspired. British India, encompassing the territories of today's Pakistan, Bangladesh, and Sri Lanka as well as India, was the crown jewel of the British Empire, an abundant source of wealth and soldiers to support London's global ambitions. India occupied a strategic position, bordering China and separated from the Soviet Union only by Afghanistan. Once Japan entered the war, India would also be an Allied staging area for covert operations in the Far East. The target was an important one. Abe, who had studied religion at university, also found India an object of personal attraction as the birthplace of Buddhism and a land of Hindus, Muslims, and other faiths.[52]

Abe, between graduation and his voyage to India, reported for duty to Second Bureau for orientation. He entered the British section of Second Bureau's Sixth Section, under Lt. Col. Sugita Ichiji, one of the Army's few Anglo-American intelligence experts. Sugita's British section was smaller than most sections in Second Bureau, consisting then of a single subordinate staff officer, a lone translator, and one clerical worker. Abe began by reading into his account, poring over the reports of successive resident army officers. Much of the information came from Japanese businesses and individuals resident there. Abe worked hard, determined to be nothing less than the Army's leading "India hand" before going on his assignment. While in Second Bureau, he also assisted in the analysis of British affairs. He worked at one point on the confrontation between Japan and Great Britain over the British settlement at Tientsin, where the Japanese had sealed off the area in an effort to flush out Chinese guerrillas.[53] Abe also tried his hand at reporting on the gathering crisis in Poland. Abe judged that Britain would go to war in response to a German invasion. In late 1939, he was also visiting the Nakano School to lecture twice a week on Britain's position in Europe and on British colonial policy.

In August 1940, after a year spent working at Second Bureau, Abe received his orders from Lt. Gen. Sawada Shigeru, the vice chief of staff. He was to proceed to India, where he would gather intelligence on British political and military developments. Abe left Kobe on the ship *Lima Maru*, arriving at the port of Calcutta on 28 September. It happened that Japan entered into the Tripartite Pact with Germany and Italy the day before, an event that must have further impressed upon him the importance of his mission. He reached Bombay, his final destination, on 3 October. There, he began playing the role of a consulate clerk while executing his orders.

Abe went about his mission in Bombay, bolstered both by his professional experience and personal circumstances. His time at the Nakano School and stint at Second Bureau provided the first. The arrival of his wife, Hanako, constituted a personal advantage. The two had married in March 1940 after a professor who had been Abe's mentor at Rissho University had introduced her to him. Hanako arrived by a later ship in the company of another Nakano School graduate who was on his way to an assignment in Afghanistan. She reached Bombay on 15 November.

Mrs. Abe had learned of her new husband's intelligence background only after the wedding. No doubt surprised, she immediately began preparing to help him in his covert career. While he was training at the Nakano School and working at Second Bureau, she enrolled in an English course and honed her typing skills. Once in India, she monitored the local press for him, bringing to his attention items of likely intelligence value. She also gave him cover for his trips around Bombay. To allay the suspicions of British intelligence officers, the two would walk together about the city. In India, unlike Japan at that time, it was the norm for married couples to stroll about town together.

Posing as a clerk at the Bombay consulate, Abe monitored Britain's belated military buildup in Asia. Abe took note of the trains loaded with troops of Britain's India Army as they passed through Bombay on their way to bolster the defenses at Singapore, the linchpin of Britain's empire in Southeast Asia, and other points east. His travels about town also took him at times to the port. In mid-November 1941, he spotted two battleships and a cruiser. Abe, returning to the consulate to consult some naval reference works, judged that the battleships were the HMS *Repulse* and *Prince of Wales*. He promptly reported his observation, providing one link in the intelligence chain that would end with Japanese pilots sinking the two battleships near Singapore at the start of the war.

Abe's assignment to India ended when Japan invaded British Malaya on 8 December 1941 as part of a general offensive that included the attack against Pearl Harbor and the invasion of the Philippines. Much against her wishes, Hanako had followed orders to return to Japan with other civilian residents. She and their newborn daughter had sailed home in early November on the *Hiei Maru*, the last repatriation ship that left India before the war.

Following the onset of hostilities, Abe was relocated together with other Japanese diplomatic personnel from Singapore, Burma, Addis Ababa, and Ceylon to a town in the foothills of the Himalayas, there to cool his heels while Japanese and British authorities negotiated an exchange of interned officials. Once arrangements had been made, he left Bombay on an exchange ship on 13 August 1942. Crossing paths with British diplomats at the transfer site at the port of Lourenço Marques in Portuguese East Africa, Abe boarded the *Tatsuta Maru* for Shonan. There he met Col. Iwakuro Hideo and three younger graduates of the Nakano School. Iwakuro, a founding father of the Nakano School, had recently taken charge of a field intelligence organization conducting Indian operations. Abe then returned to Tokyo, where he joined lieutenants Ishii Tadashi and Makizawa Yoshio, recently repatriated from their respective assignments in Mexico and Colombia, in Second Bureau's Sixth Section (Europe–U.S.). There he remained as an intelligence analyst throughout the rest of the war.[54]

Prewar Scorecard

Army leaders had begun a belated program to develop military intelligence alongside muscle as Japan faced vexing challenges from surging Chinese nationalism and a formidable Soviet Union. The Nakano School and the Noborito Research Institute were among the products of the Army's efforts. In an army that inculcated unquestioning execution of orders and a fiery patriotism, the Nakano School began encouraging its shadow warriors to think creatively. They were to know the enemy, not simply fight him. Such knowledge would be the strength underlying whatever technical skills in martial arts, safecracking, or the like in their covert quiver. From such knowledge, too, would flow empathy. A competent intelligence officer must, whatever his personal beliefs, be able to grasp the basis of his opponent's beliefs and actions. He must be able to imagine himself in the shoes of the enemy. The Nakano School at its start appeared to have recruited wisely and trained well to develop a cadre capable of such thinking.

The Nakano School, despite its firm foundation, was working within a hostile military culture. Regular officers in general had scant regard for intelligence. The nationalist culture of the time, fanned by the military and civilian authorities, worked against a sophisticated approach. How graduates of the Nakano School would function in such an atmosphere remained to be seen. Compounding the problem was the issue of time. Had the Nakano School quietly opened its doors in 1918, or even 1928, rather than 1938, the Japanese Army would have had the time to train a large cadre of intelligence officers without the pressure of war. They would have risen through the ranks to influence military attitudes and policies. Years of foreign intelligence from the school's graduates would have reached Tokyo's leaders. Instead, a handful of young lieutenants had been in the field for two years or less when the bombs fell on Pearl Harbor. The graduates of the Nakano School would now have to operate in the midst of a global war.

2

EARLY VICTORIES

Subverting Indian Army on the Road to Singapore

Lt. Abe Naoyoshi learned upon returning to Tokyo in the latter half of 1942 how far the Japanese Army had taken operations against India. The British had repatriated Abe, who had been gathering intelligence under cover as a consular official, along with other Japanese diplomatic personnel from South Asia. He then resumed working on India and other British intelligence issues at Second Bureau. During Abe's internment, Lt. Gen. Yamashita Tomoyuki had taken Singapore. Operating in the shadows of Yamashita's Twenty-fifth Army had been a number of Abe's fellow intelligence officers from the Nakano School. They had contributed to Yamashita's stunning victory by undermining the morale of the Indian units that formed the backbone of British defenses at Singapore and the rest of the Malay Peninsula. The officer in charge of the subversion campaign was one of the Japanese Army's foremost propagandists.

Maj. Fujiwara Iwaichi, a native of Hyogo Prefecture, had graduated in the Forty-third Class of the Military Academy in 1931 and received a commission as an infantry officer. His early achievements had taken him through the elite General Staff College, which he graduated in 1938. That same year, Fujiwara participated as a staff officer in the successful Japanese campaign to capture the Chinese port city of Canton. Sent to Tokyo to recover from a bout of paratyphoid, Fujiwara received orders to report to Second Bureau's Eighth Section in August 1939. His early work there involved operations to break Chinese resistance. One such operation was the installation of dissident

Nationalist leader Wang Ching-wei as chief of a collaborationist Chinese regime in Nanking. Fujiwara then turned his attention in late 1940 to a study of the propaganda required for the coming war with Great Britain and the United States. He also lectured at the Nakano School.

Fujiwara concluded from his research that Japan would do well to portray the war to the peoples of Southeast Asia and the Indian subcontinent as one of liberation against the West. Influencing his thinking were such works as Okawa Shumei's *White Rule over Asia*. The author was a prominent advocate of pan-Asian ideology and action. His Okawa Academy taught Asian languages and area studies to Japanese who operated throughout Asia against Western colonial interests. Some of his students participated in intelligence operations alongside graduates of the Nakano School.

Fujiwara feared that Japan, condemned as an aggressor by the West since the seizure of Manchuria in 1931, was losing the propaganda war. To parry Western accusations, Fujiwara read deeply the works of Okawa, surveyed the writings of other Japanese, and toured Southeast Asia from March to May 1941. His subsequent recommendations helped to set the tone for Japanese wartime propaganda. Fujiwara was later pleased to see generals Homma Masaharu and Imamura Hitoshi make use of his ideas in the propaganda campaigns of Asian solidarity executed in their respective invasions of the Philippines and the Netherlands East Indies.[1]

While Fujiwara was preparing Japanese propaganda for the coming war, his superior in Eighth Section was overseeing the development of a fifth column in Southeast Asia. Lt. Col. Kadomatsu Shoichi, an infantry officer from Kagoshima Prefecture, had only recently taken charge of a unit in Second Bureau's clandestine section when he visited Bangkok in July 1941 to assess the local situation. His host was Col. Tamura Hiroshi, military attaché and director of Japanese intelligence throughout the region. Tamura briefed Kadomatsu on Japanese covert ties to the region's Indians and Malays.

According to Tamura, the efforts to cultivate Indians resident in Southeast Asia were the most important of his operations. His chief Indian contacts were members of the Indian Independence League (IIL). Banned as a subversive organization in India and Great Britain's other colonies, the IIL had a Bangkok office that communicated with Indian nationalists around the world. Tamura also briefed Kadomatsu on his efforts to develop ties to nationalists of the majority Malay community of British Malaya.

Tamura also kept in contact with a Japanese bandit chief in Malaya who went by the Malay name of Harimao (Tiger). The Japanese military attaché turned to Harimao as part of a broader reliance on resident Japanese to support regional intelligence activities. The local Japanese were valuable because they knew the local areas, peoples, and languages. Tamura also ran his operations with the aid of such Japanese trading companies as Showa Trading, Dainan Koshi, and Mitsui & Co. Showa Trading ran Japanese weapons to Thailand. Dainan Koshi, its headquarters in Saigon, was established by the military to provide cover for intelligence activities. Mitsui was, and remains today, one of the world's top trading companies. All served as elements of what one Japanese writer termed the "advance guard" of Japanese imperial expansion.[2]

After Kadomatsu returned to Tokyo, Fujiwara shifted his attention to the development of a fifth column in Southeast Asia. On 18 September, less than two weeks after Japan's Imperial Conference ratified the decision to fight Great Britain and the United States, Fujiwara took command of an intelligence agency tasked with building a fifth column. Six men from the Nakano School formed the core of the new Fujiwara Agency. Four civilians rounded out the organization. On the day the Fujiwara Agency came into being, Fujiwara and his men assembled at Imperial General Headquarters to receive their orders. Present were the Japanese Army's vice chief of staff, the director of Second Bureau, and the chief of Eighth Section. The Fujiwara Agency was to proceed to Bangkok. Under the supervision of Col. Tamura Hiroshi, the members would raise a native fifth column in Malaya that would operate behind the lines once they went ashore. Fujiwara, having received his orders, then took his men to the Shinto shrines of the Emperor Meiji and Yoshida Shoin to pray for the success of their mission.

At the end of September, the Fujiwara Agency's members quietly left Tokyo for Bangkok. Fujiwara and Yamaguchi Hitoshi, a member of Eighth Section and alumnus of the Nakano School, made their way to Fukuoka's Gannosu airfield. Fujiwara and Yamaguchi entered Bangkok under false names, posing as members of the Japanese Foreign Ministry. Three of the Fujiwara Agency's men slipped into Thailand in the guise of employees of the trading companies Dainan Koshi,

Hidaka Yoko Trading, and Mitsubishi Corporation. Another member posed as a hotel bellboy. Also joining the Agency in Thailand was another operative from the Nakano School, previously assigned to the military attaché office under Colonel Tamura, as well as seven resident Japanese and two native Taiwanese. With Bangkok as the main base, the Fujiwara Agency established branches throughout Thailand. The southern region bordering Malaya, the planned starting point for the coming campaign for the peninsula, received particular attention.

Once established in Bangkok, Fujiwara began in earnest to build a fifth column of Indians and Malays. In early October, Fujiwara met IIL Secretary General Pritam Singh through Colonel Tamura. Singh had earlier welcomed to Bangkok three Hong Kong Indian fugitives whom Fujiwara had sent in secret from Japan. As the date approached for the Japanese invasion of Malaya, Fujiwara and Singh held a series of talks that produced on 1 December an agreement committing the IIL to support Fujiwara's covert agency. The two organizations were to collaborate on operations to aid Yamashita's Twenty-fifth Army by gathering intelligence, disseminating propaganda, and organizing volunteers into a force to liberate India. In addition, the Japanese Army would open the way for communication between local operations and the Indian nationalist Subhas Chandra Bose, then in Berlin broadcasting propaganda and raising a force from the ranks of Indian Army soldiers taken prisoner by the Germans in North Africa.

On 4 December came the military cable informing Fujiwara that Japan would go to war in four days against Great Britain and the United States. He learned that his organization would henceforth operate under the command of Twenty-fifth Army. Fujiwara immediately sent Yamaguchi to coordinate with Twenty-fifth Army Headquarters in Saigon. There, Fujiwara's subordinate met a number of staff officers, including Lt. Col. Tsuji Masanobu and Lt. Col. Sugita Ichiji. Sugita, senior intelligence officer on Yamashita's staff, had only the month before been in Tokyo, directing the Anglo-American intelligence section at Second Bureau. Yamaguchi, once he had briefed the staff of Twenty-fifth Army on the situation in Thailand and coordinated arrangements for the coming campaign, returned to Thailand.[3]

On 8 December, approximately an hour before Japanese pilots struck Pearl Harbor, elements of General Yamashita's Twenty-fifth Army began landing at Kota Bharu on the east coast of Malaya. Other military units left their starting points in French Indochina, crossing into Thailand on their way to northern Malaya. Leading the Fifth Imperial Guards Regiment from Phnom Penh was none other than Col. Iwakuro Hideo, one of the Nakano School's founders. He had taken command of the regiment that summer, after several years as a staff officer at Imperial General Headquarters.

The next morning, Major Fujiwara flew from Bangkok with Yamaguchi, Singh, and nearly a dozen other Japanese and Indian operatives to Twenty-fifth Army Headquarters at Singora, in southern Thailand, for his orders. As established in the recent agreement with Singh, the Fujiwara Agency was to operate with the IIL as well as the Malay Youth League and the Japanese bandit Harimao to gather intelligence and feed propaganda to the local population. Fujiwara promptly sent his men into action.

One of Fujiwara's most important decisions at the war's onset was to accept Pritam Singh's proposal to return Indian soldiers who had surrendered back to the front lines to assist the Fujiwara Agency in convincing other soldiers of the Indian Army to lay down their arms. In a first attempt, Yamaguchi and another Japanese operative returned several surrendered Indian soldiers across the lines into an Indian Army camp. The Indian collaborators, true to their word, soon returned with roughly a dozen Indian soldiers and news of low enemy morale.

The Fujiwara Agency from that time had considerable success in talking individual soldiers and even entire units into surrendering. Japanese radio appeals for Asian solidarity and other subversive programs for months had targeted the British Army's heavily Indian units in Malaya and Singapore. Outflanked, overrun, and isolated far behind the lines by the quickly advancing Japanese, Indian soldiers surrendered in droves. In one incident, Fujiwara and Singh negotiated the surrender of an isolated Indian battalion around Jitra in northern Malaya. Fujiwara found among the prisoners a company commander who immediately impressed him with his military bearing and pride. Returning Fujiwara's greeting, the prisoner shook his hand and said, "I am Capt. Mohan Singh."

Mohan Singh's rank and bearing made an immediate impression on Fujiwara and his superior at Twenty-fifth Army, Sugita Ichiji. The Indian captain struck them as an excellent candidate to lead Indian prisoners in the Fujiwara Agency's operations. As a test, Fujiwara put Mohan Singh in charge of eighty captured Indian soldiers. The soldiers under Singh's orders then helped to maintain order for the Japanese in Alor Star after the main force had left to continue its advance on Singapore. Seeing him in command of the prisoners, Fujiwara decided to make him his principal Indian assistant. Backing his decision was Sugita; Twenty-fifth Army's chief intelligence officer was the foremost promoter of the Fujiwara Agency. Sugita helped by assigning Lt. Kunizuka Kazunori to the Fujiwara Agency to look after Mohan Singh and the other Indians. Kunizuka, an intelligence officer from Fifth Division, had earlier shown a good command of English and a talent for dealing with Indians.

Sugita and Fujiwara then set about convincing Mohan Singh to become the leader of a force built from the ranks of surrendered Indian Army soldiers. Sugita arranged a meeting with General Yamashita to impress the Indian captain. On 20 December, Sugita, Fujiwara, and Yamaguchi took Mohan Singh and Pritam Singh to meet Yamashita. According to Yamaguchi, the general stressed for Pritam Singh the IIL's importance and assured Mohan Singh of his regard for Indian soldiers as fellow Asians. The two Indians reportedly left the meeting impressed by the "depth" of Yamashita's interest in India's independence and the "nearly limitless" aid he had promised them. Fujiwara then hosted a banquet for the two Indians. The scene of the Fujiwara Agency's members and Indian POWs sharing a meal of Indian food together moved Mohan Singh, who had resented the British officers for their attitude of racial superiority and aloofness from Indian troops. Fujiwara had won him over.

From the start, Mohan Singh showed that he was no mere puppet. The day after his meeting with Yamashita, after talking with other Indian Army POWs, Singh presented Fujiwara with a list of conditions for his assuming command of the proposed Indian National Army (INA). He asked for Japanese military support; a relationship of cooperation, rather than subordination, with the IIL; control over all Indian Army prisoners; release of all Indian volunteers to the INA; and treatment of the INA as a military ally. Once Fujiwara assured Mohan Singh that Yamashita accepted his conditions, the captain agreed to join the Fujiwara Agency's operation. For the rest of the campaign, the Fujiwara Agency's Japanese operatives and Indian collaborators worked to convince members of the Indian Army to surrender. Their efforts netted some twenty-five hundred surrenders by 11 January, a month before the British surrender in Singapore. Once General Sir

Percival surrendered the British forces on 15 February, the Fujiwara Agency had tens of thousands of prisoners, a windfall of POWs from which to build the INA.[4]

The Patriotic Bandit

The Fujiwara Agency conducted its second major operation, developing a fifth column within the native Malay population, with the help of a patriotic Japanese bandit. Tani Yutaka, born in Kyushu's Fukuoka Prefecture, was taken as a baby in 1911 by his parents to Malaya, where his father opened a barbershop. After living for a time with relatives in Fukuoka to attend school in Japan, Tani returned to Malaya to help his father. In 1931, the young Tani returned to Japan to take his compulsory military physical. He was rejected as too short for military service. Tani then opted to stay in Japan to work.

It was during this period that tragedy struck. Japan's seizure of Manchuria in 1931 had enflamed anti-Japanese sentiment among Chinese in Southeast Asia. In November 1932, rioting Chinese residents had set fire to his father's barbershop and killed his eight-year-old sister. Tani returned to Malaya, consumed with hatred for the Chinese and the British colonial police. He blamed the latter for failing to protect his family. In revenge, he turned to a life of crime, robbing trains and stealing from the British and Chinese at the head of a large band of Malay and Thai bandits. The slight Japanese youth, considered too slight for military conscription, had become the bandit Harimao.

Tani, with his knowledge of the Malay language, his contacts with the native population, and his demonstrated talent for irregular operations, soon came to the attention of Japanese intelligence. In Bangkok, Col. Tamura Hiroshi had quickly grasped the young man's value. In 1941, as Japan prepared for war, the military attaché moved to recruit him. Tamura called to his office one Kamimoto Toshio, an intelligence veteran working in Bangkok at Showa Trading.

Kamimoto, making contact with Tani, appealed to the young man's patriotism as a Japanese in asking him to work for the Fujiwara Agency. Tani readily agreed to work for his fatherland. Through his Malay contacts, he reported on the British troops stationed on the peninsula and provided topographical intelligence that the Fujiwara Agency used to produce a military map of Malaya. When the Japanese

Army invaded Malaya, Tani led his men to harass British units and gather intelligence. While tramping through Malaya's jungle trails, he contracted a severe case of malaria. When Fujiwara finally met him several days before the fall of Singapore, Tani was wracked with fever as he waged his guerrilla campaign. Outside Kuala Lumpur, he derailed a British supply train and conducted other acts of sabotage.

Tani had eluded the British but could not shake off his illness. An alarmed Fujiwara sent him to an army field hospital at Johore on the day the British surrendered, then to a larger Japanese hospital in Singapore. Fujiwara paid a final compliment to the patriotic bandit when, visiting the dying man in the hospital, he informed Tani of his designation as an official of the Japanese military administration. When Tani died of malaria the following month, Fujiwara sent a personal message to his mother in Fukuoka and had his remains flown home. Fujiwara also had a ceremony conducted at Yasukuni Shrine, where Tani was enshrined as a war god. A veteran propagandist, Fujiwara then arranged to have made in Japan a major motion picture to tell the story of Tani's service to his fatherland. Fujiwara convinced the Japanese motion picture company Daiei to make the movie. *Marai no Tora* (Tiger of Malaya), starring the dashing actor Nakata Koji in the title role, hit Japanese theaters in 1943.[5]

Seeds of Doubt

Lt. Gen. Sir A. E. Percival's unconditional surrender of Singapore on 15 February to General Yamashita presented the Fujiwara Agency with a windfall. The Agency, responsible for handling Indian Army POWs, had expected no more than ten thousand or so prisoners. The news that close to fifty thousand soldiers of the Indian Army had surrendered was stunning. Rising to the challenge, Fujiwara sent Yamaguchi the day after the surrender to arrange with the British commanders for the Indian soldiers to be sent to a former horse track called Farrar Park. Yamaguchi arranged for their delivery on 19 February. Meanwhile, other Agency members scoured the city for supplies.

Fujiwara, understanding that the mass surrender of Indian Army troops presented an opportunity for propaganda, prepared a rally to convince the prisoners that their loyalty as Asians should lie with Japan. On the afternoon of 19 February, Fujiwara strode up to the microphone at one end of Farrar Park to speak before some forty-five thousand Indians assembled before him. Lieutenant Kunizuka interpreted his remarks into English, and then an Indian officer relayed the remarks in Hindi. Fujiwara asserted that Japan was waging its war in order to liberate Asia from Western colonialism. He assured his audience that Japan had no designs on India. Finally, he appealed to the assembled prisoners to help liberate India by joining the IIL and INA. Those who did so, he promised, would be no longer prisoners but allies. In a show of what was likely a mixture of genuine emotion and prudent calculation, the assembled multitude greeted his remarks by roaring their approval and tossing their hats into the air. Pritam Singh and Mohan Singh followed Fujiwara with their own ardent appeals for their fellow Indians to join them in the struggle. The event, captured on film, was a piece of grand theater, staged by one of the Army's finest propagandists.[6]

Unfortunately for Fujiwara, ill fate was to follow his rousing start. Mohan Singh acted as though he had assumed supreme command of fifty thousand Indian soldiers for his campaign into India. He thus soon came into conflict with the Japanese. The Twenty-fifth Army, via the Fujiwara Agency, almost immediately requested that more than nine hundred Indian POWs be furnished to guard British prisoners, serve as auxiliaries in antiaircraft units, and work in military labor units elsewhere. Mohan Singh reluctantly agreed to this initial request from Fujiwara for laborers.[7] While still holding Fujiwara personally in high esteem, the INA commander soon doubted the good faith of the Japanese Army.

Meanwhile, Japan's leaders had decided to raise Indian policy to a higher level. Early in 1942, two lieutenant generals arrived in Malaya from Tokyo to review the status of the Fujiwara Agency and INA. In March, Army Chief of Staff General Sugiyama himself inspected the INA while on a tour of Southeast Asia. That same month, Imperial General Headquarters staged an international conference of Indian leaders in Tokyo. Chairing the event was Rash Behari Bose, a man who had long been Japan's favored Indian nationalist.

Rash Behari Bose had waged a terrorist campaign against British rule in India before the First World War. Involved in an attempted assassination in 1912 that wounded Lord Hardinge, viceroy of India, and discovered in another plot in 1914, Bose had fled India that year for Japan. He there learned Japanese, married the daughter of Soma

Aizo, prominent owner of the Nakamuraya, and took Japanese citizenship. The protection of the powerful rightist Toyama Mitsuru shielded Bose from the demands of Great Britain for his extradition. While his connections made him a natural choice for the Japanese as chief Indian collaborator, Fujiwara dismissed "Nakamuraya Bose" as too Japanized and lacking in stature to lead.

Indian leaders from throughout Japan's new southern empire gathered at Tokyo's Sanno Hotel for the conference, known as the Sanno Conference. It was an event that signaled the greater profile that Indian operations were assuming. Such a visible program would require the attention of someone above the rank of major. For Fujiwara, whose small band of intelligence officers had worked wonders in subversion and sabotage during the drive on Singapore, the Sanno Conference marked the end of the road. Indian operations had grown too important to leave to a major and a handful of junior officers. Fujiwara nevertheless would remain involved in Indian operations for most of the war. Most of his men from the Nakano School would work under the successor organ in an ambitious program to subvert British rule in India.[8]

Diplomats and Spies in the Dutch East Indies

Tokyo desperately needed to acquire oil from the Netherlands East Indies. The lack of oil in Japan was the empire's Achilles' heel. There were some oil fields in Niigata Prefecture, on the Japan Sea, but they yielded only a few barrels for every one hundred required. Without oil, the empire's factories would come to a halt. The formidable carriers and battleships would remain helplessly in port. There would be no fuel for the tanks or trucks at the Soviet border in Manchukuo. Oil was vital.

Washington, seeking to pressure Tokyo into halting the war in China, had terminated on 26 January 1940 the bilateral commercial treaty. The move threatened to disrupt the supply of American oil, iron ore, and other key commodities to Japan. Without oil, in the American calculation, the Japanese would fold. China would remain independent, and open to American commercial interests. The Japanese, however, having already expended a great amount of blood and treasure in their undeclared war, had no intention of bowing under American pressure.

Tokyo looked south to secure an alternate supply of oil. In the Netherlands East Indies lay some of the globe's richest oil fields. The center of the Dutch oil industry was in the region of Palembang, in the swampy interior of giant Sumatra, the island opposite the Malay Peninsula. Prime Minister Konoe Fumimaro sent Trade Minister Kobayashi Ichizo to the colonial capital of Batavia, now Jakarta, for talks starting 13 September to secure exports of oil and other needed raw materials. But Dutch colonial officials feared that supplying the Japanese would be tantamount to a condemned man selling rope to the hangman. When Tokyo joined Berlin and Rome on 27 September in the Tripartite Pact, the Dutch saw all the more reason to refuse. Rather than submit at some near date to an invasion by a Japanese war machine fueled on Palembang's oil, the Dutch sought refuge in alliance with the Americans and British. Kobayashi left with empty hands in November. Yoshizawa Kenkichi, a former foreign minister, then arrived for negotiations on 2 January 1941 to push Japan's agenda. The talks ended in failure on 17 June.[9]

Diplomacy, however, is only one path to a nation's goals. Espionage is another. While diplomats parleyed in Batavia, men of the Japanese Army gathered the intelligence required to seize the colony by force. In fact, Ambassador Yoshizawa's retinue included a trio of officers whose collecting of information beyond the bounds of the oil talks angered colonial authorities. A Japanese diplomatic cable from Batavia to Tokyo on 27 June reported Dutch military displeasure over the snooping of military officers Oga, Ishii, and Maeda. The three had been planning to depart Batavia on the *Kitano Maru* on 15 July. The indignant Dutch demanded that they sail home early on the *Asama Maru* on 3 July.[10]

When the three officers departed, however, the Japanese Army still retained a formidable intelligence network. In early 1941, while Yoshizawa was negotiating in Batavia, Lt. Maruzaki Yoshio arrived at the Japanese consulate in Surabaya, a key city on the eastern end of Java. He had graduated as a member of the Nakano School's First Class in the summer of 1939, then gone to AGS Second Bureau for a grounding in the intelligence issues of the day. There, he worked at the Sixth Section on Anglo-American issues.

In December 1940, Maruzaki received from AGS his assignment to Surabaya. Working under cover as a consulate employee, he gathered basic data on a variety of issues relevant to impending military operations. Among those issues were relations between Europeans and Indonesians, the colony's ethnic composition, and relations among the various peoples. He also reported on the colony's history, geography, culture, politics, government, and religion.

Also on Java was Lt. Niiho Satoru, Maruzaki's classmate from the Nakano School. Based in Batavia, Niiho worked under cover as a reporter for Domei News Agency. From the colonial capital, Niiho gathered information on the Dutch oil industry. His assumed identity was ideal for his task. As a reporter, he had a reason to travel about the colony, asking questions and collecting data. On a couple of occasions, Maruzaki and Niiho met. For security, they would stay within their roles and pretend to have only recently met each other.[11]

The senior military intelligence in the area was Major Kuriya Tsugunori, the attaché in Batavia. As Tokyo made final preparations from the summer of 1941 for war, AGS pressed the attaché for the necessary intelligence. On 22 October, the army's vice chief of staff cabled Kuriya, instructing him to report on Dutch military training and troop dispositions. He also received tasking on air combat methods and the organization, types, number, and location of aircraft in the colony. On 6 November, AGS cabled an order for Major Kuriya to return to Tokyo. En route, he was to contact the military attaché in Bangkok, Col. Tamura Hiroshi, and the Tomi Agency, a military intelligence organ based in Saigon. Until the arrival of the next attaché, according to AGS orders, Maruzaki and Niiho were to handle Kuriya's responsibilities.[12]

Beyond Kuriya and the two men of the Nakano School, the thousands of Japanese resident on the islands were invaluable sources. Merchants, fishermen, and masters of myriad other trades, they knew from years of residence a thousand details. They spoke the local languages. They were patriots who would serve Japan loyally when duty called. The Japanese consulate in Batavia cabled Tokyo on 31 July to counsel safeguarding such assets for future use. Dutch colonial officials had viewed Japan as an enemy since September 1940, date of the military's first advance into French Indochina. Three days before the cable, the Japanese had moved into the southern part of French Indochina. From the naval base at Cam Ranh Bay on the South China Sea and from camps in Cambodia, the Japanese had clearly taken positions to launch offensives against the Netherlands East Indies and the other colonies.

The Dutch were aware that Japanese residents were passing information to the fatherland. Consul General Ishizawa Yutaka, who had assumed that Japanese residents would simply remain in place, now feared the "wholesale arrest of resident Japanese." Rather than risk losing them, Ishizawa counseled, "It would be better to have such [residents] return to Japan early, keeping a list of their names and addresses" for future use. Tokyo wisely concurred. On 13 November, the Foreign Ministry cabled Ishizawa to order returned to the fatherland those "Japanese nationals familiar with conditions in the Dutch East Indies and those knowing the languages."[13]

Parachutes over Palembang

The question was a thorny one. How could Japan seize the vital oil fields at Palembang before Dutch demolition teams destroyed them? The Japanese Army could hit the beaches on the north coast of Sumatra, then fight through Dutch defenses up the Musi River to Palembang. The Royal Netherlands Indies Army (KNIL), a slight colonial force constituted to quell local rebellions, could not defeat Asia's greatest military. However, the KNIL would be expecting an amphibious assault. Japanese casualties could be considerable. Moreover, it would take time for the invaders to sweep aside the defenses and slog their way through the hundred kilometers of swampy terrain to Palembang. The Dutch would have more than enough time to demolish the refineries and the oil fields.

The Nakano School was behind the Army's plans to capture intact the Dutch oil fields. In April 1941, Col. Ueda Masao, assistant commandant at Nakano School, received an order from AGS Chief of Staff Sugiyama to survey the islands as a prelude to invasion. Ueda in turn had briefed Maruzaki and Niiho that they were to include information on Palembang among their intelligence objectives. An army should not blindly march into an area. Maruzaki and Niiho were to supply planners with the basic information, from describing the lay of the land to listing likely collaborators in the area who would light the way.

Now, how to overcome Dutch defenses before the demolition charges blew? Apart from a slog up the Musi River, there was no other land route. Pegunungan Barisan, the mountainous spine running down Sumatra's south coast, ruled out that route. The swamps to the east lacked a water route comparable to the Musi. The army would take to the air. In advance of the main force going ashore at the mouth of the Musi, paratroopers would quickly seize Palembang before the defenders had time to destroy the oil facilities. The expected invasion from the island's southeast up the Musi River would run into heavy losses, and the time needed would risk destruction of oil fields and refineries. Rather than going ashore, the invaders would attack from the sky. There remained, however, a host of details to resolve in advance. The Japanese Army had paratroopers, but none had experience in jumping into oil fields or neutralizing Dutch demolitions.

AGS turned again to the Nakano School. Maj. Gen. Kawamata Taketo, the school's commandant, in November ordered Okayasu Shigeo, a statistics instructor, to produce a basic survey on the oil industry. With several assistants, he conducted a preliminary search through the open literature readily available. While lacking in glamour, mining the mountains of open sources, done properly, yields veins of vital information. Newspapers, industry journals, insurance reports, and technical blueprints are worth their weight in gold. Intelligence professionals the world over have long understood the value of open sources. In Washington, for example, analysts of the OSS found much of what they required during the war at the Library of Congress.

Kawamata, after receiving Okayasu's open-source survey, ordered him to prepare a second report. The statistician, aided by Lt. Koizumi Toshihiko of the school's proving unit and several others, left Tokyo for Niigata on 8 December to inspect the oil fields and draw further details from company personnel there. In Niigata, the importance of their mission must have hit home, for the day they departed the capital was the same that pilots of the Imperial Japanese Navy reduced to twisted metal the American battleships at Pearl Harbor. War had come.

Following the Niigata survey, having learned the technical details of the oil industry, Okayasu's team gathered intelligence in direct support of a paratroop operation at Palembang. They were to gather topographical intelligence, examine techniques to prevent destruction of the refineries, and prepare lists of those expected to cooperate with the Japanese. With Japan at war, the team could not directly survey the oil fields. They turned for information to Japanese companies that had been operating in the Netherlands East Indies. From a whaling company and the Mitsui trading company, they obtained aerial photographs of the oil fields. Reproducing the photographs, the team then analyzed them to determine the location of refinery buildings, guards, and other key features. From a company executive with Palembang experience, the team gleaned details on the city of Palembang and its Dutch garrison.

The Nakano School also arranged special training for the paratroopers. Select members came from Kyushu to Tokyo for briefings from Okayasu, Koizumi, and others involved in the survey. The background talks ended with the new year. While other Japanese greeted 1942 in family gatherings with toasts of sake and ceremonial dishes, Okayasu and the paratroopers traveled to a Japanese oil field. For the first two days of the new year, they made practice jumps among some of Japan's few oil derricks.

Men of the Nakano School would also jump with the paratroopers. Since the previous November, ten lieutenants and sergeants from the school had been attached to Sixteenth Army Headquarters, set up within the General Staff College. Among them, Lt. Hoshino Tetsuichi and five others received orders to jump into Palembang. Like the paratroopers, the six were barely old enough to shave. They left for Kyushu on 9 January. From the Nyutabaru air base in Miyazaki Prefecture, paratroop headquarters, they flew with the soldiers on 15 January for the front. Hopping from Taiwan to Cam Ranh Bay, then to Saigon, Phnom Penh, and Bangkok, they finally reached their jump-off point on the Malay Peninsula on 10 February.

Then the Nakano School's men ran into trouble. The six had planned to jump with the first wave. Instead, they learned that they were all relegated to the second jump. That day, they chased after harried staff officers seemingly intent on avoiding them. That evening, Hoshino rapped on the door of a lieutenant leading one of the units. Hoshino stoutly protested the exclusion. He argued that his group knew better than anyone the terrain, the facilities, and the placement of the demolition charges. While at the Nakano School, he himself had studied Malay, the lingua franca of Indonesia. Departing from fact, he also claimed to have previously scouted out Palembang. His wrangling worked. Before the night was out, he had secured from the regiment commander a spot on the first jump. The other five, however, would go with the second wave.

On 14 February, Hoshino was in the air with the squad leader from whom he had wrangled a spot, going to battle with propaganda leaflets and military currency strapped to him. He had tossed and turned in bed the night before. Would he alone be able to accomplish what the six were to have done? He was to pacify the local people with propaganda, round up the technical personnel, disarm the demolition charges, and otherwise secure the oil facilities. He had studied Malay at the Nakano School, but would he be able to communicate? How accurate was his intelligence? With these worries haunting his mind, he had greeted the dawn after a sleepless night.

As he flew over Singapore, he could see dark smoke rising from the beleaguered bastion of Britain's Asian empire. Lt. Gen. A.E. Percival was a day away from surrendering the city and more than fifty thousand troops in what would cap the greatest disaster ever to befall the British Army. As the Japanese formation flew over Sumatra and made its way above the Musi River towards Palembang, the squad leader called Hoshino to the jump door and pointed out the refinery tanks some three thousand meters below. "We're going. You follow me!" he shouted. Hoshino, inexperienced in parachuting, thus found himself jumping second in the invasion of Palembang.

Hoshino hit the ground without mishap, then ran with others through a rear gate of a refinery. Coming upon a group of Indonesians huddled in an air raid shelter, he passed out leaflets declaring, "The Dutch Army is the enemy of the Japanese Army. People of Indonesia are our friends. We have come down from the skies. Everyone, please put your mind at ease." Questioning them, he learned that there were approximately 350 troops in the area, without tanks or armored vehicles. The paratroopers would be sufficient to capture Palembang. Hoshino raced about the air raid shelters. Interrogating three captured Dutch technicians, he confirmed his earlier information and questioned the three on the location of demolition charges. Told there were none, he then took two soldiers with him around the refinery, slipping quietly from one spot to another to confirm the absence of wires and charges at key points.[14]

The first company of paratroopers had secured much of the Palembang area, defended by a Dutch battalion. The defenders still held Sungaigerong, a few kilometers northeast of Palembang, by the end of that day. Indeed, the paratroopers were in danger of a devastating assault the next day. Fortunately, the second company of paratroopers descended on Palembang that morning. Then the main force hit the beaches and began moving up the Musi. Hoshino found his five Nakano School mates among the second wave of paratroopers that day. The airborne companies welcomed the amphibious units that night. Allied forces retreated east across the Sunda Strait for Java.

The airborne assault had caught the enemy unawares, leaving them no time to destroy the oil industry. The Nakano School had played its part in one of the most successful paratroop operations in history. With the Japanese Army in possession of Palembang, Hoshino and his colleagues then began in earnest the tasks of disseminating propaganda to the Indonesians, registering refinery employees for future use, securing the facilities, and preparing the way for the occupation troops and Japanese petroleum engineers who were on their way.[15]

Deception by Radio

It was Lt. Tarora Sadao who hit upon the idea of deceiving the enemy with false radio broadcasts. He was a handsome young officer, with a simple and sincere face masking a sharp mind. When he had grown his hair long while at the Nakano School, the boyish Tarora seemed more a college student, or even a high school senior, than an army officer in his early twenties. Like many in the Army, he was a native of Kyushu, born in 1917 in Oita Prefecture on the island's northeast side.

In the weeks following Pearl Harbor, he was an intelligence officer on the headquarters staff of Southern Army in Saigon. By February 1942, he was overseeing shipments of arms to Burmese fighting alongside the Japanese Army in Burma and hosting Asian nationalists who came calling to Saigon. Tarora was also administering the affairs of the Indian POWs who were surrendering in droves to Maj. Fujiwara Iwaichi's agency as Japanese forces pushed down the Malay Peninsula towards Singapore. Radio was another area of responsibility. Tarora had been involved in broadcasting appeals from Saigon to Indian Army troops to lay down their arms. When Singapore and Rangoon fell, he worked to turn the captured radio stations into propaganda platforms. Tarora also handled the NHK (Japan Broadcasting Corporation) radio personnel, foreign correspondents, and propagandists who came to Saigon to write, illustrate, broadcast, and publish the material aimed at winning Asian hearts and minds. Saigon was a humming hub of activity.[16]

One day, Lt. Col. Otsuki Akira called Tarora into his office. Since the previous November, Otsuki had been the senior staff intelligence officer at Southern Army. With Japanese forces taking control of Sumatra, Bali, and other outlying islands of the Netherlands East Indies, time was running short before Gen. Imamura Hitoshi's force sailed from Cam Ranh Bay to invade the central island of Java. Otsuki tasked Tarora with delivering a plan to prevent the Dutch from destroying the natural resources on Java. That night, wracking his brains for an idea, Tarora recalled a briefing from his days at the Nakano School. One of the instructors, lecturing on Germany's invasion of Poland, had described how a German propaganda team had occupied the central radio station in Warsaw several days before the city's surrender. The team had broadcast to the world that the Polish capital had fallen. The ploy had thrown Polish troops and foreign governments into confusion. Tarora was inspired to try his hand at a similar gambit.[17]

Tarora and other intelligence officers were daily monitoring Java radio broadcasts, which included instructions for the destruction of natural resources and industrial infrastructure. A central station at Bandung, in the mountains near Java's western end, relayed broadcasts to roughly a dozen stations around the island. Since the Bandung station transmitted with far less power than Saigon mustered, Tarora and others decided to try overpowering the Dutch station from Saigon. They would suppress KNIL orders and issue their own. Needed were technicians, a committee to put together authentic announcements, including a Japanese foreign correspondent, someone from another local station, a Japanese consular official recently withdrawn from Java, a military staff intelligence officer, and Tarora.

Tarora put together and directed a "special broadcast section" comprising technical and editorial staff. Among them were a consular official with recent service in Java and several Japanese with Netherlands East Indies experience, as well as a Dutchman, a Malay, and an Indonesian. Tarora's outfit would broadcast in Dutch and Malay. The section monitored Dutch broadcasts to plot program schedules, study their contents, and note the voice characteristics of the various announcers.

While Tarora and his team did the groundwork, Otsuki ran interference at higher levels. First, he needed permission from the commanders of Southern Army and Sixteenth Army. Second, broadcast facilities in Saigon belonged to the French, who had chosen collaboration over the loss of their colony. Otsuki called on Consul Uchiyama Iwataro to seek French approval. Whether it was Uchiyama's diplomatic finesse or French resignation in the face of the Japanese juggernaut, Tarora received the green light for his project.[18]

Once Sixteenth Army sailed from Cam Ranh Bay on 18 February and hit the beaches of Java on the twenty-eighth, Tarora sent his team into action. On the morning of 2 March, Saigon took a first stab at deception, playing music during a lull in broadcasts from Bandung. The next day, Tarora's broadcasters went into gear. Broadcasts from Saigon changed or canceled orders to mobilize or to destroy resources. They also beamed news of Indonesian unrest and rebellion. Two days later, the Japanese monitored Dutch broadcasts warning against bogus information and counseling listeners to pay close attention to the voices of the announcers. When Imamura's troops took Bandung that day, Tarora's team started broadcasting false news from the front, greatly exaggerating the extent of Japanese advances. Saigon also cited bogus news from London and Washington radio that the British and Americans had already written off Java as a lost cause.

Five days later, Tarora moved to block a possible withdrawal of KNIL troops from Bandung through the port of Cilacap on Java's south central coast, some 150 kilometers west of Yogyakarta. Tarora's broadcast reported that a strong Japanese force was approaching the same port from the south. That evening, while monitoring international radio beams, they picked up a broadcast from London that cited Bandung in reporting that a Japanese force had reached the port. It was a grand moment for all in the room, as Tarora and his colleagues let loose with joyous whoops of "banzai!"

Once the Dutch had surrendered, those involved in the radio deception learned a bit about blowback. When propaganda is released into the world to influence or deceive foreign audiences, there is the risk of it coming back to confuse domestic listeners as well. In fact, Japan's Domei News Agency reported to its domestic audience the bogus broadcasts from what supposedly was the Bandung station. When Lt. Col. Otsuki went in the middle of 1942 to Tokyo on temporary duty to IGHQ, he came under fire for Sixteenth Army's landing troops at Cilacap without Tokyo's approval. The tension ended when Otsuki explained that reports of the landing were a Nakano School fabrication. Both Otsuki and his questioner enjoyed a chuckle. Tarora had caught not only the Dutch but also his own military in his deception.[19]

3

WINNING, THEN LOSING, HEARTS AND MINDS IN BURMA

It was time to close the Burma Road. By 1940, a skirmish at the Marco Polo Bridge three years earlier had escalated into general warfare between Japan and China. The Japanese generals were frustrated. They had assumed a major show of force would result in a quick Chinese capitulation. The warlords had made one concession after another for the past twenty years. Now, to their chagrin, the Nationalist leader Generalissimo Chiang Kai-shek was showing some spine! Worse, he had retreated into the vast interior, kept in the fight with foreign assistance. The Japanese generals were determined to shut off the foreign lifeline to the Chinese Nationalists. One major supply route to the Nationalists ran via the British colony of Burma to Yunnan Province in southwest China. Chungking, the Chinese capital since the fall of Nanking in 1937, was in neighboring Szechwan Province. Running from Burma through the adjacent Chinese border province of Yunnan, the supply route ended in the Nationalists' mountain redoubt of Chungking.

Sending supplies down the Burma Road was part of Great Britain's efforts to prevent the Japanese from subjugating China. In Tokyo, AGS officers estimated that some ten thousand tons of supplies were reaching the Nationalists each month via Burma.[1] Such British support for Generalissimo Chiang Kai-shek enraged Japanese military officers. The anger of Maj. Ito Samata, then, was well founded. Thoughts of the Burma Road were likely among those that pushed him to plot a takeover of the British consulate in Kobe. Not long after the Kempeitai arrested Ito for his unauthorized plan, however, AGS ordered another officer to look into ways to shut down the Burma Road.

Burma in 1940 was a British colony ripe for subversion. In the nineteenth century, Great Britain had waged a succession of wars to conquer Burma and add the rich lands to its Indian Empire. The proud Burmans, the dominant people of Burma, soon suffered several humiliations. First, long masters of the region, they now suffered the insult of alien rule. The British deepened their sense of grievance by pushing them to the periphery in their own land. Great Britain opened Burma to immigration from India. Overseas Chinese also flooded into the colony. The newcomers seized much of the economic high ground, controlling much of the commerce. Moreover, the British turned to the practice, tried and true, of divide and rule. Burma's new overlords favored the Karens, Kachins, and other ethnic minorities over the dominant Burmans. The British turned the colony's rice fields into a granary for its Asian empire. British political control and Indian commercial influence fueled Burmese resentments and fed Burma's nationalist movement. Britain's belated steps to appease Burmese sentiment, including institution of limited self-government in 1923 and Burma's administrative separation from India in 1935, failed to satisfy nationalist demands for independence.

Closing the Burma Road

The Japanese were well aware of Burman resentments. Helping their Asian brothers to oust the British seemed an attractive policy. Burmese nationalism would be for Japan's military planners the sword with which to cut off the British aid going up the Burma Road.[2] Among those in Burma seeking independence were activists of the nationalist Thakin (Master) Party. Notable among its leaders was a young man named Aung San. He had early started seeking to free his country from British rule. While a student at Rangoon University, Aung San had won election in autumn 1935 as secretary of the Rangoon University Students' Union (RUSU). Expelled in 1936 with a classmate for editing an article by the RUSU president that called for dismissing a faculty member, Aung San and his colleague became the center of student protests that spread to students in high school.

Under pressure, Rangoon University reversed the expulsion. The reinstated student leader was elected RUSU president in 1938.

That same year, Aung San became a founding member and leading figure of the Thakin Party. Part of a nationalist coalition, the Thakin Party was a grouping of leftists and revolutionaries of other political leanings united by a desire for complete and early independence. As secretary general, Aung San led his party's delegation in 1940 to India, where he met Mohandas K. Gandhi, Jawaharlal Nehru, and other leaders of India's Congress Party. The British banned the Thakin Party following the onset of the war with Germany on account of the hostility that Aung San and other party members showed to their overlords while the British were fighting for survival against Hitler's war machine. It was during this unsettled time that young Aung San's path crossed that of one of the Japanese Army's more remarkable individuals.[3]

The Japanese officer who received an order in March 1940 to gather intelligence on the Burma Road assignment was Maj. Suzuki Keiji, then in charge of the Army General Staff's marine transport section. Commissioned an infantry officer after graduating as a member of the Military Academy's Thirtieth Class in 1918, Suzuki had begun building his career as one of the few Anglo-American experts in an army almost entirely concerned with the challenges of Russia and China. Following his graduation from the elite General Staff College in 1929, Suzuki had operated clandestinely for three years in the Philippines, compiling intelligence on military topography to support Army plans for invasion.

Piercing dark eyes and a fierce mustache were external signs of Suzuki's willful character. Sugii Mitsuru, who had first known Suzuki on Taiwan when the latter was serving there as a young lieutenant, found his character from the start to be "wild" and "rough." Sugii, a native of Kyushu's Kumamoto Prefecture, was one of those Japanese who viewed a southward expansion into Asia as Japan's destiny. Similar to many natives of Kumamoto, a major source of Japanese immigrants in the Americas and the Asia-Pacific, he left Japan to find his destiny. His fate was not to settle as a farmer in Peru or a shopkeeper in Palau, as so many others from his prefecture did. Rather, he lived a restless life. Sugii spent ten years, from 1925, wandering Southeast Asia and traveling through the Americas and Africa. He then joined an organ of Japanese expansionism, the Shanghai office of the Asia

Development Board. It was there that Suzuki recruited him into his service.[4]

Part of Suzuki's drive stemmed, perhaps, from the obscurity in which he labored. Toiling in the fields of intelligence in the Imperial Japanese Army, he was on a career track inferior to that of the elite colleagues working as staff operations officers. Worse still, he was covering Anglo-American affairs. While Japan's military planners could not neglect the possibility of conflict with Great Britain or the United States, they devoted the lion's share of their attention to the pressing issues of China and the Soviet Union. Military planners had, indeed, declared the United States a hypothetical enemy several years earlier. They had even earmarked several divisions for an invasion of the Philippines. Yet, Anglo-American intelligence was an afterthought in the overall scheme of things. In the words of one intelligence veteran, the place of Suzuki and the other Anglo-American intelligence experts was that of "stepchildren" in the Army.[5] It was this galling position, perhaps, that accounted in part for his wild and fierce determination. He would rise from obscurity! That character, which would at times drive him beyond official sanction in his covert operations in Burma, would later lead to his downfall.

In June 1940, the Japanese Army in China advanced to the northern border of French Indochina to observe France's termination of aid to Chungking. The French, surrendering Paris to the Germans the same month, had been in no position to refuse the Japanese demand for an end to the French supply line. The move took Japan one step closer to achieving two key objectives. The advance permitted Tokyo to shut off the flow of French aid that had quietly been making its way from the northern port of Haiphong into China. In addition, the Japanese Army had advanced another step closer to seizing the West's colonies. On 28 June, Suzuki left Japan from the port of Hakata in northwest Kyushu. His orders from AGS were to observe the situation in Burma and report his findings to Tokyo.

On his way to Rangoon, Suzuki paid a visit to Col. Tamura Hiroshi, the Japanese military attaché in Bangkok. Thailand, located on China's southern border between British Burma and French Indochina, was then the only independent nation in Southeast Asia. Its political status and strategic location made Bangkok, like Istanbul in Turkey, one of the world's foremost centers of espionage. Events in Europe were further enhancing Bangkok's importance. Earlier that month, Italy had joined Germany in declaring war against Britain and France. Several days later, Hitler's Wehrmacht advanced in triumph into Paris. Britain was fighting with its back to the wall. France had already given up the fight. Japan had reached a fork in the road. What was happening in the region? Bangkok was the center of the regional network gathering the intelligence needed should Tokyo decide to pluck the colonial fruit of Southeast Asia. The Japanese Army simply could not blunder blindly into the region. Intelligence officers would shine a light in the darkness. Their topographical intelligence, enemy orders of battle, and lists of collaborators would guide Tokyo's warriors in a region AGS strategists had long neglected.

Col. Tamura, a native of Hiroshima and a member of the Military Academy's Twenty-eighth Class, worked as the top intelligence officer in the region. He was another of the Japanese Army's handful of Anglo-American intelligence veterans. Early in his career, October 1928 to December 1931, he had preceded Suzuki in gathering intelligence in the Philippines. Tamura had then served a first tour as military attaché in Bangkok from 1936 to 1938. Following a few months in Hong Kong and less than a year as chief of public affairs for Twenty-first Army, Tamura had returned to Bangkok for a second tour as military attaché in 1939. At the time Suzuki paid his visit, Tamura was directing Japan's intelligence operations throughout the region. When Suzuki appeared at his office, Tamura welcomed his junior colleague warmly.[6]

Suzuki, following his meeting with Tamura, left Bangkok for the Burmese capital of Rangoon. He entered Burma under the name Minami Masuyo. His cover story was that he had come to Burma as a newspaper correspondent for Japan's *Yomiuri Shinbun* and as secretary of the Japan-Burma Association. He reached Rangoon on 10 July. Suzuki, assisted by Sugii Mitsuru and other associates earlier recruited in Tokyo, turned to a resident Japanese trader and Buddhist priest from Japan's militant Nichiren sect to secure introductions to leading members of Burma's Thakin Party. Suzuki determined through his contacts that the Thakin Party was eager to accept arms and training from Japan in its struggle to oust the British from Burma. In late September, he learned of a promising development. Thakin Party General Secretary Aung San and another party member had evaded arrest by the British and made their way from Burma to the Chinese port city of Amoy. Suzuki contacted the Japanese Army in

Taiwan to request that someone locate the two. Leaving one of his associates in Rangoon, Suzuki then left Burma with Sugii in early October to return to Tokyo.

In reporting his findings to his superiors, Suzuki concluded by calling for the Army to aid the Burmese in overthrowing British rule. Impatient to start the ball rolling while his report made its way from one desk to another, Suzuki acted on his own authority to have Aung San sent to Tokyo. Undeterred by the lack of army funds, he turned for financial aid to a supportive sugar company executive whom he had previously recruited as part of his venture.

As for Aung San, who had reached Amoy in August, the Amoy SSA had picked him up early in November. Once in Army custody, Aung San and an associate agreed to travel to Tokyo. The two were astute enough to understand that their hosts were likely to send them to Japan in any event. When they landed at Haneda Airport a few days later, Suzuki was waiting there to meet them. The Japanese officer made a strong impression on the young Burmese. Aung San later recounted how Suzuki had welcomed them to Japan by offering them women, a point of hospitality that the exhausted men declined. Aung San also recalled later how Suzuki had boasted to them of having killed Russian civilians, including women and children, in Vladivostok during the Siberian Intervention. Now, Suzuki told his two guests, the Burmese must fight in the same pitiless way against the British.

Suzuki's superiors, when they learned of Suzuki's unauthorized guests, dressed him down for acting on his own in bringing the two Burmese to Tokyo. Having registered their displeasure regarding his unsanctioned initiative, however, AGS then approved Suzuki's plan to subvert British rule in Burma. The move had more to do with the dynamics of military bureaucracy than with the force or logic of the major's argument. In effect, the Army accepted the plan in a bid to prevent the Navy from making Burma its exclusive preserve. A reserve naval officer had returned to Tokyo in September 1940 to lobby the Navy to support Burmese nationalists.[7] It was the prospect of the Army's rival service stealing a march on them that brought action on Suzuki's proposal. In December, Eighth Section of AGS Second Bureau coordinated with the Navy General Staff's Third Bureau, its intelligence counterpart, for a joint Burma operation under Suzuki's direction.[8]

On 1 February 1941, the joint Army-Navy organ to subvert British rule in Burma was established under Imperial General Headquarters. Its name, the Minami Agency, was a play on words. Minami was both Suzuki's cover name and the Japanese word for "south." It was a worthy name for an organization whose mission was to execute covert operations in support of Japanese military interests in Southeast Asia. Its overt name was the Southern Corporate Research Society.[9] Among those attending the formal inauguration ceremony were Army Chief of Staff Lt. Gen. Sugiyama Gen and Navy Vice Chief of Staff Vice Adm. Kondo Nobutake.

The Minami Agency's initial mission was to assist Aung San and other Burmese nationalists in overthrowing the British. To this end, Colonel Suzuki's organization was to make the arrangements to smuggle small arms and explosives into Burma and to train a cadre of Burmese who would lead a guerrilla movement. If all went well, Aung San and the others would rally Burmese and pose an increasingly strong challenge to the British colonial garrisons. Naturally, no Japanese would go into Burma. Nor would the British find any Japanese weapons among the insurgents. The Japanese hand was to remain hidden, giving Tokyo's diplomats plausible deniability should the British protest. In the latter half of 1941, following the initial phase, the Minami Agency would move to launch the guerrilla operation by inserting the arms and trained cadre into Burma.

At the core of Colonel Suzuki's operation were men of the fledgling Nakano School. Direct oversight of the Minami Agency at Second Bureau's Eighth Section was the responsibility of Capt. Ozeki Masaji, who served at the intelligence school as an instructor. Among the first graduates assigned under Colonel Suzuki within the Minami Agency were captains Kakubo Naomi and Kawashima Takenobu, as well as lieutenants Yamamoto Masayoshi, Noda Takeshi, and Takahashi Hachiro. All five were among the Nakano School's first graduates. Others followed. A number of naval officers completed the roster.[10]

The Minami Agency quickly went to work, establishing an intelligence network in Thailand. The agency's first members began arriving in early February. Suzuki arrived in Bangkok to set up his headquarters on 24 February. He directed his men to establish branches at Chiang Mai and other strategic points in Thailand. While British intelligence officers were operating from Bangkok, the threat to the operation was far less than that posed by the countless police, soldiers, and informants in neighboring Burma. The Agency's members assigned to the outlying branches surveyed the roads leading from Thailand to Burma and gathered other topographical intelligence. The branches were also to help Burmese nationalists cross the border and, once the uprising was in motion, to smuggle arms into Burma.[11]

Launched with great expectations, Japan's sole joint military intelligence operation soon sank under the weight of interservice rivalry and suspicion. The Agency's divisions surfaced early. Suzuki, during his earlier trip to Rangoon, had spurned a Burmese activist favored by the Japanese Navy in favor of a man of his own choosing, Aung San.[12] Once the Agency had set up operations in Bangkok, relations between its Army and Navy members worsened in an alarming way. Before long, Suzuki was directing Army members to investigate and tail Navy members of his agency. The end of the joint venture came when one Navy officer grew so distressed over Army surveillance that he went to the naval attaché's office to seek relief. There ensued a local "summit" in late August between Col. Tamura Hiroshi and the naval attaché in Bangkok.[13] In the end, the two services settled on withdrawing the navy members. The Minami Agency at that point became entirely an Army undertaking.[14]

Despite the early breakdown in interservice cooperation, the Minami Agency managed to gather and train a group of Burmese nationalists from Aung San's Thakin Party. Suzuki, using the contacts he had made while chief of the Army's marine transport section, arranged with Japan's Daido Shipping Company for his men to travel as seamen aboard the *Shunten Maru*, a company merchant ship that sailed between Japan and Burma.[15] Including Aung San, thirty young Burmese nationalists constituted the Burmese cadre that the Minami Agency was to train. Their names would go down in history as the Thirty Comrades. For certain Japanese, those for whom the Second World War was a glorious lost cause of Asian liberation, the Minami Agency's mentoring of the Thirty Comrades was an important chapter of history.

With Tokyo authorizing June 1941 as the date for instigating an armed uprising in Burma, the Minami Agency began in March to put its Burmese members through rigorous training at a secret camp in Sanya, a town hidden in the interior of Hainan, an occupied island off China's south coast. Today a booming tourist destination of discotheques and fun in the sun, Hainan then was an obscure island where Chinese emperors had long banished those who offended them.[16] The isolated tropical isle was an ideal setting for secret training.

Capt. Kawashima Takenobu, a graduate of the Military Academy's Forty-eighth Class prior to his training at the Nakano School, served in the Minami Agency as Suzuki's right-hand man. It was Kawashima who took overall charge of training. Lt. Izumiya Tatsuro, another graduate of the Nakano School, ran the First Training Squad, which was responsible for training the Burmese who were to assume leadership positions in the uprising. Among Izumiya's charges was one Shu Maung, alias Ne Win ("Brilliant as the Sun"). Izumiya saw that the young man's frail appearance masked a keen intellect and fierce fighting spirit. Ne Win impressed him both with quickness in absorbing lessons and his ardor in wielding the bayonet in training. Izumiya's student would later rise to the rank of general in postwar Burma before seizing power in 1962. Other Nakano School graduates were on hand to run the Burmese through a grueling course designed to turn the green political activists into seasoned guerrilla leaders. The training ranged from map reading to bayonet practice. The Burmese trained with weapons captured in China. Since their planned uprising was to appear an indigenous affair, the trainers avoided using Japanese equipment. Plausible deniability would be implausible if the British captured guerrilla rifles embossed with the imperial chrysanthemum found on Japanese weapons.

While the Minami Agency's grueling training taught the Thirty Comrades the essentials of guerrilla warfare, the exhausting and harsh regimen also showed the Burmese the dark side of working with Japan. There was, first, the demanding drilling that their Japanese trainers imposed. The Burmese also had to endure certain distasteful aspects of Japanese nationalism. This included starting each morning with the Burmese nationalists having to join their trainers in bowing in the direction of the imperial palace in Tokyo. Worse, the June target date for the uprising passed without the Japanese sending them into Burma as promised. In October, the training shifted from Hainan to a camp in southern Taiwan.[17] Izumiya later recalled the atmosphere at the time, noting that a "mood of estrangement began to set in."[18] Resentment rose to the point that Aung San discovered on his return from a trip to Tokyo that his comrades were on the verge of rebelling against their trainers. He dissuaded them from revolt, but the experience early tempered the enthusiasm of the Thirty Comrades for cooperation with Japan.[19]

From Subversion to Invasion

The Minami Agency and its Thirty Comrades had fallen victim to shifting priorities determined at Imperial General Headquarters. Suzuki's superiors in February 1941 had ordered him to prepare to instigate an armed uprising in Burma. However, they put the operation on ice once Japan's leaders decided to launch a conventional military invasion of the American, British, and Dutch colonies in southeast Asia. By the time the uprising was to have begun, Tokyo was preparing to go to war. Hitler's invasion of the Soviet Union on 22 June, Operation Barbarossa, had convinced Japan's leaders that they had to enter the war before they "missed the bus." If Hitler vanquished Stalin, what right would the Japanese have to Siberia? Even worse was to contemplate German demands for the Asian colonies of Britain, France, and Holland.

An imperial conference on 2 July ratified Japan's policy of joining Germany and Italy in the fighting without resolving the dispute between those in the Army, keen on invading the Soviet Union, and the Navy's demand to sail for Southeast Asia. In September, another imperial conference started the formal countdown to a Japanese strike south, set for 8 December. Requiring a placid front behind which to prepare its surprise assaults, Imperial General Headquarters could not afford the risk of executing the program for the Burmese uprising as planned. So it was only after troops of the Imperial Japanese Army had already gone on the offensive in Southeast Asia that the Minami Agency could prepare to take the Thirty Comrades across the Thai border into Burma as part of the Japanese offensive campaign.[20]

On 8 December, the same day that would live "in infamy" for President Franklin Delano Roosevelt and an American public outraged by the Japanese Navy's surprise attack on Pearl Harbor, the Fifteenth Army of Japan's Southern Army entered Bangkok from French Indochina without opposition. Thai leaders, correctly assessing the balance of power between the Japanese juggernaut and their own meager forces, took the path of alliance with Japan rather than suffer outright conquest. The Thais would later show the supple nature of their diplomacy by abjuring their wartime ally once Japan had lost, thereby escaping punishment at the hands of the victorious United Nations.

On 20 December, Fifteenth Army Headquarters launched its campaign for Burma by ordering one of its divisions to capture Moulmein. As for the Minami Agency, Southern Army placed it under the command of Fifteenth Army on 23 December. In the next several days, Kawashima, Izumiya, and other Agency trainers brought Aung San and their other Burmese collaborators from Taiwan to Saigon, the site of Southern Army General Headquarters. The Minami Agency had shifted its Thailand operations to Saigon on the eve of the war. On 28 December, Minami Agency members and their Burmese charges reached Bangkok. Suzuki then organized a volunteer force of resident Burmese, the Burma Independence Army (BIA), in which the Thirty Comrades would play leading roles under Agency direction. Some two dozen Nakano School graduates, including Kawashima and Izumiya, constituted the core of the BIA's Japanese "advisers."[21]

Colonel Suzuki, having seen shredded his original plan for leading an insurrection, lobbied hard to include the Minami Agency in the Japanese Army's campaign for Burma. His demands met with rejection. The commanding officers had no wish to have Suzuki's irregular forces complicate their conventional plans. Suzuki failed in a conference on 13 February with the commander of the Fifty-fifth Division, slated to lead the drive to Rangoon, to gain permission to operate in the division's area of responsibility. Suzuki had sought to accompany Fifty-fifth Division in the campaign for Moulmein. Instead, he had had to settle for leading his force into Burma from the north. The main part of Suzuki's BIA crossed the border only on 7 February, entering a region populated not by ethnic Burmans but by minority peoples on the whole hostile to the dominant Burmese and sympathetic to the British.[22]

Leading his force, Suzuki conducted more a psychological operation than a conventional military campaign. He borrowed the Burmese legend of a liberating warrior named "General Thunder," appropriating that name for his identity. He cut a dashing figure, riding through Burma astride a white horse. As T.E. Lawrence had operated to free the Arabs from Turkish rule in the First World War, gaining glory as Lawrence of Arabia, so Suzuki aimed to play a heroic role in lifting the British yoke from Burma.[23] With few men at his command, Suzuki's force fought harassing actions against small enemy units. He also struck at British authority by attacking the local police and other native officials of Burma's colonial administration. Suzuki's small force also attracted an enthusiastic response from many Burmese as word spread of its presence. The BIA, according to one British historian, undermined British morale by stoking fears of Burmese "fifth column activities."[24]

Contributing to British fears of a native fifth column was Ne Win, one of the Minami Agency's original Thirty Comrades. On 14 January, ahead of the Japanese Army's invasion, Ne Win left the Thai town of Raheng for Rangoon with five fellow Burmese and two Nakano School graduates serving in the Minami Agency. Nearly two weeks later, the men reached a tributary of the Salween River separating Thailand from Burma. Once across the river, Ne Win and his Burmese compatriots parted company with their Japanese advisors and made for the Burmese capital. Reaching Rangoon on 2 February, over a month before the Japanese Army's entry, Ne Win made contact with other Burmese patriots and began organizing guerrillas to harass the British in the rear. Once Rangoon fell in March, Ne Win served as principal assistant to Captain Kawashima in organizing the BIA before the young force departed with the Japanese on a campaign for northern Burma.[25]

Even as the BIA fought for independence, however, Southern Army began issuing instructions for a Japanese military government. Burma, adjoining the vast expanse of India, Great Britain's remaining bastion in Asia, was vital both for its position as the western border of Japan's new empire and for the abundant raw materials that were vital for Japan to continue waging war. Prime Minister Tojo Hideki had referred to Burmese independence in a speech before the Imperial Diet on 21 January 1942, raising the hopes of Aung San and the Minami Agency's other Burmese activists. However, Imperial General Headquarters on 22 January declared that Burma would fall under Japanese military administration until the granting of independence at some unspecified date.

On 31 January, Fifteenth Army's Fifty-fifth Division entered Moulmein, its first major objective in Burma. The Division's commanders, who had earlier barred the Minami Agency and BIA from operating in its area of responsibility during the fighting, then prohibited Suzuki's men in Moulmein from conducting political activities or recruiting for the BIA. While Fifty-fifth Division immediately began laying the groundwork for a military administration, the local office of the Minami Agency was consigned to an obscure house on the outskirts of town. Activists of the Thakin Party, the source of the Minami Agency's Burmese activists, had no role to play in Moulmein. Their experience gave them their "first taste of disillusionment with the Japanese Army," according to Izumiya. The Burmese "learned for the first time that the Japanese Army was distinct" from the Minami Agency.[26] The Burmese operating under the Minami Agency learned, as did the disillusioned Arabs who fought the Turks with T.E. Lawrence and lived to see the British and French partition their lands, that imperial interests trump ideals of liberation.

Neither Tokyo nor Southern Army General Headquarters, responsible for securing the security of the region, had any desire to complicate matters by granting independence to Burma. Propaganda would take a back seat to security. Army commanders would not risk their western flank, with the British Army in India and Chiang's Nationalists to the north, by setting the Burmese free. So it was that Southern Army released on 9 February the outline of its plan for military government in Burma. On 8 March, the day that Fifteenth Army marched in triumph into Rangoon, Southern Army issued in detail the plans for military rule.[27]

Suzuki adamantly opposed the plan for military government. He immediately began lobbying Fifteenth Army to reverse its decision once he reached Rangoon on 13 March. Was it some messianic delusion, a mundane ambition to have his Minami Agency play the role of advisory organ to an independent Burma, or some combination of the two, that drove him? Whatever the motive, Suzuki argued his case in repeated meetings with Col. Nasu Yoshio, Fifteenth Army's vice chief of staff. Nasu hailed from the same class of the Military Academy as Suzuki, but the old school tie failed to move Nasu in the least. Suzuki not only failed to sway his old classmate or the other staff officers of Fifteenth Army. His forceful arguments succeeded in giving them the impression that he had "gone native." Colonel Nasu at one point in their talks accused Suzuki of speaking irresponsibly and demanded to know whether he was "still a Japanese." Suzuki, frustrated by his failure to sway Fifteenth Army brass, poured forth his frustration after each meeting to his assistant Kawashima and other officers of the Minami Agency.[28]

While making his case for independence, Suzuki also continued to direct the BIA's operations in Burma. In Rangoon, he prepared the BIA to march north as part of the next phase of the Japanese Army's Burma campaign. Aung San, with his Japanese advisers, commanded the BIA's northern expedition. As during the initial invasion, the BIA engaged minor enemy units and eliminated local colonial officials. Suzuki himself also joined the campaign, directing the BIA against pro-British Karens. By the end of May 1942, the BIA had gained considerable combat experience. Starting with thirty members as an initial cadre, the BIA had grown to a force of nearly thirty thousand. Suzuki's force had also acquired considerable stocks of captured weapons.[29]

End of the Minami Agency

Despite Suzuki's determined arguments and the BIA's exploits, however, the British retreat from Burma to India marked the end of both the Minami Agency and the BIA. On 11 June, Southern Army issued orders for the Minami Agency's dissolution. Suzuki left Rangoon for Tokyo on 15 July, his new orders directing him to report for duty there with the Imperial Guards Division. The Nakano School's Kawashima, Izumiya, and the other Japanese intelligence operatives received new duties in Fifteenth Army's military administration of Burma. Soon thereafter, most of the Japanese members of Suzuki's disbanded agency received transfers to new assignment areas. Izumiya, for example, reported to Southern Army General Headquarters in Saigon to brief Lt. Tarora Sadao, another graduate of the Nakano School, on the Minami Agency's activities. Izumiya then took a new assignment in counterintelligence.[30]

Whatever the disappointment of Colonel Suzuki and his Japanese subordinates, the Thirty Comrades and other Burmese working with the Minami Agency must have suffered a keener sense of betrayal. Burma's new Japanese rulers refused both to grant independence or even to accept Aung San and other nationalists of the Thakin Party as their political intermediaries with the people of Burma. Southern Army, disinclined to work with ardent young nationalists, turned instead to Dr. Ba Maw, an older and more flexible nationalist who had held office in the British colonial administration. Ba Maw, plucked by the Kempeitai in May 1942 from the jail cell into which the retreating

British had thrown him, immediately became chief executive of the Burmese administrators who carried out the orders of Fifteenth Army.[31]

Aung San, denied a political role, became commander of the Burma Defense Army (BDA), a garrison force much reduced from the BIA that Suzuki had raised. The BIA, a force of thirty thousand under the Minami Agency, disappeared once the Japanese Army had secured Burma. In its stead was born on 27 July 1942 the BDA, a token force of only some three thousand men. With the Minami Agency's departure and Suzuki's transfer to Tokyo, only Captain Kawashima and a few other veterans of the operation remained to train and direct the new Burmese force.

Ne Win took command of the BDA's First Battalion. Serving as the BDA's chief military "advisor" was Capt. Noda Takeshi, a remaining member of the Minami Agency. Several of Suzuki's old subordinates stayed with him to direct the BDA. Aung San, Ne Win, and other members of the Thirty Comrades, far from commanding an independent army, suffered the indignity of serving as officers in a puppet force, subject to the "guidance" of their Japanese "advisers." The Japanese Army's dreaded Kempeitai shadowed leading Burmese and subjected those suspected of dangerous political views or espionage to interrogation under torture. Under such conditions, Burmese tolerance for Japanese rule would last only so long as Southern Army remained firmly in control of its new empire.

By all appearances, Suzuki's exploits as commander of the Minami Agency and BIA made little impression on his superiors. The military brass of Fifteenth Army had barred him from operating alongside the Fifty-fifth Division during the drive for Rangoon. They had ignored his repeated calls for immediate Burmese independence. Even a limited independence, such as Suzuki's apparent dream of the Thakin Party leading Burma under the guidance of his Minami Agency, was too much for the narrow vision of Southern Army's leading officers.

In any event, Suzuki enjoyed only limited success in his career after his adventure in Burma. A year after his return to Tokyo, Suzuki received a promotion to major general. However, he then spent much of the rest of the war involved again with military transport. His last wartime connection with Burma came in August 1943. Japan by then had finally moved to grant independence to Burma on 1 August.

When Ba Maw, Aung San, and other Burmese leaders came to Tokyo later that month to pay their respects to Prime Minister Tojo, the Japanese Army called Suzuki from his post in Hokkaido to attend the reception.[32]

Lt. Tarora Sadao, a Nakano School graduate who had dealings with the Minami Agency from his intelligence post at Southern Army General Headquarters in Saigon, viewed Suzuki as a tragic figure. The British military officer T.E. Lawrence, renowned as Lawrence of Arabia, had worked during the First World War with the Arabs, whom he had sincerely admired, to free them from the rule of the Ottoman Turks. Lawrence's promises had proven empty, however, when London joined Paris after the war to share the spoils of the fallen Turkish Empire's Arab lands rather than grant independence to their inhabitants. In the same way, according to Tarora, Suzuki had sincerely worked with the Burmese toward the goal of winning their independence from British rule. He had given his word that Burma would be independent, then tried to keep it by arguing without success for revocation of Japan's military administration. For his pains, Suzuki's superiors treated him as an irresponsible officer who had "gone native," then steered his career into a dead end.[33] Suzuki's associate Sugii also saw Suzuki as another Lawrence. Knowing Suzuki's wild character since his early military career in Taiwan, Sugii later wrote that Suzuki's downfall was inevitable from the start.[34]

Colonel Suzuki, Captain Kawashima, and the Minami Agency's other shadow warriors had done much to win hearts and minds in Burma. The Thirty Comrades had linked their aspirations to Japan. Once the Japanese Army rolled into Burma, tens of thousands of youths sought to join the BIA. Suzuki's superiors, in a chain leading from Rangoon through Saigon to Tokyo, then squandered their assets. Rather than channeling Burmese enthusiasm into an alliance, they clamped an iron military administration onto Burma. With victory in hand, they disbanded the Minami Agency and scattered its expertise to the four winds. Colonel Suzuki's dreams ended in the "tragedy" of thwarted ambition. Compounding Suzuki's personal tragedy was the tragic inability of top Japanese commanders to see the strategic possibilities of enlightened rule, if not outright liberation.

For the Japanese Army's leaders, their early failure to see the value of the Minami Agency or to understand the depth of Burmese nationalism sowed the seeds of later tragedy. First welcomed in Burma as a liberating force, the Japanese Army neglected to respect Burmese nationalism or to treat the Burmese as other than members of a conquered and occupied nation. Belated and nominal independence, granted too late in 1943, did little to change the nature of the occupation. For Japan's leaders, the only vision of "independence" for conquered territories was the sham model built in Manchukuo, their puppet empire. Having set Burmese ambitions ablaze in ousting the British, the Japanese squandered the goodwill they had earned by imposing a harsh and humiliating military administration. Had Japan's generals risked granting Burma freedom from the outset, had they trained the early BIA into a true army to fight alongside them, rather than reducing it to a token force, they could have exacted a far greater price for the Allied reconquest of Burma.

Aung San's promotion to defense minister of "independent" Burma and commander of its modest armed forces, redesignated the Burma National Army, did little to satisfy the young nationalist's resentment at the Japanese Army's continued domination of his country. With the British fighting their way back to Burma in any event, he would have been a fool to hold firm in solidarity with the Japanese. Aung San and other Burmese nationalists, sorely disappointed, returned Japanese disdain for their aspirations by biding their time for an opportunity to revolt. In the end, the decision to treat Burma as an occupied nation rather than as an ally would leave Japan in the war's last months to face both Allied invasion from India and a Burmese revolt behind the lines.

4

INDIA: SUBVERSION, INVASION, RETREAT

Birth of the Iwakuro Agency

The Japanese Army launched in March 1942 a major operation to destroy British rule in India. The subcontinent had long been the "jewel in the crown" of Great Britain's global empire. At its height, British India bordered Iran in the west and Thailand in the east, ranging from the snow-capped peaks of the Himalayas along the southern border of China in the north to the lush island of Ceylon in the Indian Ocean to the south. In addition to India itself, the lands once administered as British India are today Pakistan, Sri Lanka (Ceylon), Bangladesh, and Burma. Nepal and Bhutan, on India's northern frontier, were bound to British India by treaties limiting their autonomy but stopping short of formal integration into Britain's Indian empire.

Lord Curzon, who served with distinction as Viceroy of India from 1899 to 1905, aptly captured India's vital importance: "As long as we rule India we are the greatest power in the world. If we lose it we shall drop straight away to a third-rate power." The subcontinent was an immense source of wealth. From 1880, India was the leading market for British manufactured exports. In the years following the First World War, India absorbed more production from the British isles than Australia, Canada, and South Africa combined. India's colonial overseers also worked to develop the subcontinent to yield great quantities of cotton, indigo, jute, and tea.[1]

India was also vital to the British Empire as a source of soldiers.

Britain's subjects on the subcontinent already numbered well over 200 million by the time of the first imperial census in 1871. From India's multitudes, Great Britain built the Indian Army, which both guarded the subcontinent and fought overseas for the empire in both world wars. In the First World War, 800,000 of India's 1.4 million troops followed the British flag to foreign battlefields. Their contribution was roughly equal to the total number of men mustered by Australia, Canada, New Zealand, and South Africa combined. Some fifty thousand Indians served in Europe. Many more fought in the campaigns for Gallipoli, Mesopotamia, Egypt, Palestine, and German East Africa. By the time the guns had ceased firing, some sixty-five thousand Indians had died for King George V.

The Indian Army, which had compiled a creditable record in the Great War of 1914–1918, loomed as a threat to Japan's gains in 1942. Beyond the frontier of Burma, Great Britain retained control of the men, resources, and territory of the subcontinent. India remained viable as a base for a future Allied return to Southeast Asia. Japan's military planners could expect that the Indian Army would play a key role in any such campaign. In fact, Great Britain would draw on India's population of 390 million during the war to put 2.5 million of the subcontinent's subjects under arms. The Indian Army would fight not only against the Japanese in Southeast Asia but against the Italians and Germans in Abyssinia, Greece, North Africa, and Italy. Depriving Great Britain of this base would be a major step towards securing Japan's new empire.[2]

The Japanese Army, unprepared in 1942 to conquer India, opted instead to foment rebellion. The man chosen to execute the Japanese High Command's policy was Col. Iwakuro Hideo. He was, according to a Japanese who covered Washington affairs for Japan's Domei News Agency, "engagingly frank, of great energy, and with an alert brain, a man with boundless enthusiasm for the work to which he was assigned."[3] Iwakuro's star had been on the rise since he had played a key role in founding the Nakano School. In February 1939, he won promotion to the post of chief of the Army Affairs Section of the Military Affairs Bureau, one of the Army's key policy posts. The Army Affairs Section was involved at the highest level in the general direction of Japanese policy. It was as section chief, for example, that Iwakuro informed Hoshino Naoki, the Japanese official who directed Manchukuo's industrial development, of the Japanese Army's decision that he join the cabinet of Prime Minister Konoe Fumimaro. Hoshino duly joined the Konoe government as chief of the powerful Cabinet Planning Board.[4]

In February 1941, Iwakuro quietly left Japan for the United States on a mission to seek a settlement with Washington on China. He went first to New York to discuss the issues with Herbert Hoover. The former president, still a leading figure in the Republican Party and a man of influence, warned Iwakuro that the two sides should reach agreement by summer or risk a war that would "set civilization back five hundred years." Iwakuro then went to Washington. There he joined Adm. Nomura Kichisaburo, who was appointed ambassador to the United States the same month that Iwakuro received his assignment, in informal discussions with Secretary of State Cordell Hull and other American officials. Despite the wide gulf that separated the two nations over China, Iwakuro left a decided impression in Washington. In his memoirs, Hull remembered him: "Iwakuro had all the virtues and shortcomings of a Japanese Army officer. He was a very fine type, calmly poised, very sure of himself without being annoyingly self-confident. He could, of course, see only his Army's viewpoint, not ours or the real interest of Japan."[5]

In August, having failed to win American understanding for Japan's position in China, Iwakuro returned to Tokyo. With him he carried a Japanese intelligence report from New York that indicated the overwhelming war potential of American industry. The report, compiled by Col. Shinjo Kenkichi from information provided by over fifty Japanese companies in New York, estimated that America's war potential, measured by steel production capacity and other indices, was between ten and twenty times that of Japan. Iwakuro spent the latter half of the month arguing in vain before top military and civilian leaders against Japan's going to war against the United States. The die was cast. Iwakuro then left Tokyo for French Indochina, in effect exiled there by War Minister Tojo Hideki for his contrary views. In Cambodia, Iwakuro took command of the Fifth Imperial Guards Regiment, which he led shortly thereafter in the march on Singapore.[6]

A greater chance for glory came when Imperial General Headquarters turned to Iwakuro to subvert British rule in India. Tojo Hideki, who had become prime minister in October while retaining his war ministry portfolio, doubtless approved of the selection. Iwakuro had a proven track record in intelligence and administration that recommended him for the assignment. Even better, from Tojo's point of view, the mission would take Iwakuro far from Tokyo.[7]

Such was the background behind the launching of the Iwakuro Agency on 25 March 1942 in Saigon. On the basis of the Sanno Conference that he and Fujiwara had attended earlier that month, Iwakuro put together an organization that resembled less a covert unit than a diplomatic mission. His agency was to develop propaganda for Indians resident throughout Asia, train Indian commandos and infiltrate them into India, maintain covert contacts with Indian nationalists inside India, and organize the INA.[8]

Iwakuro's organization included a stellar staff, testimony to his connections. Two of his top recruits were Takaoka Daisuke and Koyama Makoto, both legislators in the Imperial Japanese Diet. Takaoka, who also had gained distinction as one of Japan's few "India hands," oversaw political affairs. Koyama, a fiery young legislator known as the "Tiger of the Diet," took charge of a covert training base for Indians at Penang. Takaoka had graduated in 1923, a student of Indian languages, from the Tokyo School of Foreign Languages. He then served as an advisor to the colonial government in Taiwan, directed the Japan-India Association, and wrote a book on India before entering the Diet. Koyama was a bit of a swashbuckler. He had worked on the crew of a Japanese ship chartered by the Italian Navy during the First World War before entering the Diet.

Iwakuro's pull also extended to his fellow military officers. In charge of general affairs for Iwakuro was Lt. Col. Maki Tatsuo, a former assistant military attaché in Berlin with a track record at IGHQ as an able administrator. Col. Saito Jiro, a veteran of the War Ministry's press section, took charge of propaganda. Maj. Ogawa Saburo, a blunt officer from Kyushu, took charge of the military section, which was responsible for directing the INA.[9] Lt. Col. Kitabe Kunio, who headed the Iwakuro Agency's Burma branch, was a veteran military advisor who had cut his teeth in Manchukuo and North China.[10] Graduates of the Nakano School served in the Iwakuro Agency as adjutants to Iwakuro's section chiefs and by holding other key posts. Such individuals included a few holdovers from the Fujiwara Agency, such as Yamaguchi Hitoshi, assigned to the propaganda section, as well as numerous new members.

The Iwakuro Agency, consisting at first of some 250 members, would grow in time to more than 500, stationed in Bangkok, Singapore, Rangoon, Saigon, and Hong Kong. In short, Iwakuro had put together a large organization that enjoyed ample funds and the most impressive expertise on India ever assembled in a Japanese military organization.[11] Kunizuka Kazunori, who had served under Fujiwara before working for Iwakuro, was so awed by his new associates that he later described feeling like a "male Cinderella" surrounded by royalty. Kuwahara Takeshi, another member of the Agency, offered acerbic praise of Iwakuro's political acumen, suggesting that he would have made a better politician than he did a soldier.[12]

The Iwakuro Agency came into being at the height of Japan's triumphs. The Dutch on Java had surrendered their oil-rich colony to the Japanese on 9 March, one day after the Japanese Army had marched into Rangoon. In the Philippines, Gen. Homma Masaharu's December invasion had quickly driven Gen. Douglas MacArthur's troops to the Bataan Peninsula, where they were facing the stark choices of starvation or surrender in a hopeless fight. On 23 March, the Japanese Navy occupied India's Andaman Islands as a first move of an operation to drive the British Navy from its base at Ceylon. There was talk of Japanese and German forces meeting in India.

In April, however, Lt. Col. James Doolittle led a group of bombers from the decks of U.S. aircraft carriers in the first American bombing raid on Tokyo. Doolittle's raid did little real damage but deeply shocked and enraged Japan's military planners. The Japanese Navy responded by drafting plans to seize Midway and Hawaii to deprive the Americans of bases from which to launch further raids. The result was a disastrous loss at Midway.

On 1 May, the Iwakuro Agency moved its headquarters from Saigon to Bangkok. One of Iwakuro's first moves was to stage a major conference of Indian leaders as an encore to the Sanno Conference. Some two thousand Indians from throughout Asia, including some 160 leaders of the IIL and INA, gathered at a Bangkok theater that month to discuss India's independence. Between the opening and closing sessions of 15 and 23 May, open to the public, the delegates met behind closed doors to discuss the details of independence in alliance with Japan. Those attending the public ceremonies included the Japanese, German, and Italian ambassadors as well as Thailand's deputy foreign minister. Highlights of the conference included ringing calls from conference chairman Rash Behari Bose and other speakers for Indians to throw off the yoke of British oppression. The finale was the reading of a telegram from Subhas Chandra Bose in Berlin, who lavished praise on his Axis allies and called on Indians to take up arms with them in the independence struggle. The audience responded to the message with thunderous applause and cries of "Long live the revolution, long live the two Boses!"[13]

Iwakuro, having staged a rousing spectacle, put his agency into gear. He devoted a good deal of his organization's resources to training agents for covert action on the Indian subcontinent. On the island of Penang, lying off the west coast of the Malay peninsula, Koyama Makoto set up a covert training center at a Japanese submarine base. Under him were a number of Japanese civilians, including a graduate of Okawa Shumei's academy. Graduates of the Nakano School constituted the core of the center. There were also a number of Indian assistants and trainees. The center consisted of several sections. The Raghavan (R) Section included the Swaraj (Independence) Institute, run by N. Raghavan, a local version of the Nakano School for Indians. Iwakuro Agency members from the Nakano School instructed select Indian youths in intelligence, subversion, CI, and propaganda to prepare them for infiltration. The Osman (O) Section trained Sikhs from the Punjab. The Gilani (G) Section, run by an INA officer named Gilani, chiefly handled Muslims. The Nepal (N) Section was responsible for operations involving Nepalese soldiers, commonly known as Gurkhas, whose loyalty, long knives, and courage had earned them a particular reputation among troops of the Indian Army. Kamimoto Toshio, who had earned good marks for liaison with the Japanese bandit Harimao in the Malaya campaign, received a new assignment in N Section. Last to be established at Penang was a section for infiltrating operatives into Ceylon.[14]

The Iwakuro Agency selected some fifty Indians for training at Penang, then sent them by submarine to India to gather military intelligence, assess popular attitudes, contact nationalists, and incite subversive acts. One group went ashore near Karachi. A second group landed south of Bombay.[15] The Agency's Burma branch also sent agents along the frontier of India to subvert any British Indian troops still in the area. Others went across the border to gather intelligence. Finally, from early January 1943, men of the Burma branch began training agents to parachute into India.[16]

The Iwakuro Agency also applied much of its talent toward producing propaganda. Singapore was the base for the Agency's radio broadcasts in English, Hindi, Bengali, and other regional languages. Iwakuro's men also produced pamphlets and leaflets deriding British rule and urging Indians to revolt. One leaflet showed an Indian pushing aside a curtain to reveal to a shocked Prime Minister Churchill and two Indian servants the scene of two Burmese in native dress chasing out of Burma a British soldier in tattered uniform. The cartoon's caption read: "All British colonies are awake. Why must Indians stay slaves? Seize this chance, rise." Most leaflets put their message across by using cartoons that depicted such scenes as the Amritsar Massacre of 1919, when a senior British officer in Punjab ordered his troops to fire into an unarmed crowd of demonstrators. Iwakuro also enjoyed the service of a famous Japanese illustrator who came from Singapore to lend his talents to the cause.[17]

For all Iwakuro's talents and resources, he was unable to incite revolt in India or prevent rebellion among the Indians in his service. The British had long kept their Indian Empire under strict surveillance. Subhas Chandra Bose was impressed while a student at Cambridge after the First World War by how liberal and tolerant he found England, "having been brought up in a police-ridden atmosphere" in Bengal. British wariness over subversion had only grown stronger with the outbreak of the war with Japan.

In India, British police and intelligence officers were able to round up many of Iwakuro's agents. When one party of agents went ashore near Bombay in April 1943, the British acted quickly on an informant's tip to intercept them.[18] The British also countered Iwakuro's propaganda, beaming their own radio programs from Delhi with the help of such Indians as Nirad C. Chaudhuri, a former political secretary to Sarat Chandra Bose, the prominent Bengali nationalist and elder brother of Subhas Chandra Bose. In November 1942, Delhi broadcast the news that one of Iwakuro's Indian agents had defected to the British during an operation originating in Burma. The British had a field day with the defection of the agent, Maj. R. Dhillon, broadcasting Dhillon's allegations of growing discord within the Iwakuro Agency's Indian program and his charges that Rash Behari Bose was but a Japanese puppet and that the INA was only a show force.

News of Dhillon's defection reached Iwakuro in early November, while he was inspecting his Burma organization. With Iwakuro was Maj. Fujiwara Iwaichi, his predecessor in Indian operations, who had become an intelligence staff officer at Southern Army. Iwakuro at once summoned Lieutenant Colonel Gill, his senior Indian officer in Burma. Iwakuro, Fujiwara, and other Japanese officers grilled Gill, repeatedly accusing him of ordering Dhillon to defect. Iwakuro, not satisfied with Gill's protestations of innocence, turned him over to the Kempeitai for further questioning.[19]

By late November, Iwakuro was facing a crisis. In spite of his keen intellect and political acumen, he showed none of Fujiwara's knack for dealing with his Indian partners. Not only did Iwakuro show none of Fujiwara's warmth or sincerity towards the Indians, he disapproved of the man Fujiwara had chosen as INA commander. Mohan Singh, in Iwakuro's view, was too "hot-blooded." Iwakuro also cared little in general for the Indian prisoners who volunteered for service in the INA. The Japanese Army drilled its officers and men to prefer an honorable death to the dishonor of surrender. Iwakuro thus had little respect for Indian officers who had compounded the shame of surrender by betraying their original oath of loyalty to Great Britain's Indian Army, which they had joined on their own initiative in the first place. Iwakuro had noted with contempt the rush of INA volunteers when Indian POWs heard at one point that those who did not join would work as laborers to build airfields and other military facilities.

Iwakuro also had to contend with Indian officers displeased with the INA's role. Mohan Singh, encouraged during the Malaya campaign by Fujiwara, demanded to invade India at the head of a large army. Iwakuro, in no way bound by Fujiwara's promises, made it plain that the INA would remain a small force dedicated to serving as a component of his intelligence program. The Iwakuro Agency would use the INA's men for radio broadcasts, agent infiltration, and other covert activities. Photographs of INA soldiers on parade would serve the purpose of propaganda rather than preparation for a true military campaign. Mohan Singh thus had nominal command of a small force of only fifteen thousand men who were outfitted with nothing but surrendered British equipment. Moreover, Iwakuro ignored Mohan Singh's demand for control of all Indian POWs. The Japanese Army dispersed many Indians not serving in the INA to toil in labor detachments throughout Southeast Asia and the Southwest Pacific.[20]

It was Iwakuro's misfortune that Mohan Singh refused to accept quietly his role. Following the Bangkok Conference in May, Iwakuro had sent to Tokyo on behalf of the IIL and INA a list of proposals for what the Indian leaders regarded as an alliance of equals. Officers at

Imperial General Headquarters received the list with indignation, considering them even more "unreasonable" than those of their client regime in Nanking. Gen. Tojo Hideki, concurrently premier and war minister, took the petition as evidence that Iwakuro was letting his Indian collaborators run wild.[21] After considerable delay, Tokyo offered a vague reply that only angered the Indians and convinced them that Iwakuro lacked clout. Iwakuro's troubles grew when the IIL accompanied the Iwakuro Agency's headquarters transfer in early autumn from Bangkok to Singapore, following the move of Southern Army there from Saigon. The presence of the IIL and INA in the same city exacerbated an increasingly bitter leadership struggle between Mohan Singh and Rash Behari Bose. The ambitious INA commander had only contempt for the IIL's leader, whom he saw as a puppet and mocked as "Nakamuraya Bose." The IIL's leader insisted that the INA came under his political authority. Mohan Singh also repeatedly threatened not to cooperate with the Iwakuro Agency unless his demands were met.[22]

Matters came to a head at a conference held on 7 December. Iwakuro accused Mohan Singh and his supporters of acting under the influence of "pro-British and fifth column elements." Fujiwara Iwaichi seconded Iwakuro's accusation while softening the charge against his protégé by suggesting that he was the victim of bad advice. Failing to break the impasse, the exasperated Iwakuro arranged with Southern Army General Headquarters to remove the thorn from his side. On 8 December, the Kempeitai informed Mohan Singh that they had arrested Gill, one of his chief supporters, on espionage charges stemming from the Dhillon defection the previous month. On the same day, the Japanese also disarmed the INA to forestall any possible revolt. On 29 December, Iwakuro summoned Mohan Singh to his office, where he relieved him of his command. As Mohan Singh left the building, the Kempeitai arrested him. He would spend the rest of the war a prisoner.

Iwakuro, having purged and disarmed the INA, then had to pick up the pieces. He ordered Major Ogawa, chief of his agency's military section, to find a new commanding officer. Ogawa settled on Lt. Col. J. K. Bhonsle, a graduate of the elite British military academy at Sandhurst and one of the most senior Indian officers to join the INA. Iwakuro also had to shore up his operation's political structure. Rash Behari Bose had proven reliable during the crisis, but the very closeness of his ties to the Japanese made him suspect as a leader in the eyes of many Indians. Bhonsle was in favor of inviting Subhas Chandra Bose from Berlin.[23] Moreover, Iwakuro and the visiting director of military intelligence, Maj. Gen. Arisue Seizo, both agreed at that time on Subhas Chandra Bose as the leader best suited to rebuild the Japanese Army's Indian operations.[24]

As for Iwakuro, he had to take responsibility for the mess. The defection of Dhillon, subsequent arrest of Gill, and final arrest of Mohan Singh had provided grist for the Allied propaganda mill and set back Japan's campaign of winning Indian hearts and minds. Iwakuro had launched his agency with outstanding resources and high expectations. Commanding an organization of some five hundred men and spending huge sums of covert funds, he and his subordinates had failed to deliver corresponding successes. Under pressure, they had resorted to sending to Southern Army General Headquarters reports whose positive tone often masked real problems.[25] Once Iwakuro had arrested the INA commander, his own days were numbered.

Iwakuro's reputation likely suffered from the presence of Major Fujiwara as a staff intelligence officer with Southern Army. Fujiwara, whom Iwakuro had replaced at the height of his success after the fall of Singapore, had taken enormous pride in his Fujiwara Agency and his role as father of the INA. Fujiwara viewed dimly Iwakuro's lack of empathy for his Indian collaborators. Fujiwara thought that Iwakuro would have done well to retain his F Agency, or at least to have retained him. Instead, Iwakuro called to his organization many veterans of Manchukuo and North China, whom Fujiwara believed represented the Japanese Army at its overbearing worst. Fujiwara apparently thought that his continued presence at the top of Indian operations would have kept Mohan Singh in line. In the end, Iwakuro received orders in March 1943 to join Twenty-fifth Army. His new task was to serve in the military administration of Sumatra in the conquered Netherlands East Indies.[26] For a man whom some had once regarded as a future candidate for war minister, the transfer marked the end of his rise. Despite a promotion to major general the same month, Iwakuro effectively went into exile.[27]

The Hikari Agency

Imperial General Headquarters in Tokyo, determined to rebuild its Indian program after Mohan Singh's arrest, turned to Adolf Hitler for a solution. In Berlin was India's leading nationalist in exile, Subhas Chandra Bose. The rounded face, glasses, and features hid a fierce character. The fiery Bengali had once shared the political limelight in India with Gandhi, Nehru, and other leaders of the Congress Party. His political stature attracted the attention of Second Bureau in Tokyo, which had arranged several years earlier to put Chiang Kai-shek's estranged Nationalist Party colleague Wang Ching-wei at the head of Japan's client regime in Nanking. Japanese intelligence officers saw in Bose a charismatic figure around whom to rally Asia's Indian population. The hurdle now was to convince Hitler to release his Indian protégé to Japan.

The object of Second Bureau's interest was seemingly destined to play a leading role in the drama of Indian independence. Subhas Chandra Bose was born on 23 January 1897 into a prominent Hindu family in Bengal. His wealth and intelligence earned him a place at Cambridge University. It was expected that a man of his intellect and background would join the elite Indian Civil Service upon graduation, then the conventional path to success for Indians in the British Empire. Although he placed fourth when he sat for the examination in 1920, Bose rejected that path, foregoing the comforts of the elite civil service and the expectations of his parents by resigning his commission. He chose, instead, to follow the rocky trail of a political activist in the cause of India's freedom. A passage from an unpublished autobiography highlights his thinking at that time: "I believe we shall get Home Rule within ten years and certainly earlier if we are ready to pay the price. The price consists of sacrifice and suffering. Only on the soil of sacrifice and suffering can we raise our national edifice. If we all stick to our jobs and look after our own interests, I don't think we shall get Home Rule even in fifty years."[28]

He joined the Congress Party, rising through the ranks to prominence as one of its leaders. Stints in British jails also marked his career. Bose objected to the political philosophy and tactics of Gandhi, who led opposition to British rule while preaching a politics of nonviolence. Bose from early in his career leaned toward armed resistance. N.C. Chaudhuri, political secretary to Bose's elder brother from 1937 until December 1941, when he joined the British in wartime propaganda, later recalled the younger Bose's demonstration at a Congress session held in Calcutta in December 1928: "In it Subhas Bose gave a theatrical display of militarism. He organized a volunteer corps, put the volunteers in military uniform, and even provided steel-chain epaulettes for the men of the simulated cavalry of the volunteers." Chaudhuri, whose differences with Bose and the direction of Indian nationalism led him to leave postwar India to live in England, ridiculed Bose. In his account of the demonstration, he noted with irony that the nationalist Bose wore a military uniform made by a British tailor from British cloth.[29]

Bose's search for Indian independence took him in the 1930s to continental Europe, where he met Adolph Hitler and Benito Mussolini. He also fell in love with Emilie Schenkl, a young Austrian woman he first met in 1934. His love for her overcame his earlier determination never to marry until India was free. Having proclaimed his celibacy, however, he felt constrained to marry her in secret to avoid the political repercussions he thought would follow a public renunciation of his vow.

Back in India, Bose's political star was on the rise. He became lord mayor of Calcutta in his native Bengal, then president of the Congress Party. In the end, however, failing to displace Gandhi in his bid to lead the party, Bose lost his position as president. He then took a more radical stance on Indian independence in opposition to the Congress Party leadership. The British authorities arrested Bose on charges of sedition in July 1940, placing him under house arrest. Bose, facing political eclipse at home, escaped from India to throw in his lot with the Axis in Europe. His first step on his journey was in crossing the Northwest Frontier into Afghanistan. In Kabul, in danger from the British agents operating in that city, Bose secured from the Italian ambassador a false passport. As Signore Mazzotta, Bose entered the Soviet Union en route to Germany. On 28 March 1941, he flew from Moscow to Berlin.[30]

In Tokyo, Imperial General Headquarters was showing an interest in the fugitive Indian leader. Around the time that Bose arrived in Berlin, AGS directed Ambassador Oshima Hiroshi to report on him. Oshima, a retired lieutenant general who had served in Berlin as military attaché before his appointment as ambassador, delegated the task to Col. Yamamoto Hayashi, a soft-spoken aviation officer serving in the military attaché office. In late October, with permission from the German Foreign Ministry, Oshima and Yamamoto invited Bose to the Japanese embassy. The Bengali immediately impressed his Japanese hosts. He first remarked how impressive he had found Okakura

Tenshin's book on pan-Asian solidarity, *The Ideals of the East*, then bluntly asked the two officers to justify Japan's undeclared war in China. Yamamoto, overlooking his guest's blunt manner, thereafter invited Bose to see him once every week or so.

Bose's interest in Japan was already well established by the time that he met Oshima and Yamamoto. Like many Asian nationalists, he was of two minds concerning the Japanese. He was both impressed that Japan had withstood Western colonialism and defeated a European power, Russia, in war. On the other hand, Japan's actions in China disturbed him. An article published in 1937 captured his sentiments thus:

> Japan has done great things for herself and for Asia. Her reawakening at the dawn of the present century sent a thrill throughout our Continent. Japan has shattered the white man's prestige in the Far East and has put all the Western imperialist powers on the defensive—not only in the military but also in the economic sphere. She is extremely sensitive— and rightly so—about her self-respect as an Asiatic race. She is determined to drive out the Western Powers from the Far East. But could not all this have been achieved without Imperialism, without dismembering the Chinese Republic, without humiliating another proud, cultured and ancient race? No, with all our admiration for Japan, where such admiration is due, our whole heart goes to China in her hour of trial.[31]

On 16 February 1942, the day after Singapore's surrender, Bose requested a meeting with Oshima and Yamamoto. Visibly excited by the news, Bose requested that the Japanese send him to Asia. In Berlin, he had succeeded only in establishing a small force, his Indian Legion, drawn from Indian Army prisoners taken in North Africa.[32] Bose's dream of leading his Indian Legion with the German Wehrmacht across the Soviet Union into India had faded, however, with the Soviet Red Army's major counteroffensive in December 1941. With the Japanese in possession of Singapore and pushing forward towards Rangoon, Bose was aflame with a new vision. He could see the victorious Japanese Army at the eastern frontier of India, and he in command of hundreds of thousands of Indian prisoners and residents of Southeast Asia. He had only to leave his German patrons. Oshima and Yamamoto were somewhat taken aback on hearing his proposal. Assigned only to maintain contact with Bose, they had not suggested that he leave Germany. The two officers promptly cabled Tokyo to report Bose's proposition.

While Oshima and Yamamoto endured Bose's repeated queries regarding Tokyo, Imperial General Headquarters was slow in responding. In Rash Behari Bose, the Japanese already had an agreeable and trusted Indian to front for them. Tokyo also had to take Berlin's interests into account. Subhas Chandra Bose, an impassioned orator who spoke several languages and composed his own propaganda, was a valuable asset. The Germans also consulted Bose on affairs of the Middle East and India, an area where their own expertise was relatively thin. Moreover, the Germans were planning to use Bose, following their ultimate victory, as an element of their postwar India policy. Tokyo thus made German consent a condition in late 1942 for bringing Bose to Asia. Oshima informed Bose of Tokyo's response, then arranged a meeting with Hitler. The German dictator, perhaps thinking Bose would do more harm to the British Empire from Asia, agreed to let Bose go. Yamamoto then departed Berlin for Tokyo in December via the Trans-Siberian Railroad to prepare for the Bengali's arrival.

Having secured Germany's assent for Bose to go to Asia, the Japanese Army then had to consider an appropriate route. Simply traveling with Yamamoto on the Trans-Siberian Railroad was out of the question for Bose, a fugitive subject of the British Empire; the risk that the Soviets would turn him over to their British allies was too great. Tokyo also rejected Berlin's proposal to fly Bose over Soviet airspace to Japanese-occupied Inner Mongolia, for the Japanese saw the offer as yet another German ruse to bring them into the war against the Soviets. A plan to fly him from Italy to Malaya was also scrapped. In the end, the Axis allies decided to send Bose from the occupied French port of Brest on a German submarine. Ambassador Oshima threw Bose a farewell party in February 1943. Bose then sailed from France on a German submarine. The U-boat made for Greenland before turning south and running down the middle of the Atlantic Ocean to avoid Allied patrols. Off Madagascar, the German submarine made contact with a waiting Japanese submarine, onto which Bose transferred. Thus he arrived in the occupied Netherlands East Indies. On 6 May, at a Japanese naval base north of Sumatra, Colonel Yamamoto greeted Bose when the exhausted Bengali stepped onto land.

Yamamoto, who had succeeded Iwakuro as director of Indian

operations, promptly escorted Bose to Tokyo for meetings with Japanese leaders. Lodging his charge at the Imperial Hotel on 16 May, Yamamoto arranged a series of meetings with the chiefs of the army and navy general staffs as well as with the navy minister and foreign minister. At the Imperial Hotel that first day, Bose also met Maj. Gen. Arisue Seizo, who, as chief of military intelligence, had ultimate responsibility for Indian operations and, hence, for Bose. Yamamoto also took Bose on a tour of Yokosuka Naval Base as well as a number of schools, factories, and other sites. Bose met Prime Minister Tojo around 10 June. Tojo, who had found little to his liking to date in his army's Indian operations, found Bose's forthright character and energy impressive. Tojo met Bose a second time on 14 June, promising Japanese aid but avoiding a clear answer to the Bengali's request for a Japanese invasion of India.

Bose made his public debut in Japan on 19 June, when he spoke before some sixty Japanese and foreign reporters at a press conference at the Imperial Hotel. He began with an apology for speaking in an enemy language, English, then launched into an impassioned recitation of his years of struggle for India's independence. He lauded Japan as a champion of Asia since its victory over Russia in 1905, then predicted ever-closer ties of friendship between Japan and an independent India. Two days later, Bose broadcast on Japan's NHK his first radio address to India from Asia. On 23 June, his Japanese hosts arranged for him to speak before a crowd assembled at a conference hall in Tokyo's Hibiya ward. Having made a strong impression on his hosts, Bose then left Tokyo with Colonel Yamamoto for Singapore.

Yamamoto, who had led his charge through Tokyo without mishap, now had to transfer the mantle of Indian leader from Rash Behari Bose to the more prominent Bengali nationalist. In Tokyo, he had brought the two Bengalis together for a first meeting, at which the older Bose had accepted his eclipse. On 4 July, Yamamoto orchestrated a mass meeting of the IIL in Singapore to announce the transfer. The two Indians informed the IIL of their mutual regard as Subhas Chandra Bose assumed the leading role. Early in July, Japanese radio broadcasts gave prominent coverage to the INA's first formal military parade, reportedly given before Bose in Singapore. The Bengali leader capped the spectacle with a rousing address, according to the Japanese broadcast. It was grand theater, if not a portent of an imminent march on India. American intelligence officers monitoring radio broadcasts touting the INA reported that "Tokyo proceeds to use the young army as a propagandistic if not a military weapon."[33]

In seeking to shake Great Britain's grip on India, Bose certainly had his work cut out for him. He was late in arriving in Asia, where his presence had greater potential to impress Indian audiences than did his previous Berlin address. It was one thing to broadcast appeals from remote Germany, and quite another to take to the airwaves from India's eastern doorstep. However, the time of greatest agitation in India was likely in the past. In the summer of 1942, a nascent "Quit India" campaign by India's Congress Party posed a threat to British rule. India's nervous rulers moved quickly to throw cold water on the sparks of unrest, its efficient intelligence and police services targeting and arresting Gandhi and other Congress organizers across the subcontinent. More than 100,000 would fall into the British dragnet. Bose, then, faced the challenge of fanning revolt when those most likely to heed and act upon his words were behind bars.[34]

Bose's arrival on the scene helped the Japanese Army move beyond the propaganda setbacks of Dhillon's defection and the arrests of senior INA officers. The Japanese further moved to improve the image of their Indian operations by assenting to Bose's demand to form a government. On 21 October, the IIL staged a mass meeting in Singapore to approve the creation of a Provisional Government of Free India (PGFI). Bose assumed the portfolios of prime minister and foreign minister. The IIL ratified Bhonsle as commander of the INA. Rash Behari Bose retained a role as supreme adviser to the PGFI. Subhas Chandra Bose, now chief of a Japanese-backed government in exile, declared war on 24 October against Great Britain and the United States. With a flair for the dramatic, he also ordered the minuscule INA to begin preparations for an offensive. Yamamoto, having produced the affair, then arranged for his charge to fly to Tokyo to join Japan's other Asian allies in a celebration of pan-Asian solidarity.[35]

Bose arrived in Tokyo on 31 October for the Greater East Asia Conference. Bose, the only leader whose government held no territory, attended as an observer. Prime Minister Tojo presided over the conference, held at the Imperial Diet during 5–6 November. Gathered together were Japan's Asian allies: Nanking's Wang Ching-wei, Manchukuo's Prime Minister Chang Ching-hui, Philippine President Jose Laurel, and Burmese Prime Minister Ba Maw. Notably absent was the prime minister of Thailand, the only allied nation not a Japanese creation. Bangkok, bowing to Japan's invitation for a representative but wary of appearing too close to an ally already on the defensive, sent in the prime minister's stead Prince Wan Waithayakon.

Bose, lacking territory, compensated in displaying his abundant gift of oratory. He issued a ringing call for Asian solidarity to liberate India. Ba Maw responded by declaring that there would be no liberation for Asia without independence for India. The assembled representatives of Japan's wartime empire also expressed their unstinting support for the PGFI in the struggle against Great Britain. For Bose, the Greater East Asia Conference was a golden moment. In the words of one British historian, he was "the outstanding politician among those in Asia who collaborated with the Japanese, though he was the one who ruled over no territory."[36]

Colonel Yamamoto, in addition to staging Bose's Asian debut and subsequent public appearances, had other responsibilities as Iwakuro's successor as director of the Japanese Army's Indian operations. When Yamamoto had assumed this assignment in May 1943, he had signaled a fresh start by renaming the Iwakuro Agency the Hikari Agency. The Japanese word "hikari" (light) indicated how, as light came from the east, so would aid for the liberation of India. Yamamoto shifted the agency's headquarters to Burma, in line with the PGFI's declaration of war and an imminent offensive. Lieutenant Colonel Kitabe retained his position as chief of the Burma organization. Major Ogawa continued to direct the INA. Capt. Kaneko Akira, an alumnus of the Nakano School, took command of the agent center at Penang following Koyama's return to the Imperial Diet in Tokyo. Other graduates of the Nakano School, many of whom had joined Indian operations under Iwakuro, constituted the backbone of the Hikari Agency. Maj. Fujiwara Iwaichi accompanied the INA to Burma, transferring from Southern Army General Headquarters to the intelligence staff of Fifteenth Army Headquarters in Rangoon. Under Yamamoto, the Hikari Agency continued beaming radio propaganda to India. Agency operatives, trained at Penang and a covert site in Burma, continued to infiltrate India by submarine and aircraft, reporting back political and military intelligence. Reporting on the Allied buildup in eastern India was of particular importance as Japan had gone from the offensive onto the defensive in the middle of 1942.

Apart from a new commanding officer and name, the role of the

Japanese Army's agency for Indian operations also changed. This was due to the decision at Imperial General Headquarters to approve a plan for an invasion of northeast India in 1944 to forestall the Allied invasion expected from the same area. Southern Army had first considered invading India in 1942, when the British had retreated in disarray from Burma and Indian leaders had launched the "Quit India" movement at the nadir of British fortunes. The Tokyo High Command had authorized Southern Army to prepare an invasion of northeast India, only to run into the strong opposition of Lt. Gen. Mutaguchi Renya and other local Japanese commanders in Burma who rejected as impossible a campaign through the untracked jungle of the frontier. Ironically, successful Allied raids on Burma from India subsequently persuaded Mutaguchi and other doubters. Mutaguchi's new faith in a ground campaign and an ominous Allied buildup in India revived Japanese invasion planning. Tokyo gave the green light in September 1943 for Fifteenth Army to begin preparing for an invasion of northeast India.

The Hikari Agency's primary role became one of combat support. Yamamoto's organization was to direct INA raiding units in the campaign for Imphal. As the war had turned increasingly against Japan, Imperial General Headquarters had grown increasingly interested in deploying small commando units alongside conventional forces. In Burma, Col. Komatsubara Akio, formerly chief of the proving unit at the Nakano School, had already created a commando squad called the Mori Unit. In advance of the Imphal campaign, his unit joined the Hikari Agency.[37]

On 7 January 1944, in line with its combat support role, the Hikari Agency received a new designation: the Southern Army Raiding Units Headquarters. Prior to the redesignation, Yamamoto had already begun sending his men, with the exception of those in Singapore and Penang, forward to their new duties. In the middle of January, Lt. Gen. Isoda Saburo arrived in Singapore to take command of the new commando headquarters. Isoda had served for two years as the last military attaché in Washington before Pearl Harbor. Repatriated to Japan, he had then taken command of a division in China. Yamamoto remained as Isoda's senior staff officer.

Isoda shifted the headquarters from Singapore to Rangoon, the better to direct guerrilla operations in the coming campaign. Colonel Kitabe, the Hikari Agency's chief in Burma, assumed command of the new headquarters' Indian Department, responsible for political and military direction of the INA. Lt. Col. Ogawa Saburo continued as the officer immediately responsible for INA military control. Colonel Komatsubara took command of the Raiding Department. The Headquarters combat command center was established with Fifteenth Army Headquarters at Manmyo, in central Burma. Along the border facing Imphal, Isoda's Headquarters fielded a string of operations sections. As in past operations, graduates of the Nakano School constituted the core of the operations, comprising more than 130 of the 500 members. In addition to the many men who remained prior to the redesignation of the Hikari Agency, many new graduates and veterans operating elsewhere on the continent silently entered Burma to join the campaign for northeast India.[38]

Isoda discovered, upon taking command of his new assignment, that Bose was tenacious in his demands, even when some seemed to have little grounding in reality. Yet, after Iwakuro's disastrous arrest of his INA commander, an even greater fiasco could be expected from a falling out with a leader of Bose's stature, so the Japanese saw the need to offer him some concessions. For the Imphal campaign, Bose lobbied the Japanese for the INA to fight at the front lines as regular combat units. He also demanded a major advance by the INA and Japanese Army from the Akyab into Calcutta, his political base. His ambition was to lead an uprising of his fellow Bengalis that would end in his triumphal entry into Calcutta. Bose simply seemed unwilling to see or accept that the Japanese Army had no intention of launching a campaign to conquer India on his behalf. Mutaguchi's goal was simply to secure the Imphal area of northeast Asia, the area from which the British and Americans were planning to retake Burma.

Isoda, seeking to placate Bose, brokered agreements on the PGFI's role in the military campaign and expected occupation of Indian territory. INA soldiers would fight as whole units to the extent possible, rather than in small detachments with Japanese units. The Japanese also agreed to turn over administration and policing duties to the PGFI after securing the Imphal area. Bose, his mind racing ahead, even spoke of his desire to make his triumphant entry into Imphal in an open sedan, accompanied by top Indian and Japanese officials. He went so far as to outline a plan to use the INA First Division as the core of his military government for northeast India. Mutaguchi accommodated Bose by agreeing to such details that lay outside the scope of immediate combat considerations. On matters of substance, however, such as the Bengali's demand to invade the Chittagong region, the Japanese stood firm in their rejection.

With great fanfare, Bose sent the INA off to battle. The Indian troops created a stirring spectacle as they marched forward, chanting "On to Delhi!" Yet, the Japanese Army had no plans for a ground campaign to take Delhi. The INA First Division went to the front as part of the Japanese Fifteenth Army. Its primary mission was to execute raids against enemy positions. Attached to Fifteenth Army divisions were smaller INA detachments whose men were to gather intelligence and induce fellow Indians in the Indian Army to desert or surrender. With the Indian units were Japanese intelligence officers to direct them. A former Nakano School instructor directed the INA's First Raiding Regiment. Numerous Nakano School graduates were seeded throughout the INA units to guide them. Thus did Isoda's organization lead the INA into battle.

It was in March 1944 when the Japanese Fifteenth Army finally began marching for India. By then, the Japanese had already lost control of the skies. The Japanese soldiers and their Indian auxiliaries fought with little protection from Allied air attacks, assaulting an entrenched enemy abundantly supplied by air while they relied upon a trickle of arms and rations borne by men and pack animals over trackless mountains to the front.

While the Fifteenth Army's regular divisions were learning how formidable Allied defenses had grown since 1942, Isoda's commandos and INA soldiers were confronting other problems. Japan's Indian auxiliaries proved largely incapable of executing one of their primary missions, that of inducing soldiers of the Indian Army to cease fighting. Morale within the Indian Army was incomparably higher at Imphal in 1944 than in the hopeless defense of Singapore in 1942. Two years earlier, Fujiwara's small band of Japanese operatives and captured Indians had swayed thousands of Indians to lay down their arms. In the fighting for northeast India, the INA's megaphones, loudspeakers, and propaganda leaflets failed to convince troops of the Indian Army to desert to what already was obviously a losing cause. INA units also had difficulties at times in finding Allied Indian soldiers. INA soldiers operating with Thirty-third Division in the campaign's northern area, for example, ran into the elite British soldiers of V Force and local levees of pro-British ethnic minorities. Other INA soldiers, assigned to the south, found themselves confronting British African troops.[39]

When Fifteenth Army's desperate divisions failed in Mutaguchi's ill-considered plan to take northeast India, the surviving members of Isoda's commandos and INA soldiers joined their comrades that July in a nightmarish retreat to Burma. The Japanese soldiers and their Indian auxiliaries struggled through the green hell of the unforgiving jungle, suffering from air attacks, disease, and starvation. Many who had survived the battle at the front or the covert operations behind the lines perished in those trackless hills. In all, some sixty thousand Japanese died in the Imphal campaign. Without sufficient rations to feed their own troops, Japanese commanders showed no special consideration for their Indian auxiliaries. Many of the INA's soldiers deserted at that time. Mutaguchi had failed to take the area from which the Allied offensive would soon come. Worse, he had broken the Japanese Army in Burma in the attempt. The western frontier of Japan's new empire was now open to invasion.

The disastrous incursion into India, which destroyed Mutaguchi's army, also spelled the end of Isoda's commando headquarters and of the INA's days as a fighting force. In June 1944, Isoda and Kitabe returned from an inspection of the Japanese front lines to draft plans for a reduced INA. With the INA's First Division destroyed in the campaign, the Japanese designated Second Division as the INA's primary combat unit. In the campaign's aftermath, however, the INA retained little value as either a fighting force or even as an exercise in propaganda. INA soldiers other than those from Second Division were slated to dig ditches, build fortifications, transport Japanese Army supplies, and provide other rear-echelon support. In short, Isoda was turning the INA's soldiers into coolies. Their lot was to be no better than that of other Indian prisoners already toiling at the Japanese bastion of Rabaul and elsewhere.

For the shadow warriors, Imphal had proven a costly campaign. Many of the Nakano School's graduates, who directed INA units at the front or operated behind the lines, never returned to Rangoon. More than fifty of 133 graduates of the Nakano School under Isoda's command died at Imphal or related operations. Isoda, who had overseen the Hikari Agency's growth and redesignation as Southern Army Raiding Units Headquarters, directed the unit's shrinking and renaming once again as the Hikari Agency in January 1945. Yamamoto

Hayashi, promoted to major general in August 1944, left the Hikari Agency to command the Nakano School in March 1945. One of Isoda's burdens following Imphal was dealing with the ceaseless and increasingly unreal demands of Subhas Chandra Bose. The indefatigable Bengali kept pressing the Japanese to recognize him as a head of state and support him in ejecting the British from India. The Japanese tried placating him. Having first permitted Bose to organize his PGFI, the Japanese then met his demand for control of Japan's occupied Indian territory, the Andaman and Nicobar Islands, by declaring the islands under his authority. Continued Japanese "responsibility" for defense of the islands, however, left Bose no more in control of the islands than the Emperor Pu-yi was in possession of Manchukuo.

In late October 1944, Isoda took Bose to Tokyo. The determined Bengali saw the trip as an opportunity to bypass Isoda to secure directly from Tokyo a Japanese ambassador to his government. He was also anxious to see whether the recent fall from power of Tojo, who resigned in July to take responsibility for the Japanese loss of their island bastion of Saipan, would effect Japanese support for his cause. Bose found Japanese officials in Tokyo less than forthcoming. Following an audience with Emperor Hirohito and courtesy calls on Prime Minister Koiso Kuniaki and other key civilian and military leaders, Bose saw that his hosts were offering him form rather than substance.

Even the form was galling. Midway through his stay, his hosts shifted him from the state guesthouse to the Imperial Hotel, which he took as shabby treatment for a visiting head of state. Maj. Gen. Sato Kenryo, chief of the Military Affairs Bureau, and Maj. Gen. Arisue Seizo, director of Second Bureau, sought during talks at the Imperial Hotel to deflect Bose's demands. They proposed that, instead of normal diplomatic representation, he accept relations on the Manchukuo model. Just as the senior military officer in Manchukuo also served as ambassador to that puppet empire, so the Japanese Army proposed to bestow on Isoda the concurrent title of ambassador to the PGFI. Bose, however, adamantly opposed the Manchurian solution.

The Japanese responded with a concession designed to save face. They agreed to send a diplomat, Hachiya Teruo, to the PGFI. The Hikari Agency, however, would retain authority for the execution of the Japanese Army's Indian operations and would continue to direct both the PGFI and the INA. As for another of Bose's demands, that Japan equip the INA with Japanese weapons in addition to the limited British stock captured at Singapore and elsewhere, the Japanese offered not the slightest concession. The INA would end the war with the bulk of its equipment the aging British weapons taken in 1942. At the end of the year, following a visit to the ailing Rash Behari Bose, Isoda escorted his difficult charge back to Rangoon to face the Allied invasion.[40]

Squandered Opportunity

The early promise of Fujiwara's Indian operations faded once the campaign for Singapore ended. Iwakuro's impressive skills at organization failed to produce remarkable results against the formidable police and intelligence organizations that kept a lid on Indian unrest during the darkest days of the war for Great Britain. Only when the tide had turned strongly against Japan did Tokyo agree to send Indian troops under Japanese command into India. Ill equipped and pitted against an entrenched enemy continuously supplied with air drops, the INA retreated in defeat with the Japanese Army back to Burma. All the efforts of Fujiwara, Iwakuro, and the scores of Nakano School officers under them failed in a program that conceived only a minor role for the Indians until their military relevance had passed.

5

PHILIPPINES: SPIES IN MANILA, COMMANDOS IN THE JUNGLE

In December 1944, long after Japan's early victories in the war had begun fading and the Allied offensive had begun accelerating, Lt. Onoda Hiroo and comrades of his from the First Class of the Nakano School's Futamata Branch flew into Manila. The Japanese Army had opened the Futamata Branch in September that year to train soldiers in commando tactics. As the tide of war was turning increasingly against Japan, the Japanese Army was turning to special warfare to counter the increasing military advantage of the Allied forces. Men of the Nakano School had first demonstrated the value of unconventional warfare in eastern New Guinea. Lightly equipped with small arms and special incendiary grenades developed at the Noborito Research Institute, the men had led a number of successful raids against Allied troops in the "green hell" of New Guinea's jungles. Now others from Futamata Branch would apply their special training to the Philippines.

Futamata Branch

On 1 September 1944, some 220 young reservists and soldiers on active duty assembled for a ceremony saluting them as the first class of the Japanese Army's new training center for special warfare. One young reserve officer, Onoda Hiroo, came with knowledge of China and the Chinese language that he had acquired over several years as an employee of the Tajima Yoko trading company in Hankow and during a subsequent tour of duty as a soldier in China. Suetsugu Ichiro, his classmate and friend, had lived in Korea prior to joining the military, when he had returned there on duty. Onoda's other class-mates also had backgrounds or service records that had caught the eyes of military recruiters searching for men to train as commandos. Various unit commanders, tasked with forwarding soldiers who held promise for special operations, had sent their top three or four men to the Futamata Branch, designated as East Unit 33.[1] Futamata is today part of the city of Tenryu, Shizuoka Prefecture, which lies between Tokyo and Nagoya. On an unimposing military site, in class-rooms housed in a few wooden buildings of unexceptional appear-ance, the Japanese Army launched a program to train the young soldiers as an elite cadre who would lead others in unconventional warfare.

By the time Onoda and his classmates began their training at Futamata Branch, the Japanese Army had long since passed from the attack to an increasingly beleaguered defense. Not long after the Japa-nese Navy had suffered a severe blow at Midway in June 1942, the Army met disaster trying to wrest back the small island of Guadalca-nal. American forces had landed in August on the island, vital for its strategic location in the South Pacific and its airfield. Ever greater efforts over the course of months to retake Guadalcanal yielded the Japanese Army nothing but casualties as the fight for the island turned into a major showdown between the United States and Japan. The pouring of ever more resources into that distant island contributed to the decision by the Japanese Army at the end of 1942 to call off its plans for a final assault on the Chinese capital at Chungking. On 31 December, finally accepting the inevitable, Imperial General Head-quarters decided to withdraw the surviving Japanese forces from Gua-dalcanal.[2]

Also in eastern New Guinea, the part of the giant island held by Australia before the war, the Japanese suffered reverses. New Guinea, the world's second largest island, holds a strategic position north of Australia's key east coast, across the Coral Sea. At the war's onset, Japan had planned to seize Port Moresby on the island's south coast. Control of the island's major city would give Japan a base from which to attack or even to invade Australia. At a minimum, the Japanese Army needed to hold eastern New Guinea in order to prevent the

United States from pouring men and matériel into Australia as a base from which to launch a southern offensive against Japan's newly won empire.

In May 1942, the Japanese Navy canceled the planned amphibious assault on Port Moresby after taking heavy losses in its narrow victory over the U.S. Navy in the Battle of the Coral Sea. In July, Maj. Gen. Horii Tomitaro landed his South Seas Detachment on New Guinea's east coast for an overland invasion of Port Moresby across the forbidding Owen Stanley Range that runs like a jagged spine through the island's center. Without proper advance reconnaissance or supply, the army detachment pushed through the dense jungle along a trail running through some of the worst terrain in the world. By September, Horii's men had succeeded in pushing aside Australian opposition to come within thirty miles of the city. By then, however, the Japanese Army was engaged in its losing fight over Guadalcanal and had no men or supplies to spare for Horii. His South Seas Detachment was ordered on 25 September to withdraw. Starving, staggering along the trail through New Guinea's "green hell," the detachment's survivors eventually made their way back to the coast.

Demonstrated Success in New Guinea

It was in eastern New Guinea where corporals Tanaka Tatsuo, Yamada Masatsugu, and thirteen other noncommissioned officers of the Nakano School first demonstrated to the Japanese Army the potential of guerrilla tactics against superior forces. Tanaka, born in Nagasaki, had crossed the Sea of Japan at the age of sixteen to seek opportunities in the colony of Korea. Working days at the stately Chosen Hotel in Keijo (Seoul) and attending evening classes at the Zenrin School of Commerce for two years, he graduated in March 1940. Immediately volunteering for military service, Tanaka became a year later an NCO candidate with a unit in Nagasaki. The next year, following a recommendation by his regimental commander and a discreet entrance examination in Fukuoka, Tanaka entered the Nakano School. A photograph of that time shows him nattily attired in a dark suit and tie, a fedora perched atop his head and a handkerchief placed in his breast pocket completing the young intelligence officer's "uniform." Tanaka graduated thirteen months later, in April 1943. Two months earlier, the Japanese withdrawal in defeat from Guadalcanal had begun. With the security of Japan's southern defenses in doubt, Tanaka traveled to Ujina to await his ship south.

Ujina, Hiroshima's port, had been a key military embarkation point since the Sino-Japanese War of 1894–95. Gathered there, awaiting their departure, were Tanaka and fourteen fellow graduates of the Nakano School. Among his comrades was Yamada Masatsugu, a classmate and fellow Nagasaki native. There was also Takara Hirosuke, a senior alumnus from the southernmost prefecture of Okinawa, and Kato Masatane from Hokkaido at the northern end of the empire, with the other men of the school hailing from points in between.

Tanaka and Yamada, classmates at the Nakano School, were close friends among the group heading south. While waiting in Ujina, they were part of a trio who most often frequented the bars and cabarets of Hiroshima. In Palau, the chain of islands in the Carolines transferred from German control to Japanese administration since the First World War, Tanaka took Yamada and Takara with him to town after wangling a special pass from a military official he knew on shore. For several days, they enjoyed the tropical scenery in what would be their final respite from the war that awaited them.

From Rabaul, the formidable Japanese fortress on the eastern tip of New Britain, Tanaka, Yamada, and most of their comrades flew west to New Guinea. Separated from Australia only by the Torres Strait and the Coral Sea, New Guinea was to have been the base from which Japan's military machine was to enter the continent. The Battle of the Coral Sea, at most a minor Japanese victory over the opposing American fleet in May 1942, had disrupted the Japanese Army's planned amphibious landing at Port Moresby. A Japanese force had next toiled through hellish jungle and mountain terrain of the Kokoda Track in an effort to reach Port Moresby. Its occupation would have given the Japanese a good port from which to invade Queensland, just across the Torres Strait, and other Australian objectives to the south. Within sight of the city, out of supplies and suffering from starvation, the Japanese detachment had withdrawn. The Japanese had then turned from offense to defense. Facing well-supplied Australian and American forces, the Japanese had stoutly defended their position at Buna for two months before those who had not fallen to enemy fire or starvation withdrew in January 1943.

Short of men, weapons, and food, and with supply growing ever less certain as the Allied noose of air and sea superiority drew tighter around New Guinea, the Imperial Japanese Army was in increasingly desperate straits. On 1 August 1943, in a camp some fifty kilometers east of Madang, Tanaka, Yamada, and their comrades formed the backbone of the IJA Eighteenth Army's Saito Special Volunteer Corps, led by Lt. Saito Shunji. He, along with lieutenants Nakamori Shigeki and Komata Yozo, was a commissioned officer who had trained at the Nakano School. Each took command of three squads. Leading each squad of fifteen men was an NCO from the Nakano School. Tanaka and Yamada were two of Nakamori's three squad leaders. The 135 men of the nine squads were Taiwanese aborigines, renowned for their stamina and hunting prowess. Born and raised in the mountainous jungle interior of Taiwan, they would be fighting in their element in New Guinea.

The Nakano School had first sent men to an island for a military operation at the war's onset, when the school was involved in the creation and execution of a plan to capture the Dutch oil fields at Palembang by airborne raid. In 1943, Tanaka, Yamada, and other graduates of the school had arrived in New Guinea to apply their special skills against a rapidly deteriorating situation. They were to gather topographical intelligence, win the hearts and minds of the island's aborigines, whom both Japanese and Allies were recruiting, and lead commando raids against Allied airfields and units. For several weeks, Tanaka, Yamada, and their fellow squad leaders trained their Taiwanese troops at weapons handling, infiltration, and night attack.

On 3 September, the Saito Special Volunteer Corps left their training grounds for their first raid. Marching south into the interior, they reached the Kainantu area in the Eastern Highlands Province. Their mission was to attack a nearby Australian camp. After first scouting their objective, four squads left their base on the night of 22 September. Tanaka and Yamada were two of the four attack leaders. Each of the four NCOs had three men under his command. Each member carried a bomb, consisting of five kilograms of explosives joined to four hand grenades, and two incendiary devices. The latter, developed at the Noborito Research Institute, produced a heat above two thousand degrees with the design of killing enemy soldiers and destroying matériel. All carried firearms as well, with the NCOs sporting in addition a pistol, sword, and five hand grenades.

From their scouting report, the attack leaders knew the camp lay on both sides of a native track. With an officers' barracks and several huts, the camp contained a force of approximately three hundred men. Tanaka and Yamada were to lead their men into the left side of the camp while the other two squad leaders infiltrated on the right. Yamada was to set off an explosive at the command tent to signal the start of the raid. Following the initial bombing attack, the squads would use their incendiaries and, as necessary, grenades to finish off the enemy. With words of encouragement from Lieutenant Saito and a ritual drink of sake, the attackers left for the enemy camp.

As they crept through the tall grass under a dark sky whose clouds largely obscured the moon, they saw occasional random fire from the Australian camp. Closer still, they could see the native huts, built on stilts, under which were heaped arms and ammunition. All was quiet. Yamada's bomb exploded first. Tanaka immediately lit his own and threw it under his targeted hut. A dozen explosions rocked the camp in a moment, then came more as the burning structures started setting off the heaps of ammunition and grenades. Startled, alarmed Australian soldiers rushed about the camp, shooting their small arms wildly into the dark, as Tanaka and Yamada gathered their men at a rendezvous spot. The eight raiders then dashed into the camp, shooting any defenders they found. Without a single casualty, the four squads returned to their base. By their count, they had destroyed two barracks, eleven huts, three trench mortars, and some three hundred shells; killed more than sixty soldiers; and wounded another eighty. Short of supplies, they had also taken back a number of machine guns, automatic weapons, some five thousand rounds of ammunition, and a hundred hand grenades. The sole disappointment was the discovery that they had inadvertently blown up all the enemy camp's rations.[3]

Saito's raiders followed their first raid with a series of successful assaults against enemy units. A second operation, executed several days later in a neighboring village, ended with three hundred enemy killed or wounded, against no casualties for the Nakano School's men. Similar results came with a series of raids lasting through the middle of October. The operations proved so successful that Imperial General Headquarters in Tokyo recalled Lt. Nakamori Shigeki to brief the results. Maj. Gen. Arisue Seizo, who directed Japanese military intelligence as chief of Second Bureau, and other officers at Imperial General Headquarters found the briefing most impressive.

Arisue decided that the Nakano School, which since its founding had concentrated most of its resources on intelligence, would devote more of its energies to irregular warfare.

Impressed that commando units were able to wreak havoc behind enemy lines with few resources, Tokyo moved to develop the Japanese Army's special warfare capabilities. One result was the addition of raiding units during 1944 to the Second Area Army in the New Guinea area. The Second Raiding Unit, constituted under Second Area Army in July, wracked up impressive results. Under Maj. Kawashima Takenobu, a Nakano School graduate who had served as Col. Suzuki Keiji's right-hand man in the Minami Agency's Burma operations, other men of the Nakano School formed the unit's core. Some forty graduates of the Nakano School led more than four hundred Taiwanese aborigines against the Allies in New Guinea and Morotai. General MacArthur conceded that Kawashima's forces inflicted considerable damage on his forces at Morotai.[4] Another result of successes in the New Guinea area was the opening of the Nakano School's Futamata Branch to meet the increased demand for training in special warfare.[5]

Commando School Days

On 1 September 1944, Lt. Col. Kumagawa Mamoru welcomed the First Class to the Futamata Branch. He was the facility's first commandant. With him were his deputy and roughly a half dozen instructors, all top-notch officers of field rank. Each instructor had knowledge of foreign countries and languages, having served overseas at Japanese diplomatic missions. Also present at the ceremony was Arisue. As a sign of the importance that Japan's military intelligence chief accorded special warfare training, he and other senior army officers would make a point of attending later Futamata Branch entrance and graduation ceremonies as well as inspecting the center at other times.[6]

The atmosphere at Futamata Branch, like that at the main Nakano School, was relatively liberal. Rather than having students parrot rote answers to set questions, the men at Futamata Branch were encouraged to think for themselves. The first lesson Onoda Hiroo's instructor gave his class was that there were no set methods in guerrilla warfare. Each student would have to confront each situation with individual creativity and initiative. Kumabe Taizo was surprised at the liberal atmosphere of Futamata training, which from start to finish he found free of the "army stink" he had known in the military until then. Kumabe marveled that students were even allowed to hold critical views of the emperor. Criticism at that time of Japan's "living god" was forbidden in Japanese society. For soldiers to take a detached or critical attitude toward the emperor was extraordinary.[7] In fact, however, the center's commandant and his staff were simply encouraging their students to develop the habit of the analytical and independent thinking required of intelligence officers. As at the Nakano School, students at Futamata Branch received instruction grounded in imperial ideology and "spiritual education." Preparing to wage war in the shadows, they remained soldiers of an army founded on the basis of imperial rule, a military in which the emperor was the commander in chief.

Another point that Kumagawa and his staff drilled into their students was that each was to stay alive to accomplish his mission. The instruction was at odds with the prevailing ethos in the Japanese Army that called for an honorable death before the "dishonor" of surrender. Japanese military leaders based that precept on a Japanese martial tradition that held that the way of the warrior was death. The Japanese Army built on that tradition, praising units that fought to the last man and despising prisoners. In one case, officers who returned from Soviet captivity following the Japanese defeat at Nomonhan in 1939 were each handed a pistol. Left alone with the weapon, the repatriated officers did what was expected by committing suicide to expiate their "shame."

Breaking such an ingrained military culture was one goal of Futamata Branch instructors. As the war turned against Japan, regular soldiers increasingly turned to a final, suicidal bayonet charge against the enemy when hope of victory had disappeared. Students of the Futamata Branch were forbidden to take that way out. Onoda, who in his previous military training had been taught how to die, learned at Futamata Branch that his duty was to live for the sake of his mission. For Japan's shadow warriors, staying alive at all costs was imperative, no matter how great the shame of having other Japanese regard one as a traitor or coward. In the event that escape proved impossible at some point in a future mission, Onoda was to surrender rather than kill himself. In death, he was useless to Japan. As a prisoner, he could still serve by feeding his captors bogus intelligence.[8]

While the spirit of instruction at Futamata Branch was similar to that at the main school, its duration was much briefer. Whereas many students spent a year at the Nakano School, those at Futamata Branch completed their intense course in three months. The routine consisted of eight hours of instruction each day, followed many nights by studying until midnight. Lt. Yamamoto Fukuichi, a member of the First Class, after the war fondly remembered his time of "dedicated application" at Futamata Branch as one of the most positive and formative of his life. In that short period, the students learned the techniques of reconnaissance, infiltration, demolition, propaganda, CI, military topography, and military government in occupied territories.

Much of the guerrilla training took place as field exercises along the Tenryu River. Students trained to destroy military sites. In one field exercise, a student disguised as a farmer scouted the Hamamatsu Air Base, looking for targets and guards before planting dummy explosives on aircraft and hangars. Within the training center's compound, they also went through physical training and honed their skills at kendo, karate, and marksmanship. Much of the training at Futamata Branch struck Onoda as similar to that of Japan's fabled ninja. In fact, he and his classmates practiced such traditional stealth techniques as walking up against a wall to avoid casting a shadow. For their graduation exercise, Onoda and his classmates were given the scenario of an American force that had invaded Japan. In response, the students put together a plan to destroy an occupied airfield and capture the enemy commanding officer.[9]

Graduation

In December, Maj. Gen. Arisue Seizo visited Futamata Branch, this time to attend the First Class's graduation ceremony. By the end of 1944, Japan was in increasingly dire straits. Some thirty thousand Japanese soldiers on Saipan had fought and died in a futile attempt to deny the island bastion to the United States. Saipan fell in early July, its capture bringing down Prime Minister Tojo's government later that same month. On 10 October, an American strike force conducted a major raid against Japan's southernmost prefecture of Okinawa, gateway to Japan's main islands. On 20 October, American forces went ashore at Leyte, an island in the middle of the Philippine archipelago. Several days later, heavy losses at the Battle of Leyte Gulf marked the end of the Japanese Navy's Combined Fleet as an effective opponent of the U.S. Navy.

Increasingly unable to oppose the Allies by conventional means, Japan's desperate military leaders turned to the unconventional. At the close of the debacle at Leyte Gulf, the Japanese Navy let fly with its "Divine Wind" tactics against the invaders. As supposedly divine winds (known in Japanese as *shimpu* or *kamikaze*) had scattered the invasion fleets of Kublai Khan in the thirteenth century, so Japanese pilots of the twentieth century would drive away the U.S. Navy's task forces. Japanese pilots taking off from airfields in the Philippines flew their aircraft directly at the American ships. One Japanese pilot tore through the flight deck of the carrier *St. Lo,* setting off explosions that sank the ship a half hour later. Other planes punched holes through the flight deck of the carriers *Santee* and *Suwanee.*[10] The concept, put forward by Vice Adm. Onishi Takijiro, the "father" of the kamikazes, was for each pilot to trade his life and plane for one enemy ship. The Japanese Navy's "special attack forces," better known to the incredulous Americans as kamikaze, thus took to its final conclusion Japan's martial tradition of death as the way of the samurai.

The men who finished training at the Nakano School's Futamata Branch in December were under explicit orders not to kill themselves under any circumstances. Like the kamikaze, however, their missions would take them to the same places where Japanese commanders intended to wage the nation's final battles: the Philippines, Okinawa, Kyushu, and elsewhere in the home islands. Following their graduation ceremony, the men of the Futamata Branch's First Class went their separate ways. Somewhat more than half the graduates left Japan proper for overseas missions in the Philippines, French Indochina, the East Indies, Burma, Taiwan, Korea, and elsewhere.

Onoda Hiroo was one of about twenty men who received orders for the Philippines. Less than half the class took positions throughout Japan. Some joined comrades from the main Nakano School for duty throughout the islands of Okinawa Prefecture, which the Japanese judged would be the next battle site after the Philippines. Lieutenants Suetsugu Ichiro and Yamamoto Fukuichi were among some twenty graduates assigned to duty with Western District Army Headquarters in Fukuoka, Kyushu, where their task was to organize guerrilla forces as part of the island's defense. Others went to the Tokyo area and into the far north of Japan. While the kamikaze pilots hurled their aircraft into American ships and infantrymen fought and died on the front lines overseas, the Futamata Branch's shadow warriors left quietly on their missions.

Landing in the Philippines

In December 1944, Lt. Onoda Hiroo and his fellow operatives from the Futamata Branch flew into territory where the Nakano School had sent few of its men in the war's early years. Unlike the campaigns for Malaya and Burma, the Japanese Army had conquered the Philippines without the Nakano School's shadow warriors. This is not to say, however, that intelligence played no part in the Philippines campaign. Gen. Homma Masaharu had directed the invasion on the basis of intelligence gathered over two decades by such intelligence officers as Tamura Hiroshi and Suzuki Keiji. Following Fujiwara Iwaichi's earlier work on propaganda, the Japanese Army in the U.S. colony worked to separate the Filipinos from their American overlords and win them over to the Japanese side. While many Filipinos did join American officers in resisting the Japanese, Manila's prominent families promptly joined the new government under Tokyo's aegis.

None of this early activity, however, involved the direct participation of the Nakano School's men. Only in November 1942, while hundreds of the school's graduates were already operating elsewhere in Southeast Asia, did two graduates transfer from Imperial General Headquarters to Manila for CI duty with Fourteenth Army. Capt. Sukawa Michio, a member of the Nakano School's First Class, took command of Fourteenth Army CI. The other Nakano School alumnus served under him.[11]

By 1944, the Japanese Army in the Philippines was facing a widespread guerrilla movement and the prospect of an imminent return of Gen. Douglas MacArthur, who had escaped to Australia in 1942. From the time Gen. Jonathan Wainwright surrendered the American forces in the Philippines to General Homma in May 1942, a number of American and Filipino officers had disappeared into the countryside to continue the fight. Alone, they would have posed little threat. However, they were able increasingly to enlist popular support as time passed. In 1942, the triumphant Japanese had found no shortage of collaborators among the Philippine elite, members of the same families who had held privileged positions under the Americans. Indeed, many of the same illustrious families had earlier transferred their loyalties from their Spanish overlords to the Americans when the United States had seized the islands from Spain in 1898. The Japanese installed Jose Laurel, a graduate of Yale University, as president and staffed his government with other members of Manila's high society.

The Japanese Army's frequent brutality soon made the new overlords objects of hatred for many Filipinos. Army officers imprisoned and executed Filipinos sympathetic to the United States. Victims included even a few prominent Filipinos, such as Justice Minister Jose Abados Santos. Many Japanese soldiers continued their army's habits, acquired in China, of slapping local men on the street who failed to bow to them, raping women, and stealing what appealed to them. One commando of the Futamata Branch ruefully admitted after the war Japan's sorry record in the Philippines. Spain, he noted, had bequeathed Christianity in three hundred years of rule. The United States had given the islands roads, cars, and Hollywood movies in fifty years of colonial administration. The Japanese, however, had only taken from the islands in their brief occupation.[12]

Negating their potential appeal as liberators of fellow Asians from the yoke of Western colonialism, the Japanese gave every indication that they considered the Philippines less an allied nation than an occupied territory. One small example was the renaming of Manila's Dewey Boulevard, named after the American admiral whose victory over the Spanish fleet in 1898 had added the Philippines to the American overseas empire. Taking down Dewey's name from the boulevard was in order as a symbolic step in erasing signs of colonialism from the capital. However, the Japanese showed poor judgment in calling the street by the Japanese name of Heiwa (Peace) Boulevard, rather than bestowing the name of some prominent Filipino hero on the boulevard.[13]

As popular hatred of the Japanese grew, the Japanese Army struggled to contain an insurgency fanned by rising expectations that MacArthur would make good his public promise to return. MacArthur's Allied Intelligence Bureau (AIB) began infiltrating agents and ferrying supplies to the Philippines by submarine as early as 1942. In return, the AIB sowed the seeds of rebellion and reaped a bountiful harvest of intelligence. Guerrilla activity was the most remarkable in the Visayas, due in part to the earlier execution of the popular Jose Abado Santos and the activities of the American guerrilla leader Lt. Col. James Cushing.

As the war's tide turned, the Japanese waged a relentless campaign against the guerrillas. The Kempeitai exploited its vast network of agents to infiltrate the anti-Japanese groups. The Army succeeded at times in cracking the simple guerrilla code and catching some of the guerrillas. Army operatives also worked in disguise from a number of false fronts in Manila, including a lumber company, to gather intelligence. One Nakano School officer named Oki Nobuo recalled that he used "English and a pistol" in his duties, which included donning a tuxedo and mingling at elegant dance parties to gather intelligence. Completing this beau tableau of a city of intrigue was a German agent of French descent named Rita, known as the "Mata Hari of the Orient." She was a beauty who spoke several European languages as well as Tagalog, the foremost language of the Philippines. Her contacts in Manila's high society provided the Japanese with a good deal of intelligence. Behind the glittering façade, however, were the mean streets of Manila. Life was perilous on both sides. Guerrillas assassinated Filipinos who collaborated with the Japanese, while the Kempeitai tortured captured guerrilla suspects to pry from them information on their networks and intentions.[14]

In March 1944, Fourteenth Army's CI organization moved from army headquarters into a building in downtown Manila. There its staff set up shop as the Institute of Natural Science. In addition to the sign out front identifying the occupants as members of a research institute, samples of seeds from tropical plants and other props were arranged to set the scene. Naturally, the intelligence officers working there dressed in civilian clothes, generally khaki pants and tropical shirts.

Maj. Taniguchi Yoshimi, a native of Kagoshima and member of the Military Academy's Forty-fifth Class, had both trained and taught at the Nakano School. In Manila, he directed Fourteenth Army CI operations from the building housing the bogus Institute of Natural Science. His organization was responsible for gathering intelligence, controlling the Philippine puppet government (Malacanang Section), directing the Filipino police, guiding Filipino politicians, and detecting guerrilla communications, a task handled by two sections (one section tapped telephones, the other monitored illegal wireless transmissions). Taniguchi's team also ran a number of branches outside

Manila on the main island of Luzon as well as in Cebu and elsewhere in the archipelago. As Nakano School members gradually arrived in the Philippines, they came to form the backbone of Fourteenth Army's CI organization. By September 1944, when Taniguchi became the head of Fourteenth Army CI, a total of twenty-four were working under cover at the Institute.[15]

Raiding American Airfields on Leyte

By the autumn of 1944, the Japanese were desperately defending their empire against General MacArthur's drive from the south and Admiral Nimitz's advance from the east. The Japanese Navy had lost over half its aircraft carriers and carrier airmen in June fighting in the Marianas. The Army had lost thirty thousand men in a failed attempt to stop the Americans from seizing Saipan in July. Increasingly imperiled were the lines of communication between the Japanese home islands and the southern possessions that held the oil, rubber, and other raw materials vital to Japan's war effort.

Determined to hold firm, Imperial General Headquarters moved to bolster the Philippines. In September, Tokyo transferred Gen. Yamashita Tomoyuki, the Tiger of Malaya, from his tour of "exile" in Manchukuo, where a jealous Tojo had buried him, to command the redesignated Fourteenth Area Army in Manila. Yamashita, having taken Malaya and Singapore early in the war from numerically superior British forces, was now to resist the vastly greater American armada bearing down on him. At his disposal were a mere thirteen lightly equipped divisions and several brigades. The greater part of his forces was on the main island of Luzon. His Thirty-fifth Army, under the command of Lt. Gen. Suzuki Sosaku, was responsible for Leyte in the central Philippines.[16]

In October, General MacArthur made good on his vow to return to the Philippines. For more than two years, he had pushed aside every obstacle, including a competing U.S. Navy plan for an assault on Taiwan, to return to the site of his earlier defeat. On 20 October, he sent his men onto the beaches at Leyte. Waiting for his soldiers was a stronger force than Yamashita had thought wise. Southern Army, contrary to the Tiger of Malaya's wish to marshal his meager forces for a decisive battle on Luzon, had ordered him to reinforce Suzuki at Leyte. Yamashita reluctantly obeyed, sending two of his precious divisions south. Japan's Navy also threw much of its remaining strength into the defense of Leyte. On 24 October, the Japanese Navy lost four carriers and the super battleship *Musashi* in the Battle of Leyte Gulf in a futile attack against the invasion fleet. The engagement, which failed to deter the American armada, marked the end of the Imperial Japanese Navy as a conventional fighting force.

In desperation, the Japanese Navy unleashed its special attack forces against the invading fleet. As divine winds had saved Japan from the Mongols nearly seven hundred years earlier, so the kamikaze were to scatter the latest invasion fleet. On 25 October, the first kamikaze hurtled down from above towards the American fleet. Crashing his bomb through the flight deck of the carrier *Santee*, the Japanese pilot took sixteen American lives and wounded another twenty-seven crew at the cost of his own life. The attacks were terrible. William Owens, a member of the U.S. Army's Counter Intelligence Corps (CIC) who went ashore at Leyte, described in his memoirs the emotions the pilots inspired in him: "Their expressed aim was to sacrifice life and plane to bolster Japanese morale and inspire terror in the enemy. In the latter goal they succeeded." Owens wrote his account as a witness, having seen a Japanese pilot fly his aircraft into a landing ship at Dulag, on the east coast of Leyte.

> He kept on target and with a crunch of metal on metal went nose first into the transport. Flame and smoke rose, first from the plane and then from the ship. Soldiers swung themselves over the rails and into the water. In a few minutes no more came over the rails. In a few minutes more the steel plates amidships were a shimmering red. A funeral pyre, the ship was gutted to the waterline. If sacrifice was a way to Yasukuni, the pilot had made it. Soldiers who reached the shore would not talk to me. They wandered in a daze, their words disconnected mutterings of fear and grief and hatred.

Admiral Onishi had discovered in the kamikaze a terrible new weapon for a navy no longer able to defeat the Allied fleets through conventional means.[17]

As the American troops began their bitter fighting to take control of Leyte, moreover, the Japanese Army would launch its own special attacks. In January 1944, the Japanese Army had formed the First Raiding Company (Unit *Sho* 1781) on Taiwan. The commanding officer and nearly all his subordinate officers were graduates of the Nakano School. The unit's men were Taiwanese chosen for their hardiness and fighting spirit. In June, the unit transferred to the Philippines, where it came under the command of Fourth Air Army. At a base south of Manila, the unit trained for its mission as airborne assault troops. The pilots were to land their transport planes wheels up to bring the raiders into the enemy camp as quickly as possible. The men spent their time in honing their commando tactics. In November, the First Raiding Company left Luzon for Leyte to fight as part of Suzuki's Thirty-fifth Army. By late November, Suzuki was facing an increasingly desperate situation. Despite reinforcements from Luzon earlier that month, he was fighting a losing battle. The Americans had seized the airfields at Dulag, Burauen, and Tacloban. Once in full operation, those airfields would contribute greatly to American air supremacy. In late November, Yamashita ordered Suzuki to neutralize the airfields at Dulag and Tacloban and to seize those at Burauen.

Late on the night of 26 November, Lt. Naka Shigeo, a graduate of the Military Academy's Fifty-second Class who had trained at the Nakano School, directed five fellow shadow warriors and eighty Taiwanese of the First Raiding Company's Kaori Parachute Squadron into four transport aircraft. They flew south for their target. At 0245 hours, three transports suddenly appeared in the dark sky over Dulag, then landed wheels up at the airfield. From the transports rushed the commandos. The airborne raiders succeeded in destroying or damaging a number of American aircraft and supplies, according to the Japanese account of the operation, but the failure of participating Japanese ground units to reach the area turned the raid into a suicide mission.

Lieutenant Naka, his Nakano School comrades, and their Taiwanese troops all died in the attack. Radio Tokyo broadcast a description of the operation as "most successful." According to the U.S. Army, three transports had made a crash landing in the area that night. All aboard one plane were reported killed on landing. Most of those from the other two simply melted into the jungle without accomplishing anything. Despite intelligence reports prior to the assault, Twenty-fourth Corps had dismissed the danger of the Japanese seizing the airfields, taking no serious measures to bolster their defenses. The Kaori Parachute Squadron's assault had served notice to MacArthur's forces that Thirty-fifth Army was determined to take back the airfields.

Fortunately for Suzuki's raiders, Twenty-fourth Corps apparently failed to learn its lesson from the November assault. At dawn on 6 December, Japanese ground units launched a surprise assault on the Buri airstrip near Burauen. They took the men there by surprise. The Japanese raiders bayoneted many of the two hundred American service and artillery troops in their sleep or as they stumbled in terror for their weapons. The survivors, after offering token resistance, fled the scene. American airborne and infantry units later managed to drive off the Japanese and retake Buri at 1800 hours.

As dusk was coming over Leyte less than an hour later, however, Japanese transport aircraft suddenly appeared over the airfields. At Dulag, Lt. William Owens and other members of his CIC detachment, looking up to see the aircraft above, spotted parachutes opening like "white blossoms" over the airfield. Japanese fighter escorts sprayed the ground with machine gun fire, while bombers dropped their payloads on the planes parked on the ground. American P-38s burst into flames, illuminating a scene of chaos as Japanese ground units fought their way from the jungle onto the airfield. Parachutists landed at Buri, taking back control of the airstrip. Another unit hit the ground fighting at the San Pablo airstrip, also near Burauen. For the next several days, the Japanese raiders fought tenaciously against American counterattacks. By 11 December, however, the airfields were back in American hands. The surviving commandos then began to fight their way north towards the Japanese lines. Many of the Nakano School's men in the raids, including Lt. Toyoda Masao, died fighting around the airfields. Others made it through the American lines to join Thirty-fifth Army units still fighting in the north of Leyte. The last surviving raiders of the Nakano School on Leyte died fighting on 8 July, only a month before the war's end.[18]

Taniguchi's Shadow Warriors

In Manila, Major Taniguchi and his shadow warriors were preparing for the coming invasion of Luzon. On 15 December, in a prelude to the main act, MacArthur's men went ashore at Mindoro, seizing the neighboring island as a base for use in the invasion of Luzon. During the landing operation, a Japanese kamikaze pilot flew his aircraft into the flagship *Nashville*, killing more than 130 men on board and wounding another two hundred. Among the dead was Brigadier Gen. William C. Dunkel, commander of the landing force. Several days after the Mindoro landing, Major Taniguchi greeted Lieutenant Onoda, who had flown from Japan on 17 December with twenty-one classmates of the Nakano School's Futamata Branch to Clark Airfield. Taniguchi also took command of another group of twenty-six shadow warriors from the main Nakano School. Taniguchi first briefed his new arrivals on the situation in the Philippines, then assigned them to their missions. Some would join an agency ordered to remain behind in Manila after Yamashita's army withdrew in advance of the invasion to the hills north of the city. Others were to take positions in outlying areas. Gathering intelligence and leading raiding units were to be their primary responsibilities.[19]

On 26 December, Major Taniguchi escorted Onoda Hiroo, Yamamoto Shigeichi, and four other members of the Nakano School to Eighth Division, located at an army base outside Manila, for their new assignments. Onoda received orders to lead guerrilla operations on Lubang, a small island northwest of Mindoro. Yamamoto and another comrade were to lead a raid against an American airfield at San Jose. Two others were to organize guerrilla operations on Mindoro. The sixth man from the Nakano School was to remain at division headquarters.

The six men received a briefing at division headquarters from Lt. Gen. Muto Akira, Yamashita's chief of staff, who was visiting the base to inspect the troops. Muto expressly warned the men to execute their missions under any circumstances, contrary to the Army's doctrine of suicide before surrender: "Fight on, even if it should take three years or five. No matter what, we will return for you. While even a single soldier remains, use that soldier to continue fighting, even if you have to live on coconuts. All right? Let me repeat, suicidal banzai charges are absolutely forbidden. Is that understood?" Onoda was riveted to hear the senior commander's exhortation. His comrade Yamamoto, a fellow native of Wakayama Prefecture who had gone through Futamata Branch with him, also encouraged him. Yamamoto, considering his orders for an airfield assault at San Jose, told his friend that he expected to die soon. He exhorted Onoda to stick to what he predicted would be a long mission on Lubang.[20]

Onoda arrived on the island with orders to deny the Americans the use of its pier and airfield. He was also to organize guerrilla operations and gather intelligence following the enemy's landing. Onoda immediately ran into opposition from other officers of Lubang's two hundred Japanese troops. The tangled lines of authority included officers responsible for an army garrison, air intelligence officers, and navy personnel. Onoda had no authority to command any of those units. He could only lead and advise. The army officers refused to cooperate with Onoda. They had their own orders to transport the island's fuel stocks to Luzon and evacuate their personnel. They also objected to Onoda's plan to destroy the airfield, which they argued would be needed again after Japan regained air superiority. Nor could he convince the garrison commander to allow him to prepare his men for guerrilla warfare. Their mission, as soldiers of the Imperial Japanese Army, was to repulse the invaders or die fighting. Onoda could do little more than convince them to allow him to set explosive charges to the pier. He also assembled bits of aircraft and local materials into dummy planes as decoys to bait the American pilots into wasting ammunition. His dummy aircraft "invariably" drew U.S. aircraft fire.[21]

Onoda was not long on Lubang before he reported his greatest intelligence finding of the war. In the first week of January, perched atop a ship that had grounded on a coral reef, Onoda spotted ships of the American armada steaming for Luzon's Lingayen Gulf. Onoda immediately made radio contact with Fourteenth Area Army Headquarters, reporting that more than a hundred warships and twice as many support ships were on their way north to the gulf. His intelligence proved valuable to General Yamashita. Years later, at a meeting of military veterans at the Army Officers' Club in Tokyo, Taniguchi claimed that Onoda's reporting was of assistance in Yamashita's defense of Luzon. If so, then Onoda's warning was possibly what triggered the ensuing kamikaze assault. When Rear Adm. Jesse Oldendorf's invasion fleet reached Lingayen Gulf, waves of pilots flew for his ships. They succeeded in sinking the minesweeper *Long* and damaging the battleships *New Mexico* and *California*. In all, twenty-five ships of the invasion fleet were sunk or damaged at Lingayen Gulf.[22]

MacArthur's men went ashore to find that Yamashita had already withdrawn his main force into the hills north of Manila. The Tiger of Malaya intended to wage a protracted fight to tie down the American forces for as long as possible. Major Taniguchi and a number of his shadow warriors had retreated to positions previously arranged in northern Luzon. Members of his Malacanang Section had already spirited President Jose Laurel and other top Filipino collaborators away from the city for refuge in Japan. Most of the remaining defenders in Manila were naval personnel under the command of Rear Adm. Iwabuchi Sanji, who was not under Yamashita's authority.

Among those who remained in Manila as MacArthur's men advanced on the city were graduates of the Futamata Branch assigned to the Nanmei Agency. The organization operated under cover as a local branch of Japan's South Seas Development Company. Under the command of Major Yamaji, the group's mission was to stay in Manila after the Americans captured the city. Yamaji's men were to pass the intelligence they gathered to Yamashita's forces in northern Luzon. They were also to carry out acts of terror and sabotage behind enemy lines. Nakajima Akifumi, one of those assigned to Yamaji's unit, joined others in his unit who were extracting confessions from suspected guerrillas. There, he saw Rita, who was using her talent for languages in the interrogations. In the end, Rita reportedly survived the fighting in Manila to slip away to northern Luzon with other members of the Nanmei Agency. Slated to leave the Philippines for Yokohama in January, she died under unclear circumstances before making good her escape.

Once MacArthur's forces had begun to fight their way into the city in the first week of February, Major Yamaji conducted his agency's operations from Rear Adm. Iwabuchi's headquarters. Much of his team's work involved demolishing buildings to clear lines of fire for Iwabuchi's men. On 11 February, under Iwabuchi's orders, Yamaji led his agency out of Manila. He and his men would continue fighting until American forces later surrounded and killed them.[23]

Onoda's War

Lieutenant Onoda was in despair as the American soldiers combed Lubang for Japanese stragglers. A small American force had landed on Lubang on 28 February. At the crucial moment, Onoda was unable to detonate the explosives. Either the explosives had failed, or local Filipino guerrillas had cut the wires. In any event, Onoda had failed to deny the Americans the use of the pier. Nor had he succeeded in his attempts to convince the Japanese officers on the island to destroy the airfield before the landing. He described his sense of failure in the following words: "I had disgraced myself as a secret warfare agent."

Despite the failure, Onoda realized that he was the only officer capable of attacking the enemy behind the lines. He had received instruction in jungle fighting at Futamata. He resolved to attack an enemy encampment to relieve some two hundred Japanese soldiers hidden in the mountains from the threat of attack. He thus decided, despite his training at Futamata Branch, that he would have to lead an attack and die like a Japanese soldier. On the night of 2 March, Onoda led fifteen men through the jungle towards an American camp. He had no thought of surviving the fight. Drawing his sword and casting aside the sheath, he crept along a dark mountain trail. Again, however, he tasted bitter disappointment. The enemy, perhaps fearing a night attack, had recently decamped. Onoda did not fight that night.[24]

In the days that followed, Onoda regained his resolve to stay alive to accomplish his mission by gathering intelligence. Driving the Americans off Lubang or inflicting serious damage was out of the question. The sight of chewing-gum wrappers littering the island, evidence of the abundance of American supplies at a time when hungry Japanese soldiers were desperately foraging for food, left Onoda with a sense of defeat. By the middle of March, only around three dozen of the original two hundred Japanese soldiers remained alive on Lubang. Onoda was the only officer left. To avoid detection, he had the soldiers split into smaller groups. In the latter half of April, Onoda's group scattered after coming under fire. At the planned rendezvous site, Onoda later found only Cpl. Shimada Shoichi. A week later, Pvt. Kozuka Kinshichi found them.[25]

While Onoda and the two soldiers were evading American patrols, MacArthur's men were engaging Yamashita's dwindling forces in northern Luzon and eliminating the last pockets of organized resistance in other areas. Few of Onoda's fellow shadow warriors survived. On their arrival in the Philippines, the men of the Futamata Branch had been assigned to Yamashita's forces in three groups: *Shobu*, including the hill town of Baguio and points north on the upper end of Luzon; *Kenbu*, placed on the island between Manila and Lingayen Bay; and *Shinbu*, covering southern Luzon, including Manila, as well as the neighboring islands of Mindoro and Lubang. Few men in the *Shinbu* group survived. On Mindoro, taken by MacArthur's force as the preliminary assault before the Luzon landing, four of the five guerrilla leaders from Futamata Branch died. In southern Luzon, nine of eleven perished. In central Luzon, only one of the four classmates survived the fighting. Only in the mountains of northern Luzon, where Yamashita was directing the last of his troops when the war ended, did half of the men (nine of eighteen) assigned to the *Shobu* group survive.[26]

In all, sixty-six of the Nakano School's ninety-eight operatives in the Philippines died there in the war's final months. Ono Tadao, one of those in the *Shobu* group, was still fighting when a Japanese emissary arrived in his area on 15 September with the news that Yamashita had surrendered. A full month had passed since the broadcast of Emperor Hirohito that announced the war's end. Two weeks before the emissary's appearance, representatives of the Japanese government had signed the surrender documents on the deck of the battleship *Missouri* in Tokyo Bay. Only when orders arrived from Major Taniguchi, however, did Ono surrender.[27]

On Lubang, Lieutenant Onoda first received notice of the war's end in late August. Filipino troops exchanged fire with his little band, then dropped leaflets before withdrawing. According to the message, the war had ended with the emperor's broadcast of 15 August. Onoda chose to disregard the leaflets as a ruse. At the end of 1945, an American B-17 flew low over Lubang, scattering more leaflets. Written on them was an order from General Yamashita to surrender. Finding some of the order's wording and composition odd, however, Onoda and his men decided that the new leaflets were yet another American forgery to trick them into surrendering. In the absence of explicit orders from Major Taniguchi, Onoda remained with his men in the jungle. For him, the war had only just begun.[28]

A converted Japanese "Sally" bomber that landed with its wheels up during a Japanese commando raid on the Americans' Yomitan airfield on Okinawa, May 1945. The Japanese raiding party of 168 men, which included ten from the Nakano School, intended to knock out the airfield so Japanese kamikazes would not be intercepted by American fighters. *National Archives*

The raid on Yomitan airfield was a disaster for the Japanese, as illustrated by the fallen commandos in the foreground. Four of the twelve planes carrying the commandos had to turn back due to mechanical problems, and seven of the remaining eight planes were shot down before they reached the airfield. *National Archives*

Lt. Gen. Kawabe Torashiro (left), vice chief of staff of the Japanese Army, and Maj. Gen. Charles A. Willoughby, Gen. Douglas MacArthur's intelligence chief, proceeding to a surrender conference, August 1945. At the time the photo was taken, the two men were still adversaries, and Kawabe considered ordering Nakano School veterans to wage a guerrilla war against the occupying forces. However, Kawabe soon became convinced that the Japanese would benefit from developing good relations with the Americans, so the plans for guerrilla war were never implemented. Kawabe and Willoughby developed warm ties and collaborated on intelligence matters. Willoughby sought assistance from former Japanese intelligence officers to improve U.S. Army intelligence about the Far East and to hunt down Soviet agents, real or imagined, in Japan. *National Archives*

Col. Charles Tench (seated at left), a member of Gen. MacArthur's advance party to Japan, and Lt. Gen. Arisue Seizo (seated at right), intelligence chief of the Japanese Army, await MacArthur's arrival at Atsugi airfield, September 1945. Arisue had approved the contingency plans for a post-surrender guerrilla war, but he concurred with Kawabe's judgment that Japan would gain more from good relations with the Americans. Arisue became MacArthur and Willoughby's most important ally on intelligence matters and an indispensable liaison between Japanese officials and the Americans. *U.S. Army Signal Corps/MacArthur Memorial Archives*

Gen. Okamura Yasuji, Japan's top general in China, affixes his seal to a surrender document on September 9, 1945, in Nanking, China. Yasuji had roughly one million soldiers under his command at the time of surrender. The Chinese Nationalists later turned to General Okamura for aid in rebuilding their shattered forces. The Japanese and the Americans, wanting to prevent Mao's Communists from solidifying their control of China, had Okamura send Nakano School veterans to Taiwan to help retrain Chiang's army. *National Archives*

6

NEARING THE END

The Japanese Empire was in dire straits by early 1945. American and British forces were retaking the colonial territories they had lost some three years earlier. Allied fleets were strangling the empire's sea lanes, restricting the flow of supplies and soldiers. American aircraft were penetrating the empire's defenses to strike the Japanese home islands.

Disarming the French in Indochina

Allied victories were even sending tremors through French Indochina, long a stable rear base for military operations. French Indochina consisted of Tonkin, Annam, and Cochin China, respectively the northern, central, and southern parts of what is today Vietnam, as well as Laos and Cambodia. The French had backed the Nationalists in Japan's undeclared war against China, permitting American oil and other supplies to flow through the port of Haiphong and, by rail via Lao Cai, across the border to Chiang Kai-shek's beleaguered forces. The French lifeline, along with the British route through Burma, had kept China in the fight before Pearl Harbor.[1]

Germany's defeat of France in June 1940 ended French aid to the Chinese and opened Indochina to the Japanese. The Japanese Army had first stationed troops in French Indochina in September 1940, taking positions in the north of Vietnam several days before Tokyo, Berlin, and Rome formed the Tripartite Alliance. In July 1941, the Japanese military entered the southern part of French Indochina in preparation for war. France's collaborationist Vichy regime of Marshal Philippe Petain, anxious to preserve its sovereignty, accepted the move. Under the Darlan-Kato accord of 29 July, the Japanese gained the right to station forces in French Indochina, under the pretext of "joint defense," at eight airfields and naval bases at Saigon and Cam Ranh Bay.[2]

Under the accord, Indochina became a rear base for support of Japanese operations elsewhere. Saigon became the headquarters for Southern Army during much of the ensuing war. In order to save its colonial possessions in Asia, the Vichy government of France gave its full cooperation to Japan during the war. It was from Indochina that aircraft of the Japanese Navy had sortied to sink Great Britain's *Prince of Wales* and *Repulse* at the war's opening. The Japanese Army broadcast propaganda from French facilities in Saigon throughout Southeast Asia and as far as India. Damaged ships were repaired in the local French shipyards. Trade increased.[3]

As the conflict's tide turned against Japan and her Axis partners in Europe, however, the French began to stir. They had, after all, only allowed the Japanese to station military forces to avoid losing their colony. Against some thirty-eight thousand troops under French command, of whom only the seventy-five hundred who were French could be counted as reliable, the Japanese had approximately sixty thousand men stationed in the colony. The Japanese, for their part, had been tolerating the continued administration of the French colonial authorities as a temporary expedient. From the start, the Japanese Army had been supporting local nationalists to undermine French authority. Inviting Subhas Chandra Bose to Saigon had been one of the more overt manifestations of this policy.[4]

Charles De Gaulle, leader of the Free French in opposition to France's Vichy regime, had entered Paris in triumph at the head of Allied forces in August 1944. But French Indochina remained under the administration of Adm. Jean Decoux, with whom De Gaulle had poor relations. In secret, De Gaulle designated Gen. Eugene Mordant, who had recently retired as commander of the French army in Indochina, his "representative" there. Decoux, incredulous to learn from Mordant's successor that the two generals were in secret communication with De Gaulle, offered to resign. Instead, he received instructions to stay in place. Furthermore, De Gaulle secretly instructed Decoux to operate according to a group of generals and senior local officials who would guide the French "resistance" in Indochina. Intelligence officers, arms, and equipment started coming from India into Indochina beginning in October.

The Japanese Kempeitai and military intelligence network, operating throughout French Indochina, did not fail to detect the French actions. There, as elsewhere, Japan's military police and intelligence officers ran an extensive network of agents and informants. The French colonists, for their part, were indiscreet. There was increasingly open talk of retaking control of the region as news of Axis losses circulated. The Kempeitai let the clandestine activities continue as a way to gauge their extent while preparing to strike at their roots. The Japanese knew before long that General Mordant was De Gaulle's man in Indochina, among other aspects of the French operations. As Jean Sainteny, a French intelligence officer who entered Indochina from his wartime base of operations across the border in China immediately after the Japanese surrender, ruefully admitted in a postwar history of French Indochina, "The secrets of whites, in Asia, are very difficult to keep!"[5]

Aware that French covert plans and Allied military victories were threatening its hold on Indochina, the Japanese Army prepared to disarm the French and undermine their ability to resume control after the war. The Japanese had not intended to liberate Indochina's peoples during the war, but they were determined to destroy the basis for any postwar resumption of Western rule.

As elsewhere, men of the Nakano School were to execute the Japanese Army's programs. In December 1942, the Army had assigned a number of Nakano School graduates to French Indochina, subsequently organizing them as the Akira Agency. The Agency directed three operations sections, one each for northern, central, and southern French Indochina. These operations squads were known collectively as the Yasu Unit. Members wore an arm band displaying a rising sun with the Chinese character "an" (pronounced in Japanese also as "yasu"), the first two Chinese characters for An-nam. These men would act as the spearhead of Japanese actions against the French.[6]

In December 1944, Lt. Gen. Tsuchihashi Yuichi arrived in Saigon to take command of the newly established Thirty-eighth Army and bolster the region's defenses. Tsuchihashi was eminently suited to his new task. He had previously held the concurrent posts of vice chief of staff in the China Expeditionary Army and military attaché to Wang

Ching-wei's puppet regime in Nanking. He also served before the war as military attaché in Paris. In addition, Tsuchihashi had once before confronted the French in Indochina. In early 1940, while chief of Second Bureau in Tokyo, he had gone to Hanoi to seek an end to the flow of supplies to the Chinese via the port of Haiphong. In speaking to Gen. Georges Catroux, then the director-general, Tsuchihashi had at first taken a friendly tone. As a former military attaché at the Japanese embassy in Paris, he quite likely admired the French, as he told Catroux. Faced with Catroux's refusal to guarantee an end to the supplies or to permit him to ascertain that no material was entering China, Tsuchihashi had taken a belligerent tone with Catroux. The meeting had ended badly, with the French general brusquely showing him the door.[7]

A dozen operatives from the First Class of the Nakano School's Futamata Branch for guerrilla warfare arrived that same month, joining their senior colleagues in the Yasu Unit. Under the direction of Lt. Col. Hayashi, a Kempeitai officer attached to the staff of Thirty-eighth Army, the Yasu Unit's members planned their operations. The first stage involved gathering intelligence on the local French armed forces, spreading propaganda, taking into custody key members of the Annamite royal government, and strengthening the underground organization of Vietnamese independence activists. They were also preparing for the second stage, when they would join in the armed attacks against French forces, conduct battlefield propaganda, destroy French garrison facilities, sabotage French factories and commercial enterprises, and engage in other special operations. In the third stage, following the elimination of French authority, the Yasu Unit's men were to keep watch over Emperor Bao Dai, help establish a Vietnamese administration under Prince Cuong De, strengthen Japan's intelligence network, participate in the organization of coastal defense units, and organize guerrilla units in the interior. With the French locked away, a pliant emperor and a pro-Japanese prince under their authority, the coast defended, and the interior primed for guerrilla warfare, the Japanese Army would have created the best conditions possible under which to contest an Allied invasion.[8]

Key to Japanese plans was controlling the Emperor Bao Dai, who ruled Annam in name only from the imperial city of Hue. Capt. Kaneko Noboru, chief of covert operations for Annam, had responsibility for taking him into custody at the crucial moment of the Japanese attack. Kaneko, a graduate of the Nakano School, had as his lieutenants two junior officers from the school. On 6 February, Kaneko and his subordinates passed in disguise through a gate of the great wall encircling Hue. Posing as a Japanese university professor, Kaneko established his operation in a trading firm's office made available to him through the Japanese trading company Dainan Koshi. The company, established by the Japanese Army as a cover organization, had operated in French Indochina since before the war. In Hue, Kaneko and his men gathered intelligence on the disposition of the city's French garrison and awaited the arrival of regular Japanese military units.[9]

On 8 February, Lt. Gen. Numata Takazo, Southern Army's chief of staff, returned to Saigon from Tokyo with orders from Imperial General Headquarters to disarm the French as part of the final defense of Indochina. The next evening, immediately following the Japanese ultimatum to Admiral Decoux, the Japanese Army swung into action. Within Hue, Kaneko's unit wrested the keys from city guards to open one of the city's great gates to the Japanese troops positioned outside. French resistance in Hue proved unexpectedly stiff, particularly around the walled palace. At dawn, however, the Japanese colonel directing the assault called over Kaneko to the palace to search for the emperor among the Vietnamese notables in custody. Kaneko, accompanied by an interpreter from Dainan Koshi, at one point peered through the window of a luxury automobile. Seated in the back were a man and woman of noble appearance. Kaneko had found Emperor Bao Dai and his wife. The young intelligence officer immediately proclaimed to Bao Dai the end of French rule and the beginning of a bright, new chapter in Vietnam's history. The young emperor shook Kaneko's hand, professing in turn his profound gratitude to Japan and his expectations of friendly relations.[10]

In spite of stiff resistance at Hue and Hanoi, the Japanese subdued and disarmed the more numerous French forces in short order. Most of the fighting was over in twenty-four hours. In Kunming, China, where Jean Sainteny was operating as commander of a French military mission, communications from Indochina revealed the sudden, desperate events unfolding. From the base at Langson came a hurried message sent in the clear: "Under attack since 9 March at 10:30; situation is difficult; we urgently need air intervention." No such aid came. The Japanese took the base the morning after their night attack, then executed its commanding general for refusing to sign the document of surrender.

For several weeks, minor French resistance continued at Dienbienphu and other isolated sites in the north, but the issue was never in doubt. Apart from a few thousand soldiers who escaped under the leadership of two French generals across the border into China, French forces were disarmed and imprisoned. On 11 March, the Emperor Bao Dai renounced the French protectorate over Annam and proclaimed Vietnam's independence. In Cambodia, Prince Norodom Sihanouk followed suit on 17 March. The French flag was also struck in Laos. The Japanese Army, having removed the threat of French treachery, moved to establish its new client regimes and build up Indochina's defenses. Meanwhile, a new problem emerged from the jungles of northern Vietnam, as national communist leader Ho Chi Minh and his Vietminh rejected collaboration and conducted raids against the Japanese.[11]

Endgame in Burma

While Japanese covert operations in tandem with regular troops had eliminated in March 1945 the French threat to Japan's hold on Indochina, the Japanese Army's shadow warriors in Burma were powerless to stop the Allied juggernaught that was rolling south towards Rangoon. During this time of Japanese reverses, the Nakano School's operatives attached to the Japanese Army in Burma worked in the shadows to gather intelligence, form guerrilla units, and carry out raids against airfields and camps. In spring 1945, however, the loss of Mandalay and Meiktila spelled the end of Japanese rule in Burma.

As Japanese fortunes ebbed, the Japanese Army's poor treatment of their Burmese allies came to haunt them. Aung San, one of Col. Suzuki Keiji's original Thirty Comrades in the Minami Agency, had long resented the Japanese military government in Burma for pushing him and his comrades of the Thakin Party aside. The Japanese had opted for the more established Ba Maw as their chief collaborator, leaving Aung San and other young nationalists with lesser roles as officers in Burma's token army. Japan's tardy granting of independence to Burma in 1943 and the redesignation of the local armed forces as the Burma National Army (BNA) did nothing to placate the young Burmese officers. The issue of Japanese sincerity aside, the writing was on the wall for the Burmese to see: Japan was losing the war. Word of Aung San's discontent reached British intelligence officers as early as 1943, too early in the war for the British to act upon it. By early 1945, however, they were in secret contact with anti-Japanese Thakin activists.[12]

On 1 January 1945, British intelligence received word that the BNA, with some eight thousand men, was preparing to fight the Japanese. The British immediately launched operation Nation, the plan to cooperate with Burma's anti-Japanese movement, sending teams of intelligence officers into Burma to gather intelligence and contact the movement. On 9 March, British in the field reported the beginning of desertions from BNA units and relayed a Burmese request for arms. By the middle of the month, the British learned that the entire BNA would turn against the Japanese. They also learned that Aung San had recently paraded his BNA units in Rangoon before leading them from the city on the pretext of going to battle against the British.[13]

By the middle of March, the Kempeitai and other Japanese intelligence organs had caught wind of the incipient revolt by their Burmese auxiliaries. Under the confused and desperate circumstances, however, the Japanese refrained from acting. Japanese officials even hosted a banquet for Aung San in honor of his departure from Rangoon, although many or most suspected what would happen once he and his troops were in the field. On 24 March, 180 cadets of the Burmese Military Academy deserted, killing some of their Japanese instructors before disappearing into the jungle. By 27 March, the Japanese had a full-scale revolt of the BNA on their hands. Some twenty of the roughly one hundred Japanese serving as liaison officers to the BNA died at the hands of Burmese soldiers. Aung San and his men proceeded to carry out guerrilla raids against the Japanese. In one sense, the Burmese were paying them back for the years of oppressive military government and Kempeitai terror. In addition, Aung San was establishing his credentials as leader for postwar Burma in advance of future negotiations with the British. It simply would not do for him to await passively the return of his nation's former overlords. Fighting before the war ended would strengthen his hand later.[14]

The Japanese, facing harassing attacks from the BNA, also had dispirited INA troops on their hands. The INA, never a true fighting force, proved of little value in the defense of Burma. First, they were still equipped only with captured British rifles and other light arms.

Without their own tanks or heavy artillery, they were unprepared to face the advancing British military forces. Under the command of the outstanding Lt. Gen. William Slim, a product of Great Britain's Indian Army, Indian officers and men fought valiantly. Their exploits stood in stunning contrast to the dismal record of their brothers in the INA. Of the twenty-seven Victoria Crosses awarded for the Burma campaign, twenty went to Indians. In contrast, INA soldiers repeatedly surrendered en masse. The experience of Slim's 161st Brigade on 23 April was typical. "As it drove south it rounded up parties of dispirited INA, whose only anxiety appeared to be to find out where to 'report in.' Quantities of abandoned rations and equipment lay everywhere; the few Japanese stragglers who were met died fighting or committed suicide rather than surrender."[15]

Maj. Kuwahara Takeshi, a graduate of the Military Academy's Fifty-second Class as well as the Nakano School, was one of the shadow warriors in Burma trying to direct the disintegrating INA. Kuwahara, after joining the Hikari Agency the previous year and participating in the disastrous invasion of northeast India, had received orders in February 1945 to take command of the INA's Second Division as its "liaison officer." On 20 April, after coming under attack by British tanks, the Indian commander of INA Second Division's First Infantry Regiment had sent word to the British that he wished to surrender. Kuwahara, retreating south that same night, encountered the INA regimental commander waiting for the British to take him prisoner. Fortunately, the Indian permitted Kuwahara to continue south rather than make a "present" of him to the British. Kunizuka Kazunori, another INA advisor, would later favorably contrast the "loyalty" of Japan's Indian auxiliaries with the "betrayal" of the Burmese. While the dispirited Indians surrendered in droves, he remarked, at least they refrained from actively "joining hands with the enemy British Army and cutting Japanese necks as one would cut a melon."[16]

Kuwahara, upon reaching Twenty-eighth Army Headquarters in the Pegu Mountains of central Burma, met Maj. Gen. Iwakuro Hideo, by then that army's chief of staff. Iwakuro, once director of the Japanese Army's Indian operations, now had little use for his INA auxiliaries. Japan's Twenty-eighth Army lacked the supplies to feed and equip the INA, which was showing little inclination to fight in any case. Iwakuro told Kuwahara that he was cutting the INA loose. The Indians were now on their own, free to fight or surrender as they wished. Iwakuro's one stipulation was that INA units were to stay away from the Japanese holding out in the Pegu area. Iwakuro's order spelled the end of the INA, which soon thereafter completely fell apart. One division commander noted in his journal on 4 May: "The Japanese have left us completely in the lurch. They are running themselves and are not bothering about us." The following day, he noted the withdrawal of all Japanese liaison officers. Kuwahara rejoined Twenty-eighth Army that month, taking command of a unit charged with river crossing operations.[17]

As the war was coming to its end in Southeast Asia, the Japanese Army grew anxious about an INA revolt. Southern Army considered disarming INA units. At one point, a staff officer of Southern Army raised the idea with Col. Kagawa Yoshio, a staff officer of the Hikari Agency. Kagawa without hesitation opposed strongly a proposal that he was sure the region's resident Indians as well as the INA would see as a betrayal. Kagawa also reported the proposal to Lt. Gen. Isoda Saburo, still in charge at that time of the Hikari Agency. Isoda also registered his "absolute" opposition. Southern Army thus abandoned its plan to confiscate the INA's arms.[18]

Losing Comrades in New Guinea

The NCOs of the Nakano School in New Guinea had enjoyed a reputation throughout the Imperial Japanese Army (IJA)'s Eighteenth Army for their remarkable raids since mid-1943. Arriving in one supply base, Tanaka Tatsuo and his comrades received extra rations from the meager military stores on account of their exploits. Japanese soldiers were no longer able to best an enemy incomparably larger and better equipped in conventional battles. But the raiders had time and again burst into an enemy camp with explosives and weapons, sending those not blown apart or shot fleeing into the night.

Tanaka, Yamada Masatsugu, and a baker's dozen of other NCOs from the Nakano School had been putting their lessons to good use in New Guinea. In addition to scouting, infiltrating, and demolishing enemy positions, the Nakano School NCOs surveyed the topographical features of the interior and worked to win the hearts and minds of tribal natives. With tact, as well as rice and other commodities, the Nakano School's men had won over local chiefs. At one point, Tanaka had convinced Gen. Adachi Hatazo, the top Japanese commander on

New Guinea, to meet an important chief. Native friendship gained them intelligence on enemy troop movements and countered enemy efforts to turn the local people against them. The natives also guided Japanese units on hidden jungle trails, offered them food, and carried equipment for them. Maj. Gen. Nakai Masutaro, the commander of the detachment within Twentieth Division that bore his name, praised the shadow warriors for their work. Equivalent to having another regiment was the worth of the topographical surveys and the tribal support they had given his detachment during his campaign against an opposing American division, in Nakai's estimation.

While Tanaka, Yamada, and their comrades had the solid training of the Nakano School to thank for their early string of raids, executed without a single casualty, fortune doubtless played its part. For, while the elite band of NCOs held to their proven ways of scouting, infiltration, and attack, their early good fortune faded over time. In December 1943, in the heat of an attack against an enemy unit, Capt. Ishii Toshio yelled out to his unit to take cover as a grenade fell. A fragment wounded Ishii in the neck. A few meters away, Lt. Komata Yozo, leading a squad, was drifting in and out of consciousness, a gaping hole in his left side. Ishii ordered Tanaka to get Komata back to the field medical unit, then returned to the attack. The raid succeeded, without further casualties, but Komata's wounds took him from New Guinea to a hospital in Japan.

In February 1945, Tanaka and his comrades in a group led by Lieutenant Ishii fought furiously alongside two other Japanese units to escape encirclement by superior enemy forces near the coast. While they eluded their opponents, seized more than 250 hand grenades and other booty, and killed an estimated 150 men, the Japanese raiders took serious losses. Sergeants Shindo Seiichi, Kobayashi Takeo, and Shinohara Takeo died in the fight. More than thirty of their men suffered death or injury. In more than four hours of fighting an enemy ten times their number, under naval shelling and inferior in arms and supplies, Tanaka and most of the raiders had survived. When he had time to reflect, Tanaka was beset by guilt for having lived while classmates of the Nakano School had died.

By May, the Japanese Army no longer could confront the enemy in conventional battle. Indeed, Allied control of the skies and waters around the island had made starvation a mortal foe for soldiers of Eighteenth Army. Even the elite raiders of the Nakano School could no longer count on regular rations. Happily, their raids netted them enemy food stores as well as clothing, boots, and weapons in short supply. Fortune, too, would smile on them at times. Once, while digging foxholes near a river, the men turned up some welcome clams. On another occasion, they found that some lizards had fallen in their foxholes and, again, the malnourished men enjoyed some unexpected protein. When the enemy was nowhere near, the NCOs could send their hardy Taiwanese out to track game. On the coast or along rivers, they would occasionally drop a hand grenade or two into the water, scooping up the fish that would rise stunned from the blast.

It was during these desperate times that Tanaka and Yamada, separated during an earlier reorganization, again joined forces. In a letter delivered by Tanaka to Captain Ishii, Yamada had pleaded to rejoin his Nakano School classmate for a "last chance" to "run wild" with his comrade. His wish granted, Yamada joined Tanaka and Hashimoto Suekichi as unit leaders in an attack on Dagua airfield. The Japanese had earlier lost control of the facility to the enemy, who were now using the rehabilitated airfield against them. Leading nearly 150 men, the Nakano School's Tanaka, Yamada, and Hashimoto were to attack the airfield, destroying its aircraft and facilities. Tanaka and Yamada were to lead fourteen men to demolish the airfield. The others would provide support.

In the darkness, Tanaka and Yamada led their men through the perimeter into the Dagua airfield. Setting explosives on aircraft, a fuel tank, a pipeline, and other objectives, the men dashed outside to take cover. A moment later, explosions rocked the air and flames lit the night sky as the explosives blew apart aircraft, ammunition ignited, and fuel burned. Met by Hashimoto, all returned to safety.

The next day, the group made their way in haste towards Tokoku Pass, a choke point controlling access to the Japanese forces assembled in the mountainous interior to the south. Their mission this time was to eliminate an enemy camp there. Hashimoto, Tanaka, and Yamada were to lead a total of fifty men in the attack. As in earlier raids, the Nakano School's NCOs caught the enemy unawares, sending those who survived the hail of grenades and automatic gunfire fleeing into the jungle.

Tanaka, determining the camp secured, had ordered his men to gather food, weapons, and ammunition when he realized that Yamada was missing. Seized with dread, he ran to his comrade's position. On a hill some hundred meters away he found his friend. Shot through the stomach, Yamada lay dying. Tanaka yelled encouragement, telling him they had seized the camp and urging him to hold on. "Tanaka, I'm done for," Yamada replied. He then called out, "Father, mother, I'm going ahead of you!" At the threshold of death, Yamada cried, "Long live His Majesty the Emperor!" Then he was gone. Tanaka had lost his closest comrade, his fellow classmate from Nagasaki, who had endured with him the months of combat, hunger, and malaria in the "green hell" of New Guinea.[19]

Tracking the Gathering Storm in the Soviet Far East

By early 1945, Japan's Kwantung Army in Manchukuo was growing increasingly worried that the Soviet Red Army across the border was preparing to launch an offensive. In Europe, the Soviets were pushing the Germans back from their early gains in Eastern Europe. Stalin, the month following the Red Army's taking of Warsaw in January, had made a secret commitment to President Roosevelt and Prime Minister Churchill at Yalta that the Soviet Union would enter the war against Japan three months after the fall of Germany. The Red Army, liberating Budapest two days after Stalin's promise and driving the German Army from Hungary in early April, was poised to take Berlin.

Moscow then turned its attention east. Soviet Foreign Minister Vyacheslav Molotov informed the Japanese Foreign Ministry on 5 April that the Soviet Union would not be extending the neutrality pact the two nations had inked in April 1941. Later that month, Soviet tanks bulled their way into Berlin. Along the Trans-Siberian Railroad, the conduit for Soviet reinforcements from the Far East to the West in the war's early months, now came Soviet forces from Europe heading east.

Japan's leaders had no reason to expect mercy from Stalin. In the latter half of 1941, after having signed the neutrality pact with Moscow, Tokyo's leaders had seriously considered Adolf Hitler's call for Japan to invade the Soviet Far East while Germany drove towards Moscow from the west. The Kwantung Army had even mobilized for invasion, designating their preparations the Kwantung Army Special Maneuvers. In the end, however, the Army had bowed to the Japanese Navy's demand for war in Southeast Asia and the Pacific against the United States, Great Britain, and the Netherlands. The Army's decision to strike south stemmed from the Navy's compelling arguments for assigning priority to the conquest of the West's colonies as a source of oil and other key resources. Memories of the crushing defeat inflicted in 1939 on the Kwantung Army by the Soviets at Nomonhan, at the border between the respective client states of Manchukuo and the Mongolian People's Republic, also entered into Japanese calculations. The Japanese Army chose to refrain from invading Siberia until such time as Hitler had decisively defeated the Soviets in Europe.

Capt. Baba Yoshimitsu, a young intelligence officer serving in the Kwantung Army, knew by the spring of 1945 that Japan's time for invading the Soviet Far East had long passed. Born in Korea in 1918, Baba had graduated from P'yongyang Higher Middle School before joining the Army in 1939. His early years in Korea and his promise as a soldier soon earned him assignment to the Nakano School, from which he graduated in 1941. Soon after the Kwantung Army Special Maneuvers had ended that same year, Baba arrived in Manchukuo for duty with the Chientao SSA. The agency operated in southeastern Manchukuo's Kirin Province, a strategic area bordered to the south and east by Korea and the Soviet Maritime Province. The Chientao SSA was based in Yenki, a key city on the rail line between Harbin in central Manchukuo and Tumen, the rail terminal nearest the vital Soviet military port of Vladivostok.

The Chientao SSA, given its proximity to both the Korean and Soviet borders, worked chiefly to eliminate Korean guerrilla activity in the area and to conduct intelligence activities against the Soviet Union. Roughly eight of every ten residents of Chientao were ethnic Koreans, many of whom had left Korea after Japan absorbed the peninsula into its empire in 1910. The area's Korean population was the sea in which swam Korean guerrillas. One, Kim Il-song, emerged after the war to lead communist North Korea.

Purging the area of Kim Il-song and other communist guerrillas was one of the Chientao SSA's chief tasks. Despite the difficulties of pursuing committed communist insurgents through the wild region's forests and mountains, the Chientao SSA worked with other Japanese military and police units in driving Kim Il-song across the border into the Soviet Maritime Province by the end of 1940.[20] Pacifying the area under the SSA's direction was the Chientao Special Force, a unit of Korean officers and men who hunted their communist brethren.

According to Gen. Chang Ch'ang-guk, a Korean graduate of Japan's Imperial Military Academy who headed the Joint Chiefs of Staff in postwar South Korea, the Chientao Special Force had the reputation even among the Japanese as the "ever-victorious Korean unit." A few years later, after the postwar division of Korea into Soviet and American spheres of influence and the outbreak of the Korean War, Korean veterans of the Chientao Special Force would again lead pacification campaigns. This time, they would fight, under American direction, against Korean communist guerrillas.

While the Koreans of the Chientao SSA occupied a special position within the Japanese military, they were far from alone. Given the bitter memories Koreans have regarding the colonial period, it is instructive to note that more than half a million young Korean men volunteered from 1938 until the end of the war to serve in the Japanese forces. Furthermore, the Japanese only selected fewer than twenty thousand of the applicants to wear the imperial uniform. The numbers dwarf the small bands of Korean guerrillas who fought against the Japanese from bases in Manchukuo or China.

Compiling intelligence on the Soviet Union was the Chientao SSA's other key duty. Given the difficulty of obtaining Soviet intelligence, the agency employed a full range of techniques: agent infiltration, document exploitation, radio communications interception and decryption, topographical surveys, and defector interrogation. The agency also prepared for wartime execution of planned covert operations against Soviet targets and beamed radio propaganda across the border.[21]

Baba, as commander of an intelligence company in the Chientao SSA's Third Battalion and as director of the SSA's covert intelligence section, conducted defector interrogations as one of his principal duties. The early rise and later fall in the number of Soviet soldiers crossing the border reflected Soviet fortunes in the Second World War. When Baba had first arrived, the demands of debriefing Soviet defectors kept him busy. In the war's first years, soldiers attributed their defections to hunger and war weariness, evidence of the desperate circumstances under which the Soviet Union was fighting. As the Soviets stiffened their defenses, then went on the offensive later in the war, however, Baba saw a decline in defections.

He also detected other ominous trends. As the Soviets neared Berlin, signaling the end of the war in Europe, the Chinese, Koreans, and other peoples living under Japanese rule in Manchukuo began to show signs of restiveness as Japan's prospects grew increasingly dark. From the start of 1945, Baba was also aware of an increasing flow of Soviet troops and equipment into the region along the Trans-Siberian Railroad. The influx spiked sharply in May, following Germany's surrender. Baba and his fellow intelligence officers grew concerned that they were witnessing a buildup for an invasion that could come as early as that summer.[22]

Harada Tokichi, from his hidden observation post in the Manchukuo Consulate at Chita, a Soviet city lying along the Trans-Siberian Railroad to the northwest of the border between Manchukuo and the Mongolian People's Republic, was also growing increasingly alarmed. Harada, like Baba a graduate of the Nakano School, was monitoring Soviet troop trains as they rumbled east. Harada had arrived at the consulate in late 1944 to gather intelligence on Soviet preparations for an invasion of Manchukuo.

In a number of ways, he represented the Nakano School's ideal. Harada had graduated in 1935 from what is today the Osaka University of Foreign Studies, his specialization Mongolian. Following a stint of employment at an electric power company in Kyushu, Harada was drafted in 1938 into a regiment from his home prefecture of Fukuyama. After successfully applying for officer candidate training, he received orders in November 1939 to report for duty at the War Ministry. That the Army had chosen him for the Nakano School was unclear to him at first. He had a definite idea of his new mission only at the point he and some thirty other candidates, dressed in civilian clothes, gathered in a room of the War Ministry in Tokyo to hear Vice Minister Gen. Anami Korechika exhort them to serve the empire as covert warriors.[23]

Harada graduated from the Nakano School in late 1940. Lt. Gen. Tojo Hideki, then minister of war, attended the ceremony, which took place without diplomas or even a printed class list. After a month's assignment at Second Bureau's Fifth (Soviet) Section, Harada received orders for Manchukuo. At Mutankiang, a key city up the rail line from Yenki in central Kirin Province, Harada joined the local Military Police Agency Annex. Posing as a civil servant and police investigator of the Manchukuo government, Harada worked as an intelligence officer in the Kwantung Army, cooperating with the Japanese Kempeitai and Special Higher Police (Tokkotai) to detect and double Soviet agents.

After some success in Mutankiang, Harada received orders to report for similar work at the annex in Mukden, where his targets were the agents of the Chinese Communists and Nationalists as well as those of the Soviet Union. Without the power of arrest, Harada and his intelligence colleagues had to rely on the cooperation of the Japanese military and special police forces. The arrangement had its frustrations, as Harada faced the perennial problem of intelligence officers working with police, that of police inclined to make an immediate arrest rather than allow a suspect to remain free as an intelligence source.[24]

In late October 1944, Harada arrived in the guise of a diplomat at the Manchukuo Consulate in Chita, where the rail line from Manchouli on Manchukuo's western border extended to the Trans-Siberian Railroad. Among the consulate's functions was providing lodging for Japanese travelers, many of them intelligence officers acting as couriers, waiting in China for their train on the Trans-Siberian Railroad. The diplomatic mission, established in 1932, also functioned as an intelligence outpost of the Kwantung Army. By 1945, the Chita Consulate had also become an established posting for graduates of the Nakano School. Lt. Watanabe Tatsui of the First Class, arriving for duty in 1939, was the first. Several others followed before Harada came. All operated under pseudonyms, working as diplomatic personnel or, in at least one case, as a consulate driver.

Harada was one of five Japanese military personnel, three of whom were from the Nakano School, working at the consulate. In early March, Harada found a Soviet train bound east at the city station, filled with troops and weapons that he determined had come from the fighting in Europe. It was yet another disquieting indication of looming disaster. In late February, three Japanese couriers en route to Moscow on the Trans-Siberian Railroad had earlier spotted Soviet military units moving east.

The time had come to pay even more attention to the Trans-Siberian Railroad. On 29 April, after holding a ceremony in honor of the emperor's birthday, the consulate's intelligence officers began monitoring the railway from a hidden observation post located between the roof and ceiling at the rear of the building. The intelligence officers, peering through a telescope, could see some three hundred meters of the Trans-Siberian Railroad. From that day, Harada spent much of his time peering through the telescope for signs of Soviet troop movements. When he and his colleagues spotted troops and equipment going east or gleaned related intelligence from couriers, they cabled reports to Imperial General Headquarters, leaving Tokyo little room to doubt a Soviet invasion. It was simply a question of predicting the date. In early June, Chita Consulate warned Kwantung Army Headquarters and Imperial General Headquarters that, in their estimate, there was a high probability that the Soviets would invade Manchukuo in the July–August period.[25]

Preparing for Japan's Last Stand

By spring 1945, the Japanese Army was well into preparing for the coming invasion of the Japanese home islands. At Matsushiro, in the mountains of central Japan's Nagano Prefecture, the Army was building a massive underground shelter to house Imperial General Headquarters. The subterranean command center also included quarters for the emperor and his retinue as well as communications rooms for directing military operations and broadcasting propaganda to the Japanese people. Dispersed throughout the prefecture were four army airfields. In June 1945, the Military Academy's three thousand cadets followed their instructors in withdrawing from Sobudai in Kanagawa Prefecture. Leaving the Tokyo area behind, they headed inland for their final quarters in mountainous Nagano Prefecture.

Japanese corporations essential for continuing the war also transferred production facilities from Japan's major industrial centers to the mountains. Mitsubishi Heavy Industries, for example, was constructing underground military factories for its Zero fighters and other weapons in two separate cities of the prefecture. In all, Japanese companies would shift nearly six hundred factories from more vulnerable sites to Nagano Prefecture by the summer of 1945.[26]

In the early months of 1945, the Japanese Army's covert institutions were also preparing to play their role in Japan's last stand. The Army had designated the Nakano School as the "general headquarters" of the nationwide guerrilla campaign planned in defense of Japan. Maj. Gen. Yamamoto Hayashi, a former chief of the Hikari Agency who had assumed command of the Nakano School in March 1945, immediately began overseeing preparations for moving the intelligence training center. Yamamoto, given several candidate sites, chose Tomioka in Gunma Prefecture as the Nakano School's last location. Tomioka, with its location in the interior of central Japan and proximity to Imperial General Headquarters' underground command post at Matsushiro in neighboring Nagano Prefecture, seemed the best site. Yamamoto then mobilized trains, ox carts, and carriages as well as his students, staff, local veterans, and high school students in Nagano Prefecture to relocate the Nakano School from Tokyo to the grounds of the Tomioka Higher Middle School by April. Over the same two months, the Noborito Research Institute left Kanagawa Prefecture, its staff and equipment dispersed to several sites in Nagano Prefecture. Of the Japanese Army's major covert warfare facilities, only the Nakano School's Futamata Branch remained in place.[27]

Well in advance of the withdrawal to Tomioka, the Nakano School had begun preparing to organize and direct Japan's guerrilla war. In March 1944, Maj. Gen. Kawamata Taketo, then commandant of the Nakano School, sent one of his subordinate officers to Burma to gather materials on special operations. The officer returned after nearly two months in the field. Lt. Col. Tejima Haruo, chief of the Nakano School's testing unit, used the results of the field survey in drafting guidelines for demolition, infiltration, and other aspects of guerrilla operations. At Tomioka, a number of the Nakano School's graduates gathered data relating to Japan's capacity for waging war in the home islands. Among those working on the study was Maj. Kimura Takechiyo. A member of the Nakano School's First Class, Kimura had begun his covert career before Pearl Harbor in Latin America. He and his colleagues determined that the Nakano School would mobilize the population throughout Japan to fight the invaders.

From one end of Japan to another, the Nakano School's shadow warriors and others constituted cadres of instructors who began drilling soldiers, reservists, and civilians for the coming fight. Women and children joined in the training, which included martial exercises with sharpened bamboo spears. Certain critics in Japan and elsewhere later decried such civilian training, ridiculing the notion of "bamboo spears against B-29s." Such criticism misses the point. The Nakano School was not training civilians to wield their spears against American bombers in the sky but against the American foot patrols they were preparing to ambush in Japan's rice paddies and mountain forests.

In April, the Nakano School also began its preparations for guerrilla operations in the event of Japan's surrender and occupation by the Allies. Majors Maruzaki Yoshio and Sakai Isamu, both members of the Nakano School's First Class, were among those involved in the creation of the Izumi (Spring) Unit. Like water flowing forth from an unseen spring, covert members of the Izumi Unit would spring forth from their underground organizations throughout Japan to wage campaigns of assassination and terror against the Allied troops and Japanese collaborators. To lead the campaigns at the local level, graduates of the Futamata Branch were chosen and assigned to their home prefectures. The Izumi Unit was one of the Nakano School's most secret programs. Even at Tomioka, few knew of its existence. As spring gave way to summer, the Izumi Unit's shadow warriors returned quietly in civilian guise to their hometowns.[28]

7

BATTLE OF OKINAWA

Lt. Gen. Ushijima Mitsuru had few illusions in March 1945 regarding his role in Okinawa. Months before, Tokyo had declared the Philippines to be Japan's Tennozan, or the decisive battle where Japan would stand firm. At Tennozan, a mountain west of Kyoto, the great warlord Toyotomi Hideyoshi had won in 1582 a decisive victory in his bid to rule Japan. Since that time, Tennozan had come to mean a battle that would decide victory or defeat. In March, having lost Manila, Tokyo declared in a ringing announcement that Okinawa would now be the empire's Tennozan. Tokyo had declared that the defense of Japan's southernmost prefecture would decide the empire's fate. The general cast in the role of Hideyoshi, however, knew that his stage was far from ready for the bloody performance expected of him.

Ushijima was a scholarly infantry officer from Kagoshima, whose lords in feudal days had held suzerainty over the island kingdom that later became an integral part of Japan. In August 1944, he received orders to prepare Okinawa's defenses as commander of the newly formed Thirty-second Army. Leaving Tokyo, where he had been commandant of the Military Academy, Ushijima arrived at the capital of Naha a month later. By that time, the United States had breached the supposedly impregnable Tojo Line in the South Pacific, annihilating in the process Thirty-first Army on Japan's island bastion of Saipan.

Ushijima had few resources with which to forge a defense of his islands. Earlier plans for an active defense were rendered null by the futile diversion to the Philippines of units marked for Okinawa. The diversion left Ushijima with no choice but to prepare for a defensive campaign of attrition. Ushijima knew that, in fact, Okinawa would be no Tennozan, for there was no chance of victory. His role was to extract as high a price as possible in exchange for Okinawa. Imperial General Headquarters underscored his fateful role by further canceling the planned transfer of the Eighty-fourth Division on Shikoku. The airfield at Ie Shima, only recently completed, was ordered destroyed. No Japanese aircraft would sortie from there to attack the American fleet. Ushijima was simply to hold the islands for as long as possible while the Japanese Army prepared for the true final defense of Japan on the main islands.[1]

Ushijima had as his area of responsibility a chain of islands, the Ryukyus, which stretch in the north from the waters south of Kyushu all the way to Taiwan, off the south China coast. The island of Okinawa, at only twelve hundred square kilometers, accounts for slightly more than half of the archipelago's land area. Once an independent kingdom, although paying tribute to both China and Japan, Okinawa came under Japanese authority when the Shimazu clan of Satsuma subjugated the islands in 1609. Following the Meiji Restoration of 1868, and the abolition of Japan's feudal system, the islands became imperial Japan's southernmost prefecture in 1879.

Ethnically distinct, relatively poor, and distant from Japan's other prefectures, Okinawa was an isolated, semitropical outpost of the empire. Poverty drove many of the prefecture's inhabitants to leave the islands for menial labor in Osaka and other Japanese industrial centers. The islands also lost to emigration the many Okinawans who left to labor in the Philippines, Hawaii, the mainland United States, and Latin America. The prefecture also stood apart in its peaceful tradition, alone in the empire for having no local army units. In clear contrast to the many generals who hailed from Fukuoka, Kumamoto, and Kagoshima on neighboring Kyushu, cradle of Japanese civilization and a font of its martial spirit, no native sons of the Ryukyus had ever risen to prominence in the imperial military.

In March 1945, Ushijima was grimly preparing to defend the island chain against what would be the mightiest invasion fleet of the Pacific War. Adm. Raymond Spruance had under his command more than fourteen hundred warships and merchant vessels for Operation Iceberg, the American campaign for Okinawa. His armada included seventeen aircraft carriers under Vice Adm. Marc Mitscher and the four carriers of Vice Adm. Bernard Rawling's British Pacific Fleet. On board the American ships were Lt. Gen. Simon Bolivar Buckner's

Tenth Army, consisting of the Marines' Third Amphibious Corps and the Army's Twenty-fourth Corps.[2]

Setting the Stage

To defend Okinawa against an Allied invasion force vastly superior in warships, aircraft, tanks, ammunition, and other conventional equipment, Ushijima planned to conserve his meager forces by bloodying the enemy from entrenched positions. Any attempt to meet the invaders on the beaches or in open combat would simply be suicidal. Ushijima also planned to rely to a great extent on special operations to supplement his conventional forces. Army and Navy pilots were to trade their lives for Allied warships and troop transports. Suicide boats were to race from hiding to explode against the hulls of the armada's ships. On shore, raiding units were to destroy strategic enemy facilities while sowing panic and confusion behind the lines. On remote islands of the chain, intelligence officers were to keep their superiors informed of enemy movements and lead local inhabitants in fighting. In Okinawa, as elsewhere, men of the Nakano School would play a key role in the Army's special operations.

In September 1944, lieutenants Murakami Haruo and Iwanami Hisashi arrived in Naha to form the Third and Fourth Raiding Units. The two officers had graduated as members of the Imperial Military Academy's Fifty-fifth Class at Sobudai before training at the Nakano School. Each officer had under his command four second lieutenants as company commanders as well as two sergeants to handle intelligence and communications. Those dozen men, as well as several others attached to the raiding units, all came from the Nakano School. Serving in each of the two units were some four hundred elite soldiers. Murakami and Iwanami also had at their disposal local Okinawan men conscripted for labor, communications, and intelligence.

In all, more than a thousand Okinawan men served in an auxiliary force called the Blood and Iron for the Emperor Duty Units (BAIF-TED units). One such unit, consisting of 150 student conscripts from the prefecture's Third Higher Middle School in Nago, was attached to the Third Raiding Unit's headquarters and companies as intelligence auxiliaries. Thirty-second Army had mobilized all male students in the middle schools and above into BAIFTED units, training them in guerrilla activities and infiltration techniques. Of the many Okinawans who served in scouts units, the most famous since the war was former Okinawa Governor Ota Masahide, who served as an intelligence auxiliary attached to Thirty-second Army Headquarters in Shuri Castle.

Unlike other commando units, which were put together by infantry commanders and their subordinates in Okinawa, Murakami, and Iwanami, the Third and Fourth Raiding Units received their orders directly from Imperial General Headquarters. While coordinating with Ushijima and his senior intelligence officer, the two raiding units were to operate independently in the field.[3]

Arriving with Murakami and Iwanami in Naha that September was Lt. Hirose Hideo, a classmate at both the Imperial Military Academy and the Nakano School. Hirose's assignment was to serve on the staff of Thirty-second Army. Working under Maj. Yakumaru Kanenori, head of Thirty-second Army's S-2 (Intelligence), Hirose was to spend much of his time directing those of his fellow Nakano School graduates whose assignments placed them on one remote island or another of the Ryukyu chain.

Throughout the myriad smaller islands of Japan, the military was posting lone soldiers to organize local inhabitants into guerrilla units, establish island defenses, and remain in place in the event of an island's occupation in order to report on enemy movements. In Tokyo, Imperial General Headquarters had established in June 1944 an Army special operations unit to oversee remote-island operations. In December, eleven graduates of the Nakano School assembled in Tokyo to receive their covert assignments in the Ryukyu chain. Sergeants Kikuchi Yoshio and Sakai Kiyoshi were among members of the Nakano School who received orders directly from Army Chief of Staff Gen. Umezu Yoshijiro to travel under alias to Thirty-second Army. Lt. Akutsu Toshiro, one of several students at the Futamata Branch ordered to proceed upon graduation to Okinawa, was also selected for a mission on one of the archipelago's remote islands.

Sakai entered Okinawa in December, posing as a journalist of the prominent newspaper *Asahi Shimbun*. He arrived to find Naha, the capital, devastated in the wake of an October air raid. Akutsu, who sailed safely into the port of Naha on 27 December from Kagoshima, found the city "completely destroyed." Naha's ruined aspect impressed on him that he had indeed entered a war zone.

On 16 January, following some initial intelligence assignments, five sergeants from the Nakano School and six members of the Futamata Branch assembled at Thirty-second Army Headquarters. In the office of the commanding officer, the men received their orders. Sakai was to proceed to Hateruma, an island east of Taiwan at the southernmost part of the Ryukyu chain. Kikuchi Yoshio received an assignment for Iheiya, situated at the northern end of the archipelago. Akutsu Toshiro learned that he was to go with another member of the Nakano School to Yonaguni, the westernmost island of the Ryukyus. The other seven shadow warriors drew assignments to other small islands. Through an arrangement with Okinawa's governor, the men left for their various posts in the guise of schoolteachers. Outside the classroom, the men would organize the local residents into guerrilla units for the coming battle. After receiving their orders, Sakai and his comrades attended a banquet that night, given in their honor by Yakumaru and his subordinates on Thirty-second Army's intelligence staff.[4]

Sakai, posing as a teacher by the name of Yamashita, arrived the following month on the isolated island of Hateruma. The local residents, immediately noticing his fair complexion and long face, recognized him as a "Yamatojin," or Japanese from the main islands. His soldierly bearing and vague background as a teacher left the islanders curious about his true identity. The large orange crate he brought with him was certainly odd for a teacher. In it were Sakai's military uniform, swords, pistols, hand grenades, explosives developed at the Noborito Research Institute, and a wireless set. He also had special pens, also courtesy of Noborito, designed to release bacteria into an enemy's water supply. Sakai had trained at the Nakano School to use such pens. He was to infect Hateruma's wells in the event of an American landing. Meanwhile, he organized the island's youths into defense units, taught judo in the evenings, and exhorted his charges not to fear death. Such actions, while today no longer part of a Japanese schoolteacher's duties, were at that time consistent with Sakai's cover. Teachers had been drilling local students since around 1943 in preparation for a decisive battle. Even the young girls, organized into *Himeyuri* (Red Star Lily) units for nursing and other duties, each received a single hand grenade and the order to use it as a suicide weapon in the event of imminent capture.

On Iheiya, Kikuchi also landed with weapons and wireless. Calling himself Miyagi, he came in the guise of a teacher, too. As part of his defensive preparations, he hid in a mountain hut his supply of explosives. Shaped like tubes of toothpaste, the explosives were products of the Noborito Research Institute. Outside the classroom, Kikuchi ran the youths through military drills. The small island rang with the cries of the young men as they stabbed at straw dummies with bamboo spears.

Akutsu was one of the two operatives who went ashore at Yonaguni, a remote island much closer to Taiwan than to Okinawa. His luggage included two wooden boxes of explosives. Akutsu's background had well equipped him for his mission. After attending reserve officer training school, Akutsu had entered the Nakano School's Futamata Branch in September 1944 as a member of the First Class. In three months of intense training, Akutsu had learned the essentials of guerrilla warfare. He had trained with his classmates in demolitions operations. In one class exercise, his task was to stage a mock attack against the local Hamamatsu Air Base. Dressed in peasant garb, he had conducted a survey of the airfield's defenses and vulnerable points before placing dummy charges on aircraft and hangars.

On Yonaguni, Akutsu divided his time between his cover assignment to teach at a local school and his covert assignment to train island residents in guerrilla warfare. Acquiring the nickname "Yamato Sensei" (Mr. Yamato) from residents who evidently found the fair, fit young man from the main islands somewhat exotic, Akutsu was a popular teacher who regaled the islanders with stories of Tokyo's subways and cinemas. For Yonaguni's residents who had never seen the bright lights of one of the world's major capitals, his tales must have sounded wondrous indeed. The island's inhabitants must also have found the teacher's extracurricular activities stimulating. Nearly every night, Akutsu trained several dozen youths and veterans in guerrilla warfare. He also cached his explosives, arms, and food in anticipation of an American invasion.[5]

The Battle Begins

On 23 March 1945, the Allied forces heralded the coming invasion with an air raid. American warships the next day pounded the southern end of Okinawa, where the Japanese defenses and civilian population were concentrated, to soften up the island further before the start of amphibious operations. In another opening move, the Americans unexpectedly wrecked one of the Japanese special attack forces.

As a prelude to the main landing on Okinawa, an American force first moved to secure the Kerama Islands. The group of islets, oppo-site Naha off Okinawa's west coast, was to serve as a safe harbor for refueling and repairing ships during Operation Iceberg. Inadequate intelligence on the American side also was a factor in uncovering the special unit. Due to the poor quality of aerial photographs of the area, American intelligence officers feared that a group of blurred objects on one of the Kerama Islands could be coastal batteries. In order to eliminate the danger such guns posed to landing operations on Oki-nawa, the Army Seventy-seventh Division went ashore on 26 March. Once on land, the soldiers routed the Japanese defenders and discov-ered that the blurred objects were in fact the buildings of a sugar refinery. What they also found, however, were more than 350 bomb-laden suicide boats that the Japanese were waiting to launch in night attacks against the American ships that were soon to begin operations in the area. If undetected, the boats could have played havoc with the American armada.[6]

The Japanese, although suffering a major setback with the loss of their suicide boats, did succeed in launching wave after wave of spe-cial attack aircraft against the invasion fleet. The Americans and Brit-ish had been sending air raids against Japanese airfields in Kyushu, Taiwan, and elsewhere in an effort to disrupt the *kamikaze* attacks they knew were coming. Still, the Japanese managed to let loose their Divine Wind against the invasion fleet. The day after the loss of the Kerama Islands, seven Japanese aircraft dove towards the American fleet. One pilot sacrificed his life to destroy two fourteen-inch guns and inflict sixty casualties on the battleship *Nevada*. Another pilot's crash left more than a hundred men either dead, injured, or missing on board the destroyer *O'Brien*, putting the ship out of action. Attacks of the Divine Wind against the British Pacific Fleet damaged the car-rier *Indefatigable* and caused the destroyer *Ulster* to withdraw for repairs.[7]

On 1 April, Easter Sunday, American soldiers went ashore on Okinawa's west coast above Naha. The marines of Third Amphibious Corps were assigned the island's central and northern areas, including the city of Nago and the Motobu Peninsula. The soldiers of the Army's Twenty-fourth Corps were to advance south, where the Japanese defenses were concentrated. The First and Sixth Marine Divisions, landing at Kadena on Okinawa's East China Sea coast, were to secure the northern two-thirds of the island, sparsely populated and dominated by hills and jungles. At the landing sites, however, Ushijima's troops were nowhere to be seen. Indeed, the Americans landed virtually unopposed. Before noon, the Americans had taken without opposition the island's two main airfields at Yomitan (or Yontan) and Kadena. The day of the landing was not only Easter but also April Fool's Day. During that first day on the island, the Americans encountered fewer than twenty Japanese soldiers. What sort of trick was Ushijima playing?

Ushijima had in fact permitted the Americans to land unopposed as part of the Japanese Army's evolving strategy against Allied amphibious operations. Imperial General Headquarters had concluded from previous losses on Pacific islands that it was simply futile to try to defeat a vastly superior landing force on the beaches, where the defending soldiers were exposed to naval bombardment and aerial attack. Tokyo had devised in response a strategy of meeting an enemy invasion from well-fortified positions dug into mountains, caves, and other natural defenses well within an island's interior. In fact, the Japanese Army's Second Bureau put together a manual on U.S. island campaigns based on fatal lessons learned in earlier attempts to "annihilate the enemy at the water's edge." Intelligence officers then briefed commanders in the field on the findings. Lt. Col. Hori Eizo, one of Second Bureau's officers responsible for writing the manual, arrived in Manila in time to brief General Yamashita just before the Americans landed at Leyte. Tokyo's new strategy probably figured into Yamashita's withdrawal from Manila to the hills of northern Luzon. The departure from the earlier Japanese practice of brave, but futile, suicide charges enabled Yamashita to continue fighting until the war's end.

Protected from enemy ships and aircraft, the Japanese defenders would then cut down the exposed soldiers advancing on their positions. Ushijima and Col. Yahara Hiromichi, his methodical senior staff officer, applied Tokyo's strategy with grim determination. Rather than resist at the point of landing, they positioned most of Thirty-second Army in the island's interior to the north of their headquarters at Shuri Castle. On 5 April, soldiers of Twenty-fourth Corps ran into this Shuri Line, coming under heavy fire in the mountain terrain. The Battle of Okinawa had now begun in earnest.[8]

By 8 April, Ushijima's men had stopped the advance of Twenty-fourth Corps, pouring down a deadly fire from their entrenched positions in the hilly terrain. As Thirty-second Army held firm, Imperial General Headquarters unleashed a series of combined Army-Navy attacks. The series of mass suicide assaults bore the name of Floating Chrysanthemum (*Kikusui*). The name of the flower, associated with Japan's emperors, was intended to lend a certain beauty to the certain death facing the men executing those one-way missions. Those of the Navy's Fifth Air Fleet and Army's Sixth Air Army subjected the Allied armada to an ordeal throughout the Battle of Okinawa. Particularly harrowing was the second Floating Chrysanthemum operation of 12–13 April, when nearly two hundred pilots hurtled toward the enemy ships floating below. The Japanese Divine Wind sank the destroyer *Mannert L. Abele* and scored numerous other hits. In all, nearly fifteen hundred aircraft flew in ten Floating Chrysanthemum operations between 6 April and 22 June, sinking twenty-six ships and damaging another 164.[9]

On the northern two-thirds of Okinawa, Murakami Haruo's Third Raiding Unit and Iwanami Hisashi's Fourth Raiding Unit did their best to harass the two Marine divisions on their advance north to Nago. Starting with eight hundred soldiers between them and a battalion of local men organized as a home guard, the two commanders raided supply dumps and camps. Throughout the north, particularly in the Kunigami area, stretching between Nago and the island's northern tip, men of the raiding units continued sniping at Marine patrols, cutting camp telephone lines, and generally keeping the Marines on their guard. Murakami and Iwanami accounted for an undetermined number of the 236 dead and 1,061 wounded in the Sixth Marine Division by the time northern Okinawa was declared secured on 20 April. By Murakami's accounting, his Third Raiding Unit had killed or wounded some one hundred American soldiers and demolished numerous ammunition and fuel dumps, food depots, and military vehicles. Iwanami's Fourth Raiding Unit claimed similar accomplishments in its area of operations.

Reflecting the determination of their commanders, Japanese morale in the raiding units was high. The contrast with the disgraced conventional force of two thousand under the ineffective Col. Udo Takehiko was a clear one. Udo had abandoned in unseemly haste the strategic town of Nago, the entrance to the Motobu Peninsula opposite the nearby island of Ie Shima and its airfield. When Udo appeared one night at Murakami's camp, he found a sign at the headquarters: "Udo's Defeated Little Remnant Gang Not Admitted."[10]

Raid on Yomitan

Following the considerable damage inflicted in the early Floating Chrysanthemum operations, however, American combat pilots flying from the captured airfields at Kadena and Yomitan began intercepting many of the kamikaze pilots well before they could reach their intended targets. Japan's Sixth Air Army Headquarters then began planning a raid to knock out the two airfields for a period of between ten days and a month. With the threat of land-based combat air patrols eliminated and other American fighters absent while their carriers withdrew from the area for refueling every ten days or so, the Floating Chrysanthemum operations would be better able to inflict heavy losses on the invasion fleet. To execute their plan, Sixth Air Army turned to an elite airborne commando unit. Among the nearly 150 men of the unit were ten from the Nakano School.

During this period, Japan's efforts to scatter the Allied armada suffered not only from enemy combat air patrols but also from differences between Japan's rival services. The Navy, which had all but ceased to exist after the Philippines campaign, was in favor of making Okinawa into the empire's true Tennozan. The Navy High Command advocated throwing every special attack plane available against the Allied fleet there. The Army, on the other hand, was already writing off Okinawa as a loss. Senior Army officers preferred to hold most of their aircraft and men in reserve for the coming fighting on the main islands. Imperial General Headquarters was thus slow in giving the green light for Sixth Air Army to conduct the raid. Only on 2 May did the Army's chief of staff grant authorization. The commandos then flew to central Kyushu. They were to sally forth from the Army's Kengun Airfield in Kumamoto. The airfield, newly built, was still untouched by Allied bombers.

On 22 May, the ten commandos from the Nakano School gathered in some woods near their barracks to sing one more time the school song before flying the next day. A young lieutenant named Tsujioka, overcome with emotion, wept as he thanked his colleagues for their cooperation and encouraged them to commit their lives and fight as planned. Lt. Ishiyama Toshio ventured to cheer him, saying,

"Tsujioka, smile, smile! This is the way a man goes." Inclement weather delayed their flight from the following day until 24 May. By the time the ten young men boarded the twin-engine bombers that would take them to their fate, each had composed a final poem. Lt. Watanabe Yusuke, a sensitive man fond of philosophy, turned to the poetic image of falling cherry blossoms as an allusion to the young men who were soon to sacrifice their lives for the empire:

Young cherry blossoms in bloom deep within a mountain,
For His Majesty's sake, it is a pleasure to fall

The buoyant Ishiyama composed a more militant, less literary line: "Step over our corpses and go forward!" Their moment of destiny was at hand.[11]

Early on the night of 24 May, 120 commandos boarded twelve Army bombers for their one-way journey to Okinawa. With ten commandos and a crew of four in each bomber, 168 men left to raid Okinawa. Fate was against them from the start, however. Four of the pilots almost immediately had to bring their aircraft back to earth in forced landings after their aircraft suffered one mechanical failure or another. As the eight remaining bombers put Kyushu behind them and passed over Ie Shima around 8:30 en route to their targets, American radar alerted antiaircraft crews on the ground. The sky lit up with intense streams of fire from the ground batteries. Seven of the eight bombers were shot out of the sky before they could land. At Yomitan airfield, one bomber set fuel drums on fire as it crashed to the ground.

The sole surviving bomber, a Mitsubishi Ki-21 (or Sally), came sliding across Yomitan's fighter strip, sparks flying as the plane's belly scraped the coral surface. From the aircraft leaped a group of eleven commandos armed with grenades, incendiary devices, and rifles. All hell broke loose. The Japanese ran through the airfield, throwing their grenades and explosives at the parked aircraft and fuel dumps, shooting at all in their path. The U.S. Marines manning the airfield responded by letting loose with submachine guns, rifles, and pistols.

It was all over the next morning, when the last commando was shot dead. Three Japanese had died in the Mitsubishi bomber, probably killed by antiaircraft fire. Ten others had fallen around the airfield. A lone Japanese soldier killed at nearby Zampa Point was apparently the last member of the raiding party. Another fifty-six commandos had perished in the four bombers that crashed. Among the fallen Japanese were Ishiyama, Watanabe, and seven other men of the Nakano School. Only one of the ten survived, when mechanical failure forced his bomber's crew to execute a crash landing shortly after takeoff.

With only one of the original twelve bombers landing on Okinawa, the handful of commandos had killed two Marines and wounded eighteen others. They had also blown up eight aircraft, including two Corsairs and four C-54 transports, and damaged another twenty-six planes. They had also set on fire seventy thousand gallons of aviation fuel. Even so, Yomitan was back in operation before noon that day. From Thirty-second Army Headquarters at Shuri Castle, Col. Yahara had watched the flares illuminating the night sky over Yomitan. Knowing that the raid would have little effect in the end, he was moved all the same by the bravery of the commandos.[12]

The Curtain Falls

While Lt. Gen. Ushijima and Col. Yahara had held the line above Shuri Castle throughout April against an American pressure that grew daily, the two officers failed to resist the determined assaults of Lt. Gen. Cho Isamu. The fierce chief of staff of Thirty-second Army, whose shaved head, glasses, and moustache gave him a passing resemblance to Tojo, was dead set against following to the end a strategy of attrition that confined soldiers of the Imperial Army to caves and trenches. Cho was one of the many Japanese officers who believed in the offensive as the only worthy tactic for a Japanese soldier. He and the younger staff officers of Thirty-second Army had protested from the start a plan that appeared simply to leave them on the defensive until they had expended all their ammunition.

In the Philippines, General Yamashita had a few weeks earlier endured the same strident entreaties from his own staff officers, eager to order an immediate assault from the hills against the Americans. The Tiger of Malaya had held firm in his strategy of attrition, with the result that he was still fighting long after Manila fell.

On Okinawa, the reserved Ushijima and Yahara were unable to resist the fiery Cho's unrelenting demands. On 29 April, the Emperor's birthday, Cho chaired a meeting of Thirty-second Army to seek a consensus to go on the offensive. Present were Col. Yahara Hiromichi, the senior staff officer; Maj. Nagano Hideo, the senior operations officer; Maj. Yakumaru Kanenori, the senior intelligence officer; and the staff officers in charge of the air force, communications, and logistics. Alone among those present, the others all approving of Cho's proposal with enthusiasm, Yahara warned of the futility of an offensive and recommended sticking to the strategy of attrition that was keeping the American forces largely in check. Cho, shedding tears of emotion, appealed to his senior staff officer: "I know you must be thinking many things, but let's die together! Please agree to this offensive." Opposed to Cho's proposal, and foreseeing its failure, Yahara in the end bowed before the group's consensus. Ushijima then reluctantly approved a major counteroffensive for 4 May.

A barrage of Japanese artillery at dawn signaled the start of Thirty-second Army's attack. For the first time in the campaign, Japanese soldiers emerged from their caves and foxholes in a major northward movement against American positions. The casualties from the overwhelming American ground, air, and naval firepower were immediate and unsustainable, and the ground gained was negligible. The very next day, Ushijima ordered his men to halt the offensive and return to their previous defensive positions. Ushijima had lost some five thousand men. The offensive had expended so much ammunition that each Japanese artillery piece was allotted only ten shells per day thereafter. Cho's offensive had achieved nothing, serving only to hasten the day of their final defeat.

The end for Thirty-second Army as a conventional ground force came the next month. On 19 June, having already withdrawn his headquarters from the ruins of Shuri Castle to a cave farther south, Ushijima issued a final order for his men to continue fighting. Three days later, he and Cho committed suicide in the samurai manner, each turning his own sword against himself in a ritual disemboweling (*seppuku*, or *hara-kiri*). Yahara, ordered to escape to make a final report to Tokyo, shed his uniform and left the final headquarters.

For the Nakano School's men, the end of Thirty-second Army as a conventional force marked the beginning of their main mission. Hirose Hideo had died in battle on 3 June, but his classmates Murakami Haruo and Iwanami Hisashi were still commanding the Third and Fourth Raiding Units. While the U.S. Marines had declared northern Okinawa secured on 20 April, the two Japanese officers were still leading raids, particularly in the Kunigami area north of Nago. In one incident, Japanese guerrillas ambushed and killed on 13 June two members of the Counter Intelligence Corps (CIC) operating on northern Okinawa's Motobu Peninsula. In another incident, guerrillas executed a village chief who had been cooperating with the CIC. Murakami and Iwanami's units were among the guerrilla forces carrying out such operations in the closing weeks of the battle. While most of the shooting had ended, American patrols and Japanese collaborators faced the danger of ambush on isolated paths or retribution at night when the guerrillas stole into the villages or refugee camps.

On 25 June, Murakami learned of Ushijima's death. Overcome by a determination to follow his commander in death, Murakami readied his men for a final attack on Kadena airfield that he set for 1 July. By the eve of the attack, however, he had regained control of his emotions. Murakami realized that a suicidal attack against the airfield would be contrary to his mission as a guerrilla commander. Instead, he prepared a new plan of terror against the Occupation. He ordered his Okinawan auxiliaries to take positions in their home villages, where they would pose as refugees. Other members of his unit he ordered to infiltrate the American camps as laborers. When he gave the order, his men would rise against the American forces of occupation. Iwanami, who learned of Thirty-second Army's destruction when he made contact with Murakami on 10 July, similarly cached much of his equipment and sent local members of his raiding unit back to their villages to gather intelligence and await further orders.

Murakami's plan was promising. The CIC, aware that the Japanese were infiltrating behind American lines, worked mightily to screen infiltrators at the points where civilian refugees were processed before entering the camps. Lacking personnel who spoke Japanese, however, CIC had no choice but to use Okinawans as auxiliary interpreters while they hastily processed masses of refugees. In the midst of such confusion, Murakami sent the local members of his unit back to their home villages to infiltrate the camps. More than a few guerrillas must have slipped into the camps during those hectic days. The hard core of his soldiers remained in the hills.

In the end, however, events would overtake Murakami's plans when Emperor Hirohito broadcast on 15 August Japan's intention to surrender. Murakami would lead no shadow war in Occupied Okinawa. Iwanami, too, bowed to the inevitable. On 2 October, he and his company commanders came down from the hills and entered an American detention camp.[13]

On the remote island of Hateruma, the Nakano School's Sakai Kiyoshi had evacuated the inhabitants to the neighboring island of Iriomote in early April, following the American landing on Okinawa. He had overcome the reluctance of the residents to the evacuation to the malaria-infested Iriomote, threatening them with violence. The result was tragic. Hundreds of Hateruma's inhabitants, particularly infants and elderly members of the community, succumbed to the disease following the forced move.

Not far from Hateruma, on the island of Yonaguni, the war ended for Akutsu Toshiro while he was still preparing to fight. Judging his weapons caches insufficient, he had gone to Taiwan in May to request additional supplies from Tenth Area Army, which was stationed there. In Taihoku (Taipei), Akutsu had found a sympathetic counterpart in Maj. Makizawa Yoshio, a member of the Nakano School's First Class. Makizawa, who had begun his covert career in Colombia shortly before Pearl Harbor, was now establishing guerrilla forces on that island as head of an intelligence annex there. Makizawa had made sure that Akutsu received the supplies he requested. Having succeeded in gaining enough explosives, small arms, and food to outfit a company of soldiers, Akutsu returned to Yonaguni in early July. He then had his guerrillas cache the weapons and food in secret caves. Preparations continued, his select young men and veterans receiving instruction in handling the explosives and small arms. Akutsu also oversaw the training of women and girls, who ran through their defense drills with bamboo spears.

The end came the following month. Akutsu had learned from a visiting ship's captain on 11 August of the destruction from a new type of weapon of Hiroshima and Nagasaki. Six days later another ship brought him a newspaper announcing the imperial surrender of 15 August. Not wishing to risk bringing down the wrath of the American occupation forces upon the island's residents or himself, he dumped all the incriminating evidence of his mission into the ocean on 2 September. Despite his extracurricular activities as guerrilla trainer, Akutsu escaped the attention of American officials. Holding fast to his cover as a teacher, Akutsu sailed safely on a repatriation ship into the port of Kagoshima on 9 January 1946.

At the northern end of the Ryukyus, Kikuchi had also moved to another island. Leaving Iheiya for a smaller island nearby, he made prior plans for resistance against the Occupation. Kikuchi remained on the island, sticking to his cover as a teacher. But popular anger among the Japanese against their leaders, who had led them to war and ruin, soon proved Kikuchi's undoing. In the initial months of the Occupation, Japanese denounced their compatriots to the American authorities in countless letters and interviews. So it was that one of the islanders betrayed Kikuchi. Acting on an informant's tip that the local teacher was in fact an intelligence officer of the Nakano School, American soldiers arrested him in November. In his first weeks in detention, Kikuchi underwent interrogation on his mission, the organization of Thirty-second Army's command structure, and other questions related to the battle of Okinawa. In February 1946, Kikuchi was sent to an internment camp in another part of the Ryukyus. Marked for special handling as an intelligence officer, Kikuchi was then transferred to Tokyo.[14]

Deadly Gateway to Kyushu

Lt. Gen. Ushijima had fought tenaciously on Okinawa. Apart from yielding briefly to his chief of staff's exhortations to go on the offensive, Ushijima had kept largely to a strategy of attrition. He thus extracted a high price in troops and time from the American invasion force. Only on 2 July came the formal declaration of American victory and an end to Operation Iceberg. The American armada had spent nearly three months on a campaign to seize one small island, more than double the forty days originally planned. The Japanese defenders had also managed to kill during that time some 12,500 members of an invasion force vastly superior in men, firepower, and supplies. Including those killed in action, American combat casualties came to nearly fifty thousand. Many of those Americans were killed without ever landing on Okinawa, for the Divine Wind sank over thirty ships and damaged nearly four hundred. While the Japanese had suffered even greater losses, they had bought time for defense of the main islands. They had also demonstrated a determination to suffer appalling losses to bloody the invaders. If the Allies suffered sufficient losses, public opinion could even pressure their leaders to negotiate a settlement short of unconditional surrender.[15]

For Imperial General Headquarters, Ushijima's defense of Okinawa had proven a model of military-civilian joint action. Local conscription of Okinawans into auxiliary units had contributed a third of the approximately one hundred thousand Japanese who defended Okinawa against U.S. Tenth Army's 183,000 men.

Despite their place at the bottom of Japanese society, perhaps only somewhat higher than that of the Koreans and other subject peoples of the empire, the residents of the Ryukyus had proven pathetically loyal and brave. The Nakano School's operatives and the Kempeitai, who had kept watch for signs of disloyalty, fearing that the many Okinawans who had resided in the United States or had relatives there constituted a potential enemy fifth column, observed firsthand the popular loyalty . In any event, little was left to chance. The Army had issued a warning that Okinawans caught speaking to one another in the local dialect, incomprehensible to the Japanese of the main islands, would be considered spies and punished accordingly. Japanese soldiers were also ordered to execute any Okinawan found to have in his possession any of the American leaflets, which littered the island, that promised protection for those who surrendered.

Perhaps to the surprise of Japan's military authorities, the local residents had proven not only loyal but a genuine asset in the fighting. Schoolgirls in their teens joined nursing units. Boys served in student auxiliaries. Adults, armed with spears and farm tools, formed units of the Home Guard. When the dust had settled, some sixty-six thousand regular Japanese troops had died in battle. Only seventy-eight hundred had surrendered or been taken prisoner. Some 60 percent of the Home Guard members died in the fighting. Fully half the student auxiliaries perished. Including noncombatants, more than 120,000 civilians lost their lives in the Battle of Okinawa. Residents on a small outpost of empire, considered "peripheral" Japanese, had endured unspeakable suffering. Those who fought and died alongside the Imperial Army's regular soldiers contributed to a defense that made Okinawa the most costly American victory of the Pacific War to date.

To the north loomed a greater island with many more residents. The much larger Army and civilian population dug into the mountains and forests of Kyushu promised to make the next stop on the road to Tokyo an incalculably more bloody one.[16]

8

PREPARING FINAL DEFENSES

Imperial General Headquarters in Tokyo was racing against time in preparing the final defenses. Japan's military leaders, in position three years earlier to subdue China and oust the Western powers from their Asian colonies, seemingly failed to keep in step with the accelerating Allied counteroffensive. On 6 February 1945, the Japanese Army created five new area army headquarters and eight military districts for the home islands and Korea. The area army commanders and chiefs of staff were to hold concurrent positions in the area military districts, giving them overall command of the region's military and civilian defense activities.

The Japanese Army then launched a crash program to raise fifty divisions. At the time, only eight regular divisions and fourteen depot divisions were in Japan. A mere three depot divisions guarded Korea. With more than three million Japanese already serving overseas, the Army turned to youths and older men to fill the ranks of the new divisions. Conscription came in three waves. The first levee came on 28 February, gathering conscripts for sixteen coastal divisions. The second call-up was ordered on 2 April, for eight "decisive battle" divisions. On 23 May, military authorities made plans to conscript in July the numbers necessary to fill another nineteen divisions.

There were two types of units to defend Japan. One was the coastal defense unit, whose members were to meet the Americans on the beaches. Without much equipment, they would face massive naval and aerial bombardment. Their fate was sealed. In dying, these Japanese were simply to make the invaders pay a price as they came ashore. Beyond the beaches would be waiting units more heavily equipped to fight the "decisive battles." If events unfolded as Japan's strategists hoped, the bloodied and weary invaders would advance inland to their destruction by this second echelon.

On 8 April, Imperial General Headquarters laid further plans for defense. Anticipating that the Americans would seek to isolate Japanese units, the Army Command divided Japan into two areas of responsibility. A general army was responsible for defending an area. Each area's top officer commanded five area armies. The First General Army, under the command of Field Marshal Sugiyama Gen in Tokyo, would defend northeastern Honshu, Hokkaido, Karafuto (the southern half of Sakhalin), and the Chishima (or Kurile) islands. The Second General Army, under Field Marshal Hata Shunroku in Hiroshima, was responsible for the defense of Osaka and other parts of Honshu west of Hakone, as well as the islands of Shikoku and Kyushu. The Army High Command also disseminated orders to prepare for the final defense of Japan. The Ketsu (Decisive) Operations, seven in all, were plans to deal crushing blows to the American invaders. Among the plans, Operation Ketsu No. 6 covered Kyushu. Ketsu No. 3 was for the Tokyo area.[1]

Preparing to lead the Allied invasion of Japan was Gen. Douglas MacArthur. A man of consuming ambition, MacArthur planned to lead an invasion force in a campaign whose scale would dwarf the Normandy landings of his rival and former subordinate, Gen. Dwight D. Eisenhower. Conquering the insular empire would also erase MacArthur's earlier reverses and frustrations. Given the impossible task of defending the Philippines at the war's onset three years earlier, MacArthur had left in early 1942, under Washington's orders, for Australia ahead of his doomed force's surrender. Then, leading a campaign from Australia north towards Japan, the ambitious commander cultivated contacts in the press and among Republicans in Congress to build his reputation as a military genius who was winning the war against Japan on a shoestring and in spite of Washington's policy of "Europe first." He tested the political waters in the 1944 presidential election, when he allowed certain Republicans to circulate his name as a candidate for the party's nomination. If all went according to plan, MacArthur could well turn the conquest of Japan into a wave of popularity that would sweep him into the White House.

MacArthur planned to wage his campaign in two stages. The first was named Operation Olympic. In November, waiting for the end of the season when typhoons plagued Japan, MacArthur would send roughly 350,000 troops under Gen. Walter Krueger's Sixth Army onto the beaches of Kyushu. Once the island was secured and turned into a base for aircraft and supplies, MacArthur would execute Operation Coronet, the invasion of Honshu. Under this second operation, planned for early 1946, MacArthur would lead an even larger force, including six American infantry divisions transferred from Europe as well as several British Commonwealth divisions. MacArthur would go down in history as the greatest general of all time. Assuming, that is, that he could overcome the Japanese defenders.[2]

First Line of Defense in Kyushu

Well before the battle for Okinawa, the Japanese Army High Command had begun preparing a far more formidable defense for Kyushu. The southernmost of Japan's four main islands and the closest to the continent of Asia, Kyushu had faced past invasions. Northern Kyushu, opposite the Korean peninsula, was where the Japanese had repelled two successive Mongol invasions by Kublai Khan in the thirteenth century. Stout hearts and typhoon winds had beaten back an invasion by the world's most formidable empire seven centuries earlier. Imperial Japan's generals were readying Kyushu once again to repeat the feat.

Kyushu is a large island of more than thirty-six thousand square kilometers, nearly half again as large as Sicily. Dominated by forested mountains in the interior and rugged coasts with few major beaches or large harbors, Kyushu offered the Japanese Army natural defenses far more favorable than those afforded by such exposed Pacific islets as Guadalcanal. Outgunned, isolated, and overrun, the Japanese Army at such flyspecks in the Pacific as Tarawa and Iwo Jima had made U.S. forces pay dearly in blood for every inch of the battlefield. The Japanese were going to extract an immeasurably greater price in Kyushu. Interior fortifications among the large island's mountains lay beyond the reach of the big guns of the U.S. Navy's warships. The island's caves and mountains sheltered the defenders from American air raids. Perhaps most important was location. Kyushu's proximity to the main island of Honshu and the Korean peninsula meant that the Japanese Army's troops and equipment had only to cross narrow straits to reach the island.

In the first round of national mobilization in February, Kyushu's Sixteenth Area Army received two of the four new coastal defense divisions. In the April mobilization, Imperial General Headquarters allotted to the island's defense two "decisive battle" divisions, two tank brigades, and an armored regiment. In the May mobilization, three more divisions and four independent mixed brigades were formed under Sixteenth Area Army. Existing divisions also shifted to the defense of Kyushu. In April, Tokyo transferred from Manchukuo the Kwantung Army's crack Twenty-fifth and Fifty-sixth divisions. In May, the elite Seventy-seventh Division, earlier shifted from Manchukuo to Hokkaido, went south to Kyushu. In all, the Japanese Army by summer 1945 assembled fourteen divisions, eight independent mixed brigades, and three independent armored brigades on the ground in Kyushu. In addition, Sixth Air Army and Fifth Air Fleet were based on the island. The Army had also earmarked for Kyushu's defense a thousand suicide aircraft to attack the American armada, with another thousand kamikaze aircraft and an additional eleven hundred conventional aircraft waiting in reserve. The dispersal of these aircraft among fields newly built and in underground hangars rendered their destruction unlikely before the invasion.

In all, the Japanese Army had assembled more than seven hundred thousand troops on Kyushu. MacArthur longed to lead the greatest invasion in history, but despite his attempts to play down casualty figures, it was increasingly evident that American casualties of a quarter million were likely. For, even if MacArthur's men shot the aircraft out of the sky and struggled ashore against the coastal defenses, they would still face an island of soldiers prepared to defend their land to the death. Behind the formidable conventional forces would be uncounted unconventional ones, led by the Nakano School's shadow warriors.[3]

Shadow Warriors in Kyushu

Four members of the Nakano School's proving unit reached Kyushu in October 1944, marking the first preparations for guerrilla warfare there. From the Futamata Branch came several waves of commandos to serve as the core members of a cadre who would train the island's civilians in guerrilla warfare. Some forty men from Futamata Branch arrived in December, followed by another twenty in March and a few more in early August. Compiling military topography was one of their duties. The Japanese Army had been fighting only overseas since quelling Saigo Takamori's rebellion in Kyushu in the nineteenth century. The generals had no appropriate military maps of Japan. Compared to the Soviet Far East or China, the home islands were uncharted territory.[4]

Other shadow warriors also took up positions in Kyushu. From Tokyo came several of the Nakano School's intelligence veterans who had been working in Second Bureau. Maj. Kameyama Rokuzo, a graduate of the Nakano School's First Class, transferred from his post in the covert operations section. Capt. Itezono Tatsuo left Fifth Section for Fukuoka, as did Capt. Sakura Ichiro of Sixth Section. Capt. Makino Masahide from Seventh Section went south to serve at Kumamoto District Headquarters. They were part of a larger shifting of talent from Tokyo's intelligence headquarters to what would be the front lines after Okinawa. Lieutenant colonels Abe Kunio and Tokunaga Hachiro, both former chiefs of Second Bureau's British section, were also among those who left Tokyo for new duties in Kyushu. The Japanese Army had started late in a crash effort to strengthen its deficient intelligence capabilities. Ironically, Japan's fortunes had been in decline as the expertise of Second Bureau had grown. Japan's intelligence officers were better able than ever to report on the enemy. While the military's "eyesight" had improved, its "muscles" had deteriorated. The Japanese Army was increasingly incapable of acting on its research and analysis. For the defense of Kyushu, men trained in strategic intelligence left for the front lines.

From the continent to Kyushu came other men of the Nakano School. Araki Goro transferred from the Kwantung Army in Manchukuo to Nagasaki District Headquarters. Harada Shunichi left the China Expeditionary Army for Miyazaki District Headquarters. From Southeast Asia came Lt. Col. Fujiwara Iwaichi, whose Fujiwara Agency had operated with such success against Indian units of the British Army in the Japanese conquest of Malaya and Singapore. Fujiwara also arrived in Miyazaki Prefecture, on Kyushu's east coast, assuming the post of senior staff officer in Fifty-seventh Army. From the First Class of the Nakano School's Futamata Branch, which graduated in December 1944, arrived twenty-six shadow warriors. Lt. Yamamoto Fukuichi, one of the class, drew an assignment as a member of Lt. Col. Yakumaru Katsuya's intelligence staff in Fukuoka. His

duties included handling captured American fliers, working on plans
to mobilize the island's civilians, and publishing a military newspaper
for Kyushu. Under Captain Itezono's command were Narazaki
Masahiko, a young probationary officer, and nine of his classmates,
all recent graduates of the Nakano School. Around thirty commandos
from the First Class of the Nakano School's Futamata Branch came
to the island. In all, roughly one hundred men of the Nakano School
reached Kyushu for what must have seemed to them their final assignment.[5]

As in Okinawa, many of the shadow warriors in Kyushu were to
train and lead irregular forces in guerrilla warfare. In late January, the
Japanese Army set up a guerrilla training unit at Nichinan, Miyazaki
Prefecture, on Kyushu's southeast coast. The organization's designation, the Kirishima Unit, was the name of both the local Shinto shrine
and the mountain chain. Kirishima Shrine, dedicated to the god
Ninigi-no-Mikoto, was an apt inspiration for the unit's name. Tradition held that Ninigi-no-Mikoto was a legendary ancestor of Japan's
divine emperors. The shadow warriors adopting Kirishima as their
unit name were committed to defending the empire. The unit's mission was to teach guerrilla tactics to civilians gathered into home
guard units. In a school facing the town's feudal castle, members of
the teaching cadre prepared soldiers for what promised to be the
bloodiest campaign of the twentieth century.

Commanding the Kirishima Unit was Capt. Kishimoto Iwao, one
of several Nakano School officers in Kyushu since October. One of
the Japanese Army's leading experts on irregular warfare, Kishimoto
had already put together a manual based on Soviet and Chinese Communist documents on guerrilla warfare by partisan bands. "A Reference for Guerrilla Warfare in Japan" was the first distillation of his
research. He and others from the Nakano School later refined the
product for use on the island. "A Reference for Guerrilla Warfare in
Kyushu" was a more concrete document, with the addition of details
particular to conducting hit-and-run operations in the mountain forests and towns of the island. Disseminated throughout Kyushu, Kishimoto's document was read by those preparing for MacArthur's
invasion.

Under Kishimoto's command were some seventy men, including
several members of the Futamata Branch's First Class. One of them
was Lt. Suetsugu Ichiro. It was the task of Suetsugu and other

instructors of the Kirishima Unit to impart the lessons learned at Futamata Branch to the select noncommissioned officers assigned to the unit. Suetsugu and the other shadow warriors taught their men techniques of disguise and infiltration. After a month of training, many of the Kirishima Unit's members left for various commands throughout Kyushu, where they conducted topographical surveys, drilled local associations of reservists and women, and handled other intelligence duties. Lt. Haraguchi Shigehiko, a classmate of Suetsugu's from Futamata Branch, went solo to the Goto Archipelago of Nagasaki Prefecture. His base of operations was Fukue, the westernmost of the five major islands constituting the Goto (literally, "five islands") chain. The beautiful beaches, old Roman Catholic church, and samurai houses made the island of farmers and fishermen a charming location. Haraguchi, assigned to the district's special guard unit, had little time to enjoy Fukue's beauty. Invasion was imminent.[6]

Several trainers of the Kirishima Unit, accomplishing their training mission in May, traveled to frontline units in southern and eastern Kyushu. Kishimoto and Suetsugu, for their part, left for Western District Army Headquarters in Fukuoka. Suetsugu remained subordinate to Kishimoto, who assumed command of the headquarters staff's newly created Research Office. Kishimoto reported directly to Maj. Itezono Tatsuo, who oversaw its operations as deputy to Lt. Col. Yakumaru Katsuya, Sixteenth Area Army's intelligence chief. The covert unit's duties included drafting plans for guerrilla units throughout Kyushu. With three other shadow warriors of the Nakano School and a few women attached to the unit as support staff, the two worked feverishly, drafting plans for their classmates in the field. On many nights, the men never left the office. Rather, each would roll out a mattress atop a desk to snatch three or four hours of sleep before resuming his work.[7]

In early June, the Research Office decided to send Suetsugu to Kumamoto Prefecture to scout locations for a second Kirishima Unit. One promising site was the area around Mount Aso, a giant volcano whose massive caldera and verdant slopes were ringed by wooded hills and streams. On 10 June, Suetsugu left by train to explore the area's mountain lodges and other structures for candidate training sites. As his train headed southwest for Kumamoto, the wail of an air raid siren filled the air. Just as the train pulled into the station at Kurume, short of the border between Fukuoka and Kumamoto prefectures, a formation of American B-29 bombers appeared overhead. Bombs hurtled downward. Suetsugu took cover under the train as explosions rocked the area. Hit was the station building. The rail line to Kumamoto was also knocked out of service. Fate had spared the young operative. Suetsugu dusted himself off, apprised his headquarters of the situation, and returned from whence he came. His mission to Kumamoto had gone up in flames.[8]

As spring turned to summer and the expected autumn invasion neared, the shadow warriors on Kyushu had achieved a great deal. Kishimoto and others from the Nakano School had overseen the training of some five thousand Japanese soldiers in irregular warfare. Trainers also imparted the lessons of guerrilla warfare to more than ten thousand local veterans and other civilians. The training had consisted largely of lessons in attacking airborne troops, laying ambushes, conducting night raids, and committing acts of sabotage. Those who went through the training learned the essentials of martial arts. Given the lack of regular weapons available, the civilian combat units drilled in shooting arrows and wielding bamboo spears. The only other weapons available to them were hand grenades, pistols, incendiary devices, and swords. Japan no longer could turn back the deadly formations of B-29 bombers whose bombs rained down death and destruction on factories and families alike. Retribution would have to wait. Once the American troops reached the island, the civilian units would have their moment. As American soldiers floated downwards, dangling at the ends of their parachutes, trudged in single file along some dirt path bisecting a rice paddy, clambered up a wooded ridge, or slept in their camps, they would meet the pupils of the Kirishima Unit.[9]

Guerrillas in Tokyo

In the imperial capital, Imperial General Headquarters prepared their defenses. It was certain that, in the event MacArthur succeeded in taking control of Kyushu, the way would be clear to advance on Tokyo in eastern Japan. In February 1945, the Japanese High Command established Twelfth Area Army and Eastern District Army Headquarters in Tokyo. Comprising Twelfth Area Army, commanded by Gen. Tanaka Shizuichi, were five field armies. Learning the lessons of Saipan and Leyte, Tanaka was prepared to wage the same deadly war of attrition that Ushijima was conducting with far fewer resources in Okinawa. When the Americans stormed ashore at Kujukuri or Sagami Bay, there would be only some sacrificial coastal defense units there to bloody them. Tanaka would hold his main forces inland to deal sharp blows to MacArthur's soldiers, far from the reach of the U.S. Navy's shells.[10]

In the shadows of the regular Japanese Army would lie in wait the irregular forces, led by the shadow warriors. At the heart of the area's commando operations were men of the Nakano School. One such was Capt. Arai Fujitsugu, who received orders to organize an elite commando unit that would operate in the Tokyo area. Earlier in the war, Arai had for a time been working as a member of the Nakano School's testing unit that tried out new tactics and equipment. Before receiving orders to develop a guerrilla unit in Tokyo, Arai had been operating in China. In March 1944, the Japanese Army in Nanking had initiated a program to train mixed units of Japanese and Chinese loyal to the Nanking regime. Arai was one of the select few members of the Nakano School chosen to lead the training there.

In April 1945, having transferred to Tokyo under the Eastern District Army Headquarters, Arai took command of the program to establish a guerrilla unit for the capital area. Arai's organization was called the Yashima Unit, its designation an ancient name for Japan. He established his unit headquarters at an elementary school in Itsuka, west of Tokyo. There he assembled an elite group of hand-picked men. For Maj. Gen. Takashima Tatsuhiko, vice chief of staff for Twelfth Area Army, the Yashima Unit was his most elite outfit. It was by no means, however, the only organization for guerrilla warfare. Eastern District Army, following orders issued in March, formed a number of district guard units to enlist civilians in the guerrilla operations that would play an auxiliary role in the Japanese Army's defense of eastern Japan. Here, too, the Nakano School's shadow warriors would occupy key positions in organizing the units and training civilians. In all, close to a hundred members of the Nakano School joined the various district headquarters.

Under Arai, roughly ten officers and NCOs from the Nakano School constituted the core of the Yashima Unit. They in turn commanded approximately one hundred men. They were to execute their mission once the Americans had captured Tokyo. By then, Imperial General Headquarters would have withdrawn with the regular military units to the underground headquarters at Matsushiro in the mountains of Nagano Prefecture. Arai and his men would organize the remaining Japanese residents in the area to attack American units behind the lines. In the hill caves west of Itsuka, Arai stocked the wireless communications equipment, weapons, and provisions necessary to wage guerrilla warfare. From downed B-29 bombers, he gathered weapons, provisions, and clothing to use in future operations. His acquisitions from the downed aircraft included some one hundred small arms and ammunition. Arai also joined hands with local activists to have bamboo spears, crude hand grenades, and other weapons made.

In early August, Arai received a shock when orders came from the Eastern District Army Headquarters to move his operations from the interior of the Kanto plain to the coast. Staff officers of Eastern District Army were in effect ordering Arai to meet the enemy at the water's edge. Arai was incredulous. These men seemingly had learned nothing from the fighting to date. Arai hotly demanded in a meeting at Eastern District Army Headquarters to know why he should throw away the lives of his force in a vain defense of the beaches, where they could expect no shelter from the horrific air and naval bombardments that would proceed the landing. He grew indignant at the thought of vainly sacrificing his men, demanding, "What is the point of having them die a dog's death before fighting?" Arai pressed forcefully for authorization to follow the original plan. The staff officers rejected his case with scathing criticism typical of the worst aspects of the regular army: "Is life so precious to you? The kind of tactics you're talking about aren't written in the Military Academy textbooks." Arai had no choice but to obey orders. As he toured the inadequate beach defenses at Sagami Bay with three subordinate officers a few days later, he felt as though he were looking over his own grave. Then came his reprieve. Salvation from the stupidity of Eastern District Army Headquarters arrived following his inspection of defenses at Kamakura, when he heard the imperial radio broadcast announcing Japan's decision to stop fighting.[11]

Guerrillas in the North

In the empire's northernmost reaches, the Japanese Army also strengthened its defenses against a possible American assault. Similar to the American Wild West, the northern area was the Japanese frontier at the end of the nineteenth century. Once the home of aboriginal tribes, Hokkaido, Karafuto (Sakhalin), and the Chishima (Kurile) chain of islets strung between Hokkaido and the Kamchatka peninsula increasingly came under Japanese influence. Tokyo pursued a policy of exploration and settlement in competition with Moscow, whose influence was expanding east and south from Siberia. The Japanese had managed to secure the entire island of Hokkaido by the time of the establishment of imperial Japan in 1868. In a negotiated settlement with Moscow, Tokyo relinquished claims to Karafuto in exchange for title to the Chishima Islands in 1875. With victory in the Russo-Japanese war, Tokyo added the southern half of Karafuto to the empire in 1905.

In the first half of the Second World War, the region was the stage for important military actions. At the onset of Japan's war against the West, in December 1941, a strike force of the Imperial Japanese Navy had sailed in secret from Hitokappu Bay in the Chishima Islands to attack the American naval base at Pearl Harbor. In June 1942, at the high-water mark of Japan's successes, Japanese forces occupied the islets of Attu and Kiska at the western end of Alaska's Aleutian chain. As the war's tide turned against Japan, Tokyo suffered reverses in that region. In May 1943, American forces had overcome on Attu a Japanese garrison that fought to the bitter end. At the end of July, the Japanese secretly withdrew their troops from Kiska, leaving an empty island when American troops stormed ashore in the middle of August. With the Aleutians entirely back in American hands, the nearby Chishima chain was exposed.

Imperial General Headquarters moved to shore up defenses in the north against a possible American thrust. As part of that policy, Tokyo established Twenty-seventh Army in early 1944. Under the command of Lt. Gen. Terakura Seizo, with his headquarters on the island of Etorofu, the new army was to defend the Chishima chain. Along with other ground and air units, the meager forces in the north constituted Japan's Fifth Area Army.

With the regular troops in the north were Japan's shadow warriors. In December 1944, Maj. Gen. Hagi Saburo took command of military intelligence in the area as chief of staff for Fifth Area Army. After attending the Military Academy as an infantry officer in the Twenty-ninth Class, Hagi later gained entry to the elite General Staff

College. In an even greater mark of favor reserved for rising officers, he also graduated from a political studies course at Tokyo Imperial University. His later career included a stint from November 1937 to May 1939 as staff officer with the Kwantung Army.

Under Hagi's command served more than a hundred men from the Nakano School, including its Futamata Branch. Capt. Taniyama Kisaburo, for example, arrived at Fifth Area Army by way of Second Bureau's American section. He and other intelligence officers were part of the strengthening of intelligence capabilities against the American target.[12]

While preparing for an American invasion, Hagi kept an eye on the Soviets as well. He oversaw the activities of the Karafuto SSA on the southern half of Sakhalin. The Karafuto SSA engaged in a variety of operations, including counterintelligence, monitoring radios, tapping telephone lines, and engaging in covert reconnaissance in Soviet Sakhalin.[13]

With Japan facing imminent invasion, however, the relative weight of Hagi's activities necessarily shifted from gathering intelligence to organizing for guerrilla warfare. One of those laying the foundation was Capt. Muta Teruo. A member of the Military Academy's Fifty-fifth Class, Muta had received training in guerrilla warfare at the Nakano School. His activities on the empire's northern frontier began with his arrival at Fifth Area Army Headquarters in Sapporo, Hokkaido's capital, in September 1944. Early in November, Muta received an assignment to the intelligence section of Twenty-seventh Army Headquarters, on Etorofu near the southern end of the Chishima chain. Based on a military topographical survey, Muta issued several weeks later a manual on the essentials of guerrilla warfare on the island.

In early December, Muta led the fledgling effort to train a guerrilla force for Etorofu. His superior officer, who oversaw the program, was none other than Maj. Gen. Suzuki Keiji. Four years earlier, Suzuki had overseen the training of the Thirty Comrades, a group of young Burmese activists, as part of his Minami Agency that was to subvert British rule in Burma. Instead, following Japan's decision to go to war against Great Britain and the United States, he had seen his role reduced to a sideshow in the Japanese Army's subsequent invasion of Burma. After clashing with his superiors in opposition to the imposition of military rule, he had been transferred to a divisional staff position, then received two consecutive assignments in transportation posts before landing in Etorofu.

Muta, in order to carry out his program of guerrilla training, slated twenty-five of the best officers on the headquarters intelligence staff of Twenty-seventh Army as well as from among the three battalions on the island. Of those, fourteen were graduates of the Nakano School. Muta trained his cadre in two scenarios. One involved a night raid against enemy ships anchored in Hitokappu Bay. The second envisioned a night raid on land against the headquarters of the invading army near Hitokappu Bay. Members of the Nakano School were particularly involved in the second scenario.

In the end, however, the problems facing guerrilla resistance on Etorofu must have seemed too daunting. The greatest of the Chishima chain's volcanic isles, Etorofu extended a mere two hundred kilometers from north to south and a mere thirty kilometers at its widest. There were few places to hide. Sources of food were meager, apart from the fish on and around the island. Moreover, the island's small population, a mix of Japanese and aboriginal Ainu residents, included many aged individuals, women, and children, who would place demands on supplies while adding little to Etorofu's defense. In late January, Twenty-seventh Army Headquarters was dissolved, with most of the force shifted south to Sendai. Most of the intelligence officers went to Sapporo, headquarters of Fifth Area Army. A few remained on Etorofu. A few other shadow warriors went to Sendai.

On 6 February, as part of the plan to defend the home islands, Imperial General Headquarters redesignated Sapporo as headquarters of both Fifth Area Army and the new Northern District Army Headquarters. Gen. Higuchi Kiichiro, military commander in Sapporo since August 1942, remained in control of the newly designated military force. Hagi remained his chief of staff. To defend the area, Hagi oversaw the creation of combined military-civilian guards. A total of twenty-four such units were established on Hokkaido, another nine in Karafuto.

Hagi also organized guerrilla forces in anticipation of an Allied invasion. In June, he organized a week-long guerrilla exercise in the region around the city of Asahikawa in central Hokkaido. In late July, Fifth Area Army created the Northern Army Guerrilla Cadre Training Unit, locating it between Sapporo and Chitose. Hagi assumed command of the unit. One of his two chief instructors was Capt. Muta

Teruo of the Nakano School. In a training course conducted in late July, the unit put some one hundred young officers through a course in irregular warfare. A second running of the course was slated for early August.[14]

Holding Korea

The shadow warriors were also operating outside the Japanese archipelago. Japan's leaders had no intention of abandoning Korea. Japan had waged war with imperial China and czarist Russia in succession over Korea before formally taking possession of the strategic peninsula in 1910. Unlike Malaya and other Western colonies acquired since 1941, Korea was an integral part of the Japanese Empire. Hundreds of thousands of Japanese lived in Korea, with some five hundred thousand in the southern part of the peninsula.[15]

In the spring of 1945, Maj. Maruzaki Yoshio arrived in Korea. A member of the Nakano School's First Class, he had gathered intelligence before the war in the Dutch East Indies, operating under cover as an employee of the Japanese consulate at Surabaya.[16] Following a number of intervening missions, he now joined the headquarters of Japan's Korean Army as the staff officer responsible for "domestic" resistance. Before 1945, few of the Nakano School's shadow warriors had gone to Korea. The peninsula was quiet. With the growing threat of an Allied invasion of the Japanese Empire proper, the shadow warriors began arriving in the Land of the Morning Calm. In December 1944, four graduates of the Futamata Branch's First Class formed an annex of Korean Army Headquarters. Operating from a temple near Kwangju, South Cholla Province, they trained noncommissioned officers in the arts of guerrilla warfare. By summer 1945, at least forty-five graduates of the Nakano School and Futamata Branch had reached Korea. They took up positions from the island of Chejudo to the peninsula's south to Nanam in the northeast. Outside the capital at Keijo (Seoul), Kwangju, Nanam, P'yongyang, and Taegu were significant bases for the shadow warriors. They were to lead the guerrilla forces composed of Japanese residents and, perhaps, Koreans. The latter were of dubious value, however. While Koreans constituted the backbone of the colonial police force and a source of military recruits for the empire, popular resentment over Japanese rule was smoldering. In the event of an Allied invasion, the shadow warriors would likely face widespread Korean opposition.[17]

Killings at Aburayama

As men of the Nakano School toiled to prepare guerrilla forces to fight alongside the Japanese Army's regular units, frustration was running high at Sixteenth Area Army Headquarters in Kyushu. Due to the unrelenting pounding of American bomber crews, the headquarters staff had withdrawn from stricken Fukuoka to the city's outskirts. In the early morning of 11 August, the headquarters unit charged with monitoring foreign radio programs learned via a shortwave broadcast of Japan's intention to surrender according to the terms stipulated by the Allies in the Potsdam Declaration. Only days before, Hiroshima and Nagasaki had disappeared under atomic mushroom clouds. Two days earlier, the same day that a single American bomb incinerated Nagasaki, the Soviet Union's Josef Stalin had sent his armored legions thundering across the border into Manchukuo.

Certain shadow warriors at Sixteenth Area Army Headquarters, enraged by the recent events and the news that they would surrender without a fight, took the opportunity to turn their anger on the American fliers in their hands. The downed American aircrews had already suffered at the hands of intelligence staff officers in Sixteenth Area Army. Any Allied airman who fell into the hands of the Japanese Army could expect little mercy. Beatings and torture were the common means used to pry information from Allied prisoners of war. American aircrew suffered further. Pilots, as officers, were generally in a position to know more secrets than the average infantryman or sailor. Thus, when members of Doolittle's raiding party crash-landed in China short of friendly lines and fell into the hands of the Japanese, Imperial General Headquarters ordered them sent to Tokyo for interrogation as a source of intelligence on the U.S. military.

Moreover, the Japanese Army, outraged by the Doolittle Raid of April 1942 on Tokyo, had made it a policy to execute captured fliers. The Japanese justified the executions on the grounds that the airmen were guilty of indiscriminate bombings that killed civilians. Given Japan's dense population and the distribution of innumerable small factories and workshops throughout residential neighborhoods, almost any bombing of a Japanese target was bound to result in civilian casualties.

In addition, the U.S. Army Air Forces by the late stages of the war no longer made any pretense of limiting bombings to military targets. In the Utah desert, at Dugway Proving Ground, technicians had perfected incendiary bombs in tests against painstaking reconstructions of Japanese residences. Made of wood, paper, and straw, Japanese houses were a bomber's dream. Maj. Gen. Curtis LeMay and other air officers, eager to demonstrate the effectiveness of aerial bombardment, embraced a policy of terror bombings against Japan. Even before the atomic bombs fell on Hiroshima and Nagasaki at the war's end, LeMay and his fliers had inflicted a horrific incendiary bombing campaign against Japan's population centers. Their efforts culminated in the great raid of 9 March 1945 against Tokyo, which killed or injured some 120,000 residents and destroyed nearly a quarter million homes.

From a Japanese point of view, American aircrews were guilty of murder. That they were bombing civilians from on high rather than shooting them at ground level mattered little. The U.S. Army, which was bombing civilians as part of a terror campaign, still branded Japan's policy of executing captured airmen as murder. An editorial in the Army weekly *Yank* captured the American view of the Doolittle executions, referring to them as "open, official murder" that "cruelly and savagely violated all the rules of civilized warfare." Sadly, by this point in the bloody history of the twentieth century, warfare had long since ceased being civilized. In Kyushu, Sixteenth Area Army had already executed eight downed airmen in June. As the reality of their nation's surrender hit them, staff officers decided that they would extract a further measure of vengeance.[18]

On the evening of 10 August, Capt. Itezono Tatsuo called a meeting of around twenty shadow warriors engaged in guerrilla training. He informed them that, on the orders of senior air staff officer Col. Sato Yoshinao, all officers involved in guerrilla warfare were to participate the next morning in the execution of eight American prisoners. Itezono further informed them that karate and arrows would be used. Lt. Yamamoto Fukuichi remarked how he wished to test his skill in karate on a prisoner. Itezono had secured permission from Sato to apply his unit's guerrilla training on the prisoners as a form of live exercise. He saw it as a means of boosting unit morale for his men, recent graduates of the Nakano School who had yet to see battle. Col. Tomomori Kiyoharu, assistant chief of staff for Sixteenth Area Army, approved Itezono's request. Such blooding of new men was by no means a personal cruelty on Itezono's part. The practice was widespread in the Japanese Army, having first taken root in 1937 among Japanese units fighting in China.

The next morning, Itezono led his shadow warriors and the eight American prisoners from Western District Army Headquarters to Aburayama in the hills south of Fukuoka. In a clearing in the wooded hills, Japanese soldiers first stripped their captives and dug a number of holes. A lieutenant from a guerrilla unit then stood over a prisoner who had been forced into a kneeling position. Brandishing his sword, the lieutenant brought it down on the prisoner's neck, killing him at a blow. The next four prisoners died in similar fashion.

The captors then practiced their martial arts. When Itezono had asked for volunteers, several of the shadow warriors had begun warming up. One then stepped forward to strike several devastating karate blows to a prisoner, whose hands were pinned behind his back. The wounded man then lost his head to an officer's sword. The Japanese killed the seventh prisoner in similar fashion, Lt. Narazaki Masahiko of the Nakano School administering the coup de grace by sword. Lt. Yamamoto Fukuichi of the Futamata Branch was one of several shadow warriors who had delivered the karate blows. Col. Tomomori Kiyoharu had ordered the coup de grace by sword for each of the beaten fliers.

The captors then forced the last flier into a sitting position as Otsuki Takashi, a probationary officer from Futamata Branch's Second Class, shot an arrow at him from a distance of approximately three meters. After missing twice, the Japanese hit his target with his third arrow, piercing the prisoner's head above his left eye. The captors then forced the dying man to kneel, and one of them chopped off his head with a sword. Under a hot August sky flowed onto the green grass of Aburayama the crimson blood of eight American fliers. Executed in line with the policy of the Japanese Army, they had suffered unusually cruel deaths at the hands of Itezono's shadow warriors. When it was all over, Colonel Tomomori remarked that the men had gained valuable experience for the decisive battle to come.[19]

9

ENDING THE WAR, FINDING NEW ALLIES

As spring gave way to summer, the Japanese Army prepared to strike a crippling blow against Gen. Douglas MacArthur's invasion force. Imperial General Headquarters would either repel the invasion or extract so steep a price in American lives that Washington would negotiate for peace. Japan would escape the catastrophic fate of unconditional surrender that had befallen Germany in May.

The military planners divided responsibility for Japan's defense into two major commands. First General Army, with its headquarters in Tokyo, would defend the capital and the rest of Honshu to the north. Second General Army, with its headquarters in Hiroshima, would engage the enemy in southwestern Honshu and in Kyushu. The Japanese Army's intelligence officers predicted, correctly, that MacArthur planned to take Kyushu before making the leap to Honshu. The generals had by now turned Kyushu into a daunting fortress.

In each successive campaign against the American forces, the Japanese Army had waged an increasingly deadly defense. Military leaders had learned by 1945 how futile were the earlier "banzai" charges and vain attempts to annihilate the enemy at the water's edge. In Okinawa, General Ushijima had permitted American forces to come ashore unopposed before waging his deadly campaign of attrition from well-entrenched positions. Moreover, Okinawa had merely been a rehearsal for the coming tragedy. The Army had sacrificed Okinawa, holding nearly all its men, aircraft, and resources in reserve for the final showdown.

In Washington, President Harry S. Truman heard of the formidable Japanese defenses with alarm. MacArthur, aiming to capture the White House after the war, was eager to lead the invasion of all time. However, the estimated casualties ran as high as a quarter million for Kyushu alone. Even if the Japanese Army failed to stop MacArthur from securing a base in Kyushu for the final assault on Honshu, such a bloodbath could well turn the American public against the final campaign to take Tokyo and to win Japan's unconditional surrender. President Truman, deeply concerned over intelligence on the Japanese buildup and mistrustful of MacArthur's optimism, then played another card. The United States had recently succeeded in developing and manufacturing the world's first atomic bombs. Reports of the awesome tests in the desert suggested a way to compel Japan's unconditional surrender without losing hundreds of thousands of American lives. In a fateful decision, President Truman ordered the atom unleashed on Japan.[1]

Fallout from Hiroshima

At approximately quarter past eight o'clock on the morning of 6 August, a single bomb fell from a lone bomber in flight over Hiroshima. A moment later, much of the city disappeared. In 1937, the world had learned in horror how German bombers in the service of Gen. Francisco Franco in the Spanish Civil War had laid waste to the village of Guernica. The Spanish artist Pablo Picasso had captured the new horror of mass civilian deaths in his searing painting of the stricken town. By 1945, the lethal progress of military technology and tactics was staggering. Conventional bombs had killed hundreds in Guernica. Eight years later, a single atomic explosion extinguished 100,000 lives in Hiroshima in a hellish fireball. Roughly an equal number would die over time from radiation poisoning.

Much of Second General Army Headquarters vanished that morning under the mushroom cloud. Among the countless fallen were Okamoto Hiromi and Harada Keizo, two intelligence officers of the Nakano School assigned to the headquarters. Hosokawa Masashi, who had graduated in the First Class of the Nakano School's Futamata Branch less than a year earlier, lingered for a month before dying of radiation sickness.[2] Later on the day that Hiroshima turned to ashes, Lt. Gen. Arisue Seizo, chief of military intelligence, heard that the city had suffered enormous damage from a particularly destructive bomb. That evening, Arisue and his colleagues at Imperial General Headquarters in Tokyo heard via a monitored American shortwave radio broadcast that the United States had exploded an atomic bomb over Hiroshima.

The next day, Arisue led a survey team of a dozen military and civilian experts, including Dr. Nishina Yoshio, senior scientist for the Army's own atomic bomb project. A distinguished physicist, Nishina had studied in Europe under Lord Rutherford and Niels Bohr throughout most of the 1920s before establishing his own laboratory in Japan in 1931 at the top-notch Institute of Physical and Chemical Research. Nishina had also built Japan's first cyclotron. Ironically, the Army had abandoned its atomic bomb project as impractical only one month before the bombing of Hiroshima and Nagasaki.

Arisue's team reached Hiroshima around 5:30 that evening. The devastation was remarkable. Below the team stretched a blackened landscape where houses and buildings had stood. Here and there stood a lone tree, blasted and stripped of its leaves. At a military airfield four kilometers from ground zero, no soldier was on hand to meet them as the aircraft taxied to a stop. Only once Arisue and his men had deplaned did an officer, the left side of his face burned red and his uniform blasted in tatters, emerge from a bomb shelter to welcome them.

Arisue then went a short distance to Shipping Headquarters. He found the main building intact, but all its windows were shattered. The chief of staff for military water transport briefed him on the damage. That night, in guest quarters littered with glass shards and lit by candles, Arisue dictated his first report to Tokyo. The next day, he went for further briefings at Second General Army Headquarters and Fifty-ninth Army Headquarters. From the ruins of Fifty-ninth Army Headquarters emerged Lt. Gen. Matsumura Shuitsu, chief of staff. He greeted Arisue with the words, "This is war, so it can't be helped." The stoic Matsumura would later win election to the postwar Diet, serving there as a leading advocate for the nation's veterans before passing away in 1962.

The following morning, 9 August, Arisue abruptly left the survey in Dr. Nishina's hands and raced back to IGHQ. Word had reached him of two new disasters. The United States had just dropped a second atomic bomb, this time obliterating much of Nagasaki. Worse still, Stalin had declared war against Japan. The Soviet Red Army was invading Manchukuo. Japan's Kwantung Army, once the pride of the Imperial Japanese Army, had long since lost the strength to defend Japan's puppet empire. With its best units transferred to the home islands or the southern front, defeat was a foregone conclusion.

In Nagasaki, the nuclear attack had devastated the port city. A moment's flash laid waste to the city that had been both a center of Japanese Christianity since the arrival of the Portuguese and Spanish in the fifteenth century and Japan's window to the West during the centuries of seclusion. Tens of thousands died instantly. Others, less fortunate, lingered for days or weeks before succumbing to the radiation.

Lt. Haraguchi Shigehiko of Futamata Branch's First Class, based well offshore on picturesque Fukue, had come to Nagasaki for meetings at district headquarters when the bomb struck. Exposed to the radiation but far enough from ground zero to avoid the blast, he returned to Fukue to continue his duties. When he learned that Tokyo had decided to surrender, he was dead set against it. Returning to Nagasaki on 18 August, he demanded in a meeting with Maj. Gen. Matsuura Hoichi, commanding officer of the Nagasaki District, that Western District's men continue the fight, alone, if necessary. Kyushu's divisions had yet to fight. To accept surrender, particularly after having just seen Nagasaki devastated, must have been more than the young lieutenant could bear. Matsuura, however, had his orders.

Haraguchi, rebuffed, next headed for Kurume to argue Lt. Gen. Yokoyama Isamu out of surrender. The ailing lieutenant failed to gain an audience with the commanding general of Sixteenth Area Army. Fukushima, the vice chief of staff, could only repeat that orders were orders. Haraguchi returned to Nagasaki on 23 August, dejected and exhausted. For solace, he turned to music. Haraguchi dearly loved to play the flute. That evening and the next, he played late into the night. He also pressed the several members of the Nakano School in his district to prepare to strike at the enemy ships when they sailed into port. His comrades argued that disobeying the imperial command to lay down arms would invite harsh retaliation from the occupying troops. Worse, such an act of disobedience would violate the spirit of sacrificing one's self for the empire. Swayed by the appeal to obedience, or perhaps simply too ill, Haraguchi took no further action. He died of radiation poisoning on 25 August.[3]

Prisoners of the Soviet Union

Until the morning of 9 August, imperial Japan had remained at peace with the Soviet Union while waging war against Stalin's allies. This odd state of affairs dated from April 1941, when Tokyo and Moscow had concluded a neutrality pact. The treaty, undertaken to secure Japan's northern flank, played into Tokyo's subsequent decision to strike south. Mired in China and extended as far south as Papua New Guinea, Japan held tight in the north. Tojo turned a deaf ear to Hitler's request for an invasion of the Russian Far East. The Japanese Army had mobilized in the summer of 1941, when the ink was barely dry on the neutrality pact, to invade Siberia in the event Hitler's Wehrmacht conquered European Russia. But the Red Army had held fast that winter. By 1945, Japan's dreams of advancing in conquest to the shores of Lake Baikal had long since faded. Japanese leaders awoke to the grim reality of defending Manchukuo, Korea, and northern Japan against an increasingly likely Soviet invasion.

In desperation, Tokyo had turned to Moscow to negotiate an end to the war. In 1905, imperial Japan had avoided eventual defeat by czarist Russia through a settlement brokered by the United States. With American and British forces poised to inflict a crushing defeat, the Japanese Empire in 1945 turned again to a foreign power to broker a peace treaty. Tokyo offered Moscow a deal, proposing that the Russians join them to compel an end to the Anglo-American offensive. A combination of the Soviet Red Army and Russian oil with the Japanese Navy and natural resources from Japan's new empire in Southeast Asia would make Japan and Russia rulers of the vast Asia-Pacific region. Tokyo also dangled the Chishima Islands and southern Sakhalin, formerly Russian territories. But Japan was too late. President Roosevelt had already agreed at the Yalta Conference that Stalin would receive those in return for a Soviet declaration of war.[4]

Rather than rescue Japan, Stalin sent the Red Army into Manchukuo on 9 August. Japan's Kwantung Army had no hope of defending the borders. The generals planned to make their stand around Tunghua, near Korea. The vast plains of northern Manchukuo offered no defense against the Soviet tanks, but the difficult, mountainous terrain around Tunghua would give the Japanese defenders some chance to halt the offensive. If not, the Kwantung Army could withdraw further across the nearby Yalu River into Korea. But the Japanese defense plans fell apart as the Soviets launched an all-out offensive. Not only did the Red Army drive rapidly through northern Manchuria, but units of the Soviet Twenty-fifth Army crossed the Tumen River on 11 August to invade Korea at Kyonghung, near the borders of Manchukuo and the Soviet Union. On 14 August, Soviet marines of the Pacific Fleet went ashore at Ch'ongjin, a major port on Korea's east coast. Other marine units invaded the Chishima Islands. Still other Soviet units poured into the Japanese half of Sakhalin.[5]

Japanese soldiers, confronting the Red Army at the front, also found peril at the rear. Many Chinese and other peoples chose this moment of crisis to rise against their Japanese overlords. In one case, local tribesmen in northern Manchukuo betrayed to the Red Army the whereabouts of a Japanese Army SSA, whose members were leading some one hundred Japanese civilians to the safety of Inner Mongolia. Nearly all died in the ensuing Soviet attack. Death also came to many of the five thousand Japanese who constituted the core of the puppet Manchukuo Army. A motley force of Chinese, Koreans, Manchurians, and Russians under Japanese command, the Manchukuo Army had served largely as an auxiliary force in "bandit suppression" campaigns. But the force had often proven unreliable, the soldiers at times revolting against their Japanese officers or collaborating with the "bandits." When the Soviets came across the border on 9 August, some Manchurian units followed their Japanese commanders into battle. Others deserted. Some ethnic Chinese and Manchurian officers ordered their subordinates to kill their Japanese superiors. In Manchukuo's final days, some two hundred Japanese died at the hands of their restive troops.[6]

Few of the Nakano School's men in Manchukuo escaped death or captivity. Some died in the days of fierce fighting preceding the surrender. More than five hundred thousand officers and men of the Kwantung Army laid down their arms and awaited their fate. Their number included many of the more than 120 Nakano School graduates assigned to Manchukuo. Maj. Gen. Akigusa Shun was also among the prisoners. Akigusa, one of the Nakano School's founding fathers as well as a top Soviet expert, suffered the bitter fate of witnessing the war's end as the Kwantung Army's intelligence chief. In Harbin, he participated in the surrender talks. The victorious Russians demanded that he turn over Russian linguists from the Kwantung Army to serve as interpreters, a ploy that also served to uncover

Japan's intelligence officers. He was then detained in the city's Yamato Hotel, where began the first interrogation sessions.

Taken to Moscow, Akigusa would appear the following August as a witness at the Moscow trials of Grigory Semenov and Konstantin Rodzaevsky, two prominent White Russians linked to Akigusa as collaborators with the Kwantung Army. Akigusa reportedly died of illness while in captivity near Moscow early in 1949.[7]

The Soviet occupation forces made a priority of tracking down the Kwantung Army's intelligence officers. Many of those arrested were graduates of the Nakano School. As the Kwantung Army had gathered intelligence against the Soviet Union for years, so the Soviets had pieced together the puzzle of Japanese intelligence operations in Manchukuo. Few Japanese intelligence officers escaped the dragnet. In many cases, White Russians who had served as intelligence auxiliaries and agents turned on them. Some betrayed the Japanese in the hopes of saving their own necks. Others acted in revenge against the Japanese for the humiliations heaped on them over the years. White Russians, most Orthodox Christians and many of high status in the former czarist Russia, had suffered various indignities in the service of the Japanese. For example, the Japanese had required their Russian subordinates to bow each morning in the direction of Japan's Imperial Palace and before Shinto shrines.[8]

Among the Japanese intelligence officers caught in the Soviet dragnet was Capt. Baba Yoshimitsu, who had trained at the Nakano School before his assignment to the Chientao SSA. Counterintelligence officers of the Soviet Twenty-fifth Army, which had occupied Chientao, took him into custody on 21 August. Early in his detention, Baba spent time near his childhood home of P'yongyang as the Twenty-fifth Army advanced into northern Korea. Before long, however, his captors sent him into captivity in Siberia. Baba, along with other intelligence officers in captivity, underwent extensive interrogation.

In 1948, Baba would stand trial before a military tribunal and receive a prison sentence for engaging in anti-Soviet activities as a spy. He would then disappear for years into the Soviet Union's vast "gulag archipelago," where hundreds of thousands of Japanese soldiers toiled alongside German POWs and Soviet political prisoners. Moscow began releasing Japanese prisoners in December 1946, letting go those deemed to be pro-Soviet or determined innocent of intelligence activities and other "war crimes." Baba would emerge from captivity only in 1956, however, during a period of thaw in Japanese-Soviet relations, when Moscow released those prisoners who were former intelligence officers or had held key positions in Manchukuo.[9]

Fiery End to Indian Operations

As the Red Army rolled through the plains of Manchukuo, Subhas Chandra Bose was winging his way to Japan's crumbling puppet empire to meet the Soviets. The fiery Bengali nationalist was seeking yet another ally in his quest to free India. Maj. Gen. Isoda Saburo, responsible for intelligence operations against British India as chief of the Hikari Agency, was anxious to have Bose leave Singapore before the British returned. A week earlier, Tokyo had offered refuge to allied leaders throughout Asia. On 14 August, one day before the Emperor Hirohito's surrender broadcast, Isoda and Hachiya Teruo, Tokyo's envoy to Bose's provisional government, had urged Bose to quit Singapore for Japan. President Jose Laurel of the Philippines and Ba Maw of Burma had already taken shelter there. But Bose rejected the offer. He saw little point in hiding in Japan, where Allied forces of occupation would likely find him before long.

More important, he was still determined to drive the British from India. Six years earlier, Bose had left India to fulfill his quest in Germany. There he had broadcast propaganda to India and the Middle East, overseen the forming of an Indian Legion comprised of prisoners of war, and dreamed of entering India in glory. When the Wehrmacht failed to conquer the Soviet Union and reach India, Bose had gone to Asia to join hands with the Japanese. They, too, had now failed him, but Bose remained undaunted. When two members of the Indian Independence League had told him on 12 August of Japan's impending surrender, he had only responded with a smile, "So that is that. Now, what is next?"[10]

After Nazi Germany and imperial Japan, the Soviet Union seemed to Bose his best bet. Bose had begun thinking of working with the Soviets from the time of his third and final visit to Tokyo in October 1944, when he had paid his respects to the new government of Gen. Koiso Kuniaki. In Shanghai, on his return flight from Tokyo, Bose had met Anand Mohan Sahay, an Indian resident of Japan. Bose had requested that Sahay make contact in Tokyo with Ambassador Yakov Malik. But Foreign Minister Shigemitsu Mamoru and other Japanese officials had denied him what they termed a "useless" meeting with Malik. Following Germany's surrender in May 1945, Bose again tried to open a "second front" by contacting Tokyo through an intermediary. The Japanese in June discouraged him again, saying that it was hopeless to intercede with the Soviets for him. The decision was made that he should go to Manchukuo to contact the Soviets.[11]

In leaping from the Axis to the center of world communism, Bose was acting according to the ancient political adage that the enemy of one's enemy is one's friend. Great Britain and Russia for more than a century had competed for power in Central Asia. If London were to lose India, then Moscow stood to gain. Japanese leaders, for their part, also had their reasons for letting Bose go. Tokyo, the war lost, could still strike at London by having Bose continue subverting British rule in India from the Soviet Union.

Bose and an assistant left Saigon on 17 August for Manchuria in a converted Army bomber. To finance his new venture, Bose took with him 80 kg of diamonds and other precious items. He was flying for the port of Dairen. Once there, he planned to strike a deal with the Russians and enter the Soviet Union.[12] With Bose and his assistant was Lt. Gen. Shidei Tsunamasa, recently appointed the Kwantung Army's vice chief of staff. The plane completed the first part of its journey the next morning, landing at Taihoku Airfield in Taiwan. After lunch, Bose and the other passengers again boarded the plane. But the aircraft had barely left the ground when its port propeller broke away. The crippled bomber crashed nose first into the ground some one hundred meters past the runway. Shidei died on the spot. Bose staggered from the burning wreckage, his head bleeding and his clothes on fire. Taken to a nearby military hospital, he died that night from his burns. His last words were reportedly: "India will be free before long. Long live Free India."[13]

The Japanese, having offered Bose refuge in the last days of his life, sheltered him after his death. The Japanese Army first cremated his remains, then kept the ashes at Nishi Honganji, the largest Japanese Buddhist temple in Taihoku. On 5 September, three days after the surrender, Japanese Army officers secretly flew Bose's ashes to Tokyo. Members of the Hikari Agency and other officers then took them in secret to Renkoji, a temple of Japan's Nichiren Buddhist sect, for a secret funeral service on 18 September. Later, Japanese intelligence operatives most closely associated with Indian intelligence operations—Arisue Seizo, Isoda Saburo, Iwakuro Hideo, and Takaoka Daisuke—would form with other associates and admirers of the Bengali nationalist in Tokyo the Subhas Chandra Bose Academy. The old boys of Japanese intelligence would honor their greatest wartime partner throughout the Occupation and the years beyond.[14]

Caches and Guerrillas

Lt. Gen. Arisue Seizo knew that the war was coming to an end. The enemy was coming to Japan. An astute intelligence officer, Arisue also understood that Japan would have an opportunity to gain from the emerging confrontation pitting the United States and Great Britain against the Soviet Union. On the eve of surrender, Arisue called to his office a staff officer for a special mission. Capt. Amano Terumi had worked in Fifth Section of Arisue's Second Bureau since graduating from the Nakano School in 1941. He was one of the few members of the Nakano School still at Second Bureau. Most of the others had transferred to various army commands to fight on the front lines in the final battle for Japan. In Fifth Section, Amano had gathered intelligence in the Soviet Union while acting as a diplomatic courier on trips to and from Moscow along the Trans-Siberian Railroad. He had also posed once as a sailor to gather intelligence on Nakhodka, where he had spent a week secretly sketching the port. Most of his work at Fifth Section had involved military topography.

In his office, Arisue instructed Amano on his new mission. He was to gather up his section's topographical intelligence and hide it. He was to keep hidden the Japanese Army's detailed intelligence on Manchuria and Siberia until such time as Arisue could use it as leverage with the United States. Arisue was astute in seeing the advantage in having Soviet intelligence at hand to offer the United States. He was not the only intelligence chief to prepare such caches. Gen. Reinhard Gehlen, wartime chief of the Wehrmacht's Soviet intelligence organization, Fremde Heere Ost (FHO, or Foreign Armies East), had ordered his men several months earlier to hide his crates of Wehrmacht intelligence in the mountains of Bavaria as bargaining chips with the Americans.

Amano, assisted by a lieutenant, gathered the secret documents and placed them in fourteen large trunks. On the afternoon of 15 August, following the Emperor's surrender broadcast, Amano and his assistant left on their mission. The two parted company, each with a share of the intelligence. Amano took his trunks to Hyogo Prefecture. His assistant went to Mie Prefecture. Each year, in the absence of other instructions, they were to meet at the Isei Shrine in Mie Prefecture on 15 August to confer on the disposition of their documents.[15]

Arisue, having arranged the intelligence caches as bargaining chips, also approved a plan for fighting in the event the Occupation proved unbearable. Involved was Maj. Inomata Jinya, a member of the Nakano School's First Class. Inomata had worked largely against the Soviet target since graduating in 1939 from the Nakano School.

When surrender seemed inevitable, Inomata had approached Col. Shiraki Suenari with a proposal for resistance. The young officer had already discussed fighting the Occupation forces with majors Hata Masanori and Tarora Sadao, both early graduates of the Nakano School. Shiraki, chief of Second Bureau's Fifth Section, knew Inomata from the days when the young intelligence officer had served under him in KAHIS. In advance of the Occupation, proposed Inomata, the Army should prepare caches of weapons and supplies. Intelligence officers of the Nakano School, resident in their hometowns throughout Japan, would monitor and report on the actions of Occupation authorities in their area. If need be, they would wage a guerrilla campaign against the foreign troops and Japanese collaborators. Shiraki approved of Inomata's concept, wrote a memo outlining his plan, and sent the document up the chain of command. Arisue then approved it, as did his superior, Lt. Gen. Kawabe Torashiro, the Japanese Army's vice chief of staff. The next step was to instruct the Nakano School. Shiraki ordered Maj. Tarora Sadao to go to Tomioka, Gunma Prefecture, to pass the new orders to the Nakano School.[16]

Well before Inomata made his proposal, AGS had pondered how best to wage guerrilla warfare in the home islands. The Nakano School, tasked with planning irregular combat involving civilians, had devised principles of guerrilla warfare and put together a covert organization. Within the Nakano School, unknown to Inomata and nearly everyone else, certain soldiers moved beyond the school's basic curriculum. The Nakano School had prepared a unit to wage guerrilla warfare in the home islands. The instructors were members of a select group. Among them was Capt. Komata Yozo, who had fought with distinction as a commando leader in the "green hell" of New Guinea. Maj. Yamamoto Kiyokatsu, one of several instructors who had researched and field-tested guerrilla tactics, was another leader. The unit's name was Izumi, or spring. Its members would well forth, like water from underground, to wage war.[17]

In advance of the Nakano School's closing, the members of the Izumi Unit had left to prepare for guerrilla warfare. Some returned to their original regiments. Others, posing as civilians, quietly went home. Even within the Nakano School, few knew of the Izumi Unit's existence. The elite members of the secret unit had undergone intense training between June and August. Much of the focus was on using explosives. They also learned how to take advantage of the mountains and valleys running throughout Japan, to enlist civilians in their terror campaigns, and to use civilian runners to avoid radio interception. Much of the teaching was based on lessons learned in Okinawa. The reports to Tokyo from Okinawa on the use of civilians influenced the Izumi Unit's training.[18]

In Tomioka, Maj. Gen. Yamamoto Hayashi prepared to execute the order from Tokyo of 11 August that he close the Nakano School. Only days earlier, the latest class of students had arrived to begin their training. Two days later, Yamamoto sent two subordinates to Tokyo for details on the coming surrender. That same day, he ordered the destruction of the school's secrets. Billowing clouds of smoke rose over the school as secret documents, weapons, and communications gear burned to ashes. It was a scene repeated throughout the Japanese Empire, as military officers and civilian officials set their secrets ablaze.

Imperial General Headquarters also took care to eliminate evidence of its secret projects at the Noborito Research Institute. On 15 August, Army Affairs Section ordered the destruction of all materials pertaining to the military's "special research." First on the list was the Noborito Research Institute and its balloon bomb program. Also listed was the Kwantung Army's Unit 731, which had conducted lethal experiments on captives to develop biological weapons.[19] From the Noborito Research Institute's dispersed sites in Nagano Prefecture and elsewhere rose smoke from burning documents and materials. At one of the laboratory sites, the unit commander gave his forty subordinates a final order. They were to disperse as members of an underground resistance network. If summoned, they would wage guerrilla warfare against the coming Occupation.[20]

On the morning of 15 August, Yamamoto called an assembly in the courtyard of the Nakano School. At noon, they all listened for the first time on the radio to the voice of their emperor. In silence, they heard him call on his subjects to "bear the unbearable" by accepting surrender. Once the radio fell silent, it was time for Yamamoto to conduct his final ceremony as commandant. After issuing final instructions in a voice wracked with emotion, he approached the Nanko Shrine, which he had ordered brought from Nakano when the school had withdrawn to Tomioka. As his final act as commandant, Yamamoto set the shrine ablaze. The Nakano School had ceased to exist.

Later that day, the students began leaving for their hometowns, where they would lie low and await further instructions. The staff also dispersed, following a final meeting that evening marked by tears and a last singing of the school song. Only a few individuals remained the next morning to continue disposing of weapons and equipment. Some they distributed to local troops, police, and government officials. They buried other weapons at the school in the event of a future uprising. By late August, their work done, the last of the Nakano School's members left Tomioka.[21]

Attending the Nakano School's final ceremony at Tomioka were most of the instructors from the school's Futamata Branch. After receiving the same day their orders to close their training center, they returned to break the news to the students of the Fourth Class. On first hearing the order to close Futamata Branch, the students swore continued resistance and refused to leave. The commandant settled the dangerous situation by promoting each student to sergeant and ordering him to return to his prior unit. Then, following orders received at Tomioka, the staff and students set to destroying the school's ammunition and equipment. As of 25 August, three days before General MacArthur's advance party touched down at Atsugi Air Base, the Futamata Branch was no more.[22]

Hiding an Ally and a Prince

The men of the Nakano School were ready to wage war against the Occupation forces. Some also planned to defy the victors by hiding two fugitives. One, Ba Maw, was the wartime leader of Burma. The

British were determined to find him. A second plan was to hide a Japanese prince to ensure the survival of the imperial line in the event that the Allies executed Emperor Hirohito and his family. The two plans emerged in the final, feverish days before surrender. Senior graduates of the Nakano School, alerted to the government's decision to accept the surrender terms stipulated in the Potsdam Declaration, met in Tokyo the night of 10 August to discuss what action to take. Maj. Inomata Jinya was among members of the assembled First Class.

They listened as Lt. Col. Shiizaki Jiro called on them to join him and other officers in thwarting the surrender. Shiizaki impressed many of his listeners with his forceful appeal. Maj. Kubota Ichiro, one of the Nakano School's First Class, was among those ready to join the plot. Just as officers appeared on the verge of backing the plotters, Maj. Hata Masanori joined the heated discussion. Hata, an officer in Second Bureau's Fifth Section, had worked for a time on German intelligence after training at the Nakano School. Speaking with the cool detachment of a professional intelligence officer, he warned his colleagues against joining an insurrection that had no prospect of saving Japan. Hata argued as an expert on Germany. He pointed out Hitler's error of fighting the enemy to the point of collapse on German soil. Hata called on his comrades to reject rebellion in the interest of reconstructing Japan. He won over his audience. Kubota and the others declined to join the doomed plot. Shiizaki and other young officers involved failed to win the backing of senior military commanders. Several days later, after the insurrection failed, Shiizaki committed suicide.[23]

Having rejected one course of action, men of the Nakano School elected another. Lt. Col. Hirose Eiichi, a specialist in communications intelligence, was the AGS point of contact for the Nakano School. Meeting in secret with a few senior members of the Nakano School, he put on the table a proposal to safeguard Japan's imperial line. In surrendering, Japan was risking the security of the emperor and his family. The Soviets had brutally murdered their own Czar Nicholas II and his family. In the United States, opinion polls were showing that roughly a third of Americans favored Hirohito's immediate execution; roughly another third called for his trial as a war criminal, imprisonment, or exile.[24]

Hirose's plan was to take young Prince Michihisa of the imperial Kitashirakawa family into hiding to ensure the survival of the line in the event the Allies executed the others. Hirose viewed the young prince, a grandson of Emperor Meiji, as close enough to the throne to be regarded as a legitimate successor without being so close as to attract the attention of Occupation authorities when he disappeared. Hirose's intention to safeguard a distant relation was a sound one. In fact, Arisue had only just rejected the proposal of another military officer to hide Crown Prince Akihito on the grounds that the Occupation authorities would immediately notice his absence and go hunting for him.[25] Hirose's choice also stemmed from his having attended the Military Academy with the father of the young prince, so he knew the family. He had recently visited them in June, on his return to Tokyo from inspecting the mammoth underground military headquarters under construction at Matsushiro, Nagano Prefecture.[26]

At the same time that Hirose was convincing members of the Nakano School to carry out his plan to safeguard the imperial line, Japan's Foreign Ministry enlisted their aid in hiding a fugitive Japanese ally. Ba Maw, in retreat from Rangoon, had fled Southeast Asia at the war's end to avoid capture, or worse. A few days before the Japanese surrender, British aircraft had riddled with bullets a house occupied by him. Ba Maw had left Burma in the company of the Japanese ambassador via the Siam-Burma Railway, reaching Bangkok on 22 August. From there he had flown to Taiwan before reaching Tokyo.[27]

The Foreign Ministry had two choices regarding their Burmese protégé. One was to hand him over to the British. The other was to hide him until he was no longer a wanted man. In the end, officials of the Axis faction prevailed upon Foreign Minister Shigemitsu Mamoru to hide their ally. Ba Maw left Tokyo with a Foreign Ministry official to hide in remote Niigata Prefecture, across the mountains from Tokyo on the Japan Sea coast. Ba Maw took refuge in Rakushoji temple, his identity supposedly that of a Manchurian.[28]

In late August, Inomata met in Tokyo with a classmate to hear his report on preparations for Prince Michihisa's hiding place. Maj. Kubota Ichiro, a fellow member of the Nakano School's First Class, had some shocking news for him. Kubota had gone to the town of Muikka, in Niigata Prefecture, to seek the aid of a local resident he knew. Imanari Takuzo's patriotism as a youth leader, wealth as the owner of a ham factory, and residence in a remote corner of Japan had qualified him in Kubota's eyes as an ideal member of the operation.

However, as he briefed Inomata, Kubota learned from Imanari that the Foreign Ministry had already pressed him to hide Ba Maw. Kubota, a quick-tempered idealist from Kyushu, had readily agreed.

Inomata listened in disbelief, then argued against Kubota's decision. Hiding the fugitive Burmese would almost certainly expose their original plan. But Kubota remained firm. He insisted that abandoning a wartime ally would be immoral and leave Japan without credibility in future relations with Southeast Asia. In any event, he explained, he had already given his word. Kubota had also left Maj. Koshimaki Katsuji, a fellow classmate fluent in English, at Muikka to look after Ba Maw. In the end, Inomata yielded uneasily. There were now two operations: Azuma (East), for Ba Maw, and Honmaru (Inner Citadel), for Prince Michihisa. Financing both operations was Maj. Abe Naoyoshi, who had spent the war at Second Bureau as a staff intelligence officer in the Anglo-American section following repatriation from his covert mission in Bombay.[29]

Inomata then left on the next phase of his mission: forging a false identity for the prince. His destination was Hiroshima. In ruins, the city was the ideal place to create a false paper trail that would be difficult to trace. Meanwhile, in a remote corner of Niigata Prefecture, the fugitive Burmese leader remained in the care of several members of the Nakano School. With little to do, Ba Maw passed the time taking walks in the woods, teaching Imanari English, conversing with Koshimaki, and entertaining his hosts by singing such Japanese wartime hits as *"Shina no Yoru"* ("China Nights") at banquets.

Meeting in Manila

Japan's unprecedented decision to surrender required an extraordinary government. Following the painful decision, the government of Adm. Suzuki Kantaro resigned. His successor was Gen. Prince Higashikuni Naruhiko, who had held a number of senior positions within the Army and was also a relative, by marriage, to Emperor Hirohito. There was no modern precedent for an officer prince to take the reins of government. Japan's imperial family had reigned, not ruled, over modern Japan. But the times called for extraordinary measures. The Japanese Army, the single most important variable in the political equation, was in an uproar. Rebel officers in Tokyo, including Shiizaki, had launched a coup d'etat, killing the commander of the imperial guards in a failed bid to gain custody of the emperor and stop the pending surrender. In the field, the Japanese Army remained largely intact. Gen. Count Terauchi Hisaichi, commander of Southern Army, cabled from his Saigon headquarters that Tokyo should reject the Potsdam Declaration.

It was such military unrest, as well as a fear of popular revolution, that brought Higashikuni to lead the government. For added measure, Emperor Hirohito instructed other officer princes to convey the imperial will to Japanese military commanders overseas. Gen. Prince Kanin Haruhito went to Saigon and Singapore as imperial emissary to Terauchi's Southern Army; Gen. Prince Asaka Yasuhiko went to Nanking and Peping to brief Gen. Okamura Yasuji's China Expeditionary Army; and Lt. Col. Prince Takeda Tsunenori went to Hsinking to order the Kwantung Army to cease fighting.[30]

When Higashikuni took office as premier on 17 August, his first task was to send a mission to Manila to confer with General MacArthur's staff on the details of the coming military occupation. He appointed Lt. Gen. Kawabe Torashiro to lead a group of sixteen principal members and two interpreters. The Army dominated the mission, with seven of the sixteen principals. Another six delegates were naval officers. There were also two civilian officials of the Foreign Ministry.

The Japanese mission had a distinct intelligence coloring to it. Kawabe, an aviation officer from Toyama Prefecture, was an accomplished intelligence officer. His career included tours as military attaché to Moscow (1932–34) and Berlin (1938–39), as well as time in Manchuria as intelligence chief of the Kwantung Army (1935–36). In Manchuria, he had formed in 1936 the Asano Unit, a unit of White Russians.[31] Maj. Gen. Amano Masakazu, another delegate, had directed Anglo-American intelligence in Second Bureau. Colonels Yamamoto Arata and Takakura Morio had both held intelligence positions as senior members of Second Bureau's Eighth Section.[32] Even the two interpreters, lieutenants Otake Sadao and Takeuchi Harumi, belonged to Second Bureau. There were also intelligence officers among the naval officers. Of the two diplomats in the mission, Okazaki Katsuo was director of the Foreign Ministry Intelligence Bureau.

Kawabe's group left Tokyo on 19 August, flying in secret from Kisarazu Air Base to avoid possible attacks by opponents of the surrender. Picking up an American fighter escort en route, the delegates reached Manila the same day. Awaiting the arrival of their aircraft at Nichols Field were General MacArthur's intelligence officers.[33]

MacArthur had granted his intelligence chief, Maj. Gen. Charles Willoughby, a "prominent role" for G-2 in the Manila surrender negotiations. Willoughby had lobbied for such a role on the strength of his staff's "detailed knowledge of the strength and dispositions of the Imperial Japanese Forces" as well as the General Staff structure "and other military organs." He also won for G-2 oversight of Japan's military demobilization.[34]

Willoughby was of striking appearance and background. He was a bear of a man, muscular in build and second only to MacArthur in height.[35] Born Karl Weidenbach in Germany, son of a German father and American mother, he had left for the United States at the age of eighteen. Adopting the English form of his given name and his mother's maiden name, Charles Willoughby joined the Army, serving in France in the First World War. In his early intelligence career, he served as military attaché in Colombia, Ecuador, and Venezuela. He then spent ten years at the Command and General Staff College at Fort Leavenworth, where his lectures in military history first brought him to MacArthur's attention. Following his assignment as G-4, in charge of logistics, under MacArthur in the Philippines, Willoughby assumed responsibility for intelligence as G-2 after he withdrew with MacArthur to Australia in early 1942.[36]

As an intelligence officer, Willoughby has earned poor reviews. According to Col. Sydney Mashbir, his subordinate in charge of the Allied Translator and Interpreter Service: "Willoughby was a good combat soldier . . . He was a very gallant officer in action. Several times he rallied Philippine battalions and brought them back into the fighting. But as an intelligence officer, he was nix."[37] Even MacArthur saw Willoughby as less than great as an intelligence officer.[38]

In his favor, Willoughby showed MacArthur a loyalty that bordered on worship. According to Brig. Gen. Elliott Thorpe, MacArthur's counterintelligence chief: "Willoughby had a good deal of personal charm, and he and Courtney Whitney were the only two men I know of who could successfully flatter MacArthur and get away with it."[39] More "Prussian" than American, Willoughby would click his heels together and bow from the waist rather than nod his head. He also made a habit of kissing the hands of women he met. He was also rather sensitive about those who called him "Prussian." In a postwar interview with the historian D. Clayton James, Willoughby remarked regarding Gen. Walter Krueger, commanding officer of MacArthur's Sixth Army: "He was German born. At least I have an American mother." Such mannerisms and a deadly serious demeanor earned him the nickname "Sir Charles." A man easily upset, who would launch into tirades in a high-pitched voice, he became an object of ribbing from the more playful senior officers on MacArthur's staff.[40]

Willoughby was the point man in the impending military occupation of Japan. It was he and his staff who were on hand to greet the arriving Japanese mission. Col. Sydney Mashbir met the delegates. As Kawabe led his delegation from their aircraft onto the airfield, he strode forward to shake Mashbir's hand. The colonel moved to accept the general's gesture, when he remembered the presence of reporters and photographers on hand to record the historic moment. At the last second, Mashbir jerked away his hand. The press thus recorded what appeared to be a snub on the part of the victors. It was an awkward beginning.

What the press failed to record was far more interesting. The ensuing talks proceeded far more favorably for Japan than was apparent outside the conference room. The agenda was determined to an extent by the political ambitions of Gen. Douglas MacArthur. Having reached the pinnacle of his career as a five-star general, he now coveted the White House. As early as the 1944 election, while waging war in the Southwest Pacific, he had allowed political backers in the Republican Party to put his name into play as a presidential candidate. In Manila, the victorious general's mind was fixed on the 1948 election. Richard Nixon recalled years later how both MacArthur and Gen. Dwight D. Eisenhower, hero of Normandy and MacArthur's rival, had both coveted the Oval Office. The difference, according to Nixon, was that only MacArthur had let his ambition show. His machinations were so transparent "he gave every appearance in 1948 of running for office while on active duty in Japan."[41]

MacArthur calculated that his victories in the Pacific had given him a chance at winning his party's nomination and election to the White House. A successful military occupation of Japan would enhance his credentials as a leader. On the other hand, Japanese resistance would tarnish his record. Leading the largest invasion in history, his ambition in Operation Olympic, could have made him a hero. Fighting a thankless guerrilla war after the surrender would not play well with Americans, who wanted their "boys" home and out of the military.

Kawabe was thus in a position to turn the specter of domestic upheaval to Japan's advantage. While the Japanese mission had ostensibly flown to Manila to take orders, MacArthur's team soon found themselves negotiating the terms of what was supposed to have been unconditional surrender. Learning of the failed military rebellion in Tokyo and of unrest in the capital area among fighter pilots at Atsugi Air Base, where MacArthur was to land, the American side acceded to the Japanese request for a delay. MacArthur's advance team was to have departed Manila for Atsugi on 21 August. That same day, however, Gen. Richard Sutherland, who was presiding over the talks, agreed to Kawabe's request that the team wait until 26 August to allow the Japanese military leaders time to bring order within the military.[42] Sutherland, aware that MacArthur required Japanese cooperation to land without incident, had little choice.

In the end, MacArthur's presidential ambition and the Japanese government's cooperative posture contributed to saving Japan from direct military rule. MacArthur's staff conveyed to Kawabe's mission that Japanese officials would implement Occupation directives. Japan would retain its government, including the imperial institution. In the words of General MacArthur's history of the Occupation, his forces would gradually occupy "designated areas after the Japanese had disarmed the local troops. No direct demilitarization was to be carried out by Allied personnel; the Japanese were to control the disarmament and demobilization of their own armed forces under Allied supervision."[43]

What was behind the decision to move softly into Japan? An appreciation of the advantage of harnessing imperial prestige was one consideration. The Japanese leadership had forestalled rebellion by having the emperor announce Japan's surrender, and sending imperial princes to convey that decision to field commanders must have made an impression. Another factor was the cooperative posture of the Kawabe mission. The choice was clear: work through Japanese officials or risk continued fighting.

Apart from the threat of regular troops rebelling, MacArthur's headquarters must also have dreaded the prospect of guerrilla warfare. Willoughby, the former military history instructor, had long ago learned the danger of guerrilla war to military occupation. He drew a somber lesson from Napoleon's disastrous attempt to suppress Spanish guerrillas: "Armies of occupation in territories overrun by patriot bands are on continuous nerve-racking alert; such an army is not popular at home, in enemy country, and with itself, and watchful waiting is apt to become very tiresome." He capped his lesson by borrowing the words of the Italian statesman Count Camillo de Cavour: "You can do anything with bayonets except sit on them."[44]

MacArthur's staff likely also worried over the covert threat of the Japanese Army's illusive SSAs. American and British intelligence had long ago detected a shadowy network of intelligence officers and agents operating in China and Southeast Asia. In the Philippines, the Japanese Army had committed nearly one hundred graduates of the Nakano School. It is quite possible that MacArthur's G-2 discovered their presence on the islands. In the battle for Okinawa, dozens more shadow warriors of the Nakano School had fought. By then, MacArthur's CI agents were on the lookout for them. Lt. Frank Gibney's prisoner of war interrogation report of Shimada Akira, a civilian, pointed to the Nakano School or a similar offshoot. The report stated that Shimada had joined the Peking SSA on the recommendation of Lt. Gen Cho Isamu in 1939, "without having to attend the special school maintained for training the members of this organization."

In August, a CIC report, issued in Okinawa, pointed to the Nakano School in its listing of priority CI targets in Korea. *CIC Area Study, Korea*, in a paragraph on the SSA target, stated: "Members of the unit [sic] are well trained, being graduates of special courses of instruction in Tokyo." Despite vague knowledge of the Nakano School's role in training intelligence operatives, the U.S. Army was largely at sea. The same CIC report, for example, suggested U.S. military intelligence considered the SSAs to be a single organization, believed Gen. Doihara Kenji to be its commanding officer, and assumed its local headquarters to be in Keijo (Seoul). The CIC was wrong on all three counts. Doihara, while well known as commanding officer of SSAs in China during the 1930s, had no authority over them by 1945. As for Korea, there was no SSA in Keijo. The sole SSA on the peninsula was in the north, in Najin, North Hamgyong Province, close to the meeting of the Korean, Soviet, and Manchurian borders. Graduates of the Nakano School did serve at Najin, Korea Army Headquarters, and other units. The lack of solid intelligence on Japan's covert organizations was by no means confined to CIC. On

15 August, the day of Japan's surrender, the Military Intelligence Department in Washington issued an intelligence bulletin that included a section on the Japanese Army's technical laboratories. The classified report drew a blank as to the functions of the Ninth Technical Research Institute, or Noborito Research Institute.[45]

Fittingly, the man with the answers to their questions was MacArthur's guest in Manila. Kawabe, after all, had backed Arisue in authorizing the proposal for Nakano School veterans to monitor the Occupation. As Arisue's direct superior, moreover, Kawabe was in a position to know the details of Japanese military intelligence. In any event, whether MacArthur's intelligence staff suspected Kawabe as a key to their concerns or not, they treated him well. Following the day's discussions, Kawabe had spent the evening drinking beer with some of MacArthur's staff officers. He had come away with the impression that there were no hard feelings among the international fraternity of professional military officers. On returning to his hotel room in the early morning, he found a gift of cigarettes and whiskey, courtesy of Willoughby.

The next day, once the talks had ended, Kawabe left the conference room for the airfield in the company of Willoughby and Mashbir. Kawabe's awkward arrival, when Mashbir had refused to shake his outstretched hand, now seemed long ago. In the sedan taking the three to the waiting aircraft, Kawabe conversed freely with his new partners. With Willoughby, he spoke in German; with Mashbir, Japanese. When the car arrived at Nichols, Kawabe received Mashbir's extended hand. Willoughby then accompanied him to his seat and shook his hand. Kawabe must have been pleased at how well the mission had ended as Willoughby wished him "auf wiedersehen."[46]

MacArthur likely expected that he had struck a good bargain with Kawabe. In return for a lenient Occupation administered by Japanese officials, those same authorities would guarantee a peaceful Occupation. As MacArthur told his staff, "It is my earnest hope that pending the formal accomplishment of the Instrument of Surrender, armistice conditions may prevail on every front and that bloodless surrender may be effectuated."[47] It is possible that MacArthur's family history influenced his willingness to strike a bargain. His own father, Gen. Arthur MacArthur, had led the campaign at the turn of the century in the Philippines to suppress the guerrilla movement for independence. The stage was now set for an Occupation far different from that first foreseen. Prior to the Manila Conference, a top-secret document for "Blacklist," the occupation of Japan, predicted resistance: "It is probable that there will be resistance in some form or another to the terms of surrender . . . Under these circumstances, it may be necessary to impose certain sanctions or to employ reprisals." The document further noted that "every Japanese national is an enemy" and that "sabotage and under-ground resistance are doubly menacing because of complicated language and race psychology." Intelligence measures to implement the surrender included "arrest and/or Intelligence control" of the Kempeitai, SSA members, and those participating in other targeted organizations.[48]

Following Kawabe's mission to Manila, however, prospects seemed much brighter. In a memo for Sutherland, Willoughby did not foresee an occupation similar to the kind imposed on a prostrate Germany. He thus found fault with the "initial drafts" of instructions for the Occupation, finding a "punitive strain, based on erroneous premises" made with Germany as the model. However, according to Willoughby, "the German occupation involved the complete dissolution of a hostile Government and its ideology; Japanese occupation involves its complete maintenance and the use of a specific ideology, the Shinto basis of secular Government." He then referred to the Manila Conference: "The formal meeting with Japanese Emissaries, our requirements and their compliance, specifically provided for the utilization of military and other Governmental channels and agencies. The enormous initial discrepancy between US occupation forces and available Japanese major units is so complete that punitive or disciplinary features are impracticable now and may become fatal, if initiated prematurely." The solution was a partnership with the Japanese military in which he would play the lead role.[49]

An Oasis for Arisue

Arisue Seizo was at Atsugi Air Base on 28 August as chief of the official reception committee gathered to welcome General MacArthur's advance party. A typhoon had delayed the arrival of 150 communications experts and engineers, led by Col. Charles Tench, by two days. Briefed in advance by Kawabe on how well the Manila talks had gone, Arisue had every reason to feel confident that the Occupation would begin well. Kawabe had reported that the Americans did not appear vindictive. If circumstances required, however, Arisue had prepared for the worst. He had recently turned over six million yen to the Nakano School's last commandant, Maj. Gen. Yamamoto Hayashi, who had come to him on 18 August to obtain funds for postsurrender covert operations.

When the advance party landed, Arisue led them to a tent for refreshments. Seeing that his guests hesitated to drink the offered lemonade, Arisue downed a glass to show that he had no intention of poisoning them. Shortly thereafter, two uniformed members of the Soviet military attaché office in Tokyo appeared on the scene. Testing the waters, Arisue asked an American officer about the two Russians. The American replied brusquely that the Soviets had nothing to do with them. At that moment, Arisue concluded that the alliance between the United States and the Soviet Union would not last much beyond the end of the war. Moreover, Japan's intelligence chief foresaw that Japan would gain from the estrangement between the two emerging superpowers the margin of maneuver necessary to rise from the ashes of defeat.[50] Two days later, Arisue was again on hand at Atsugi, this time greeting General MacArthur and his staff.

The choice of Arisue to conduct initial military liaison with MacArthur's arriving forces was natural, but contentious. Given indications that MacArthur's G-2 would play the lead in liaison, it was appropriate for Tokyo to select the chief of Japanese military intelligence. Even so, Prime Minister Higashikuni had hesitated before appointing Arisue, concerned over his well-known ties to the deposed Italian dictator Benito Mussolini. Indeed, Arisue's admiration for Il Duce and love of Italy had earned him the reputation as an officer who had "gone Italian."[51] Arisue had first gone to Italy in 1928 to study military strategy; he did so until ordered to take command of a battalion in late 1931. In August 1936, he had returned to Rome as military attaché.

In a meeting to determine whether Arisue was a suitable choice, a member of Higashikuni's cabinet raised the issue of his fascist connections. Arisue averred that he had indeed liked and admired Mussolini. However, Arisue continued, he was not a fascist but a Japanese soldier. Moreover, his years of experience in Italy and North China had left him well versed in international etiquette and without any inferiority complex in dealing with Westerners. Indeed, he was skilled at dealing with them. For example, the twin punch of American atom bombs and Soviet tanks in August 1945 had led Japan to surrender. Yet, when interrogated during the Occupation on the cause of Japan's defeat, Arisue cited MacArthur's genius as a general.[52] Nor was he a stranger to issues concerning occupied territory. He had served in Japan's North China Army when that army was maneuvering to turn northern China into another Manchuria. Intelligence officers of the North China Army were those who governed occupied areas. In the end, Higashikuni approved the Japanese Army's "Italian" intelligence chief to head the reception committee.

The Higashikuni government's preparations for the Occupation far exceeded simple liaison. Tokyo prepared nothing less than a campaign on multiple fronts to influence the Occupation at every level. First, aiming for the top, the Japanese mustered every military officer, civilian official, and businessman with American experience. The Japanese Army made sure that such old "American hands" as generals Kamada Senichi, Oi Shigemoto, and Haraguchi Hatsutaro lost no time in renewing their ties to the American officers they had known before the war.[53]

Aware of religion's influence in American life, Japan's leaders also brought their prominent Christians to the fore. The Japanese authorities had long included religion as an arrow in their propaganda quiver. Hoshino Naoki, Japan's top civilian official in Manchukuo, made Muto Tomio the puppet empire's propaganda chief with the expectation that Muto would put his Christian background to good use in dealings with the West. Prime Minister Higashikuni brought into his cabinet one of Japan's most eminent Christian activists, Kagawa Toyohiko.[54]

Japan's campaign to play on religious sensibilities reached the personal level. Arisue, for example, learned that Gen. Robert Eichelberger, commanding officer of MacArthur's Eighth Army, was a Roman Catholic, so he arranged to have fish delivered to him on Fridays. How impressed the general was with the gesture is unclear. Eichelberger was far from admiring of the Japanese when he reached Japan a few hours ahead of MacArthur on 30 August. He recalled his reception in the following words: "I conferred unprofitably with a Japanese general named Arisuye [sic]." Eichelberger, chief of military intelligence for the American Expeditionary Forces in Siberia following the First World War, had faulted the Japanese for their support of the Cossack Ataman Semenov and others he deemed "murderous wretches" among the White Russians.

Japan's religious campaign surely played well with MacArthur, an Episcopalian fond of invoking the Deity in nearly every public utterance. The journalist John Gunther once described MacArthur's pleasure on receiving an autographed portrait of the Pope: "He even goes so far as to think of himself and the Pope as the two leading representatives of Christianity today. The Pope fights on the spiritual front, so to speak, while he tackles communism on the ground."[55]

While taking heed of the spiritual, Japanese officials did not shrink from catering to the carnal. On 18 August, the Higashikuni government created the Recreation and Amusements Association (RAA), an official system of brothels for the incoming American soldiers. With the considerable sum of a million yen, the RAA established a chain of "comfort stations" to serve as a "sexual breakwater" against the GI tide. The RAA would save "decent" Japanese women from dishonor while taking the edge off battle-hardened soldiers. The organization was no hidden affair. An RAA advertisement run in the 1 October 1945 edition of the *Nippon Times* began: "Grand Amusement Facilities Now Established for the Occupation Forces. Please Proceed to RAA Establishments!" MacArthur was a veteran commander who understood the reality of camp life. He simply turned a blind eye to all the "comfort" that ensued. Faubion Bowers, one of Willoughby's intelligence officers, jokingly gave Tokyo high marks for its comfort policy in an interview years later: "That's why Japan won the war."[56]

Arisue, buoyed by his positive assessment of the receptions at Atsugi on 28 and 30 August, soon had even more reason for optimism. On 31 August, he received a telephone call from the Grand Hotel in Yokohama, where MacArthur had established his initial headquarters. Arisue was delighted to hear the voice of Col. Frederick P. Munson on the other end of the line. Munson, who had landed at Atsugi the previous day, had received orders three days earlier from General Sutherland to act as liaison officer to the First Demobilization Ministry (Japanese Army) and Foreign Office. Munson was expert in Japanese military affairs and fluent in the language. He had first landed in Japan as a language student in 1932. In the winter of 1935–36, he had observed the Japanese Army while attached for six months to the Tenth Division's Tenth Field Artillery Regiment at Himeji. From Japan, Munson had gone to Peping as an assistant to Col. Joseph Stilwell, who required an officer fluent in Japanese for his reporting on the Japanese military's activities in North China.[57]

Arisue thus knew Munson from the years before the war. For Arisue, hearing Munson's voice was like "stumbling upon an oasis in the desert" or "meeting Buddha in hell." Arisue found Munson, fluent in Japanese, as a man who "understood the psychology of the Japanese and the feelings of the Japanese military 100 percent." With Munson as his guardian angel, Arisue's lingering anxieties lessened greatly. Indeed, the next twelve months of his tour in occupied Japan, Munson would run interference for Arisue against hostile members of the Occupation and work with him to lay the groundwork for the bilateral intelligence relationship that still exists today.[58]

Intelligence Partnership

Among those on board the battleship *Missouri* on 2 September for the surrender ceremony were two subordinates of Arisue. One was Col. Sugita Ichiji, the intelligence officer who had interpreted for Gen. Yamashita Tomoyuki when the "Tiger of Malaya" had browbeat General Percival, also on board, into surrendering at Singapore three years earlier. Following the fall of Singapore, Sugita had directed Second Bureau's Sixth Section and served as an instructor at the Nakano School. Prior to the surrender ceremony, acting as a representative of the Higashikuni government, Sugita had called on Munson to seek further assurances that MacArthur would tread lightly in occupying Japan. On board the *Missouri* with Sugita was Maj. Gen. Nagai Yatsuji. During the war, Nagai had headed Second Bureau's covert operations section, which had directed the propaganda broadcasts of "Tokyo Rose," a composite broadcast personality played by a number of Japanese-American women.[59]

On 4 September, two days after the surrender ceremony, Arisue received from Munson a telephone call informing him of the U.S. Army's interest in discussing with him the Japanese military's capabilities in code breaking and other aspects of communications intelligence (COMINT). Arisue was ordered to appear the following day before a Lt. Col. Hugh Erskine, one of the U.S. Army's top Japanese COMINT experts.

The next morning, Arisue called on Erskine. Also at the meeting was a second-generation Japanese-American (Nisei) interpreter. Following introductions, Erskine immediately asked Arisue to tell him about the Central Special Intelligence Division (CSID), which conducted COMINT operations under the army's chief of staff. Arisue, after hearing the Nisei's interpretation of the question, feigned ignorance of the organization's name. At that point, Erskine rejoined in fluent Japanese that Arisue knew very well what he was asking. Arisue discovered at that point that his interrogator had been born and raised in Japan. Japan's military intelligence director then withdrew to his second position. He demanded to know the purpose of Erskine's inquiry. Was it related to the search for war criminals, military history and reference, or future use against the Soviet Union and Chinese Communists?

Erskine assured Arisue that he was not gathering information to identify the Japanese Army's COMINT officers as war criminals. The American intelligence officer avoided directly addressing the other two possible reasons for the inquiry but hinted that the time could come when such information could prove of value. Arisue, relieved, began to brief Erskine on CSID. In the course of the discussion, Erskine raised the issue of the tabulating machine seized in Manila during the Japanese conquest of the Philippines. The U.S. Army used such equipment, an early form of computer, for computations in its code-breaking efforts. Erskine wished to know the missing machine's whereabouts to preclude its falling into Soviet hands. Arisue informed him that the machine was thrown into a river at the war's end. The meeting ended amicably, with Arisue prepared to discuss Japanese COMINT further.

Arisue was in good spirits as a result of the meeting. The personnel at CSID had destroyed the evidence of military COMINT activities and gone to ground for fear that the Occupation authorities would brand them as war criminals. Now Arisue knew that members of MacArthur's intelligence staff were seeking to tap Japanese expertise for use against the Soviets. He also knew that the Americans were to interview CSID's chief, Maj. Gen. Nishimura Toshio. Prior to Nishimura's interview of 9 September, Arisue met him to discuss how they should respond. Understanding that Japan stood to benefit from the growing rift between the United States and Soviet Union, Arisue and Nishimura agreed to cooperate with the Americans on COMINT against the Soviets if asked.

The American request was not long in coming. A few days after

Arisue had followed MacArthur from Yokohama to Tokyo on 17 September, Willoughby asked that he prepare a proposal for a secret Japanese COMINT organization to operate as an auxiliary of the U.S. Army. Arisue turned to his subordinate, Maj. Gen. Nagai Yatsuji, who enlisted a couple dozen COMINT veterans and began drafting a proposal. Three months later, near Christmas, the Japanese offered their present. Taken aback by the grandiose Japanese demand for a budget of nearly one million yen, Willoughby returned the proposal to Arisue for revision.

Arisue ended his account of Japan's first postwar steps toward a COMINT (now SIGINT) partnership with the U.S. military with the rejection of the first proposal. But subsequent events suggest the two sides soon reached an understanding. As one author noted in his history of the National Security Agency (NSA), Japan quickly changed after the Second World War from the U.S. military's priority COMINT target to its leading platform. In Hokkaido, the closest of the Japanese home islands to the Soviet Union, the first American troops arrived at Chitose, site of a Japanese COMINT station, in September 1945. By 1949, the Army Security Agency, NSA's predecessor, had established the Twelfth Army Security Agency (ASA) Field Station there to monitor Soviet signals. Despite the lack of details, it seems clear that Willoughby and Arisue came to some understanding.[60]

The Arisue Agency

Arisue, having headed the reception committee at Atsugi, next created an intelligence organ for liaison with Willoughby and his staff. Arisue had followed when MacArthur left Yokohama for Tokyo on 17 September. Japan's new shogun moved his headquarters to the Dai-Ichi Life Insurance Building, an imposing structure situated across the street from the Imperial Palace. Arisue, leaving behind several officers for continued liaison in Yokohama, discreetly moved his operation into the Japan Club. The building housing the club stood next to MacArthur's headquarters. Arisue's office even faced those of Willoughby and Munson, who would at times call him to a meeting simply by waving to him. Together with naval intelligence liaison run by Rear Adm. Nakamura Katsuhei, nearly thirty intelligence officers operated from the Japan Club.[61] Officially, Arisue ran what was known as the Army Liaison Committee (Tokyo).[62]

Arisue built his organization, the Arisue Agency, around veteran intelligence officers. Col. Yamamoto Arata, who operated as his chief of staff, was a leading expert on the United States. Yamamoto had achieved an impressive record as a top student at the Military Academy and General Staff College. Rare for an Imperial Japanese Army officer, he had gone to the United States rather than Germany or the Soviet Union for the postgraduate overseas assignment commonly given to the best students. Yamamoto had continued deepening his American expertise, serving a tour as assistant military attaché in Washington until six months before Pearl Harbor and ending the war as intelligence chief of the section responsible for the United States. His background had earned him a place in Kawabe's delegation to Manila the previous month.

Under Yamamoto were four veterans who served as "staff officers." Col. Tejima Haruo, one of the four, was another intelligence expert. Tejima had served for nearly three months as resident military officer in India before going to Chile as military attaché several months before the attack on Pearl Harbor. After returning to Japan in 1943, he had assumed command of the Nakano School unit responsible for testing and developing covert operations equipment and techniques. Tejima had also put together the manuals for waging guerrilla warfare in the home islands. Two junior officers, a couple of noncommissioned officers, and several support staff rounded out the operation. Maj. Yamada Kosaku, one of the two junior officers, had lectured on France at the Nakano School.

The Arisue Agency, in addition to operating in the shadows of Willoughby's G-2, also maintained close ties with Japan's formal government apparatus that was established to execute MacArthur's orders. In late August, the Government of Japan had established the Coordination and Liaison Office (CLO) as the Foreign Ministry's point of contact with the Occupation authorities. Arisue was on intimate terms with the chief of the CLO, Okazaki Katsuo, who in the war's final months had regularly met Arisue in his role as the Foreign Ministry's intelligence chief.

The Arisue Agency's general point of contact in CLO was not First Bureau, nominally responsible for military affairs and public order, but the General Affairs Bureau under Iguchi Sadao. Iguchi had been a senior diplomat in Japan's Washington Embassy in the months leading to Pearl Harbor. Purged from public office after handling liaison in several offices of the CLO, he later returned to duty to work on the San Francisco Peace Treaty (1951) and serve as ambassador to the United States (1954–1956) and to Chiang Kai-shek's Republic of China on Taiwan (1959–1962). Finally, the Arisue Agency functioned within the surviving IJA chain of command, operating directly under the War Ministry's authority. Although IGHQ was abolished on 13 September and the Army General Staff was dissolved the following month, the War Ministry functioned until December, then continued as the First Demobilization Ministry. Vestigial appendages of imperial Japan's War Ministry later remained as the Social Welfare and War Victims' Relief Bureau of the Health and Welfare Ministry[63]

Ostensibly, the Arisue Agency was simply to supply information to MacArthur's Headquarters to assist in the designation and apprehension of war criminals, the repatriation of troops from overseas, and other duties pertaining to the dismantling of the Imperial Japanese Army. In fact, the Arisue Agency functioned as the Japanese partner in the U.S. Army's budding relationship with Japanese military intelligence.

In this sense, Arisue was similar to Gen. Reinhard Gehlen, Hitler's wartime chief of military intelligence on the Eastern front. Gehlen directed the FHO, the branch of the Wehrmacht General Staff responsible for intelligence on the Soviet Union, until the closing weeks of the war in Europe. As Arisue hid his intelligence on the Soviet Union as a bargaining chip, so Gehlen had his organization's Soviet intelligence buried in the mountains of southern Germany for the same reason. In the early years of the Cold War, Gehlen's organization was a major source of information for Washington. In late August that year, around the time that Arisue received his first telephone call from Colonel Munson, officers of the U.S. Army in Europe flew Gehlen and other Wehrmacht intelligence officers to Washington for intelligence briefings on the Soviet Union.[64]

Meeting of Minds

Arisue was most fortunate to have Willoughby as his partner. The rapid collapse of the Anglo-American alliance with the Soviet Union led officers of the U.S. Army to tap the intelligence resources of Japan and Germany while the war's ashes were still warm. Arisue thus would likely have acquired the same role of partner, no matter who had landed at Atsugi as the G-2. Nevertheless, Arisue was most fortunate that the "Prussian" Willoughby came to Japan. Willoughby never for a moment harbored the slightest bit of hatred against his erstwhile Axis enemies. No sooner had he arrived than Munson had introduced him to Gen. Prince Kaya Tsunenori, a cavalry officer who had ended the war as commandant of the General Staff College. Kaya and Willoughby, the former command and general staff instructor from Leavenworth, had a most pleasant evening together[65]

Any lingering doubts that Arisue had found his oasis must have ended on the evening of 24 September at the Imperial Hotel, where Willoughby and other top brass were staying. That evening, Arisue and Kawabe dined with Willoughby and Munson. Arisue found his hosts in fine spirits. Willoughby, seeking to put his guests at ease, assured them that he saw no difference between the U.S. Army and the Imperial Japanese Army. Speaking in German to Kawabe, Willoughby decried those in Japan who were loudly denouncing the "militarists," declaring himself a fellow "militarist." Musing on the uncertain fate of military men, Willoughby averred that he could just as well be arraigned himself one day as a war criminal in some future war.

In fact, as one Occupation official later wrote of Willoughby, any Japanese with views as extreme as his was purged. The "Prussian" officer candidly revealed his views of the world in his treatise *Maneuver in War* (1939). Of Mussolini's conquest of Ethiopia in 1936, Willoughby wrote that it had cleansed the "stain" of Emperor Menelik II's defeat of an invading Italian army in 1896: "Historical judgment, freed from the emotional haze of the moment, will credit Mussolini with wiping out a memory of defeat by re-establishing the traditional military supremacy of the white race, for generations to come." As for Japan's undeclared war on China, he had framed the conflict as a choice of "red sickle or rising sun." Of course, he preferred the latter, viewing Japan as the "champion" of capitalism in Asia against communist "encroachment."

Willoughby recalled that evening at the Imperial Hotel how his heart had gone out to Kawabe upon seeing him under circumstances of the "tragedy" of defeat in Manila. As for the global conflagration that had only recently ended, Willoughby was most understanding. He called it "odd" to argue over which side was right, suggesting only that Japan had "committed errors of arithmetic." In other words,

Japan had miscalculated in going to war. Willoughby also told his guests of his exploits as an infantry officer in France during the First World War. The evening ended with Arisue and Kawabe impressed that in MacArthur's intelligence chief they had found a "man of the world" with whom they could work.[66]

Loose Ends

Arisue had early established a fine relationship with Willoughby. The two admirers of Mussolini had become friends. For Willoughby, in fact, Arisue appears to have become a confidant, a fellow intelligence man with whom he could commiserate. He never mocked Willoughby as "Sir Charles" or smirked at his Prussian ways. Willoughby would bare to Arisue his frustrations as MacArthur's intelligence chief, speak of the difficult relations between operations and intelligence in the U.S. Army, and discuss the rivalry between the U.S. Army and Navy. Hearing Willoughby's comments, Arisue found they matched the problems that had plagued him.[67]

Arisue became the source for much of what the U.S. Army understood regarding Japanese intelligence. He played a coordinating role, keeping in touch with Japanese intelligence officers who consulted with him before talking to the Americans. His position allowed him to regulate the flow of information. In the trial of Lt. Gen. Homma Masaharu for war crimes in the Philippines, for example, Arisue withheld from the American prosecution information that would have implicated Col. Tsuji Masanobu as the driving force behind the Bataan Death March.[68] Arisue also misled American investigators from the United States Strategic Bombing Survey (USSBS) on his intelligence organization. The resulting USSBS report on Japanese intelligence was pathetic. The credulous Americans accepted, for example, Arisue's word that no intelligence training school had existed in Japan.[69]

Despite Arisue's standing with Willoughby, however, he was not in a position of equality. Japan, after all, had lost the war. This left him unable to prevent the U.S. Army from plundering many of the jewels of the Japanese intelligence community. An early target was the Tokyo organization of the South Manchuria Railway Company (SMRC). One of the world's leading intelligence organs, the SMRC had amassed a treasure trove of information on China, Manchuria, and the Soviet Far East. The SMRC's reputation continues to this day. One of Japan's foremost Russian experts recalled the SMRC in a recent newspaper article, lamenting that Japan today has no comparable research organ on Russia. An affiliated office in Tokyo, the East Asia Economic Research Bureau, was known to have trained spies as well.

Within a few weeks of the surrender ceremony, MacArthur's men had sped to Fukushima Prefecture, where the Bureau had withdrawn to escape the rain of bombs on Tokyo in the war's final months. The U.S. Army hauled away numerous documents, many of them in Russian. MacArthur's interrogators also called in for questioning SMRC personnel. Horiba Yasugoro, for example, was interrogated on the fighting at Nomonhan in 1939 between Japan and the Soviet Union.[70]

MacArthur's men also targeted institutions and individuals linked to the Nakano School. Lead elements of the First Cavalry Division took possession of the Nakano School's buildings in Tokyo on 30 August 1945.[71] Men of the 441st CIC Detachment found in October elements of the Noborito Research Institute in Nagano Prefecture. MacArthur's men also called Noborito personnel into Tokyo for questioning. At the end of November 1945, the American dragnet also caught Maj. Yamamoto Masayoshi. Yamamoto, an officer of the Nakano School who had landed in northern Australia during the war to survey the coast for a possible invasion, was monitoring the Occupation with other alumni in southwest Japan when CIC called him to Tokyo. He underwent three weeks of questioning on the content of training at the Nakano School and those who trained there. CIC also reportedly compelled him to write a list of those he knew from the school.[72]

While the shadow warriors of the Japanese and American armies played at both cooperation and hide-and-seek, the Occupation ran smoothly as the weeks passed. MacArthur, backed by Washington, had avoided a guerrilla war by working through Japan's imperial institution and government machinery. Col. Bonner Fellers remembers what MacArthur told him shortly after Manila, while they were in Okinawa en route to Tokyo: "He said, 'This is very simple. We'll issue all our orders through the instrumentalities of the Japanese Government.' He said, 'When you put a man out of his house for an American, he resents it. But when somebody representing the Emperor goes to him and says, 'This house has got to be turned over to the occupation, that's the Emperor's will.' That was the genius behind the whole thing. If the Emperor had been tried as a war criminal, the war would have been on yet."[73]

Proud of their accomplishment, MacArthur and his men could not understand why some critics sought to depose, try, or even execute Emperor Hirohito. Willoughby, without revealing the deal struck in Manila, showed his exasperation at a press conference on 21 November 1945. Describing himself as "completely baffled" by criticism of MacArthur's policy of governing through the emperor and government officials, he remarked that the only alternative "was to have come in shooting." As he put it, "Either you go in without shooting or you come in shooting. Either you go in without losing a man or you count casualties in the hundreds of thousands." As Munson later explained to an American historian, "When the Japanese were told by the Emperor to stop, boy, they stopped."[74]

That same November, when American intelligence officers were interrogating Major Yamamoto, and Willoughby was defending his commander's "soft" line towards Japan, the Nakano School's Inomata Jinya, Kubota Ichiro, and others called on Arisue to seek his help in hiding Prince Kitashirakawa. Arisue in turn took them to a gangster's funeral to see a major godfather of Japan's criminal society as a possible resource.[75] While the plan to safeguard the imperial line was still in the works, certain members of the Nakano School no longer judged it necessary. The Occupation seemed too benevolent for such a course of action. With such a view, Abe Naoyoshi and other participants withdrew at the end of the year.[76]

10

FROM CACHES TO KOREA

As the Japanese put 1945 behind them, certain intelligence officers had every reason to feel satisfied. Lt. Gen. Kawabe and his delegation had struck a grand bargain in Manila in August to preserve the imperial throne and the machinery of Japan's government. Lt. Gen. Arisue had discovered an "oasis" in MacArthur's intelligence staff. He had also learned of the U.S. Army's interest in using Japan's intelligence resources for a future showdown with the Soviet Union. The prospect of the Izumi Unit's men springing from the shadows into violent action appeared increasingly remote as the Occupation took gentle hold. Meanwhile, in a remote corner of rural Niigata Prefecture, men of the Nakano School were still hiding the fugitive Ba Maw from the British. Major Inomata and several comrades were still planning to hide young Prince Kitashirakawa to ensure the imperial line's survival. As the New Year dawned, Japanese intelligence officers were holding onto their caches while they cooperated with the occupiers.

Arrests of the New Year

A Japanese informant brought the Ba Maw and Kitashirakawa operations crashing down. The CIC in Tokyo received word from a Japanese in Niigata of a "suspicious foreign monk" seen around a temple. Ba Maw's guardians had permitted the fugitive Burmese leader to walk in the woods around the temple where he was hiding. After local residents had noted the "Manchurian" monk's presence, someone had denounced him. General Headquarters (GHQ), learning that the monk was Ba Maw, lost no time in demanding that the Foreign Ministry turn over the fugitive. A Japanese official met the Burmese in Niigata to suggest he surrender. Ba Maw rejected the official's appeal, demanding instead that his handlers exfiltrate him to Korea. Failing to sway Ba Maw, his guardians had little choice but to deceive him. Imanari, the local youth leader, convinced Ba Maw to leave his refuge for a last visit to Tokyo, where Lieutenant Colonel Hirose and Nakano School officers were to throw him a farewell party before spiriting him out of Japan.

On an evening in the middle of January, Ba Maw, Hirose, Imanari, and two Foreign Ministry officials involved in hiding the Burmese leader gathered at the Marunouchi Hotel in Tokyo for the supposed farewell party. Ba Maw was in good spirits. Introduced to Hirose, he shook the intelligence officer's hand and thanked him for his help. While Ba Maw chatted with Hirose, an official left the room. A moment later, American military police burst through the door to arrest Ba Maw. Once the unpleasant affair was over, Hirose and the others remained in the room to continue the party. An hour after Ba Maw's arrest, the door again suddenly swung open as military police marched into the room with Ba Maw in tow. Livid over the betrayal, he had denounced his guardians. All left the room under arrest.

Under interrogation, the men gave the names of the Nakano School's participants in the two operations. The arrests of Kubota and Koshimaki quickly followed. On 22 January, a brief announcement of Ba Maw's arrest appeared on the front page of the *Nippon Times*. The story behind the story, of course, remained out of public view.

Inomata, the leader in the operation to hide the prince, remained at large a little longer. He was at home when police came for him in February. Fortunately, he had the presence of mind to have his wife destroy the prince's false identification papers from Hiroshima. Taken to Sugamo Prison, Inomata landed in solitary confinement on the third floor, an area once reserved for prisoners on death row. He underwent days of questioning. Brief walks in the corridor under the supervision of military police were his only exercise.[1]

While some intelligence officers sat behind bars, others remained free. The British never did find Lt. Col. Tada Minoru, a principal member of the Imperial Japanese Army's Hikari Agency who was connected to Subhas Chandra Bose. Tada had started with Bose on the Bengali leader's final journey, but parted company with him in Saigon. Once back in Japan, he managed to evade capture, dying in his hometown in Shimane Prefecture in 1951. Similarly fortunate was Arisue Seizo, who never even had to hide. Suspected of involvement in the Ba Maw affair, the intelligence chief underwent questioning by the British but denied knowledge of the Nakano School or its operations. His close ties to Willoughby, most likely, kept him out of Sugamo.[2]

In the end, Ba Maw left Sugamo in July. London probably decided on the early release to avoid complicating Asian affairs by making a martyr of him. Following a short stay at the British Embassy, he flew home to Burma to rejoin his family. The Japanese involved in hiding him were released several days later. Inomata, given a ride from the prison with his comrades, courtesy of his jailers, reflected on the changes that had taken place during his imprisonment. The new Japanese Constitution, discretely written by MacArthur's Government Section, translated into Japanese, and announced in March, retained the emperor. The threat to the throne seemed gone. As he rode through Tokyo after nearly a half year of imprisonment, Inomata wondered what it had all been for. [3]

Caches, Caches Everywhere

Ba Maw was far from the Occupation's only find. MacArthur's staff had informed Kawabe in Manila that the Japanese were to turn over their arms and account for their military facilities. Yet, soldiers of the Occupation forces found countless arms caches and war matériel hidden throughout Japan, including "an extensive underground fighter aircraft engine plant" near Tokyo and equipped pillboxes covered by dummy houses in Shikoku. Many schools hid these forbidden buried treasures, including the one in Tomioka that had sheltered the Nakano School at the war's end.[4] In January 1946, U.S. troops discovered hundreds of cases of military supplies in the ancient capital of Nara. The cache was unearthed near Nara's Daibutsu, Japan's largest statue of the Buddha. The incident inspired one wag in the Associated Press to report that the religious figure was "waiting to be demilitarized."[5] Patrols of the British Commonwealth Occupation Forces (BCOF), which occupied Shikoku and southwestern Honshu, found during the Occupation's first year "huge arsenals of arms and ammunition in vast caves."[6] Many caches remained hidden for the length of the Occupation and, in some cases, for decades to come. In 1998, a work crew dug up a Japanese tank at Sagami General Depot, once the Imperial Japanese Army's Sixth Arsenal. The tank appeared to have been buried by the Japanese at the war's end.[7]

MacArthur's GHQ declared that the unearthed caches indicated a breakdown in the Japanese chain of command, but some discoveries must have sorely tried American patience. One such case surfaced in January, the month of Ba Maw's arrest. The principal of Tomioka Middle School in Gunma Prefecture, where the Nakano School had withdrawn in the war's last months, alerted authorities to the existence of arms buried on his school grounds. An investigation revealed a cache of small arms, machine guns, and explosives. Willoughby demanded that Arisue summon those involved to Tokyo for questioning. On investigation, Arisue found that those involved were Lt. Col. Sakamoto Sukeo and Maj. Katagi Ryohei of the Nakano School. Both men were still at large. Arisue, in a meeting with Colonel Munson and Col. R.G. Duff of the 441st CIC Detachment, again sought to avoid a tough spot by dissembling. He suggested to the exasperated Americans that Sakamoto and Katagi had not buried the arms for a possible uprising. No, they were simply disposing of them when they buried them intact.

Arisue suggested that he could summon Sakamoto and Katagi to Tokyo if GHQ promised not to prosecute them as war criminals. Munson and Duff agreed to Arisue's terms. The two wanted men then appeared in Tokyo. Under little pressure to confess, they simply stonewalled their interrogators. When asked the whereabouts of Maj. Gen. Yamamoto Hayashi, the responsible officer as the Nakano School's last commandant, Katagi denied any knowledge of his direct superior. He also insisted that he and his classmates had buried the arms simply to dispose of them. [8]

End of an Army

The poor state of U.S. Army intelligence was likely one reason that Arisue could win immunity for Sakamoto and Katagi. Most American veterans had left Japan within months of the surrender ceremony; nearly all were demobilized by the end of 1946. The formidable military machine that had won the war fell apart in the autumn and winter of 1945–46.[9] Replacing the veterans were green conscripts, who in turn left Japan after a year's duty. Their replacements were far less capable. The number of Japanese local hires also increased.[10]

The Army's decline hurt its intelligence capabilities. Some of America's best minds had served in military intelligence to help win the war. Once the fighting ended, most left the military to resume their civilian lives. Professor Edwin Reischauer, a Japan hand from Harvard, stopped working on Japanese codes to go back to his academic career; he later returned to government as ambassador to Japan. CIC agents Henry Kissinger and J. D. Salinger were among those in Europe who quickly left the Army. Even talented career intelligence officers were soon gone. Military intelligence also suffered from the rotations of military personnel. Mashbir, chief of the Allied Translator and Interpreter Service (ATIS), left Japan in December 1945.[11] Munson left in the spring of 1946.[12]

The brain drain certainly hurt CIC, whose handicaps were daunting even as its agents first entered Japan. One CIC officer explained: "However seasoned CIC men were in combat, as agents they needed intensive training to deal with an alien, conquered people, whose language they did not speak, whose psychology in victory or defeat they did not understand." The sum of their training in Manila, prior to assuming Occupation duties in Japan, however, was a week of orientation. After the war, the CIC also faced a wrenching change. Having guarded the Army's secrets during the war, they now had to gather positive intelligence in Korea and elsewhere. It was one thing to censor mail. It was quite another to run agents against foreign targets.[13]

Worse still, the seasoned veterans left soon after their arrival. According to a history of the 441st CIC Detachment: "With the rapid demobilization of the Army after V-J Day many experienced CIC personnel were sent back to the United States for separation from the service. Replacements were slow in arriving and the counter intelligence work was becoming heavier . . . Replacements . . . were young, inexperienced men who required months of training after arrival." Most revealing is a note written in October 1946 by Lt. Col. Wayne Homan, commanding officer of the 441st CIC Detachment. Homan advised Col. Rufus Bratton, head of Civil Intelligence Section in Willoughby's G-2: "Most of our agents are callow youths within the 19–22 year bracket, who have no civilian experience, and not much CIC or Army training. They lack not only experience, but ability, common sense, and stability."[14]

Another problem was the personnel pool. CIC had narrowed its selection of Japanese linguist agents at the end of the war to America's minuscule Nisei community. The U.S. Army had erred throughout the war in thinking that only Americans of Japanese origin or Americans with experience living in Japan could master the difficult language. While the U.S. Navy combed America's universities for the brightest students to tackle the language, the U.S. Army put its confidence in a small population whose members were not uniformly competent. Maj. Faubion Bowers, a military intelligence officer fluent in Japanese, explained: "The Army worked on the principle that if you've ever been in Japan you had a right to be commissioned as an officer. It automatically meant you knew Japan and Japanese psychology, as well as the Japanese language. The Navy was very smart because the Navy said, 'If you have a mind that can learn anything well, then you will be able to cope with Japanese,' which is sound. The Navy went through all the leading universities and offered this program of a year's study in Boulder to the top-ranking scholars, regardless of their field, and then an automatic commission at the end. So they got all the really brilliant scholars, and, sure enough, the scholars were able to cope with Japanese within a year."

Most Nisei, born and raised in the United States, spoke little more than the limited "kitchen Japanese" they learned at home from their immigrant parents. Many learned the dialects of Okinawa, Kumamoto, and Hiroshima, the major areas of Japanese immigration, which struck some Japanese as crude and unrefined.[15] Nevertheless, always the majority of students at the U.S. Army's Military Intelligence Service Language School (MISLS), Nisei became the only students training as linguist intelligence officers after August 1945. Of the twelve hundred students who entered MISLS from September through November, all were Nisei.[16]

In short, the CIC of the war years ceased to exist early in the Occupation. Nearly all the talented veterans went home. Those who entered the CIC in the Occupation years encountered a far different service. Harry Brunette, a CIC special agent during the Occupation, recalled that "You had to be lily white to get into CIC and turn coal black to stay in." According to him, "That CIC badge was your authority to do anything. If they told you to break in and steal some documents, you did it. We'd trade with the devil if we had to."[17]

Behind that agent's cryptic remark was the tale of CIC's transformation under Willoughby. He had maneuvered since the early years of the war to wrest control of CIC from Brig. Gen. Elliott Thorpe. During the war, Willoughby had managed to dislodge one of Thorpe's men from command of the 441st CIC Detachment, only to see him replaced with another officer in Thorpe's camp. Willoughby emerged victorious in the spring of 1946, when he gained control of the Civil Intelligence Section (CIS), including CIC, and Thorpe left Japan for the United States. In short order, Willoughby turned CIC from hunting suspected Japanese war criminals and uncovering caches to monitoring Soviet residents in Japan and any Americans or Japanese he viewed as leftist.[18]

With the CIC a mere shadow of its wartime self, Willoughby turned for talent to Japanese professionals. He tapped former officials of the Special Higher Police (*Tokko*), or Japanese Thought Police, to gather intelligence on his targets.[19] Many former intelligence officers of the Japanese Army, including Japanese-Americans who had served on the Japanese side, worked for Willoughby's intelligence organization.[20]

Notorious in occupied Japan were CIC officers and Japanese working under Col. James "Cactus Jack" Canon. His infamous Canon Agency, for which he recruited heavily among Nisei, worked directly under the 441st CIC at the old Kempeitai building. According to Brunette, "They were almost always linguists, Japanese-Americans, and they were directly responsive to CIC headquarters. They'd only come into our field office to get paid and drop off sealed reports for Tokyo."[21] Canon apparently preferred Nisei, seeing them as less squeamish and talkative than other Americans.

Arisue received a request from G-2 early in the Occupation for intelligence that would enable Willoughby to tar Agnes Smedley, an American leftist prominent in various anticolonial causes, as a communist spy. In the 1930s, Smedley had known the journalist spy Richard Sorge when the two resided in Shanghai. She had later traveled throughout much of China, working part of the time as a news correspondent. During 1940 and the first half of 1941, before she returned to the United States on account of ill health, she gave lectures in Chungking, wartime capital of Generalissimo Chiang Kai-shek's Nationalist government.

Willoughby was determined to prove that Smedley had gathered intelligence in China on behalf of Sorge, a Soviet intelligence officer hanged for espionage in Tokyo in 1944. To delve into Smedley's China days, Willoughby turned to Arisue. His Japanese partner worried about gathering intelligence against a prominent American. Willoughby justified his request on the grounds of intelligence. Yes, he admitted, she was an American citizen. But he was also sure that her activities in China were linked to Sorge's spy ring.

Arisue, in need of an intelligence officer with a background in China, enlisted the aid of Col. Shigekawa Hidekazu. From May 1940, when Arisue was a staff officer of the North China Area Army, Shigekawa had been the staff officer in charge of covert operations before taking command in 1942 of an SSA in the region. Shigekawa had gathered intelligence on Smedley at that time on account of her activities at the Nationalists' remote capital.[22] While Smedley had openly promoted the Chinese Communists during the war years, Shigekawa found no evidence that she had spied on behalf of the Sorge spy ring. Willoughby nevertheless accused her of espionage in a report he issued through the Supreme Commander for the Allied Powers (SCAP) in February 1949. The Department of the Army promptly repudiated his report. Willoughby refused to relent. Although Smedley died in 1950, Willoughby peddled his slander as a friendly witness at hearings of the notorious House Committee on Un-American Activities in 1951 and the following year in his book *Shanghai Conspiracy*.[23]

Among those rumored to work for Willoughby in one way or another, including service as agents of the Canon Agency, were certain men of the Nakano School.[24] While there has never been any public identification of the Nakano School veterans or their alleged activities, it is possible that one or more were involved in the Smedley affair and other operations. During the war, Shigekawa's SSA included at least one graduate of the Nakano School. Others possibly worked for the infamous "Cactus Jack" Canon, who reputedly employed veterans of Col. Hidaka Tomiaki's wartime organization. Shigekawa and Hidaka were two of several officers in North China who operated under Col. Hongo Tadao, intelligence chief of the North China Area Army. The duties of the Shigekawa and Hidaka agencies included tapping telephone lines, intercepting radio, exploiting documents, and running agents. At least one veteran of the Nakano School served in the Shigekawa Agency, another six in the Hidaka Agency.[25]

World War III

Well before the surrender, American officials foresaw another conflict. Opposition to the Axis powers had brought together in Asia a most unlikely combination of powers: the United States, Great Britain, and the Soviet Union. Washington and London had for decades maintained cordial relations, and respective spheres of influence, in Asia. But both had sent armed forces into Siberia in 1918 in a futile attempt to strangle the nascent Soviet regime. From Moscow came a push for worldwide revolution, the Soviets letting loose endless volleys of propaganda and engaging in subversive activities throughout the world. Almost until the day Hitler invaded Poland, Washington and London had viewed Moscow as the primary threat to their interests.

Despite the alliance against the Axis, Stalin's spies, active in the United States since the 1930s, continued to gather intelligence during the war years. American officials and military officers, for their part, prepared during the war for a future conflict with Moscow. William J. Donovan, President Roosevelt's spy master as director of the OSS, was one such man. Troubled by agent reports of communists seeking to dominate resistance movements in Europe and wary of Soviet intentions, Donovan designated the USSR an OSS intelligence target in 1944.[26]

The prescient OSS chief pointed to the growing tensions during a visit to China in the waning days of the war. On 7 August, the day after Hiroshima disappeared under a radioactive cloud, Donovan arrived at an OSS base in Hsian. Speaking to a small group of his officers, he claimed that the war was over but the peace was not won. Referring to Hiroshima and the coming conflict with Moscow, he told his men that the atomic bomb gave the United States a respite during which to prepare for final showdown: "In that time, America must have friends: without them we might not survive. We must be wiser and more cunning and more dedicated than the Communists, in the years ahead, if we are to survive."[27] Donovan's concerns existed elsewhere in Washington. Vice-Adm. Charles Cooke, Navy Chief of Staff, predicted in June 1945 to William J. Sebald, a future Occupation official then with the Navy, that the Japanese would be American allies against the Soviets in a future war.[28] Concern over a future conflict also led to the Army's decision to fly Gen. Reinhard Gehlen of the Wehrmacht to Washington in August.

In Tokyo, Japanese leaders were also attuned to the threat of a conflict. At the time of Japan's surrender, Rear Adm. Tomioka Sadatoshi predicted that the Americans and Russians would soon oppose one another. Tomioka also judged that the competition between the two great powers would provide Japan the margin for maneuver and recovery.[29] Kato Masuo, a veteran Japanese newsman for the Domei News Agency, wrote in 1946 of Japanese expectations for a world war between the Russians and Americans.[30] Kodama Yoshio, wartime operative for the Imperial Japanese Navy and postwar agent for American intelligence, also predicted an inevitable clash.[31]

Moreover, certain former Japanese Army officers were working under MacArthur to coordinate intelligence and plan military operations. Col. Hattori Takushiro, a favorite of General Tojo, led Willoughby's Japanese general staff. Hattori's career in operations recommended him as director of this hidden general staff. When a senior operations staff officer of the Kwantung Army, Hattori had helped direct the small war against the Soviet Red Army at Nomonhan in 1939. He had also been a principal architect, as chief of the Army General Staff's Operations Section, of Japan's opening offensives in December 1941. Nearly five years to the day since Pearl Harbor, Hattori joined Willoughby as chief of the history staff in Japan's First Demobilization Ministry. Other than plan for war, Willoughby did compile histories during the Occupation. He oversaw the Japanese contribution to *Reports of General MacArthur*, as well as numerous Japanese military reports. Contributing to the history of Japan's war were two intelligence officers related to the Nakano School: Lt. Col. Fujiwara Iwaichi and Col. Sugita Ichiji.

Many in Japan knew that MacArthur was planning for war, including prominent Japanese, and, surely, the Soviets. Dr. Harry Emerson Wildes, a member of Government Section, wrote that many Occupation officials believed that the fifteen senior military and naval officers on Willoughby's history staff were coordinating Soviet intelligence.[32] American journalists, including the *Chicago Sun*'s Mark Gayn, also knew of Willoughby's Japanese general staff. In his account of the Occupation, Gayn quoted a speech by Willoughby before Japanese industrialists in Tokyo in September 1946. Calling the Japanese Army "first-rate," Willoughby continued: "We have just dealt with the German police state. We shall take care of the new police states that have now emerged in Europe. I know many of you are worried over the possibility of new conflicts flaring up on Japanese soil. I want you to know that when such a conflict comes, we shall be shoulder to shoulder with you."[33] A month earlier, Col. Harry Creswell, Willoughby's subordinate in charge of CIS, had argued vehemently against a purge of Japanese industrialists on the grounds that such a move would deprive the United States of experienced men needed in the coming world war.[34]

Lt. Gen. Kamada Senichi, who had run an intelligence agency in Yokohama subordinate to Arisue in Tokyo, spoke before a Japanese audience on 3 July 1947 of a coming war between the United States and the Soviet Union. He further explained that he and other veteran officers were planning military operations for such a conflict with staff officers of the U.S. Army. Japanese Communists reported Kamada's speech to SCAP. It is likely that they informed Soviet representatives in Tokyo as well.[35]

Beyond reconstituting a Japanese general staff, Willoughby was also preparing to build a new Japanese army around Hattori. Mac-Arthur's intelligence chief had early confided to Arisue that he antici-pated a need for Japan to have a national "police" force to handle internal or external crises.[36] By 1949, even Eichelberger put aside his longstanding antipathy for the Japanese military to declare publicly that he favored its reconstruction.[37]

From Caches to Cooperation

In January 1946, the arrest of Ba Maw and the associated intelligence officers of the Nakano School should have suggested that Arisue was playing a double game in his dealings with the U.S. Army. It must have been clear that responsibility for the innumerable arms caches throughout Japan ran to the top of the Japanese chain of command. Rather than a breakdown of authority, as MacArthur claimed, the caches revealed the determination of Japanese military leaders to wage war in the event of a punitive Occupation. That Willoughby continued working with Arisue suggests that MacArthur and officials in Wash-ington required the talents of Japan's veterans to keep the peace in Japan and prepare for war with the Soviet Union.

The international scene was growing dark. In March 1946, Win-ston Churchill proclaimed the death of the Anglo-American alliance with Stalin and the start of the Cold War. At Fulton, Missouri, the wartime British prime minister declared that an "iron curtain" of communist dictatorship had fallen across eastern Europe. Almost to the day of the first anniversary of V-E Day, the American public heard that "Uncle Joe" Stalin was the new enemy. The specter of a third global war haunted the West.

As in the recent war, Europe was of paramount concern in planning for war with Stalin. Firming the defenses of the European allies came first. Washington drafted its Asian policies to bolster Europe. In Southeast Asia, the United States backed France and Holland as the allies poured their meager resources down the rat hole of empire. Recipients of American aid for postwar recovery, Paris and Amsterdam were expending much blood and treasure in battling Asian nationalists in vain efforts to recover their former colonies in Indochina and Indonesia. Washington, although critical of European colonialism, was now effectively siding with colonial forces against the tide of nationalism surging across Southeast Asia.

Washington's policy of "Europe first" also shaped American actions in northeast Asia. Japan, separated from the Soviet Union by the Sea of Japan, was far less vulnerable to a Soviet invasion than Western Europe. The Soviet Navy was incapable of conducting an amphibious invasion of occupied Japan. On the other hand, the Japanese archipelago was an unsinkable aircraft carrier for the United States to use in war with Russia. From Japan, the United States could open a second front against Stalin. American bombers flying from Japanese bases could attack Vladivostok and other major military targets of the Soviet Far East. The U.S. Army and Marine Corps could stage amphibious operations from Japan against Vladivostok or, via the Korean Peninsula, invade Siberia through Manchuria. Japan was thus a vital element in Washington's emerging global strategy against Moscow.

Moreover, Japan could fill formidable intelligence gaps in Asia. The United States lacked even basic information on the Soviet Far East, let alone the detailed topographical information and other intelligence needed to conduct bombing campaigns or amphibious operations. American military planners knew little of the Soviet Red Army's past battles or present disposition in the region. Although planning for aerial reconnaissance of the Soviet Far East began at the end of the Second World War, it would only be in December 1947 that the first reconnaissance aircraft flew from Alaska over the Soviet Chukotski Peninsula. The first deep penetration of Siberia, also originating in Alaska, took place only in August 1948. Noteworthy is the crew's ending that mission by landing at Yokota Air Base outside Tokyo. Three subsequent reconnaissance flights over Siberia that summer originated at Yokota.[38]

Washington's urgent need for intelligence on the Soviet Far East put Japanese military veterans in a fine position. The former Japanese Army was unmatched in its knowledge of the Soviet Far East. The intelligence treasure trove included military reconnaissance flights conducted over Soviet territory during the Kwantung Army Special Maneuvers in 1941.[39] Flights had continued as late as 1944.[40] The intelligence from those flights would go far in filling the Pentagon's empty target folders.

In addition to air intelligence, the Imperial Japanese Army had also been rich in human experience. Japan's veterans were experts on the Soviet Far East, Manchuria, and China. From August 1918 until October 1922, the Japanese Army had units in the field during the Siberian Intervention. Not only had Japan possessed the southern half of Sakhalin from 1905; the Army had occupied the northern part between 1920 and 1925. For decades, the Japanese had been monitoring the Soviet Army across various borders. The Kwantung Army in Manchuria, the Fifth Area Army on Karafuto, the Seventeenth Area Army in Korea, and the Mongolian Garrison Army had all faced the Soviet Red Army. Finally, the Japanese Army had fought what amounted to minor wars with the Soviet Army on the borders of Manchukuo at Changkufeng (1938) and Nomonhan (1939). Those veterans knew well the region and the Red Army.

Human intelligence was a particular area of expertise. The Japanese Army had established its first SSA on the continent in 1918. Over nearly thirty years, some three thousand military personnel had served at the SSAs.[41] They had run countless agents—White Russians, Chinese, Koreans, and others—against the Soviet Union. There were also Arisue's buried maps and other documents. During the early months of the Occupation, Willoughby's G-2 was able to put his hands on some data. In addition to confiscating the South Manchuria Railway Company's materials, G-2 bought intelligence from individuals connected to Japanese military intelligence. Members of the Harbin SSA reportedly returned to Japan at the war's end at one point with intelligence, including targets for bombing, which they sold to MacArthur's GHQ.[42]

As for Arisue, he had faced repeated requests from the beginning for intelligence on the Soviet Union. While extending cooperation in certain matters, he held firm on his intelligence caches until the time seemed ripe. By the spring of 1946, when circumstances appeared favorable, he finally acted. In April, Arisue again called Captain Amano of the Nakano School before him. Only eight months earlier, Arisue had ordered Amano and an assistant to hide trunks full of topographical intelligence. Now Amano was to unearth them for Arisue to present to MacArthur's G-2. Amano and his assistant, for their part, retrieved the trunks from their hiding places with some reluctance. While they no doubt understood the value of the deal, both regretted that their superior was passing such treasures to the U.S. military.[43]

With his intelligence caches, Arisue was playing a trump card. He and his agency had established a partnership with the U.S. Army similar to that of General Gehlen in Germany. The Arisue Agency, which had existed in part to "dangle the bait of intelligence on the Soviet Union before MacArthur," in the words of the journalist Mark Gayn, quietly ceased to exist shortly thereafter. Arisue himself resigned his position in the First Demobilization Ministry in June. He remained close to Willoughby, however, assuming the position of a U.S. military "advisor" in July and keeping it until December 1956. Arisue would retain informal ties to the U.S. Army. Arisue also paid courtesy calls on Willoughby in the United States in 1959 and 1966.[44]

Continental Intelligence

Arisue kept his hand in intelligence affairs by mustering veterans for various projects. Japanese intelligence officers helped Willoughby's G-2 screen Japanese soldiers returning from Soviet captivity for intelligence. Each repatriated Japanese possibly possessed key information on some factory, road, or other project on which he had labored. By retrieving and piecing together each bit of information, Willoughby's G-2 could create an intelligence mosaic of the Soviet military-industrial infrastructure in the Far East. American intelligence was particularly anxious to detect signs that Stalin was developing atomic weapons.

The intelligence gleaned from Japanese repatriates likely held a particular interest for Washington, where a handful of officials and military officers had grasped that Soviet spies had been gathering atomic secrets from America's wartime Manhattan Project. On 1 February 1943, the U.S. Army's Signal Security Agency (SSA) launched its effort to read Russian diplomatic traffic. Intelligence gained from the project, under the code name VENONA, combined with intelligence from the FBI and other sources to show that the Soviets had stolen America's atomic secrets. Washington's nuclear monopoly, a precious strategic asset as America's wartime military forces melted away in the peacetime demobilization, was at risk.[45]

In September 1946, MacArthur's GHQ received word that the Soviet Union would soon begin repatriating Japanese war prisoners from Siberia. In November, Willoughby requested Arisue's assistance in screening the repatriates. Arisue agreed after consulting with a trio of Japanese generals at the First Demobilization Ministry. He offered Willoughby the requested intelligence auxiliaries, primarily intelligence officers with experience in Second Bureau's Soviet section. The advisors were divided into three groups, one each for the repatriation ports: the northern port of Hakodate, in Hokkaido; the central port of Maizuru, in Honshu; and the southern port of Sasebo, in Kyushu. In Europe, the U.S. Army in Germany was similarly interrogating repatriated German POWs in Operation Hermes. In the latter half of the 1940s, in the days before U2 overflights, satellite imagery, and other sophisticated collection systems, the U.S. military's worldwide program of interrogating repatriates from the Soviet Union was a key source of intelligence.[46]

At Maizuru, Maj. Gen. Sugai Toshimaro assumed command of four Japanese intelligence veterans. Sugai, with tours in Manchuria and Korea under his belt as a staff officer in the Kwantung Army and vice chief of staff for the Seventeenth Area Army, could advise the green Americans. Sugai's section assisted Lt. Wayne Takaki of the 441st CIC Detachment and the roughly dozen other Japanese-Americans under him. On 8 December 1946, the fifth anniversary of Pearl Harbor, the first repatriation ship from Siberia sailed into Maizuru. With the invaluable assistance of Sugai and his men, Takaki's unit received high marks from G-2 in Tokyo for its first intelligence report. The data, which to Sugai and his men appeared unexceptional, was a gold mine to Willoughby's G-2. The U.S. Army's maps on the Soviet Far East dated from the Siberian Intervention at the end of the First World War.

On the heels of Sugai's advisory group came a second unit of eight Japanese intelligence veterans. Seven were former military men, including Col. Maeda Mizuho and Maj. Maekawa Kunio. Maeda and his men were as impressive as those who served under Sugai. Maeda in particular had an outstanding background. In Manchukuo, he had run the Kwantung Army's detention center for defectors and suspected spies. Prisoners determined of no value were transferred to the Kwantung Army's Unit 731, which used them in experiments to develop the weapons of bacteriological warfare (BW). In the area where Korea borders Russia, Maeda had been the first chief of the Najin SSA. Established in September 1938, in the wake of the Japanese Army's clash with the Red Army at Changkufeng that same year, the Najin SSA gathered intelligence on the Soviet Union. A number of the Nakano School's men served at the agency.[47]

At Maizuru, Sugai and his men assisted Takaki and the other Americans in seeking evidence of a Soviet nuclear program. They sifted through accounts of forced labor on Soviet projects for the telltale signs of a nuclear weapons project: uranium mines, electrical power stations and lines, rail lines and roads, and military units. The presence at Maizuru of Lt. Col. Laurence P. Dowd suggested that the Americans were hunting for atomic clues. In 1944, Dowd, then an intelligence officer at the U.S. Army's Japanese school for intelligence officers at Camp Savage, Minnesota, had directed Nisei to comb through Japanese documents for clues of Japan's atomic bomb project. Information from repatriates also presumably added to intelligence from reconnaissance flights and other sources to compile Soviet orders of battle and topographical studies.[48]

The Japanese and Americans at Maizuru were quick to notice that among the various soldiers and civilians sailing back to Japan were those they suspected of being Soviet intelligence agents. Following two more ships docking in early January 1947, the CIC at Maizuru reported to G-2 in Tokyo its suspicions. Willoughby acted swiftly, with G-2 rounding up the suspects on 9 January.[49] Over time, dozens of Nisei and other CIC agents would screen the repatriated prisoners for spies in the intelligence contest between Washington and Moscow. The effort would last for years. G-2 would create huge files covering tens of thousands of Japanese. Arrests and detentions would continue during the Occupation.

Japanese intelligence veterans, including at least two connected to the Nakano School, also contributed to studies related to planning for a future war against the Soviet Union. Col. Kotani Etsuo, a lecturer on Soviet affairs at the Nakano School, worked with SCAP to produce the report *Japanese Intelligence Planning Against the USSR*.[50]

Col. Yano Muraji, who lectured at the Nakano School on the United States, edited Kotani's report and the others in the landmark series of monographs.

Of particular value in any world war with the Soviet Union was topographical intelligence on Manchuria, where the U.S. Army was woefully deficient. Given Manchuria's strategic value as a rear base for Chinese Communist forces in the Korean War and as an invasion route to the Soviet Far East, Japan's shadow warriors were almost certainly helping G-2 to prepare for a third world war. As noted above, Col. Hattori Takushiro had joined Willoughby's shadow general staff in the guise of writing history. The ruse fooled few people, and Hattori's staff was widely suspected of having participated in strategic planning during the Korean War.[51]

Early in 1951, a few months into the war, Hattori's staff began a series of thirteen reports on Manchuria. Japanese aid was essential. As stated in the editor's preface to one study: "The Kwantung Army, stationed in force in Manchukuo from the inception of the Hsinking regime in 1931 until the defeat of Japan in 1945, had accumulated a fund of firsthand local military knowledge unrivaled in other countries."[52] Among those working on the series was Lt. Col. Asaeda Shigeharu, an associate of Col. Tsuji Masanobu. Taken prisoner by the Red Army at the end of the Second World War, Asaeda had tried in vain to provoke the Soviets into attacking American forces in Korea. Released from Soviet captivity in 1949, Asaeda was again working towards a war between the two superpowers.[53]

White Unit

While some Japanese intelligence veterans were screening repatriates from the Soviet Union, others left Japan for China. Generalissimo Chiang Kai-shek's Nationalist forces had been warring against the Chinese Communists since their alliance dissolved in bloodshed in 1927. The simmering civil war, interrupted in 1937 by Japan's undeclared war against China, had erupted again with the end of the Second World War. The Nationalists, following initial victories, ran into disaster in Manchuria. By 1947, the Communists were in control of most of northern China and on the offensive.

The Nationalists had enlisted Japanese in the struggle from the moment of Tokyo's surrender. Chiang and the many officers under him who had received military training from the Japanese, either in China or at the Imperial Military Academy in Tokyo, were well aware of the prowess of Japanese officers. The Japanese Army had made a strong impression on generations of Chinese by overwhelming China's tottering Ch'ing Empire in 1895 and defeating czarist Russia in 1905. Chinese leaders had then invited Japanese to instruct at various military academies. Following the Nationalist Revolution of 1911, which brought down the Ch'ing Dynasty, many Chinese attended the Japanese Military Academy. Apart from Chiang, among those who trained in Japan were generals Ho Ying-ch'in and Chang Chun. Even as late as 1935, fifty Chinese students had been training at the Imperial Military Academy. Overseeing the Chinese students was Col. Kono Etsujiro. An intelligence veteran expert in Chinese affairs, Kono later directed several SSAs and held the post of supreme political advisor to the Manchukuo Army before his death in 1944.[54]

Gen. Ho Ying-ch'in, who had graduated in 1916 from Japan's Military Academy, showed the utmost respect in Nanking when he accepted in 1945 the surrender of more than a million Japanese under his former military instructor, Gen. Okamura Yasuji. Ho showed deference to Okamura despite the Japanese general having waged a brutal war of "kill all, burn all, loot all" against the Chinese.[55] Despite a toll of death and destruction in China far surpassing that elsewhere in Asia, Chiang permitted the repatriation of numerous officers whom the Americans, British, or Dutch would surely have hanged as war criminals for similar offenses against their citizens. Col. Tatsumi Eiichi, commanding officer of the Third Division in central China, possibly owed his life to such calculations and connections. Shortly after the Japanese surrender, Tatsumi received a visit from Gen. Tang Enpo. The two officers had a high regard for one another based on past dealings. As a result, Tatsumi and nearly his entire division sailed home in May 1946.[56]

The Nationalists brought Japanese officers into the postwar civil war as intelligence auxiliaries. One such Japanese was Col. Tsuji Masanobu. Revered by some in the Japanese Army as a "god of operations," Tsuji had directed much of the intelligence and operations planning behind General Yamashita's capture of Singapore in early 1942. Tsuji was also responsible for the thousands of Chinese massacred after the fall of Singapore and the thousands of Americans and Filipinos killed in the Bataan Death March. Eluding the British in

Southeast Asia at the war's end, disguised as a monk, he secretly made contact with Chiang Kai-shek's operatives in Bangkok on 28 October. Tsuji boldly demanded that Chiang's local intelligence operatives escort him to China, where he would propose a Sino-Japanese alliance to Chiang and Tai Li, the generalissimo's feared intelligence chief. Tsuji's bold gamble succeeded. Leaving Bangkok on 1 November under escort, Tsuji eventually reached Chungking on 19 March 1946.

Tai Li's death in an air accident while on a visit to Nanking on 24 March deprived Tsuji of his meeting with Chiang's wartime intelligence chief. But soon after the Nationalists moved their capital to Nanking on 2 May, Chiang's intelligence staff sent for Tsuji. He arrived there on 1 July, then joined Chiang's military intelligence staff. Working with him were Lt. Gen. Doi Akio and Maj. Gen. Yamamoto Hayashi. Yamamoto, the Nakano School's last commandant, had gone underground in Japan at the war's end before quietly making his way to Nanking in 1947. It is unclear whether it was due to CIC incompetence or connivance that Yamamoto escaped capture in Japan during the Occupation's early months. That he left occupied Japan for China after Willoughby took control of CIC suggests that he left with Willoughby's blessing.[57]

Welcomed by the Nationalists, Tsuji could not dissuade them from marching to disaster. Judging that the Communists were too strongly entrenched in the north, he advised against committing Nationalist forces to Manchuria before consolidating their position in central and southern China. Much to his frustration, Tsuji found his sound advice ignored.

In April 1948, Tsuji received permission from his Chinese superiors for a three-month leave of absence to go to Tokyo. In May, after meeting with the Nationalists' military intelligence chief, he left Shanghai, disguised as a professor, on a ship of Japanese repatriates. After coming ashore at Sasebo later that month, he quietly made contact with MacArthur's intelligence staff via Japanese veterans in Willoughby's employ. Tsuji was particularly close to Hattori Takushiro, the man around whom Willoughby intended to reconstruct the Japanese Army. Hattori and Tsuji had both helped direct Japan's small war with the Soviet Union at Nomonhan in 1939 as well as for the war against the United States, Great Britain, and the Netherlands in 1941. Still a wanted man, Tsuji probably had arranged his return in advance through Hattori. Once in Japan, he associated with other Japanese serving Willoughby as intelligence auxiliaries, including Kodama Yoshio and Lt. Col. Asaeda Shigeharu. While supposedly a secret, the notorious Tsuji's presence was widely known among journalists in Tokyo.[58]

Tsuji's return to Tokyo underscored MacArthur's ties to Chiang Kai-shek. In the nearly five years between the Japanese surrender and the Korean War, MacArthur's intelligence staff grew to rely on the Nationalists for much of their intelligence.[59] It would be natural, then, for Willoughby to permit veterans to serve the Nationalists. The journey of the Nakano School's last commandant to Nanking in 1947 seems a case in point. One can imagine that Yamamoto Hayashi eluded capture within Japan during the first nine months of the Occupation, before Willoughby gained control of CIC and ended the hunt for war criminals. It is harder to imagine Japanese escaping from occupied Japan by ship or plane to China. Given Willoughby's relations with Arisue and Chiang, it seems likely that Yamamoto left Japan with G-2's authorization.

Willoughby also likely sped another trio of intelligence officers on their covert mission to China in 1949. Three Japanese military advisors flew from Japan via Hong Kong to Taiwan in late October. Two of the three, Maj. Gen. Tomita Naosuke and Capt. Aratake Kunimitsu, were army veterans. The third, Cmdr. Sugita Toshimitsu, was a former naval officer. Tomita and Aratake had served together in China.[60] Each of the three men used a Chinese alias. Tomita's cover name was Pai, or White. From his alias would come "White Unit" (*Paidan*), the name for covert Japanese military advisors to Chiang Kai-shek's shattered forces on the island of Taiwan. One Japanese author who has written on the White Unit suggests the name likely was chosen for the anti-Communist connotation of "white" versus the communist "red."[61]

Aratake Kunimitsu had graduated from the Nakano School to serve as an intelligence officer at the headquarters of China Expeditionary Army. In March 1944, he had gone to Hong Kong to serve as deputy to an officer who had preceded him at the Nakano School. Their primary mission in Hong Kong was to gather intelligence on the Nationalists. Aratake was fortunate in that his agency in Hong Kong enjoyed a close relationship with the local military government, which was not always the case for intelligence officers. In Hong Kong, fortunately, the military government's chief of staff was Lt. Gen. Tada Tokuichi. A former lecturer at the Nakano School, Tada did not share the suspicious view of many regular military officers regarding covert operations.

Aratake's agency enjoyed a number of successes. In June 1944, an agent who had infiltrated a U.S. Air Force officers' club in Kweilin learned of plans for American pilots based in Chengtu to conduct an air raid against Kitakyushu. Kweilin, like most major Chinese cities, was riddled with Japanese agents. Some were among the numerous prostitutes who serviced the American soldiers in the area. Other Japanese agents posed as refugees. Another agent gathered intelligence regarding Allied plans for a counteroffensive in Burma. Aratake's agency had received commendations from China Expeditionary Army headquarters for its achievements.[62]

Aratake's next assignment was with the Twenty-third Army, where he served as deputy in an affiliated intelligence outfit. Early in 1945, he learned that a captured Chinese intelligence officer was facing execution by the Kempeitai. Aratake considered the man's execution a waste, seeing greater advantage in using the man for access to Chiang Kai-shek. Aratake conceived of using the prisoner to deliver a proposal to Chiang Kai-shek for alliance. He then proposed his idea to his superior, Maj. Gen. Tomita Naosuke. Tomita, an infantry officer from Kumamoto Prefecture, was chief of staff for Twenty-third Army as well as Aratake's direct superior. Convinced by Aratake, Tomita ordered the Kempeitai to release the prisoner into Aratake's custody. Aratake treated him well to recruit him. As part of this effort, Aratake took the man to meet two Chinese officials in the collaborationist regime at Nanking. Aratake finally sent him, escorted by another intelligence officer of the Nakano School, through the lines on his mission as messenger to Chiang Kai-shek.

By August 1948, the former prisoner had become a senior intelligence officer on Taiwan. In order to arrange for Japanese military advisors, he sent an emissary to Kobe. The second Chinese, a former official of the previous Nanking regime, was one of the two to whom Aratake had introduced him in 1945. It was then Aratake who escorted the envoy to Tokyo for discussions with Tomita. Following those talks, Aratake went via Hong Kong in secret to Taipei for talks with generals Peng Meng-chi, Niu Hsien-ming, and Li Li-po. While in Taipei, the former prisoner's wife profusely thanked Aratake and the Nakano School officer who had once escorted her husband through the lines for saving his life. In the end, the two sides reached an agreement to send Japanese military advisors to the Nationalists.

Preceding the White Unit to Taiwan was Lt. Gen. Nemoto Hiroshi, one of the Japanese Army's leading China experts. Following discussions in Japan with an emissary of Chiang Kai-shek in spring 1949, Nemoto had led a small group of advisors from a port in Kyushu in May. Nemoto arrived at Keelung the following month and remained in Taiwan until June 1952. Nemoto reportedly directed the successful defense of Quemoy in October 1949. Permitting the Chinese Communist invasion force to land unmolested, as the Japanese Army had done for the Americans in Okinawa four years earlier, Nemoto then directed the Nationalists to destroy the invasion force's fleet of junks and launch a counterattack.[63]

So it was that Tomita, Aratake, and Sugita had flown from Japan on 28 October 1949 for the former Japanese colony of Taiwan as the lead members of a team of seventeen Japanese military advisors. On 3 November, in the company of Gen. Peng Meng-chi, the trio met Generalissimo Chiang Kai-shek in Taipei. On 17 November, Tomita took Aratake to Chungking for a second meeting with Chiang, who had flown ahead of them to the mainland. The two Japanese then went to inspect the front lines at the battle for south China. They then left ahead of Chiang on a flight to Taiwan, departing the besieged mainland on 28 November. The following month, Chiang escaped the tightening noose around Chengtu by flying to Taiwan.[64] That same month, Maj. Gen. Okamoto Kakujiro, who had once given lectures at the Nakano School, left with eleven former Japanese military officers by ship from Kyushu for Taiwan; another two members of the original seventeen members of the White Unit had sailed from Kyushu in November.[65]

Tomita and Aratake occupied a key place in Chiang Kai-shek's plans to defend Taiwan and return to the mainland. Their role was particularly important in the desperate time between Chiang's flight to the island at the end of 1949 and the formal resumption of Washington's aid in the form of a 116-man Military Assistance Aid Group (MAAG) under Maj. Gen. William C. Chase in the spring of 1951. The White Unit was probably part of a secret program approved by Washington. According to Joseph B. Smith, an American intelligence officer, President Truman had approved covert aid while giving

Chiang the cold shoulder in public. In any event, Japanese press reporting of Nemoto's presence and American diplomatic reporting of Tomita's White Unit did not end their activities.[66] Chiang entrusted handling of the White Unit's training program, which included strategy, tactics, spiritual training, and anticommunist indoctrination, to his most trusted subordinates. When the White Unit opened its training center in May 1950, Chiang himself attended the ceremony.[67]

By the summer of 1951, more than fifty Japanese military veterans had quietly entered Taiwan as advisors of the White Unit. In that year, the White Unit peaked at seventy-six Japanese advisors. In all, eighty-three veteran officers of imperial Japan journeyed to the former colony to train the Nationalists by the time the White Unit ceased operations in 1964.[68]

Korean War

Col. Yamamoto Kenzo probably thought that his counterfeiting days had ended the day Japan surrendered. Yamamoto, an intendance officer of the Imperial Japanese Army, had been with Second Bureau's Eighth Section (Covert) when Col. Iwakuro Hideo had tapped him to execute the Army's counterfeiting operation against China. Yamamoto, as director of the Noborito Research Institute's Third Section, then directed his stable of talented counterfeiters in producing Nationalist yuan notes. Men of the Nakano School then had distributed the fake currency in China. In addition to counterfeiting the yuan and other foreign currencies, Yamamoto's Third Section also forged enemy documents, passports, and other identification papers.[69]

In the spring of 1948, there came to Yamamoto's residence in Tokyo's Nakano Ward a summons for him to appear at the Nippon Yusen Kaisha (NYK) Building, which housed Willoughby's men. Yamamoto had already confessed his past counterfeiting activities to American interrogators during a brief period of detention after Japan's surrender. Unsure of how much he should reveal, Yamamoto first checked with Arisue Seizo, who counseled Yamamoto to speak freely. Yamamoto then learned what interested G-2. He spent a month outlining the organization and activities of the Noborito's Third Section.[70] His interrogators found particularly impressive Yamamoto's background in forging Soviet passports and his knowledge regarding Manchurian and Soviet topography. His interlocutors then demanded his cooperation. In exchange, they offered to protect him from the Soviets and Chinese, who would surely see him as a war criminal on account of his past. Yamamoto, given an offer he could not refuse, readily agreed.[71]

In the spring of 1950, Yamamoto recruited former subordinates from Third Section. By May, he had convinced about a dozen men to join him in working for the U.S. Army. The veteran forgers went to work in a depot on the sprawling naval base at Yokosuka, which the U.S. Navy had confiscated from the Japanese Navy. A depot, where the flow of men and equipment would pass for normal, was a natural cover. The forgers, ostensibly members of a nondescript outfit, the Government Printing Supplies Office (GPSO), turned out phony passports, uniforms, and identification papers of the Chinese Communists, North Koreans, and Soviets.[72]

Ban Shigeo was another recruit. During the war, he had served in Col. Yamada Sakura's Second Section at Noborito. Ban led Subsection 1 in developing covert communications techniques, including invisible inks and the means to detect them. His wartime duties of development and dissemination had taken him far afield: China, French Indochina, Indonesia, the Philippines, and Singapore. The Japanese Army recognized him and Maj. Gen. Shinoda Ryo, Noborito's commander, with a major certificate and cash award. Japanese-American intelligence officers of the CIC visited Ban in October 1945 to query him on the explosives and CI equipment he had handled. Once the Korean War had started, the U.S. government invited him to Yokosuka. By 1951, Ban was chief of GPSO Chemical Section.[73]

The Noborito Research Institute's veteran forgers in G-2's employ produced the documents and paraphernalia that Charles Willoughby required to infiltrate agents into North Korea, China, and the Soviet Union. Among units under his control that collected intelligence were the Canon Agency, 8177 Army Unit (AU), 8240 AU, and the 308th CIC Detachment.[74] In the American zone of Korea, Willoughby's CIC relied on paid agents, rightist youth organizations, and the interrogation of refugees from North Korea or Manchuria. As in Japan, the local police were invaluable partners.

Willoughby had his intelligence network on the peninsula soon after the Japanese surrender ceremony. The CIC first hit the peninsula on 9 September 1945, when men of the 224th CIC Detachment reached South Korea. Others would soon follow. The 441st CIC Detachment in Tokyo, under Willoughby's control from May 1946, had jurisdiction over all CIC units in Korea. In a veiled dig at the fledgling CIA, a history of CIC boasted: "No other intelligence agency in Korea could claim more complete coverage than CIC." Still, CIC was not up to snuff. The only men who could function without interpreters were two Korean-speaking white agents and a dozen Nisei.

As in Japan, CIC's main function was less conducting independent intelligence activities than communicating with the local military, police, and other former officials of the Japanese Empire. An internal report noted that, with language the foremost barrier to operations, CIC relied too much on unscrupulous Korean interpreters and translators, many inherited from the Japanese colonial administration. [75] CIC also sent some refugees back north as agents.[76] These activities also required local support. According to Lt. Yon Chong, an intelligence officer of the Republic of Korea's Navy (ROKN) assigned to Tokyo under G-2, the materials for Willoughby's infiltration operations on the continent—from combat uniforms of the Chinese People's Liberation Army (PLA) to peasant coolie rags—came from the Tokyo area.[77]

In addition to the Noborito Research Institute, men of the Nakano School were probably involved in Willoughby's operations on the continent. Investigators of a major Japanese newspaper reported in a history of the shadow warriors in Okinawa that a number of intelligence veterans operated on the Korean Peninsula in the postwar years.[78] Also, according to Inagaki Takashi, a former member of the Shanghai SSA, for example, three plainclothes American military intelligence officers approached him in the spring of 1948. The Americans, apparently CIC, demanded that Inagaki, repatriated from China in 1946, return to the Shanghai area to gather intelligence related to the Chinese civil war. Inagaki, detained for six months when captured by Communists on a mission that began in April 1949, returned to Tokyo to work with CIC on other amphibious insertion operations. Willoughby apparently had formed an auxiliary organization of intelligence officers with continental experience, possibly including veterans of the Nakano School. A member of the "Japan Lobby," a group of Americans who promoted Japanese interests, writing to John Foster Dulles in January 1951 noted the availability for service in the Korean War of intelligence officers who had "formerly operated in China."[79]

At least one member of the Nakano School also reportedly joined a mission to North Korea. In November 1948, Willoughby's Canon Agency sent an intelligence team by boat to North Korea; the team included at least one veteran of the Nakano School. The team returned around 20 December after searching the Ch'ongjin, Wonsan, and P'yongyang areas to determine the extent of the Soviet Red Army's presence on the peninsula. The Canon Agency's men found few signs of the Soviets but did detect military equipment and arms of the Korean People's Army (KPA) heading south towards the border. Canon, impressed by the team's success, reportedly praised the Nakano School for the quality of its graduates.[80]

Japan's shadow warriors remained active after the Korean War erupted in June 1950. The disguises and forged documents of the Noborito Research Institute's veterans remained essential for infiltration operations. One such operation contributed to MacArthur's amphibious invasion behind enemy lines at Inch'on. In that infiltration, ROKN Adm. Son Won-il ordered Lt. Cmdr. Ham Myong-su to lead a unit on a mission to gather intelligence on North Korean defenses between the port of Inch'on and the capital of Seoul. Ham, a veteran intelligence officer who knew the area well, left Pusan on 23 August with a team of four officers and thirteen NCOs. Ham's men, operating from an island off Inch'on, went ashore dressed as KPA soldiers, security officers, stevedores, and fishermen to infiltrate the port and the surrounding area. They identified the coastal batteries on the island of Wolmi-do, discovered some two dozen machine-gun nests on another island, and searched for KPA units. Of vital importance to MacArthur's gamble to launch an amphibious assault, Ham found Inch'on lightly defended. His men detected only about one thousand KPA troops in the area. Ham's intelligence went to ROKN headquarters at Chinhae. Admiral Son then relayed the welcome intelligence to MacArthur's GHQ in Tokyo.

To confirm Ham's findings as well as Japanese hydrographic intelligence on Inch'on's dramatic tides and treacherous channels, Willoughby sent a joint Army-CIA team in Operation Trudy Jackson back to the area in late August under the U.S. Navy's Ensign Eugene Clark and ROKN Lt. Yon Chong. Yon, an energetic and capable officer, had received orders from Willoughby via Canon three weeks before the Korean War erupted to go quietly to Korea to survey the readiness of the ROK Army as well as its intelligence on the KPA. Yon, met at Inch'on on 6 June by the commanding officer of the 308th CIC Detachment, later met ROK Army Chief of Staff Ch'ae Pyong-dok and other top brass. One survey section of the Inch'on team went as far as Seoul. In addition, agents who parachuted behind enemy lines made their way to the operation's base on an island off Inch'on. During this operation, too, Yamamoto and his forgers at Yokosuka's GPSO likely furnished the uniforms and identification papers necessary to infiltrate the Inch'on area.[81]

Around the time of the Inch'on landing in mid-September, Willoughby ordered an intelligence team sent to survey the border between North Korea and Chinese Manchuria. Well before any formal U.N. order, General MacArthur had decided to take his forces across the 38th parallel all the way to the border on the Yalu River. Once again, Lt. Yon Chong left with a team, including Japanese operatives, for his mission north of P'yongyang. Reflecting MacArthur's concern over the possible entry of Communist China into the war, members of the team infiltrated the Chinese side of the Yalu River and even penetrated as far north as Mukden as well as points on the Liaotung and Shantung peninsulas. Yon's team reported Chinese were present in North Korea as early as October.[82] MacArthur, determined to unite the peninsula, chose to ignore this and other reports pointing to Chinese intervention.

The Inch'on landing, MacArthur's masterstroke of the war, illustrates well the importance of covert Japanese assistance. Indeed, Willoughby's intelligence auxiliaries likely steered their American partners to Inch'on as a suitable invasion site. At the onset of the Korean War, MacArthur's G-2 reportedly called on Japanese intelligence veterans for their advice. Willoughby's auxiliaries reportedly recommended Inch'on.[83] In retrospect, the recommendation appears a suitable one. The Japanese Army had, after all, conducted amphibious operations at Inch'on in both the Sino-Japanese War of 1894–95 and the Russo-Japanese War of 1904–05.[84] Those campaigns, and nearly forty years of colonial rule, had left the Japanese with a wealth of data on Inch'on's treacherous tides.

In addition to hydrographic intelligence on Inch'on, the Japanese also provided topographic intelligence to MacArthur's forces in Korea. Gen. Paek Son-yop of the ROK Army recalled in his memoirs receiving maps, presumably from Tokyo, printed in Japanese and English. Paek also received from Tokyo the propaganda leaflets urging communist guerrillas operating behind UN lines to surrender.[85] Willoughby himself noted in his biography of MacArthur that G-2's Geographical Branch put together maps with the help of Japanese military veterans.[86] General Paek, a veteran of the former Japanese Army, was fighting with the assistance of veteran fellow officers in Tokyo.

In the Korean War, men related to the Nakano School also proved their worth in operations against communist guerrillas. Men who had once served under Japanese officers in Manchukuo constituted much of the ROK Army's officer corps. Some officers had served before the Second World War in the Chientao SSA, waging "pacification campaigns" against Korean and Chinese guerrillas. The Chientao Special Force was a special unit of Korean volunteers formed in March 1939. The unit was one of several special "foreign units," including the famous Asano Unit of White Russians, organized under Kwantung Army intelligence officers. Lt. Col. Okoshi Nobuo, who held the concurrent positions of Chientao SSA chief and Chientao District military advisor, was the driving force behind the creation of the Chientao Special Force.

The Korean officers and men fought under Japanese command to exterminate guerrillas in the area around Chientao in southeast Manchukuo, home to more than five hundred thousand ethnic Koreans, then 85 percent of the area's population. The Chientao Special Force was apparently a component or subordinate unit of the Chientao SSA of the Kwantung Army Headquarters Intelligence Section. As in the Asano Unit and other special service agencies, graduates of the Nakano School occupied key positions in the Chientao SSA. Following the posting of the first Nakano School officer in 1940, nearly ten served in the Chientao SSA by the end of the war. Unlike some of the Chinese units under Japanese command, there was no mutiny of the Chientao Special Force. On 26 August, the Japanese commander disbanded the force of some three hundred Koreans at Chinchou, some two hundred kilometers southwest of Mukden. Under the direction of the Korean officers, the men headed home for Korea.[87]

Rigorous repression throughout Korea had long ago driven Korean independence fighters across the border into the mountains of the Chientao region. Taking advantage of the rugged terrain and large Korean population, small bands of guerrillas continued raids against Japanese and puppet forces. Kim Il-song, later dictator of North Korea until his death in 1994, was the most prominent of these guerrillas. Yet, even his exploits were minor pinpricks. Kim Il-song achieved his greatest moment in a raid on Poch'onbo from Manchukuo the night of 4 June 1937. His partisan band of roughly a hundred guerrillas killed seven policemen, wounded another seven, and destroyed the town's police station along with several other government buildings before retreating into Manchukuo once again.[88]

The Japanese responded to the provocations of Kim Il-song and other guerrillas with an increasingly effective pacification campaign. Throughout Manchukuo, the Japanese had worked to eradicate opposition to their rule by separating the guerrillas from the general population. Fortified villages, improved lines of communications, and strengthened local militias were all elements of the Japanese strategy.[89]

Even Kim Il-song failed to withstand Japanese pressure, in part played through the Chientao Special Force, which grew particularly intense from the end of 1939. Kim ultimately fled Manchukuo for refuge in the Soviet Union, crossing the border into the Soviet Far East in November 1940. He spent the war years in the Soviet Far East. Lt. Gen. Nikolai Lebedev, a staff officer of the Soviet occupation forces stationed in P'yongyang after the war, recalled that the Japanese Army's attacks had proven too much for the Korean guerrilla leader. In desperate circumstances, Kim had led his "defeated" little band over the border. For the rest of the war, he would train at a secret camp near Khabarovsk as a member of the Soviet Red Army's Eighty-eighth Brigade.[90]

Korean officers of the Chientao Special Force who survived the Second World War and evaded Soviet capture joined the ROK Army. Several rose to high positions. Of the hundreds, if not thousands, of Koreans who served in the Chientao Special Force, about a dozen rose to prominent positions in the ROK military. Paek Son-yop, the most famous, served twice as Army chief of staff before heading the ROK Joint Chiefs of Staff. Kim Sok-pom commanded the ROK Marine Corps. Yi Tong-hwa commanded an army corps before becoming commandant of the General Staff College. Kim Paek-il commanded ROK I Corps before his death in 1951.

Kim Paek-il and Paek Son-yop demonstrated particular vigor in applying their talents for guerrilla suppression, first honed in the Chientao Special Force, in South Korea. Kim Paek-il played a key role in suppressing the Yosu rebellion of October 1948. Leftists in the ROK Army's Sixth and Fourteenth Regiments in the port city of Yosu had incited a rebellion when their units were ordered to join a campaign to suppress guerrillas on the island of Cheju.[91] His talent for pacification next took him to the Chiri Mountains. Kim had just assumed command of the ROK Army infantry school, established in November 1949, as its first commandant. But an insurgency immediately required his talents. The day after the opening ceremony, Kim left for the Chiri Mountains to conduct sweeps against guerrillas in the region. Again, the veteran guerrilla fighter achieved "brilliant" results in three months of operations. His career came to an end in a fatal plane crash on 28 March 1951.[92]

Another of the Chientao Special Force's veterans was Gen. Paek Son-yop, considered by his American superiors to be the ablest general officer of the ROK Army. Gen. James Van Fleet, commanding officer of the Eighth Army and Paek's superior, considered him the ROK Army's "best fighting general."[93] Even before the Korean War erupted, Paek had applied his experience in the Kwantung Army to insurgencies in South Korea. In 1949, as commanding officer of the ROK Army Fifth Division, Paek had led sweeps against guerrillas in the Kwangju region. He had also held the post of ROK Army intelligence chief, which gave him experience on another level regarding combat against insurgents.[94]

Paek's crowning achievement as a guerrilla fighter, however, came during the Korean War. In November 1951, Gen. James Van Fleet called Paek to his headquarters at Eighth Army. Communist guerrillas in the Chiri Mountains, between Seoul and Pusan, were harassing military units and obstructing lines of communication. Government authority existed only during daylight hours. According to a popular expression: "It's the Republic of Korea during the daytime. But it's the People's Republic of Korea at night."[95] Van Fleet, determined to exterminate resistance in the area, had chosen the Kwantung Army veteran for Operation Ratkiller.

Paek, who had earned his spurs suppressing Korean guerrillas under Japanese officers, was to lead the greatest pacification campaign of his career under American command. Van Fleet had directed campaigns against leftist insurgents in Greece's bloody civil war. The American general assigned Lt. Col. William Dodds, who had served under him in Greece, to guide Paek's campaign. The Eighth Army's commander granted Paek command of the ROK Army's Capital Division and Eighth Division. Also at his disposal were the troops of the

Southwest District Combat Command, local units of the Korea National Police (KNP), and rightist youth groups.

Paek deployed his task force around the Chiri Mountains. To isolate the guerrillas and sympathetic villagers, the authorities placed the area under martial law and cut telephone service between villages. It was a replay of the past. From the late 1930s until the end of the Second World War, the Japanese and their Korean auxiliaries had eliminated or driven into the Soviet Union the forces of Kim Il-song and other anti-Japanese leaders from the mountainous terrain on both sides of the border between Manchukuo and Korea. In December 1934, the Japanese had issued an order through the government of Manchukuo for the construction of collective villages. Residents were required to move to the new settlements, which generally ranged in size from fifty to 150 households. Formed in the shape of a square, with guns placed every hundred meters along a perimeter marked by a trench, earthen wall, and barbed wire, the new villages were designed to keep guerrillas from the peasant population. Passage in and out of the villages was strictly controlled. The Japanese had concentrated villagers in the area into protected settlements and imposed a system of collective responsibility to punish the relatives and neighbors of those who passed intelligence or otherwise aided the independence fighters. Beyond the settlements, the Japanese waged a pitiless campaign, for anyone not residing in a settlement was deemed a guerrilla.

Paek in fact was conducting a campaign similar to those he had known in Manchukuo. KNP auxiliaries and youth regiments were deployed to cut off escape routes while Paek drew his noose around the mountains where the guerrillas kept their strongholds. On 8 December, Paek's forces swept the summit of Mt. Chiri. On 26 January 1952, two consecutive rings of troops closed on rebel forces, wiping out the core of the resistance. In all, Paek's men killed or captured more than nineteen thousand guerrillas by the time Operation Ratkiller ended on 15 March. A former guerrilla from the Southern Army noted in his account of the campaign that even today there are no reliable figures for casualties. He put it at more than six thousand deaths among the ROK military and police forces and well in excess of ten thousand guerrilla deaths. It is likely that more than twenty thousand Koreans in all died in that single savage episode of that tragic war.[96]

Contributing Talents to Cold War

Men associated with the Nakano School, some of whom had buried arms caches in the summer of 1945 for a possible uprising against the Occupation forces of the United States, played an important postwar role in helping the U.S. Army to gather intelligence on the Soviet Union. Their expertise was critical. In the early years of the Cold War, in the days before satellite imagery and other technical marvels of our day, Japan's shadow warriors supplied much of the intelligence. How officers of the U.S. Army must have welcomed the Japanese maps, agent reports, and other legacies of the Imperial Japanese Army's Second Bureau! Starting from scratch would have been too daunting to imagine, particularly with the constraints of a peacetime budget and personnel.

Certain veterans of or related to the Nakano School, entitled by dint of their wartime service to a quiet life in postwar Japan, enlisted in the Cold War. From the battlefields of China to the operations support facilities of Yokohama, they applied their talents against the Soviet Union and its allies. Without their help, the U.S. Army would have fought with far fewer resources. From topographical intelligence to guerrilla suppression operations, Japanese intelligence veterans played vital roles.

11

OLD BOYS IN NEW JAPAN

Imperial Japan had disappeared in the flames of the Second World War. Flowering from the ashes of war and occupation was a new Japan. The roots remained the same, but the plant appeared strikingly different. New Japan boasted in 1946 a new constitution, drafted secretly in English by officials of General MacArthur's Government Section, translated into Japanese, and imposed upon the nation. Under the new charter, the Japanese people exercised power through their elected representatives in the National Diet. The imperial throne remained as a symbol of national unity, although Japan's emperor no longer had an empire. He no longer enjoyed supreme command of a mighty military. Emperor Hirohito, who weathered the storm of defeat, put aside his uniform and white horse for a common suit of clothes. No longer reviewing the troops, he posed for photographs before a microscope to remind the public that he was an amateur marine biologist.

In new Japan, there no longer existed an Imperial Army and Imperial Navy. Article Nine of the constitution both renounced war as a sovereign right and forbade Japan even to maintain armed forces. The giant manufacturers whose factories had produced the weapons of war struggled to shift production lines to civilian uses. They began producing pots, pans, and buses instead of bullets, rifles, and bombers. Japan's conglomerates also maneuvered to avoid or survive the trust-busting policies of the Occupation's New Dealers. One example was Mitsubishi Heavy Industries (MHI), whose famed Zero fighter had dominated the skies over China and the Pacific for much of the war. MHI resulted from the 1936 merger of Mitsubishi Shipbuilding and Mitsubishi Aircraft. Broken by Occupation policy into three companies in 1950, the company would regroup as "New" MHI in 1964. Overcoming the blanket ban on Japanese aerospace R&D that lasted until the Occupation's end in 1952, MHI has long since returned to the skies. The company is manufacturing Japan's new F-2 fighter as well as missiles and other advanced military systems.

The war's ending released many Japanese from years of deprivation and regimentation. Scrambling to find food and shelter in the first desperate months after the surrender, people by and large put their lives back together as food returned to the markets and new houses rose from the rubble. Many Japanese rushed to embrace postwar pop culture, free of the thought police, Kempeitai, and neighborhood leaders who had pushed them to wear drab wartime clothing, closed the dance halls, and branded jazz as a decadent enemy influence. Women again had their hair permed. The young danced the jitterbug and other wild American steps. When the Korean War erupted, endless streams of American purchases for the soldiers at the front, as well as the countless American soldiers who dropped extravagant sums on R&R, set the Japanese economy growing. The ashes of imperial Japan progressively disappeared under the growth of new Japan.

Many of the war's survivors, however, continued to suffer. The rising economic tide brought little comfort to the countless Japanese suffering the loss of loved ones. A staggering number of soldiers and civilians had died overseas and in the home islands, leaving behind widows, aged parents, and orphaned children. Hundreds of thousands disappeared into Soviet prison camps. Many men in their middle years and youths in their teens, hastily drafted into service in Manchukuo and Korea, died in captivity. An estimated sixty thousand of roughly six hundred thousand Japanese died in the Soviet Union.

Other Japanese faced a long jail term or death sentence from Allied tribunals. Many of those sentenced were guilty of wartime cruelty, even atrocities, against Allied prisoners or civilians. Hundreds paid for their acts with their lives. In Tokyo, senior Japanese military officers came before the International Military Tribunal for the Far East (IMTFE). Their accusers charged them with plotting against peace, as if waging war were some domestic crime akin to the bootlegging of Al Capone. General Tojo and several other so-called "Class A war criminals" received the death sentence. In Yokohama, the Allies leveled charges against lesser officers, soldiers, and military civilians accused of murdering or mistreating prisoners of war. Similar trials took place at various tribunals in Southeast Asia. In India, the British brought to trial former officers of the Indian Army for joining the INA in collaboration with the Japanese. Allied courts tried more than four thousand Japanese and executed nearly a thousand. More than three hundred Japanese received life sentences, with more than three thousand receiving lesser terms in jail.

Hundreds of the Nakano School's shadow warriors had sacrificed their lives in the war. More than fifty had died during the harrowing Imphal campaign alone. Only a few of the roughly one hundred sent to the Philippines had survived MacArthur's return to the islands.[1] Many intelligence officers who survived the Red Army's offensive in the war's closing week perished in Soviet captivity. Nearly three hundred intelligence personnel of the Kwantung Army fell into Soviet hands. In one account, ten members of the Nakano School were among fifteen intelligence officers caught by the Soviet Union's dreaded counterintelligence organ SMERSH. The Soviets executed all fifteen men, twelve of them before a firing squad. Maj. Gen. Akigusa Shun, founder of the Nakano School and intelligence chief of the Kwantung Army at the war's end, died in a prison near Moscow in early 1949.[2]

In Southeast Asia, Allied tribunals put to death several members of the Nakano School. One of those executed was Maj. Niiho Satoru, a member of the Nakano School's First Class. Before Pearl Harbor, Niiho had gone to Batavia in the guise of a foreign correspondent for Japan's Domei News Agency to gather intelligence on the Dutch oil fields at Palembang and elsewhere in advance of the Japanese invasion. During the war, following a period back in Japan, he transferred to Nineteenth Army headquarters on New Guinea. Natives friendly to the Japanese would at times hand over downed Allied airmen to the Japanese. He had executed them in line with Japanese military policy.

Tried by the Dutch, Niiho was sentenced to die on 8 December 1948. The seventh anniversary of Pearl Harbor, the date suggested less a verdict of justice than vengeance. On the evening before his death, he wrote one letter each to his wife and son. In the letter to his wife, Toshiko, he encouraged her to live in the face of the hardships she would encounter without him. He also asked her to take care of their son. He described his sentence as an act of revenge, then begged her forgiveness for his inability to care for her. He assured his wife that he would die bravely the next morning, as a Japanese. Niiho's note to his son, who had been born only after he had left Japan for New Guinea, was brief. Writing that he would stand before a firing squad the next morning, he told his son how sorry he was to die without ever seeing his face. Proud of having served Japan, he assured his boy that "Wherever there is a spirit of sacrifice for your country, there your father will always be. Farewell, son."[3]

In Japan, other members of the Nakano School came under arrest for executing American fliers. On the morning of 26 September 1946, police in Kagoshima Prefecture acted on behalf of the American Occupation forces in arresting Maj. Itezono Tatsuo. Itezono had led a group of guerrilla fighters from the Nakano School in the gruesome execution of the eight American crewmen at Aburayama, in Kyushu, on 11 August the previous year. Nearly eight months after arresting Itezono, the police dragnet also caught Lt. Yamamoto Fukuichi, one of the shadow warriors who had struck karate blows against prisoners at Aburayama. At the ensuing trial in 1948, they and others present received stiff sentences. Yamamoto was sentenced to thirty years at hard labor in Sugamo Prison.[4]

Among those jailed for the deaths at Aburayama, one man later emerged from Sugamo to forge friendships in the West. Narazaki Masahiko, the kendo adept who had wielded his sword that bloody day at Aburayama, remained in jail until 1958, when the last inmates jailed for war crimes left prison. Returning to his abiding passion, Narazaki rose through the ranks of kendo. Twice, he won first place in national competitions. He was an executive of Japan's national kendo federation and president of the federation in Saitama Prefecture, north of Tokyo. He also met many foreign students of the art and instructed them in kendo's finer points. When Narazaki passed away in September 1999, his Belgian students took note. The author of an article published by the All Belgium Kendo Federation wrote that the Belgian swordsmen who knew him would remember him as an engaging instructor with a warm smile and a love of sake.[5]

Old Boys and Asia

On 18 September 1994, nearly one hundred people gathered at a small Buddhist temple in northwest Tokyo for the fiftieth anniversary memorial service for Subhas Chandra Bose. Much had changed since the first service. When Japanese military officers had brought the remains of the Indian nationalist to Renkoji in 1945, they had acted in stealth. With Japan under military occupation, a public ceremony was out of the question. Once the Occupation ended and Japan recovered its sovereignty, however, the temple became a symbol of friendship between Japan and India. A modern structure, standing two stories high and lacking the antique art treasures of the crowded tourist temples of Kyoto, Renkoji receives few visitors on most days. In 1957, however, Indian Prime Minister Jawaharlal Nehru paid his respects during a trip to Tokyo. President Rajendra Prasad visited the next year. Prime Minister Indira Gandhi was there in 1969. In the Main Hall, among the gilded ornaments, wreathed in flowers and incense, a portrait of Bose occupies a place of honor. Before this altar to Indian independence, Indians and Japanese pay homage.

To the left of the main structure on the temple grounds lies the clue to the identity of those who worked behind the scenes to foster Japanese-Indian relations through the legacy of the Bengali nationalist. Beside the building stands a bronze bust of Bose in uniform. The monument dates from August 1990, the forty-fifth anniversary of his death in the closing days of the war. At the rear of the statue is a plaque of the organization behind it: the Subhas Chandra Bose Academy. The list of its members is revealing. Among the names are those of the three officers who directed the Japanese Army's Indian operations: Fujiwara Iwaichi, Iwakuro Hideo, and Isoda Saburo. Also listed is Takaoka Daisuke, the parliamentarian who served in Iwakuro's agency. Present as well are three graduates of the Nakano School: Fujii Chikao, Kuwahara Takeshi, and Yamazaki Takehiko.

Old boys of the Nakano School also remained involved in the affairs of other nations where they had once operated. Nowhere was this clearer than in Burma. Aung San, independent Burma's first defense minister, had trained before the war as one of the Thirty Comrades under Col. Suzuki Keiji's Minami Agency. Japan's shadow warriors lost a valued comrade when he died shortly after independence by machine-gun fire from a political rival's men. In a few years, another of the Thirty Comrades rose to power. Ne Win, one of Burma's senior military officers, seized power in 1958 for two years before taking the reins in the coup of 1962. In 1966, Tokyo rolled out the red carpet when the Burmese strongman arrived on a state visit. Among those whom Prime Minister Sato Eisaku invited to the state banquet were Col. Suzuki Keiji and Capt. Kawashima Takenobu, once the colonel's right-hand man in the Minami Agency.[6]

For certain members of the Minami Agency, their Burmese days set the course of their postwar lives. As early as 1952, the year Japan recovered its sovereignty and Japanese were free once more to travel abroad, Suzuki Keiji flew to Burma on a Japanese mission to buy rice. At Ne Win's invitation, he visited Burma in December 1966. Shortly before his death in September 1967, the old colonel met Prime Minister Sato to advise him on his impending state visit to Rangoon. Years later, Ne Win honored the memory of his Japanese mentor by inviting Suzuki's widow to Burma in February 1981 to bestow a posthumous medal on her husband. When the Burmese leader paid another visit to Tokyo, in November that year, he took time to call on the colonel's widow. As a token of his respect, he presented to her a copy of the English translation of a Japanese history of the Minami Agency.[7]

The history's author was Izumiya Tatsuro, a Nakano School graduate. He had once trained Ne Win and other members of the Thirty Comrades on the remote Chinese island of Hainan. Like Suzuki, Izumiya retained his ties to Rangoon long after the war. On 27 March 1995, he was among the members of the Minami Agency in Burma at the government's invitation for the fiftieth anniversary of the Burmese armed forces. Watching the soldiers on parade from his vantage point in the stands, he must have felt the strong pull of pride and nostalgia. On the evening of 19 September 1995, the Minami Agency's surviving members held their association's final gathering. The old boys met near Lake Hamana, an oasis of greenery and water between the sprawling metropolises of Tokyo and Nagoya. Izumiya was among the assembled veterans. Attending, too, was the Burmese ambassador to Tokyo. Among the trees stands a stone monument to Aung San, whom Colonel Suzuki had brought to the area on the eve of the war.[8]

Japan had lost the war, but old boys of the Nakano School recalled proudly their service in the shadows. Yanagawa Motoshige found reason to reflect with pride on what he had wrought. His area of operations had been the former Netherlands East Indies. He had started in Bandung shortly after the invasion with six Indonesian youths, his "children," whom he trained in intelligence. He had then recruited fifty young men for his version of the Nakano School at Tanggerang, on the outskirts of Jakarta. With PETA, the Indonesian defense forces established near the war's end, the numbers grew into the thousands.

Many of those he recruited and trained would later fight the Dutch soldiers sent to reconquer the former colony. Pondering imperial Japan's defeat, Yanagawa found meaning in Indonesia's independence. He recalled that, "In the end, I would like to say that the war was not in vain. We achieved the great war goal of national liberation."

Yanagawa would remain in Indonesia after the war, watching his "children" rise through the ranks. In all, eighty-five youths had trained at Tanggerang; all but one joined PETA. From PETA came the leaders of Indonesia's military. One youth, sixteen years old when he walked into the training hall at Tanggerang, was Zulkifi Lubis. A colonel and deputy chief of staff in the Indonesian Army, his ascent ended in the late 1950s with his arrest for playing a key role in a failed coup d'etat. Maj. Gen. Kemal Idris also graduated from Tanggerang. In September 1965, he was one of the officers who led the military's suppression of leftist forces that led two years later to the withdrawal of the Indonesian leader Sukarno from power. Three decades later, as chairman of Barisan Nasional, or the National Front, he led an organization of retired senior officers in support of Sukarno's daughter, Megawati Sukarnoputri, against Muslim political forces in the wake of President Suharto's resignation. From PETA's Second Training Unit at Bogor had risen Suharto himself, who ruled Indonesia for three decades.[9]

The Manchurian Connection

Capt. Baba Yoshimitsu was one of the more fortunate of the Nakano School's men in Manchukuo at the war's end. Interrogations quickly followed the surrender, with Baba first coming under suspicion as an intelligence officer on 21 August. When the Soviet Twenty-fifth Army moved its headquarters from Chientao to P'yongyang, Baba was one of the suspects shifted there, where he stayed between late September and November. Later placed in Soviet detention facilities, Baba experienced repeated interrogation until his trial three years after the war's end. In November 1948, he stood before a military tribunal of the Volga Military District. With him were Col. Endo Saburo, once Baba's superior as chief of the Chientao SSA; Col. Takebe Matsuo, former chief of the Heiho SSA; and several other Japanese intelligence officers. Found guilty of anti-Soviet actions on account of their intelligence service, all received prison sentences.[10]

Common prisoners who survived the bitter cold and meager rations returned to Japan in the latter half of the 1940s, but the Kwantung Army's shadow warriors remained in captivity until 1956. Following negotiations leading to a resumption of diplomatic relations between Tokyo and Moscow, the last surviving prisoners sailed from Siberia in late December on board the *Koan Maru*. Some fifty of the repatriates on board were men of the Nakano School. One of them was Baba.[11] Like many of the shadow warriors who served in Manchukuo, Baba put his life back in order with the help of fellow "old boys" with backgrounds in intelligence and continental affairs. He worked for a time for Lt. Gen. Doi Akio, once his superior as intelligence chief of the Kwantung Army. Doi had established in 1950 a think tank, the Continental Problems Research Institute, to contribute to Japanese policy on the Soviet Union and Communist China. Doi's institute enjoyed a quiet influence among Japanese leaders, including such influential backers as Adm. Nomura Kichisaburo, ambassador to Washington when the bombs fell on Pearl Harbor and an influential figure in American and naval circles in the postwar period.

In 1965, Baba accepted the invitation of Dietman Chiba Saburo to serve as executive director in Japan of the Asian Parliamentarians Union (APU). He would serve Chiba in that role until the politician's death in 1979. Chiba, impressed by the anticommunist Moral Rearmament Association (MRA) and by the Asian People's Anti-Communist League (APACL), decided to establish the APU as a forum where conservative Japanese legislators could meet with other Asian parliamentarians. Chiba launched the APU in 1964 with the backing of conservative colleagues of the ruling Liberal Democratic Party (LDP), some of them connected to the erstwhile "Manchurian faction," whose notable members had included Gen. Tojo Hideki, Kishi Nobusuke, Kaya Okinori, and Hoshino Naoki. Tojo's ties to the others came from his stint in Manchukuo as chief of staff of the Kwantung Army. Kishi was the architect of Manchukuo's industrial policy. Kaya was president of the North China Development Corporation. Hoshino held several top posts in Manchukuo's puppet government. All later joined Tojo's wartime government. Kishi Nobusuke, who had governed Japan from 1957 to 1960, became APU chairman, with Chiba holding the deputy position.

As executive director of the APU, Baba established ties with many of Asia's leading anticommunists. APU members who made the greatest impression on him were President Pak Chong-hui and Prime Minister Chong Il-gwon of the Republic of Korea (ROK), both graduates of Japan's Imperial Military Academy; President Chiang Kai-shek of the Republic of China on Taiwan; and various leaders of Southeast Asia. The Korean connection was particularly developed. Baba kept close ties to retired Lt. Gen. Min Pyong-gwon, chairman of the National Assembly's defense committee, and Chang Sung-t'ae, an influential legislator of the ruling party. Among his close associates in Southeast Asia were Jose Laurel III, former Philippine ambassador to Japan. Jose Laurel's father had served as president of the Philippines under Japanese occupation. The younger Laurel had attended the Japanese Military Academy, his entry arranged by Lt. Gen. Arisue Seizo. Fluent in Japanese, the younger Laurel remained a key player in postwar relations between Manila and Tokyo for many years after the war.[12]

In 1975, Baba strengthened his Korean connections by becoming executive director of the Japan–ROK Dietmen's League. Uno Sosuke, a member of the ruling LDP, had four years earlier launched the Japan–ROK Dietmen's Friendship Society. Uno, born and raised in Korea, was a natural candidate to foster relations. Uno, unlike Baba, was a simple conscript without intelligence duties. He had been one of the first Japanese to leave the Soviet Union for home. After sailing from Nakhodka to Japan on board the *Shinyo Maru* in October 1947, he published the following year an account of his Soviet captivity, *Damoi Tokyo* (Hello, Tokyo). In 1952, by which time Uno had become a local legislator from Shiga Prefecture, the film studio Toho released a movie version of his book, *I Was a Siberian Prisoner*. Baba, also a child of the peninsula, shared with Uno the harsh experience of Soviet detention. Chairing the counterpart ROK–Japan Dietmen's League was Kim Chong-p'il, nephew "by marriage" and former prime minister to President Pak. Baba formed close ties to influential League members Yi Pyong-hui, a former ROK Army colonel.[13]

In 1976, Japanese politicians launched the Federation of Japan–ROK Friendship Societies. Chairing the federation was Shiina Etsusaburo, the former Japanese foreign minister who had concluded in 1965 the Basic Treaty with South Korea. In 1949, MacArthur's headquarters had signed on Tokyo's behalf a commercial agreement with Seoul, which led to trade and the establishment of consular ties. The bitter colonial legacy, however, prevented official diplomatic ties until 1965. Shiina was also an old "Manchurian" hand who had served under Kishi Nobusuke in Manchukuo and in Tojo Hideki's wartime government. Baba, who continued his work promoting bilateral ties, also had contact with Prime Minister Fukuda Takeo. Fukuda was a former Finance Ministry official known for having had close ties to the Japanese Army. Baba had indeed traveled a circuitous route. Born in Korea, he had graduated from the Nakano School, toiled in the shadows of covert work in Manchukuo, suffered years of imprisonment in the Soviet Union, then rubbed elbows with Kishi and other "Manchurians" to promote Tokyo's postwar interests on the peninsula of his birth.[14]

Nakano Veterans in Politics

While Baba supported politicians of the ruling party, other old boys of the Nakano School served on the front lines of postwar politics. Maj. Gen. Matsumura Shuitsu, who had lectured on propaganda at the Nakano School, won election to the Diet. An uncounted number of veteran officers launched second careers in local politics. Lt. Col. Ozeki Masaji, a veteran intelligence officer who had also lectured at the Nakano School, won election as mayor of Gifu.

In 1963, Kimura Takechiyo won election to the Diet's lower house from his native Kagawa Prefecture as a member of the ruling LDP. He joined the political faction of Nakasone Yasuhiro, a hawk with a police background in imperial Japan's Interior Ministry and a wartime stint as a naval officer. Kimura, an early graduate of the Nakano School, had operated before Pearl Harbor from the military attaché office of the Japanese Embassy in Mexico. During the war, following his repatriation in an exchange of diplomatic personnel, he served in Second Bureau's Sixth Section. At the time he first won election to the Diet, Kimura founded the International Political and Economic Research Society as a forum on Japan's strategic policy. Among the society's members was Tairadate Katsuji, who graduated with Kimura from the same class of the Nakano School and worked with him in Second Bureau's Sixth Section.

Another shadow warrior who won election to the Diet was Ishibashi Kazuya. Trained in guerrilla warfare at the Nakano School's Futamata Branch, he graduated as a member of the Third Class in July 1945. During the Occupation, he entered local politics in his native Chiba Prefecture, winning a town council race in 1947 at the age of twenty-five. In 1976, Chiba Saburo arranged for Ishibashi to succeed him in the Diet. Chiba also arranged with the influential Fukuda Takeo, who became prime minister following the 1976 elections, for Ishibashi to join his faction of the ruling LDP.

Searching for Lieutenant Onoda

On 10 March 1974, one of imperial Japan's shadow warriors emerged in Southeast Asia. Lt. Onoda Hiroo suddenly appeared one evening in a jungle clearing before Maj. Taniguchi Yoshimi, his superior from a war that had ended nearly thirty years before. Gripping his rifle and bearing a loaded knapsack, Onoda stood at attention while the former CI chief of Gen. Yamashita Tomoyuki's Fourteenth Area Army read to him an order terminating his mission. Taniguchi then barked "at ease" to his old subordinate, had him remove his knapsack, collected his rifle and ammunition, and offered him a cigarette embossed with the imperial chrysanthemum. Suzuki Norio, a young adventurer who had first run into Onoda and led Taniguchi to him, was on hand to photograph the event.

That night, Onoda talked for hours of his thirty-year mission. He spoke with pride of his alerting Fourteenth Area Army Headquarters to the American invasion fleet sailing to Manila in 1945. The next morning, he gave Taniguchi an intelligence briefing, informing his former superior of Lubang's topography and the disposition of "enemy" forces and suggesting the best places for setting up machine-gun nests. He even outlined a plan to destroy an American radar site on the island.[15]

The next day, Onoda flew by helicopter from Lubang to Manila. Dressed in a uniform, he paid a visit to President Ferdinand Marcos at Malacanang Palace. He offered his sword, which the president declined to take. Onoda then received a pardon for his thirty years of warfare on Lubang. The two men embraced before the crowd of assembled reporters and cameramen. In Tokyo, the government announced that Onoda would receive a military pension based on thirty-one years of service, that is, from the time he joined the military to the day he emerged from the jungle. However, since the Japanese Army had ceased to exist in 1945, he was not paid for his thirty years in the jungle. Onoda, considering his returning home alive compensation enough, did not seek indemnification for his service.[16]

Onoda's "surrender," more a termination of his activities, marked the end of an extraordinary mission. In the months after American forces overran Lubang in early 1945 and Japan surrendered in September, surviving Japanese soldiers on the island laid down their arms in defeat. Some forty men on Lubang surrendered during 1946. At the end of the year, however, some five hundred Japanese soldiers remained at large in the Philippines. Onoda at that time was leading three soldiers: Akatsu Yuichi, Shimada Shoichi, and Kozuka Kinshichi. One day in 1951, Akatsu left Onoda's band to surrender. In 1954, Shimada died in a shootout with Philippine forces. In 1972, Onoda lost Kozuka in another gun battle.[17]

Onoda became something of a legend during this time. In September 1946, a repatriated member of Futamata Branch reported to Major Taniguchi that his classmate Onoda was still on his mission in Lubang. Akatsu's surrender in 1951, Shimada's death in 1954, and news in 1958 of Onoda's attacking local villagers each confirmed that the shadow warrior was still alive. While searching for Onoda was impossible during the Occupation, Japan's Ministry of Health and Welfare (MHW), which included the vestigial remains of imperial Japan's war and navy ministries and had responsibility for veteran affairs, mounted a substantial search of the island in May 1959. Finding no trace of him and believing him dead, MHW issued his death notice in November that year.[18]

Careful of Philippine sensibilities, MHW had included Onoda's brother Toshio but excluded veterans of the Nakano School from the search in 1959. The veterans of Onoda's Futamata Branch class, however, increasingly joined the effort to bring him home. Lt. Suetsugu Ichiro, who had spent the last months of the war training guerrilla fighters in Kyushu, was at the forefront of the effort. In a visit to the Philippines in 1952, Suetsugu had heard news suggesting that Onoda might still be alive. Excluded from the MHW search in 1959, Suetsugu acted in Japan as an advisor. When MHW mounted another expedition in October 1972, following Kozuka's death, Suetsugu participated as the representative of Futamata Branch. During the following year, he and other classmates worked with MHW to find Onoda.[19]

When the adventurer Suzuki Norio came across Onoda in February 1973 and reported his contact to Tokyo, it was Suetsugu who arranged the dramatic termination of mission and return of Japan's "last soldier" the following year. Onoda flew on 12 March on a chartered Japanese passenger jet to Tokyo's Haneda Airport. Waiting for him there were his aged parents, an emotional flag-waving crowd, a host of reporters, and a bevy of LDP politicians eager to greet him. Following a brief hospital stay for observation, Onoda began a round of events scheduled for him by MHW. His itinerary included a visit to Yasukuni Shrine and a courtesy call on Prime Minister Tanaka Kakuei. When Onoda complained that the ministry had allowed no time in the original schedule for him to visit the graves of his fallen comrades Shimada and Kozuka, Suetsugu intervened to arrange the trips.[20]

For weeks after his return, Onoda was in the spotlight of the world's media. Newspapers around the world carried front-page photographs and stories about the slight soldier. He became a celebrity sensation in Japan, where the media reported his every move for weeks. True, Japanese soldiers had been returning to Japan since the war's end. Lt. Yamamoto Shigeichi, a classmate of Onoda from Futamata Branch, had emerged in 1956 from the Philippine jungle, where he had been since American troops had cut his unit to ribbons during the attack he led on the San Jose airfield on Mindoro during the Manila campaign. But the stream of soldiers of the first few years after the war had all but ceased over time. When Sgt. Yokoi Shoichi appeared on the American territory of Guam in January 1972, the curious Japanese media had turned the spotlight on him for a moment. Yokoi was no shadow warrior, however, simply an unexceptional NCO who had fled into the jungle with no purpose other than survival.

Onoda cut a much more heroic figure, his spare frame, intense gaze, and goatee giving him the air of a samurai who had seemingly reached Japan in a time machine. Japanese sent him tens of thousands of letters, many praising him for a stalwart character and sense of duty that postwar Japanese society had supposedly abandoned in its headlong pursuit of economic growth and private gain. A mother and her daughter even sent him a song of their own composition, "Ah, Lubang!" The foreign response to the Onoda phenomenon was a mix of wonder and disapproval. William Safire, the columnist and former speechwriter for President Nixon, referred to Onoda in a column that revealed American frustrations with Japan's growing share of America's textile market and other industrial sectors. Onoda, he sourly joked, was "the only Japanese veteran to return home to receive happy tidings" because, as "he has surely been told, Japan won World War II." The *Far Eastern Economic Review*, based in Hong Kong, wrote scathingly of the "unthinking hero's welcome" for a man who had "probably" killed "more than 30" Philippine civilians and stolen their property during his thirty-year war. The magazine also found troubling the adulation of Onoda as a "manifestation of the 'code of the samurai'" by a supposedly pacifist postwar Japan.[21]

Onoda was so popular following his return to Japan that some Japanese urged him to run for the Diet. Japan's "last soldier," however, was unhappy in the limelight. The old boy also found troubling what he saw as the withering of traditional patriotism and old virtues in a Japan devoted to the pursuit of the almighty yen. As a popular celebrity, Onoda probably could have secured a Diet seat or, without a doubt, some corporate sinecure. Finding honest work, or even walking down the street in peace, however, was impossible. Instead, the man who had spent thirty years in one jungle decided to live in another. Following the lead of his older brother Tadao, Onoda left Japan for Brazil in April 1975. Settling on 514 hectares of wild land in the Brazilian interior, close to the borders of Bolivia and Paraguay, Japan's last soldier began raising 250 head of cattle. Some thirty Japanese families in the area were also raising cattle and chickens with land acquired with the aid of the Japanese International Cooperation Agency.[22]

In 1976, Onoda married a woman introduced to him by Suetsugu Ichiro. He and his wife, Machie, worked hard to make his operation a success. In ten years, he had doubled his ranch to 1,128 hectares and was raising seventeen hundred head of cattle. He also assumed a leading role in the Japanese community. His Japanese neighbors unanimously elected him chairman of an ethnic association formed in 1978. At each New Year, Onoda would join his neighbors in a celebration that would begin with a singing of "Kimigayo," Japan's imperial anthem, and ended with copious cups of sake. Onoda also participated in creating a baseball team for the community's Japanese-Brazilian children in an effort to maintain their Japanese roots.[23]

Onoda, who kept in touch with events in Japan by reading the Japanese press of the Japanese-Brazilian community, read one day in 1980 the shocking story of a teen in Japan who had murdered his parents. The story weighed on his mind as an example of how Japan's postwar youths seemed adrift amidst Japan's prosperity. He decided to open a nature camp in Japan. Applying his experience on Lubang, Onoda opened his camp at the foot of Mt. Fuji in July 1984. Each year, Japan's last soldier returns from Brazil to run a camp where young Japanese learn land navigation; study the terrain, stars, and forest plants; and learn how to handle a knife, catch fish, pitch a tent, and apply first aid. He also trains counselors who will work in other camps. The counselors and campers then apply their lessons in survival games, living off the land. Onoda, never blessed with his own children, calls his own the thousands of children who attended his camp. They, in turn, call him "Uncle Jungle." Here, again, Onoda is seemingly on another mission for Japan.

Recovering Lost Men, Territory

In October 1997, prominent Japanese and Russians met on Sakhalin to confer on regional issues. Leading the Japanese participants to the meeting in Yuzhno-Sakhalinsk, known as Toyohara when the city served as the capital of the Japanese territory of Karafuto, were Shiina Motoo and Suetsugu Ichiro. Shiina, son of former Foreign Minister Shiina Etsusaburo, was for years one of the ruling LDP's most prominent internationalists.[24]

Following Japan's defeat in the Second World War, Suetsugu worked tirelessly to redress the wrongs that he perceived inflicted on Japan. Distraught over Japan's defeat and occupation, he almost chose suicide, going so far as to write a final note to his parents in September that year. In January 1946, he fled his home in Kyushu on a tip that American military police were shortly to arrest him for his connection to the execution of captured American airmen at Aburayama at the war's end. Several recent Nakano School graduates under Suetsugu's command had joined in the execution at Aburayama, but Suetsugu himself apparently was elsewhere that day. Reaching Hokkaido, in Japan's far north, he spent the winter there. At the end of May, convinced that his tracks had grown cold, he left Hokkaido for Tokyo with forged papers and a new identity as Miyazaki Ichiro.

In the capital, Suetsugu joined the Sound Youth Club, an organization established that March by repatriated Japanese students of Chienkuo University in Manchukuo. Renamed the Japan Sound Youth Association on 15 August 1949, the fourth anniversary of the imperial surrender broadcast, the organization became one of those in which Suetsugu would play a leading role. Under the noses of the Occupation's authorities, Suetsugu campaigned for the immediate release of Japanese imprisoned as war criminals and the return of Japanese territory occupied by the United States and the Soviet Union. The Association's activities caught the attention of the Occupation authorities, drawing in 1951 an investigation by the Special Investigation Bureau of MacArthur's General Headquarters. While the investigation report duly noted Miyazaki Ichiro as vice-chairman, the investigators apparently failed to recognize him as the fugitive Suetsugu.

Members of the Japan Sound Youth Association, whose ranks shortly grew to some five thousand members, worked in opposition to leftist activists. On May Day, marked each year by leftist rallies, they would gather as an auxiliary police force to safeguard the Imperial Palace. The site had been the target of a mass demonstration on 1 May 1946 that had shaken the Japanese authorities. Suetsugu's efforts on behalf of Japanese prisoners marked the origins of his postwar ties to Kishi Nobusuke and other Japanese leaders.

Suetsugu first stepped onto the international stage in 1952, when Justice Minister Kimura Tokutaro sent him to Manila to appeal to other delegates at a general session of the International Red Cross for the return of Japanese war prisoners from the Soviet Union and China. He then went with Hirota Yoji, an official of the Foreign Ministry who was serving as his interpreter, to the United States to press for the release of Japanese imprisoned by the United States as war criminals. At that time he made the rounds of American officials in Washington and such key figures in postwar relations as Japanese-American activist Mike Masaoka.

With Japanese sovereignty restored in 1952 under the San Francisco Peace Treaty, the Japanese held as war criminals in Sugamo Prison in Tokyo were all but free. Yamamoto Fukuichi, a shadow warrior serving a thirty-year prison sentence for his part in the Aburayama Incident, would often sneak out of Sugamo at night even during the Occupation to meet his old comrade Suetsugu at the headquarters of the Japan Sound Youth Association. Yamamoto and the others remained in the increasingly comfortable jail, however, to avoid the backlash from Washington that a formal release would have provoked. On 31 March 1956, Yamamoto formally left prison on parole. On 30 May 1958, the last eighteen such prisoners left Sugamo Prison as free men. All had been imprisoned for wartime incidents involving Americans. In recognition of his efforts on behalf of imprisoned Japanese, Suetsugu received an invitation to attend the final release ceremony. Suetsugu, outraged that the Allies had executed nearly one thousand of the four thousand Japanese found guilty of war crimes and jailed the others, felt some measure of satisfaction at seeing Sugamo empty of the men whom he considered victims of victor's justice. At a 1977 eulogy address given to the sixth general meeting of the Mataichikai, the association of the Futamata Branch's First Class, at the Gokoku Shrine in Ishikawa Prefecture, Suetsugu spoke of the "humiliating defeat in war," the arrest of Japanese as war criminals, and the "steep path" taken for the "rebirth and rebuilding of the fatherland."[25]

Not long after the Sugamo ceremony, Suetsugu helped launch Tokyo's version of Washington's Peace Corps. Before sending Japanese youths overseas, the ruling LDP in August 1961 sent future prime ministers Takeshita Noboru and Uno Sosuke, then the party's respective bureau and department chiefs for youth affairs, on a preliminary tour of Asia to gather information on aid projects. Assisting the LDP was Suetsugu's Japan Sound Youth Association, which sent a number of youth delegations to Asia to seek the views of their counterparts. In 1963, his organization joined representatives from other organizations related to international exchange, youth affairs, and agriculture to advise the LDP. Finally, Tokyo launched in 1965 the Japan Overseas Cooperation Volunteers (JOCV). First concentrating on Asia, the JOCV has since expanded its activities throughout the developing world, including several European countries of the former Warsaw Pact.[26]

Suetsugu also poured much of his tireless energy into Tokyo's effort to recover territories lost in the Second World War. His first objective was Okinawa, Japan's southernmost prefecture and site of the war's bloodiest clash between the American and Japanese armies. Recovering the prefecture would be no small feat. In contrast to Japan's main islands, the U.S. military directly ruled the Ryukyus. The U.S. Army, Navy, Air Force, and Marines turned the tiny island of Okinawa into a base for military and intelligence operations throughout Asia and as far afield as the Persian Gulf. The strategic value of Okinawa, situated off China's south coast, grew all the more when the Chinese Communists drove the Nationalists from the mainland and raised the red flag in Beijing in 1949. While local protests limited Okinawa's use as a staging area for bombing sorties against North Vietnam, the island played a key role in the war effort as a logistics base. In secret, Okinawa also served as a nuclear storage depot.[27]

Despite the Pentagon's grip on Okinawa, Suetsugu was determined to help Tokyo recover the prefecture. In November 1955, his Japan Sound Youth Association was one of some eighty organizations that formed the Conference to Promote the Return of Okinawa to the Fatherland. Suetsugu's group had previously attracted attention to the issue by staging hunger strikes against Okinawa's loss at the time of the San Francisco Peace Treaty, then by conducting programs of youth exchange with Okinawans and campaigning to send Japanese flags to Okinawa's schools. Suetsugu's actions helped to keep the Okinawa issue before the eyes of Japanese leaders, government officials, and the general public. They also worked to undermine American efforts to foster an Okinawan identity separate from Japan. The U.S. Army's CIC and other officials were producing propaganda aimed at convincing the islanders that they were distinct from the Japanese.[28]

In the wake of leftist protests in 1960 against the revised bilateral security treaty, which Japanese opposition parties opposed for tying Tokyo to Washington's global containment policy against Moscow, Suetsugu's group left the Conference due to irreconcilable differences. While a nationalist with no particular love for the United States, Suetsugu remained above all a realist. He was critical of the Japanese Left's use of the issue as a club to attack the United States, Japan's ruling LDP, and the bilateral military alliance. With Okinawa's bases critical to the Pentagon in the Vietnam War as well as any future Asian contingencies, Suetsugu knew that the key to Okinawa's reversion was unceasing political pressure combined with assurances for a continued American military presence there.[29]

When the legislator Nakasone Yasuhiro invited Attorney-General Robert F. Kennedy to Japan in 1962, Suetsugu made the rounds in advance to each man on Kennedy's itinerary, requesting that each raise Okinawa's reversion. Suetsugu had a long association with former Prime Minister Nakasone. Early in the postwar period, both were members of the National Territory Defense Research Association. Suetsugu also worked behind the scenes with Takeshita Noboru, then chief cabinet secretary, to plan the epochal visit to Okinawa of Prime Minister Sato Eisaku, which was important to the Japanese case for latent sovereignty as the first postwar trip by an incumbent premier. In 1967, Suetsugu traveled as a member of an Association-backed delegation that flew to Washington to make the case for reversion. Through the Okinawa Base Problems Study Committee, Suetsugu also participated in the bilateral conferences of academics, retired military officers, and other experts who helped pave the way for an official resolution of the issue.[30]

Suetsugu's activities supported Tokyo's policy on Okinawa. Seeking at first only residual sovereignty in the face of the reality of American military occupation, Tokyo gradually began extending "aid" to the islands to ease Washington's burden and demanding reversion. By the time Ambassador U. Alexis Johnson settled into the embassy in 1967, he found resolving the Okinawa issue his "biggest single job." From 1967, Japanese money far exceeded the American contribution. As sentiment in Okinawa and elsewhere in Japan turned increasingly anti-American as the United States used Japanese facilities to prosecute the Vietnam War, reversion became all the more a key issue. Tokyo no doubt enjoyed the growing popular antipathy towards Washington as leverage. In the end, President Richard Nixon and National Security Advisor Henry Kissinger negotiated with Prime Minister Sato the reversion of Okinawa in 1972. Nixon, assured that the military bases and overall alliance remained intact, even saw handing back Okinawa as the "most significant outcome" of his relations with Sato.[31]

With Okinawa settled, Suetsugu turned his attention to helping Tokyo to recover the territories lost to the Soviet dictator Josef Stalin in 1945. Japan has never accepted the loss of land due to Soviet invasion in the waning days of the war. Japanese could consider, perhaps, the loss of Karafuto, the southern half of Sakhalin that Tokyo had taken from Moscow as a prize in the Russo-Japanese War, as an outcome in the shifting fortunes of war. However, the loss of the Chishima (Kurile) archipelago appears to be a naked land grab. In 1855, the Treaty of Shimoda divided the island chain between Etorofu (Iturup) and Uruppu (Urup). In 1875, Tokyo traded its claim to southern Sakhalin for title to the entire archipelago. In the decades since the Second World War, Tokyo has demanded as a condition for signing a peace treaty that Moscow return the archipelago's four southernmost islands: Kunashiri, Etorofu, Shikotan, and the Habomai islets. Behind Tokyo's firm stance, Suetsugu Ichiro worked tirelessly in the wings with a succession of Japanese governments and Russian leaders.

Suetsugu was a member of the Northern Territories Issue Association. Originally established in 1961 as the Northern Territories Association, the organization has operated since 1969 as a special corporation of the Japanese government. Suetsugu also pursued the issue as secretary-general of the Council on National Security Problems. The council, which once tackled the issue of Okinawa's reversion under another name, is now at the forefront of the reversion campaign. Suetsugu worked on the council with such prominent "Russia hands" as Dr. Hakamada Shigeki. An American academic expert on Japanese-Russian relations, writing shortly before the collapse of the Soviet Union, wrote of Suetsugu as secretary general of the council heading "the most influential group on Soviet matters." For his passionate efforts to recover the islands, Suetsugu earned the nickname "Mr. Northern Territories."[32]

Much of Suetsugu's influence was due to his decades of experience in Moscow and numerous contacts among Russian leaders. His dealings with Moscow dated from May 1973, when he served as managing director for the first "Asian Peace" conference in Tokyo of Japanese and Soviet experts. Attending the fourth such conference, held in Moscow in 1977, Suetsugu made one of his most important contacts when he met Yevgeny Primakov. A former chief of the Soviet KGB, Primakov became director of the influential Institute of World Economics and International Relations (IMEMO) before Russian President Boris Yeltsin tapped him as foreign minister and then, in 1998, as his prime minister. Suetsugu also developed ties to Aleksandr Yakovlev, principal deputy to President Mikhail Gorbachev at the end of the Soviet era. In recognition of his importance to bilateral ties, Moscow awarded Suetsugu the Order of People's Friendship in 1995. Foreign Minister Primakov presented the friendship medal to Suetsugu and three other Japanese in a ceremony at the Russian embassy in Tokyo the following year.[33]

Suetsugu's ability to develop relations with such influential Russians was due, in turn, to his access to Japanese leaders. In particular, his long-standing ties to former Prime Minister Nakasone Yasuhiro and other hawks in Japanese ruling circles attracted Russian attention. Aleksandr Lebed, the retired general and leader of the Russian People's Republican Party, spoke highly of Suetsugu prior to visiting him in Tokyo in September 1997. Lebed boasted to reporters that he was to meet "people who have great authority, but who do not hold official posts," a reference to Suetsugu and Nakasone. The influential former general also called Suetsugu "a prominent public figure." In Tokyo, Lebed spoke on 18 September at the Hotel Okura as part of a lecture series organized by Nakasone's Institute for International Policy Studies (IIPS). Referring to the Northern Territories, Lebed reportedly averred that Russia had no historical claim to the islands and asked his hosts to wait for a Russian consensus on reversion to form.[34]

A key to Suetsugu's influence among Moscow's leaders was his central role among ordinary Japanese seeking the return of the islands. Supporting Japanese politicians are the displaced island residents and other ordinary Japanese. Outside the corridors of power, Suetsugu nurtured the popular roots of Japan's campaign to regain the Northern Territories. He was close to Kodama Taiko, the former resident widely considered Japan's "de facto 'ambassador'" to the islands. A child when Stalin expelled nearly twenty thousand Japanese from the Kuril archipelago, Kodama was at the forefront of the grassroots movement to recover her homeland. Suetsugu was at her side since the 1970s, helping to "polish her rhetoric and build a national movement." This combination of popular pressure and Suetsugu's guidance did much to keep the issue before the public eye. Since 1982, Japan has recognized the campaign with a Northern Territories Day on 7 February, the anniversary of a Russo-Japanese treaty in 1855 that set the border north of Japan's present claims.[35]

Since Suetsugu's influence gained him access to Japan's leaders in advance of Japanese-Russian summits, Suetsugu long weighed into the policy process in Tokyo. Prior to each major summit meeting between a Japanese premier and his Russian counterpart, Suetsugu had an advance meeting. On 29 October 1997, prior to his summit with President Boris Yeltsin at Krasnoyarsk, Prime Minister Hashimoto Ryutaro received a briefing from two senior officials of his foreign office. On their heels came a meeting with Suetsugu, who met with Hashimoto for more than thirty minutes. He briefed Hashimoto again in advance of the Kawana Summit, held 18–19 April 1998 on Japan's Izu Peninsula. Judging from published accounts of his activities, Suetsugu consistently counseled that Tokyo hold firm against aid or expanded trade relations with the Russian Far East until Moscow returned the four islands. He frequently took a hard line in private and before the press. When President Boris Yeltsin arrived in Tokyo on 8 July 1993, he made an apology in his airport speech for having cancelled an earlier trip. According to a Japanese diplomat, Suetsugu was keen on wringing an apology from the Russian president, a position a number of Japanese diplomats also favored. Former Prime Minister Nakasone had then conveyed the message to Moscow several weeks before Yeltsin's arrival.[36]

In short, Suetsugu aimed to help Tokyo recover the Northern Territories by following a game plan similar to the one that he used in the earlier campaign for Okinawa. At the Kawana Summit, Hashimoto proposed that the two nations draw a boundary between Uruppu (Urup) and Etorofu (Iturup) as part of the settlement for a peace treaty. While Moscow would continue administering the islands, agreeing to the boundary would constitute recognition of Japan's latent sovereignty, a concept used in the reversion of Okinawa. Much of Suetsugu's work involved propaganda for domestic and foreign audiences. On 7 February 1998, Northern Territories Day, an audience of fifteen hundred Japanese attended a rally organized by the Management and Coordination Agency at the Kudan Hall in Tokyo. Following a televised speech by Prime Minister Hashimoto, Suetsugu spoke to the crowd on Tokyo's efforts to regain the islands.[37]

Aid for the islands' residents was another tactic. As Tokyo undermined the American hold on Okinawa by giving money to the island's residents that Washington could ill afford, so Japanese officials were offering aid to Russian residents of the Northern Territories. Such an offer came at a time when neither the moribund local government on Sakhalin nor national officials in distant Moscow had the means to help them. As Suetsugu explained to an American reporter in 1997, the Northern Territories were of less strategic importance to Moscow, which in any event lacked "the money to support these islands anymore."

While Japanese trade, investment, and tourism could conceivably reverse the economic decline, Tokyo held back all three inputs in the absence of a peace treaty while polling opinion on the islands and in Moscow on reversion, promising that Russian residents would fare well under the Japanese flag. As part of a campaign, Suetsugu's council took space in a Sakhalin newspaper on 9 April 1998 to call for the "early resolution" of the territorial issue. Dr. Hakamada penned an article counseling Russians that it would be a "misunderstanding" to believe that Tokyo had shelved the issue while the two sides worked towards a peace treaty. He also wrote that Russian inhabitants would enjoy the right of permanent residence and basic welfare protection under reversion.[38]

Suetsugu's campaigns since the war for the release of imprisoned veterans and the recovery of lost territories from the United States and Russia resembled on the surface the noisy demonstrations of Japan's flamboyant rightists. Anyone who spends more than a few days in Japan is likely to catch sight of their sound trucks parading through city streets, bedecked in slogans of reverence for the emperor and blaring martial music from the time of the defunct imperial armed forces. These strident rightists, widely considered members or associates of the Japanese criminal underworld, or Yakuza, enjoy little popular support. Most Japanese consider them a nuisance for disturbing the peace with their raucous music and ear-splitting harangues. They, as Suetsugu did, demand that the Russians return the Northern Territories. The difference, however, is that the men in the sound trucks appear to embrace the cause more as an occasion for noisy confrontation than as a genuine issue to resolve. Suetsugu and his associates kept their distance. Kodama Taiko, Suetsugu's "ambassador" to the Northern Territories, explained: "The right wing is a huge liability for us, because the public always assumes, wrongly, that we're one and the same."

For that reason, Suetsugu likely found the sound trucks a headache. A man of the right, he was no bully. His sense of nationalism, his love of country, would be unexceptional in the United States or Britain. Americans are vocal in their patriotism. The British have a long history of ardent service in the cause of King and country. Japan, however, was on the losing side of the Second World War. Moreover, the victors took pains to portray the war as a criminal act. Burdened by the legacy of defeat and the caricature drawn at the war crimes trials in Tokyo, Japanese have largely refrained from frank expressions of patriotism and demands for their due from other countries. Suetsugu had been in the forefront of Japanese who have questioned this state of affairs. As memories of the war recede, and Japanese reflect on the bias of the war crimes trials, Suetsugu's position will increasingly be accepted in Japan as the conventional wisdom.

Old Boys in the New Army

A number of officers connected to the Nakano School made the transition from the Japanese Army to its postwar successor, the Ground Self-Defense Force (GSDF).

Maj. Kuwahara Takeshi, a graduate of both the Military Academy and the Nakano School, had directed INA's Second Division during the ill-fated invasion of India and subsequent defense of Burma. Capt. Komata Yozo, a graduate of the Nakano School who led a commando unit on New Guinea during the war and was training members of the Izumi Unit at the end, became deputy commandant of the GSDF Intelligence School and retired from the service with the rank of major general.

Maj. Yamamoto Kiyokatsu, an instructor at the Nakano School who was also involved with the Izumi Unit, also served as deputy commandant at the Intelligence School. Maj. Hirose Eiichi, the liaison officer in Imperial General Headquarters for Nakano School officers, rebounded from his postwar arrest by GHQ to command the GSDF's Northern Army. Capt. Kawashima Takenobu of the Minami Agency, a graduate of both the Military Academy and the Nakano School, after the war reached the rank of major general before retiring from the GSDF. Capt. Morisawa Kikaku, a graduate of both the Military Academy and the Nakano School, worked at the headquarters of U.S. Far East Air Forces (FEAF) during the Occupation. Following stints at the Continental Problems Research Institute and the *Japan Times*, he served in the Self-Defense Forces (SDF) from 1954 to 1970. Among his accomplishments, he wrote a bilingual dictionary of English and Japanese military terms.[39]

Lt. Col. Fujiwara Iwaichi, the intelligence officer who lectured at the Nakano School before leading his agency to suborn Indian Army units in the Singapore campaign and fathering the INA, continued to shine in postwar Japan. From 1947, Fujiwara joined Col. Hattori Takushiro in Maj. Gen. Willoughby's project to write a history of the war. In 1955, Fujiwara was one of the last four officers of the Imperial Japanese Army to enter the GSDF; the four joined under an exception to a policy that had barred from postwar military service graduates of the General Staff College who had held army staff positions.[40]

In August 1956, Fujiwara became commandant of the GSDF Intelligence School. His deputy was Yamamoto Kiyokatsu. Convinced that the Imperial Japanese Army had given short shrift to intelligence, the former Nakano School lecturer decided he would pour his energies into training officers thoroughly in intelligence and foreign languages. Whereas German, French, Russian, and Chinese had been the core languages taught officers of the Imperial Japanese Army, the GSDF Intelligence School has been training its students in English, Russian, Chinese, and Korean. English, no longer an "enemy language," is primarily for officers preparing for training at American military schools or for liaison duties with officers of the U.S. Army.

He also decided to draw upon the legacy of the Nakano School for postwar intelligence training. With the cooperation of many shadow warriors, Fujiwara had the Intelligence School's research section gather the knowledge of the Nakano School's old boys on such areas as intelligence warfare against the Chinese Communists in Manchukuo and China, propaganda in occupied territories, and operations involving various Asian peoples. The resulting documents filled a large safe. However, a successor to Fujiwara burned the precious documents in a panic when Ueda Koichiro, a senior Diet legislator of the Japan Communist Party (JCP), referred to the documents in a March 1977 session of the budget committee. The commandant, alarmed by the public allegation that the GSDF's Intelligence School was training officers for covert warfare based on the lessons of the Nakano School and by the demand to inspect his school, destroyed the evidence.[41]

Following assignments in 1960 as vice chief of staff of the Eastern Army and in 1962 as commanding officer of Twelfth Division, Fujiwara retired with the rank of major general from the GSDF and entered the field of foreign relations. In a way, he was returning to the Indian operations that he had executed with great success during the war. In 1954, shortly before joining the GSDF, Fujiwara had toured Bangkok, Rangoon, and Bombay, visiting intelligence veterans living there. One former subordinate was running the Bangkok office of the Marubeni general trading company. Another was the chief of Mitsubishi Corporation's Bombay office. Takahashi Hachiro, who had trained at the Nakano School, was working in Rangoon as an advisor to the Burmese government. Fujiwara also joined the Folks' Diplomacy Association, an organization operating under the jurisdiction of the Foreign Ministry.

In autumn 1966, he learned from Tarora Sadao, a Nakano School graduate who had served under him in Saigon, that someone had spotted Subhas Chandra Bose's sword in a Tokyo museum. Bose had received the sword as a gift of Toyama Mitsuru, the formidable rightist who had protected the fugitive Rash Behari Bose against British demands that the Japanese Foreign Ministry extradite him. Ever the propagandist, Fujiwara seized the opportunity to promote Japan's ties with India. After preparing the groundwork through consultations with Iwakuro Hideo, the Indian Embassy, INA veterans, and the Indo-Japanese Association, Fujiwara and Tarora flew to Calcutta in March 1967 to present the sword to the deceased Indian leader's nephew, who was director of an institute devoted to the memory of his uncle. The result was a grand occasion, involving the provincial governor and other dignitaries. As a secondary propaganda coup, Bose's sword went to Delhi's historic Red Fort in December. At the site of the postwar INA trials, a symbol of British rule and Indian independence, Prime Minister Indira Gandhi led a host of politicians, government officials, and other important persons to see the sword.[42]

Old Boys in Intelligence

Other than the GSDF Intelligence School, other old boys of the Nakano School applied their covert talents to Japan's postwar intelligence programs. Some joined the National Police Agency or the Public Security Investigation Agency, where they probably worked against the Japan Communist Party as well as Soviet, Chinese, and Korean intelligence operatives. A number of alumni likely joined one private investigation agency or another, adding their talents to the large pool of former police in such offices who gather intelligence for profit. Col. Yabe Chuta, who had been the Imperial Japanese Army's last military attaché in Moscow as well as a lecturer at the Nakano School, joined other military "Soviet hands" in 1947 in secretly forming an intelligence organ to monitor the JCP and Soviet Union for Prime Minister Yoshida Shigeru. The intelligence they provided likely contributed to strengthening his relationship with General MacArthur's intelligence chief, Maj. Gen. Charles Willoughby.[43]

12

LEGACIES

European Colonialism in Tatters

On the morning of 2 September 1945, representatives of the United Nations had gathered on the deck of the battleship *Missouri* to accept Tokyo's surrender. Among those following Adm. Chester W. Nimitz, the American representative, in adding their signatures to the surrender document were Adm. Sir Bruce Fraser of Great Britain, Gen. Jacques Leclerc of France, and Vice Adm. C.E.L. Helfrich of the Netherlands. The scene suggested that the British, French, and Dutch were set to resume their interrupted rule over much of Asia. Japan had humiliated the European colonial powers in driving them from Southeast Asia, but the United States had led the Allied counteroffensive that defeated the Japanese. An observer at the ceremony could have concluded that the region was safe once more for European hegemony. Nowhere was the dual nature of the Second World War more on display. Leclerc, for example, had participated in the liberation of France and the defeat of Germany. On 18 August, he had flown from France for Asia. Having fought to free his people, he was now to lead an expeditionary force to shackle Indochina once more.

Washington's European allies certainly intended to restore their imperial fortunes. True, the British in 1942 had promised India autonomy within the British Commonwealth at some point after the war. Unclear, however, were such details as when and in what form London would honor a pledge made under duress. Would the British keep a promise made during the darkest hours of the war as an expedient to avoid an Indian revolt? As for Burma, Malaya, and Singapore, the British intended to continue their rule. American intelligence officers serving in wartime India under Lord Mountbatten's South East Asia Command (SEAC) grasped the situation with the quip that SEAC really stood for "Save England's Asiatic Colonies." French forces in Indochina, released the month of the surrender ceremony from the jails into which the Japanese had thrown them six months earlier, immediately began clashing with Vietnamese intent on liberty from foreign rule. In Indonesia, where local leaders had declared independence with Japanese blessings three days after the imperial surrender broadcast of 15 August, Dutch soldiers returned to claim the islands once again for the Netherlands.[1]

However, the European colonial military and police forces failed to quell nationalist movements. The Japanese had humbled the Western powers and stirred Asian nationalists to action. When Indian sailors rioted over the Red Fort trials of INA officers, London had a clear sign that the cost of holding its Indian empire was more than the war-weary British public would bear. Independence came in 1947, after much wrangling between Hindus and Moslems led to the partition of the Great Britain's imperial crown jewel into India and Pakistan. Facing the prospects of armed struggle with Aung San, the former protégé of Colonel Suzuki's Minami Agency, London acceded in 1947 to Burmese demands for independence. The republic was born the following January. The British also made concessions in Malaya that led to a federation under British tutelage by 1948.

The French and the Dutch, less astute than the English in the face of rising nationalism, were waging vicious, losing wars to keep their Asian dominions. For the French, nine years of postwar fighting ended in the debacle of Dienbienphu and a retreat from Indochina. Gen. Georges Catroux, former governor-general of Indochina, later compared French possessions in Indochina to ancient trees, sturdy in appearance, yet uprooted and toppled "in a few minutes" by a "typhoon." The Japanese Army, which entered Indochina in 1940, had swept the French from power in March 1945 and, by stoking nationalist ambitions at the war's end, had destroyed France's Asian empire. The war had been the typhoon that took down colonies that otherwise would have stood firmly for years to come.[2]

By the time the Second World War ended in Asia, the Japanese Army had spent several years cultivating Asian nationalists and raising local armies. Men of the Nakano School had trained or led native military units from India to Indonesia. In the end, the Japanese field armies in Southeast Asia deliberately turned over many of their weapons and supplies to Asian nationalists rather than surrender them to the victorious Allies. If imperial Japan had failed to supplant the West in Asia, the Japanese Army would at least destroy the foundations of European rule. One British scholar captured the dilemma London faced in rebuilding its Asian empire after the Special Operations Executive (SOE) had supplied arms to Asian forces for wartime clandestine operations: "However, the problem of the SOE legacy in Asia was more fundamental than simply arms and training. After all, vast quantities of weapons were, in any case, available in 1945 from the Japanese, who surrendered their weapons more readily to Asiatics than to Europeans."[3]

By 1948, Washington was in a precarious position. The Americans had joined the British, French, and Dutch in Europe in a fight for freedom against Adolf Hitler, but the global alliance had linked Washington even then to imperialism and suppression in Asia. The American journalist Theodore White had a clear view of the wartime situation from the Nationalist Chinese capital at Chungking. He described London's position as follows: "The British were fighting two separate wars. In Europe they stood with all honor for the freedom of humanity and the destruction of the Nazi slave system; in Asia, for the status quo, for the Empire, for colonialism." Washington's global alliances and a policy of "Europe first" continued after the war amid rising tensions with Moscow.

Washington had honored an earlier pledge by granting independence to the Philippines in 1946, but alliances with London, Paris, and Amsterdam against Moscow put the United States before the tidal surge of postwar nationalism. As one scholar of Asian nationalism put it, "During the Cold War the United States regarded Western Europe as the ultimate domino, the area of the world that could not under any circumstances be lost to the Soviet Union. The U.S. therefore built there its strongest alliances and even went along with the futile efforts of Britain, France, and the Netherlands to reestablish their colonial empires in East Asia."[4]

The resulting danger was all too clear for those with eyes to see. An OSS analysis from August 1945 assessed the situation with a clarity that is painful in hindsight:

> The Japanese, by breaking up the European colonial system, seem to be advancing the cause of nationalism in Southeast Asia. They have

injected a new confidence in the natives and it will be next to impossible for them to go back to their old way of life. The British, French and Dutch have no positive program to offer these people, who witnessed the defeat of the European colonialists at the hands of the Japanese. The United States has a backlog of prestige over here now, but the generalities of our foreign policy must be made specific or we will soon lose this prestige.

The Central Intelligence Agency (CIA), postwar successor to the OSS, was also clear in analyzing the changes Japan had wrought. A confidential report of September 1948 from the fledgling agency neatly captured the dilemma. First, the report pointed to "the release of bottled-up nationalist activities in the Far East as a result of Japan's defeat of the colonial powers in World War II and its encouragement of local nationalism in occupied areas." Second, the CIA warned that the nationalist movement was "no longer purely a domestic issue between the European colonial powers and their dependencies." Washington's natural support for colonial independence ran the risk of alienating the primary allies in Europe in the emerging Cold War against the Soviet Union. Backing the Europeans in their futile attempts to piece back together what the Japanese had shattered, on the other hand, would be a losing bet against the "irresistible force" of nationalism, run the risk of "future disruption," and leave the West weaker over the long run.[5]

It was a tragedy of the Cold War that Washington's policymakers failed to heed the CIA's prescient warning. Facing global competition with the Soviet Union and the People's Republic of China, the United States stood against the nationalist tide in Indochina in a vain attempt to prevent a communist victory. That tide ultimately wore down the United States, as it had swept away the French colonial forces two decades earlier. In April 1975, forces of the Socialist Republic of Vietnam captured Saigon as officials of South Vietnam retreated with their American allies to the safety of ships offshore. Thirty years after Nimitz, Fraser, Leclerc, and Helfrich had put their signatures to a Japanese surrender document that seemed to signal a resumption of European rule, the forces of Asian nationalism unleashed by Japan had driven the American military from the Asian continent.

Shadow Warriors Waging Japan's History Battles

On the grounds of the Police Academy of the Tokyo Metropolitan Police Department, where once stood the Nakano School, there remains today a stone marker to the Japanese Army's school for intelligence officers. In a sense, the stone is the companion marker to the memorial to the Futamata Branch in Tenryu and the Noborito Research Institute's memorial Shinto shrine that rests in a grove of trees of Meiji University's branch campus in Kanagawa Prefecture. On 30 September 1995, almost exactly fifty years to the day that Japan surrendered, Kuwahara Takeshi and Fujii Chikao entered the grounds of the Police Academy in Tokyo's Nakano Ward to visit the monument. Both were veterans of the Japanese Army's covert operations against British rule in India. Kuwahara was a graduate of the Nakano School as well as the Imperial Military Academy. Turning to his old comrade, Fujii remarked, "Well, I guess we were Lawrence of Arabia." Kuwahara replied, "They were operations for the sake of winning the war, but I believe that our actions led to the liberation of India."[6]

As part of the heritage of the twentieth century, one of Japan's legacies was the destruction of European colonialism in Asia. The Japanese dealt a first blow to colonial prestige by defeating the Russians in 1905. Capt. Malcolm Kennedy, a British officer who served as military attaché in Tokyo after the First World War, is worth quoting at length:

> By defeating the Colossus of the West, Japan had destroyed the myth of the White Man's invincibility. Until 1905, Asian nationalism had been negligible and little more than an academic concept . . . With Japan's victory as a concrete example of what a determined Asiatic people could do, however, Asian nationalists began to dream dreams of the day when they themselves would be able to emulate Japan's achievements and become masters in their own houses.[7]

The Japanese victory exercised a lasting influence over Asia. It inspired popular nationalism throughout Asia, led numerous Chinese warlords prior to the Manchurian Incident of 1931 to have their officers and men undergo Japanese military training, and attracted Subhas Chandra Bose, the Indian nationalist who embraced the Japanese during the Second World War. Louis Allen, an intelligence officer of the British Army during that conflict, ended his history of the war in Asia with the following assessment: "In the long perspective, difficult and even bitter as it may be for Europeans to recognize this, the liberation of millions of people in Asia from their colonial past is Japan's lasting achievement."[8]

In Japan, old boys associated with the Nakano School have joined officials and other veterans in raising objections over the years to the judgment of Occupation officials and Japanese progressives that Tokyo's imperial policy was simply criminal. In 1995, the fiftieth anniversary of the war's end, several graduates of the Nakano School spoke of Japan's legacy in an article published in a prominent Japanese weekly magazine. Murata Katsumi, a veteran of the Hikari Agency, was critical of a statement by Japan's socialist premier on the issue of war guilt: "Prime Minister Murayama said it was a war of aggression, but it was not completely bad. There was also a legacy. The nations of Southeast Asia at that time were under oppression as colonial territories. I think that the military forces trained by Japan played, in effect, a great role in their independence." Izumiya Tatsuro spoke similarly of his unit's activities in Burma, saying, "I am convinced that the actions of the Minami Agency became a legacy to independence." Tsuchiya Kiso, who trained the postwar Indonesian leader Suharto and other soldiers in the former Netherlands East Indies, offered a more balanced view of the Second World War: "I am one who sees it as a war of Asian liberation. In its entirety, however, there were aspects to the war leaving it to be viewed as aggression. History is composed of countless threads intertwined. One cannot interpret them in a single word."[9]

In the years since the war, operations associated with the Nakano School have emerged in Japan as favored threads in popular history. Daiei, a major Japanese film company, turned to the Nakano School in a series of spy movies made in the latter half of the 1960s. Ichikawa Raizo, a popular actor cast in Japanese films as the hero with nothing to lose, starred as an intelligence officer of the Nakano School in six movies made between 1966 and 1968. As Japan's answer to James Bond, Ichikawa waged desperate battles against foreign spies as well as regular officers of the Japanese Army. The popular series portrayed Ichikawa as an honorable intelligence officer pitted against overwhelming forces. In *Rikugun Nakano Gakko Ryusango Shirei* (Army

Nakano School Order Ryu 3), for example, Ichikawa plunges into the treacherous netherworld of Shanghai in 1940 to uncover the plotters whose assassination of a Japanese emissary threatens to derail the search for peace with China.

Decades after Daiei's popular spy series, some nationalists turned to film to highlight certain threads of history associated with the Nakano School. On the fiftieth anniversary of Japan's defeat in 1945, a committee formed by the People's Congress to Protect Japan released a history video depicting Japan's role as the liberator of Burma and India in the Second World War. The People's Congress is now part of the Japan Conference, established on 30 May 1997 in a ceremony at the Hotel New Otani, with more than a thousand participants. A roster of principal members of the People's Congress at the time the video went on sale included Lt. Col. Sejima Ryuzo, a wartime protégé of General Tojo and postwar associate of Nakasone Yasuhiro. Another member was Horie Masao, who served as a major in the Imperial Japanese Army, rose to command the GSDF's Western Army, and then headed the Japanese Veterans' Association. Former Prime Minister Hashimoto Ryutaro, then head of the influential Ministry of International Trade and Industry (MITI), was yet another member.

The People's Committee for the Fiftieth Anniversary of the War's Termination produced *Jiyu Ajia no eiko: Indo, Myanma-no dokuritsushi* (Glory of Free Asia: A History of India and Burma's Independence) to link Japan's wartime activities with the liberation of Burma and India from British rule. The video's history relies heavily on the exploits of Colonel Suzuki's Minami Agency and Lieutenant Colonel Fujiwara's agency to make the case for Japan's wartime role as that of liberator. Izumiya Tatsuro, the Nakano School graduate who served under Suzuki in Burma, offered his testimony on film in support of that case. The emphasis on wartime episodes linked to the Nakano School possibly has some connection to the constitution of the People's Congress to Protect Japan, for the names of veterans Suetsugu Ichiro and Onoda Hiroo were listed with that of Hashimoto Ryutaro and other members of the organization behind the video.[10]

Kase Hideaki, a prominent commentator on foreign affairs and fellow member of the People's Congress to Protect Japan, is a link to the movie *Pride*. Released in 1998, the film casts Gen. Tojo Hideki as the victim of victor's justice conducted by a vengeful United Nations in Tokyo. Interspersed with scenes from the International Military Tribunal for the Far East (or Tokyo war crimes trials) are those depicting Tokyo's actions to liberate India from British rule. Subhas Chandra Bose and the INA figure prominently in the film. The focus on India is related to the composition of the movie's production committee. In addition to Kase Hideaki and Fuji Nobuo, a graduate of the Imperial Naval Academy, Kunizuka Kazunori served on the three-man committee. With a stellar cast, including the popular actor Tsugawa Masahiko in the role of Tojo, the controversial film was the first, according to the *Far Eastern Economic Review*, "to make the rightist point for a mainstream audience."[11]

Whether *Pride*'s point was simply rightist or was actually a revisionist attempt to correct flawed views long accepted as the conventional wisdom is open to debate, but the recent success of a history series shows that a Japanese audience certainly exists for such views. Three volumes of essays titled *Kyokasho ga oshienai rekishi* (History That the Textbooks Don't Teach), edited by Professor Fujioka Nobukatsu of the University of Tokyo, enjoyed popular success from the moment the first volume hit the bookstores in 1996. Fujioka, intent on choosing positive strands from Japan's part in the Second World War, included episodes related to the Nakano School. His first volume included a chapter on how the Japanese military endeavored to help India gain independence. The heroes of that essay were Subhas Chandra Bose, Fujiwara Iwaichi, Kunizuka Kazunori, and others related to the Japanese Army's Indian operations. By 1997, Fujioka's three-volume series had already sold more than a million copies.

While critics in the West, the Koreas, and China have loosed barrages of criticism against such expressions of popular nationalism, Fujioka and other Japanese "rightists" are little different than patriots in other nations. One can easily imagine the response of American conservatives, for example, if Mexican politicians each year loudly called on the United States to rewrite school history books to confess that the Mexican War was a naked land grab. American writers often portray their country's expansion from the Atlantic coast in 1776 to the Philippines by 1898, achieved by conquest and coerced sales at the expense of France, Mexico, and Spain, as a story of a divine "manifest destiny." Who in the United States, then, can cast stones at Fujioka for portraying Japan's imperial expansion in the Second

World War at the expense of the West's empires as a war of Asian liberation?

Intelligence Agency

The Nakano School, as the Japanese Army's training school for intelligence and guerrilla warfare, offers a warning today to a Japanese military making its way in a world grown uncertain since the end of the Cold War. In short, the Nakano School stands as a monument to imperial Japan's tragic neglect of intelligence.

Col. Sumi Shinichiro, who consecutively ran two SSAs in Manchukuo, explained after the war to the popular writer Shiba Ryotaro how the top graduates of the General Staff College opted for careers in operations, a trend that contributed to an overall neglect of intelligence. Indeed, the General Staff College curriculum included no substantial instruction devoted to intelligence. First Bureau (Operations) of the Army General Staff was off limits to most intelligence officers, generally excluded from the rooms where the Army's elite plotted their military campaigns. A number of intelligence veterans have written eloquently of the general slighting of intelligence within an army whose blinkered elite ran wild with a spirit of "operations first." The memoirs of Lt. Col. Hori Eizo, a staff intelligence officer of Imperial General Headquarters, include a brief reference to his having to take a train to reach his assignment, since all available aircraft were reserved for operations officers.[12]

When the Japanese Army at last noted the need for a school to train intelligence officers, establishing the Nakano School in 1938, the action came too late. Kuwahara Takeshi and other shadow warriors, reflecting after the war on the Japanese Army's fate, concluded that the Nakano School had come ten years too late. Tarora Sadao even suggested that Japan would never have gone to war in 1941 if the Nakano School had begun its training in the 1920s. Japan was well on its way to global war when members of the Nakano School's First Class left Japan in 1940 to gather intelligence overseas. By the end of the war in 1945, some twenty-five hundred shadow warriors had trained at the Nakano School and Futamata Branch, but the senior graduates had risen only to the rank of major. Had the Japanese Army founded the Nakano School in 1928, rather than in 1938, thousands more officers perhaps would have passed through its gates. Considering how much more intelligence would have been at hand and how much larger, more senior a cadre of shadow warriors would have existed to exercise its influence throughout the Japanese Army, one can understand Tarora's wistful comment.[13]

Unfortunately, the Japanese Army went to war against China, then the United States, Great Britain, and the Netherlands, on the basis of gross optimism and prejudice rather than reasoned analysis based on sound intelligence. Tojo took Japan to war in 1941, not only in blindly trusting in Germany's Wehrmacht to defeat Japan's enemies in Europe but in discounting U.S. military potential and even in blithely assuming that the numerous Americans of German descent would oppose a war against their "fatherland." On such assumptions and prejudice did the Japanese Army go to war. Sakura Ichiro, a former president of the Nakano School's alumni association, told one reporter on the fiftieth anniversary of defeat in the war, "The Japanese Army accepted intelligence as it suited them but discarded intelligence at variance with operations. Their disregard for intelligence in the end did not change."[14]

Nor, once at war, did senior officers of the Japanese Army show much understanding of winning hearts and minds or other intelligence operations in occupied areas. Izaki Kiyota, a graduate of the Nakano School's First Class, found regular staff officers and members of the dreaded Kempeitai regularly ruining his operations. Propaganda operations aimed at rallying local support could hardly counter the torture and terror many Chinese and other Asians faced at the hands of Japanese soldiers. One intelligence officer of the Shanghai SSA, for example, recalled for a postwar journalist his vivid confrontation with regular officers intent on slaughtering Chinese civilians.[15]

Japan's shadow warriors ran afoul of higher policy on numerous occasions. Tokyo's leaders had started upon a path of imperial conquest, one common to the history of each of the belligerents of the Second World War, on the pretext of liberating Asia from alien rule. Had Tokyo's aims squared with Japanese propaganda, then the war would possibly have progressed differently. The Japanese Army's intelligence operatives, at any rate, would have suffered less from the contradictions. In a postwar analysis, Maj. Gen. Imai Takeo assessed the Minami Agency's activities at the war's outbreak as successful because they fell in line with the nationalist trends of the time, thereby winning Burmese cooperation and contributing to the Japanese

Army's ouster of the British from Burma. However, the Japanese Army then squandered the Minami Agency's initial success by rejecting independence, a move that ultimately brought the Minami Agency's Aung San to lead the Burmese army in revolt in March 1945.

Similarly, the journalist Maruyama Shizuo observed in his early history of the Nakano School that the Japanese Army's covert operations had begun with early successes but ended in failure because senior officers used them only for narrow tactical purposes in seizing enemy territory. While Suzuki took seriously the Minami Agency's mission of liberating Burma, according to Burmese leader Ba Maw, Tokyo did not. In effect, the tactical successes of Japan's shadow warriors came to naught against Tokyo's policy of applying military rule to its new southern empire rather than promptly setting free the West's former colonies. In short, the Army's senior officials failed to look beyond immediate, tactical uses of intelligence to grasp its strategic value.

Considering the constraints under which Japan's shadow warriors operated, the men of the Nakano School did well. In short, as Col. Sugita Ichiji wrote, Japanese intelligence was good; Japanese leaders simply ignored it.[16] As Tokyo follows an uncertain path in the aftermath of the Cold War, more often pursuing political and military initiatives independently of Washington, Japanese leaders could well take to heart the legacy of the Nakano School. As revealed in 1977 by a legislator from the Japan Communist Party, the GSDF Intelligence School was using materials compiled from the Nakano School in its lessons. However, given the undoubted focus of Japanese military intelligence at that time on internal subversion and threats to American military bases in Japan, counterintelligence was the likely focus of the Intelligence School. Fujiwara Iwaichi recalled that Japanese leftists, resident Koreans, and other internal threats constituted the main area of concern for Japanese military intelligence in the early postwar years.

Japanese leaders, who often seek affirmation for policies and preferences in the practices of foreign nations, can take comfort in the warm reception for the Nakano School's legacy in Asia. As noted earlier, Japanese intelligence veterans were welcome advisors to the military of Chiang Kai-shek's Republic of China on Taiwan. Given the colonial ties between Korea and Japan, as well as the Cold War triangle of Seoul, Tokyo, and Washington, it would be natural to learn one day that the Korea Central Intelligence Agency and its successor organs extolled the Nakano School's spirit to their trainees. Less expected, perhaps, but nonetheless a tribute, was the assertion by a North Korean defector that his alma mater, the Kim Chong-il Political Military School, held aloft the spirit of the Nakano School as an example to its students.[17]

Shifting gradually from an almost exclusive economic focus to a greater concern for diplomacy and military affairs independent of the alliance with Washington, Tokyo has taken steps since the early 1980s to enhance its intelligence capabilities. Some observers point to Nakasone Yasuhiro's election as prime minister in 1982 as a turning point. A former police official in imperial Japan's Interior Ministry, Nakasone had also served as a naval officer during the Second World War as well as director-general of the postwar Japanese Defense Agency (1970–71). In the view of Matsuhashi Tadamitsu, a former intelligence officer of the National Police Agency, Nakasone's ascension represented a shift in power from the economic agencies to the police.

After more than ten years of planning, the Defense Agency established in January 1997 a comprehensive military intelligence agency, modeled on the Pentagon's Defense Intelligence Agency. Much is expected of Japan's Defense Intelligence Headquarters (DIH), lodged in part of the Defense Agency's new headquarters complex built atop Ichigaya, former headquarters of the Imperial Army. DIH is to integrate the imagery intelligence (IMINT) from spy satellites Japan is building, SIGINT from Japanese intercept sites, open-source intelligence (OSINT) gleaned from foreign publications, and whatever intelligence is provided by the United States and other partners.

All that is missing is an independent program to gather foreign intelligence from paid agents, or human intelligence (HUMINT). While Japan has no declared HUMINT program, Col. Mori Hideyo, an instructor at the GSDF Intelligence School, wrote in a 1996 issue of the Japanese military's journal of ground warfare of Japan's need to combine IMINT with SIGINT and HUMINT. According to a military commentator writing for a popular military magazine the following year, it was only recently that a senior Japanese officer would openly address the military's need for HUMINT.

Should Japan move to develop a military HUMINT program, nurturing overseas intelligence networks of intelligence officers running paid foreign agents, the Self-Defense Forces are likely to draw on the legacy of the Nakano School. The CIA today traces with pride its intelligence programs to the wartime exploits of the OSS, the predecessor organization established in 1941. A bust of William "Wild Bill" Donovan, the OSS chief, stands today in the main hallway at CIA headquarters in Virginia. Similarly, Japan's Defense Agency may well point to the many exploits of the Nakano School's shadow warriors to instruct and inspire its intelligence officers in their overseas activities. A bust or painting of Maj. Gen. Akigusa Shun, "father" of the Nakano School, could one day soon grace the corner of some nondescript building in an anonymous Japanese training center for operatives, if it is not already there.[18]

Setting Sun on Japan's Last Soldier

On 31 May 1998, Onoda Hiroo landed on an isolated island as part of a mission. Japan's "last soldier" had first stepped into the world's spotlight in 1974, when he ceased after thirty years his mission on the Philippine island of Lubang. Although the mass media beyond Japan's shores had lost track of him some months after his sensational return to Tokyo, Onoda remained an object of international fascination. Over the years, the Japanese public read of his life's story in several books and numerous articles that he penned. An English version of his autobiography, *No Surrender*, first appeared in 1975. That same year, he appeared at a professional luncheon of the Foreign Correspondents Club of Japan. In the late 1990s, the Naval Institute Press in Annapolis republished his story as one of its "Bluejacket Books" paperback series. His return to Lubang in 1996 received international press coverage. Later that same year, a popular Japanese military monthly magazine featured Onoda in a regular column devoted to the palm readings of prominent Japanese. Late the following year, Onoda appeared at the Blue Note Tokyo to hear an award-winning jazz musician perform her composition *Kogun* (Lone Force), a musical composition inspired by him.

In 1998 he stood behind a lectern on Okushiri, a small island west of Hokkaido. He had come to the isolated island in Japan's northern reaches to speak of the life's lessons he had learned on his thirty-year mission on Lubang and in nearly twenty years spent running a nature camp in Japan. Onoda had spoken two days earlier at Misawa Air Base, headquarters of the Japanese Air Self-Defense Force's Northern

Air Defense Force as well as the base for elements of United States Forces Japan (USFJ). In his speech, "To Live," Onoda spoke of how man cannot live alone but must remember the debt owed to society and nature. In Okushiri, he delivered the same message. Still standing erect, looking lean and fit, one of the Nakano School's last old boys was still on a mission for Japan.[19]

Pursuing His Quest to the End

The end came as Suetsugu Ichiro was still seeking the return from Russia of Japan's Northern Territories. Once the United States had bowed to Japanese pressure by returning Okinawa in 1972, Suetsugu had campaigned to regain control of the four islands north of Hokkaido that Japan had lost to the Soviet Union in 1945. In coordination with his government, but on a nonofficial track, Suetsugu developed an impressive array of Russian contacts. Yevgeny Primakov, the former KGB chief and prime minister, was only one of many prominent Russians he knew.

On 11 July 2001, Suetsugu succumbed to cancer in Tokyo, his family at his side. He had kept his eyes on his goal until the end. In September 1999, he had been diagnosed with lung cancer. In November the next year, he had learned that cancer had struck his stomach. On 11 June 2001, he had received another grave diagnosis: cancer had invaded his liver. Yet, Suetsugu never retired to enjoy his last days in leisure. On 29 June, he had led a group of Japan's Russia experts in issuing at the prestigious Japan Forum on International Relations a call for Tokyo to adhere to the longstanding demand for the return of all four islands. Two days later, his breathing labored, Suetsugu entered the hospital for his final battle.[20]

Suetsugu's passing was worthy of a veteran of the Nakano School. Having toiled in obscurity during the war and the decades that followed, he left this life without the fanfare of a front-page newspaper article. Yet, those who had stood by him in war and peace would mark his departure. The New Leaders' Association, one of the many groups Suetsugu had led, announced that representatives of a dozen organizations he had created or led would join his family in a memorial service on 30 July. Those who had trained alongside him at the Nakano School's Futamata Branch would attend with others who had worked with him after the war on restoring Japan's losses.

Acting as chief of the ceremony was one of Suetsugu's longstanding associates, former Prime Minister Nakasone Yasuhiro. He was far from the only prominent mourner. Former prime ministers Kaifu Toshiki, Hata Tsutomu, and Mori Yoshiro were there to pay their respects. Chief Cabinet Secretary Fukuda Yasuo, son of former Prime Minister Fukuda Takeo and the late premier Obuchi Keizo's daughter, Obuchi Yuko, who has inherited his Diet seat, also attended. Sejima Ryuzo, the former officer of Imperial General Headquarters and postwar chairman of the general trading company Itochu, also bid farewell. Their presence, and that of approximately two thousand other guests less well known, gave testimony to the service that Suetsugu rendered to Japan over the years.[21]

Notes

Introduction

1. This account of Onoda's return to Lubang comes from articles published during May and June 1996 by the AP news agency, *Pacific Stars and Stripes*, and the Japanese newspapers *Asahi Shimbun, Japan Times, Mainichi Shimbun, Sankei Shimbun, Tokyo Shimbun,* and *Yomiuri Shimbun*.
2. Onoda Hiroo, conversation with author, 5 July 2001.

Chapter 1

1. Fukumoto Kameji, "Renin to musunda Akashi Taisa," in *Nihon no himitsusen,* special edition of *Shukan Yomiuri* (8 December 1956), pp. 22–23.
2. Fujiwara Iwaichi, "Boryakuka," *Rekishi to jinbutsu* (August 1985), p. 68; and Hata Ikuhiko, *Showashi no gunjintachi* (Tokyo: Bungei Shunju, 1987), pp. 384–87; and Tanaka Ryukichi, "Shanhai Jiken wa ko shite okosareta," in *Bessatsu Chisei,* No. 5, *Hisomerareta Showashi* (Tokyo: Kawade Shobo, 1956), p. 181.
3. Nakano Koyukai, ed., *Rikugun Nakano Gakko* (Tokyo: Nakano Koyukai, 1978), pp. 132–33; and Kinoshita Kenzo, *Kesareta himitsusen kenkyujo* (Nagano: Shinano Mainichi Shinbunsha, 1994), p. 193.
4. Kinoshita, *Kesareta,* p. 89.
5. Hirakawa, *Ryukon,* p. 6.
6. Kawahara Emon, *Kantogun boryaku butai* (Tokyo: Press Tokyo Shuppankyoku, 1970), pp. 30–31.
7. Ariga, *Nihon,* pp. 80–81.
8. Hirakawa, *Ryukon,* p. 7; and Ito Sadatoshi, *Nakano Gakko no himitsusen: Nakano wa katarazu, saredo kataranebanaranu* (Tokyo: Chuo Shorin, 1984), pp. 109–10.
9. The Tokyo School of Foreign Languages, along with Takushoku University in Tokyo and the Toa Dobun Shoin in China, centers of excellence in teaching foreign languages and area studies, were well suited to produce intelligence officers. Toa Dobun Shoin no longer exists, but the Tokyo University of Foreign Studies (renamed after the war) and Takushoku University are today the Japanese equivalents of such American institutions as Columbia University's School of International and Public Affairs.
10. Hata, *Showashi,* pp. 311–15; and John J. Stephan, *The Russian Fascists: Trag-*

edy and Farce in Exile, 1925–1945 (New York: Harper & Rowe, 1978), pp. 70, 173, 321; and Louis Allen, "The Nakano School," in *Proceedings of the British Association for Japanese Studies*, vol. 10 (1985), Sheffield, South Yorkshire: University of Sheffield, Centre for Japanese Studies, p. 10.

11. Hirakawa, *Ryukon*, p. 6; and Ariga, *Nihon*, pp. 98–100.

12. Nakano Koyukai, *Rikugun*, pp. 19–20; and Ito, p. 110.

13. Nihon Kindai Shiryo Kenkyukai, ed., *Iwakuro Hideo-shi Danwa Sokkiroku* (Tokyo: 1977), p. 138.

14. Okawa Shumei (1886–1957), a graduate of Tokyo Imperial University with a degree in Indian philosophy, gained expertise in Asian colonial affairs while a researcher at the South Manchuria Railway Company and its subsidiary East Asia Economic Research Bureau. A leading academic in Islamic studies, he lectured at Takushoku University. Okawa established a school for Asian languages and other subjects to train Japanese to fight against Western imperialism in Asia. Iwakuro and Shiratori Toshio, a pro-Axis diplomat, were among the Okawa Academy's backers. See Foreign Ministry Diplomatic Record Office and Nihon Gaikoshi Jiten Editorial Committee, eds., *Nihon gaiko jiten* (Tokyo: Yamakawa Shuppansha, 1992), p. 105; and Nihon, *Iwakuro*, pp. 131–32.

15. Nihon, *Iwakuro*, pp. 126–27.

16. Hirakawa, *Ryukon*, pp. 7–8.

17. Hata, *Showashi*, pp. 317–20; and Nakano Koyukai, *Rikugun*, pp. 22–23.

18. Nihon, *Iwakuro*, p. 129; and "Shinsetsu: Rikugun Nakano Gakko," *Bessatsu Shukan Sankei* (1 February 1960), p. 36; and Hata Ikuhiko, *Nihon Riku-Kaigun sogo jiten* (Tokyo: Tokyo Daigaku Shuppankai, 1991), p. 609.

19. Yanagawa Motoshige, *Rikugun chohoin Yanagawa Chui* (Tokyo: Sankei Shinbun Shuppankyoku, 1967), pp. 92–93; and Kato Masao, *Rikugun Nakano Gakko: Himitsusenshi no jittai* (Tokyo: Kojinsha, 2001), p. 16. Yanagawa's given name has also been rendered as Muneshige and Munenari.

20. J.J. Lavigne, "Décès de Narazaki Sensei," http://www.bkr.be/BKR/nou velles/Narazaki.htm.

21. Nakano Koyukai, *Rikugun*, p. 22; and "Shinsetsu," p. 37.

22. Nakano Koyukai, *Rikugun*, pp. 36–37.

23. Nakano Koyukai, *Rikugun*, p. 22; and Hata, *Showashi*, p. 317.

24. Hata, *Showashi*, pp. 317–22; and Nakano Koyukai, *Rikugun*, p. 19; and Allen, "Nakano School," p. 10.

25. Nakano Koyukai, *Rikugun*, p. 24.

26. Kato, *Rikugun* (2001), p. 26.

27. Kumagawa Mamoru, "Futamata Bunko" in *Rikugun Nakano Gakko Mataichi senshi: Futamata Bunko Daiichikisei no kiroku*, Mataichi Senshi Publication Committee, ed. (Tokyo: Mataichikai, 1981), p. 21; and Fujiwara, "Boryakuka," p. 68.

28. "Rikugun Nakano Gakko Futamata Ikki 10-nin no unmei," *Sande Mainichi* (12 November 1972), p. 140.

29. Mainichi Shinbun Tokubetsu Hodobu Shuzaihan, ed., *Okinawa Senso mararia jiken: Minami no shima no kyosei sokai* (Tokyo: Toho Shuppan, 1994), p. 92.

30. Nakano Koyukai, *Rikugun*, p. 37; and Hata, *Showashi*, pp. 319–20.

31. Nakano Koyukai, *Rikugun*, pp. 31, 34–36, 38–40, 42–44.

32. Tomisawa Shigeru, *Tokumu kikanin yomoyama monogatari* (Tokyo: Kojinsha, 1988), pp. 51–54.

33. Kato, *Rikugun* (2001), pp. 27–28.

34. Yanagawa, *Rikugun*, pp. 92–94.

35. Kato, *Rikugun* (2001), p. 31.

36. Hirakawa, *Ryukon*, p. 79; and Kuwahara Takeshi, *Futo: Hito gunjin no kiseki* (Yokohama: Kuwahara Takeshi, 1990), pp. 78–80.

37. Hata, *Riku-Kaigun*, p. 652; and Takaoka Daisuke, *Mita mama no Nanpo Ajia* (Tokyo: Japan-India Association, 1939), pp. 328–29.

38. John Gunther, *Inside Asia* (New York: Harper & Brothers, 1939), p. 104.

39. Hata Ikuhiko, *Showa Tenno itsutsu no ketsudan* (Tokyo: Bungei Shunju, 1994), pp. 113–14; and Nakano Koyukai, *Rikugun*, p. 145.

40. Hata, *Showa Tenno*, pp. 113–14; and Nakano Koyukai, *Rikugun*, pp. 172, 195–98.

41. Yamamoto Tomomi, *Four Years in Hell: I Was a Prisoner Behind the Iron Curtain* (Tokyo: An Asian Publication, 1952), pp. 33–36.

42. Iwakuro Hideo, "Junbi sareteita himitsusen," *Shukan Yomiuri* (8 December 1956), p. 21.

43. "Rikugun," *Sande Mainichi* (12 November 1972), p. 140.

44. Nakano Koyukai, *Rikugun*, p. 148.

45. "Rikugun," *Sande Mainichi* (12 November 1972), p. 140.

46. Nakano Koyukai, *Rikugun*, p. 166; and Russell Warren Howe, *The Hunt for "Tokyo Rose"* (Lanham, MD: Madison Books, 1990), p. 20.

47. Nakano Koyukai, *Rikugun*, p. 160; and "Rikugun," *Sande Mainichi* (12 November 1972), p. 140.

48. Nakano Koyukai, *Rikugun*, p. 165.

49. Ito, *Nakano Gakko*, p. 263.

50. Nakano Koyukai, *Rikugun*, pp. 160, 167.

51. Hata, *Nihon Riku-Kaigun*, p. 609.

52. Nakano Koyukai, *Rikugun*, p. 150.

53. Ambassador Craigie claimed the Tientsin incident was part of a movement by a "powerful faction in the Army" to provoke a war against Britain "on an issue in which American sympathies were not directly engaged." Craigie, *Behind the Japanese Mask* (London: Hutchinson &. Co., 1945), p. 73.

54. Nakano Koyukai, *Rikugun*, pp. 150–53; and Hori, *Daihonei*, p. 77.

Chapter 2

1. Fujiwara Iwaichi, "Fujiwara Kikan no katsuyaku," *Rekishi to jinbutsu* (August 1995), pp. 106–08; and Nagasaki Nobuko, ed., *Minami, F Kikan kankeisha danwa kiroku* (Tokyo: Institute for Developing Economies, 1979), pp. 21–22.

2. Suzuki Taisuke, "Kaisen zenya: Fuun no Bankokku," *Shukan Yomiuri* (8 December 1956), pp. 63–64; and Nakano Koyukai, *Rikugun*, pp. 387–88; and Maruyama Shizuo, *Nakano Gakko* (Tokyo: Heiwa Shobo, 1948), p. 83.

3. Nakano Koyukai, *Rikugun*, pp. 387–91; and Yamaguchi Hitoshi, "F Kikan senkoki," *Shukan Yomiuri* (8 December 1956), pp. 70, 71, 73.

4. Nakano Koyukai, *Rikugun*, pp. 391–94; and Yamaguchi, "F Kikan," pp. 70, 73, 76–78; and Richard J. Aldrich, *Intelligence and the War against Japan: Britain, America and the Politics of Secret Service* (Cambridge: Cambridge University Press, 2000), pp. 41–42; and Kunizuka Kazunori, *Indoyo ni kakaru niji: Nihon heishi no eiko* (Tokyo: Kobunsha, 1958), pp. 13, 31.

5. "'Mare no Tora' no jissho," *Sankei Shimbun* (30 March 1997), p. 11; and Ikeda Mitsuo, "Marai no Harimao (Tora)," *Shukan Yomiuri* (8 December 1956), pp. 85–92; and Kunizuka Kazunori, *Imparu o koete: F Kikan to Chandora Bosu* (Tokyo: Kodansha, 1995), pp. 107–08; Estimates of the size of Tani's gang range from nearly a thousand to three thousand.

6. Nakano Koyukai, *Rikugun*, pp. 401–02; and Yamaguchi, "F Kikan," p. 79.

7. Kalyan Kumar Ghosh, *The Indian National Army: Second Front of the Indian Independence Movement* (Meerut, India: Meenakishi Prakashan, 1969), p. 95.

8. Nakano Koyukai, *Rikugun*, pp. 404–05; and Nagasaki, *Minami*, p. 23.

9. Ministry of Foreign Affairs Diplomatic Records Office and Nihon Gaikoshi Editorial Committee, eds., *Nihon*, pp. 728–29.

10. U.S. Department of Defense, ed., *The "Magic" Background of Pearl Harbor*, appendix to vol. 2 (Washington, DC: U.S. Government Printing Office, 1978), pp. A-571–72.

11. Nakano Koyukai, *Rikugun*, pp. 168, 500.

12. U.S. Department of Defense, ed., *The "Magic" Background of Pearl Harbor*, appendix to vol. 4 (Washington, DC: U.S. Government Printing Office, 1978), pp. A-481, A-489.

13. U.S. Department of Defense, ed., *The "Magic" Background of Pearl Harbor*, (Washington, DC: U.S. Government Printing Office, 1978), appendix to vol. 2, pp. A-581–82, and appendix to vol. 4, p. A-492.

14. Nakano Koyukai, *Rikugun*, pp. 490–93; and Ito, *Nakano*, pp. 215–16.

15. H. P. Willmott, *Empires in the Balance: Japanese and Allied Pacific Strategies to April 1942* (Annapolis: Naval Institute Press, 1982), pp. 267, 301; and Nakano Koyukai, *Rikugun*, pp. 493–94.

16. Ito, *Nakano*, p. 217; and Tarora Sadao, "Nanpogun kimitsushitsu," *Shukan Yomiuri* (8 December 1956), p. 98.

17. Nakano Koyukai, *Rikugun*, p. 495.

18. Tarora, *Nanpogun*, pp. 98–99; and Ito, *Nakano*, pp. 216–17.

19. Tarora, *Nanpogun*, p. 99; and Nakano Koyukai, *Rikugun*, pp. 498–99.

Chapter 3

1. Ken'ichi Goto, "Cooperation, Submission, and Resistance of Indigenous Elites of Southeast Asia in the Wartime Empire," in *The Japanese Wartime Empire, 1931–1945*, Peter Duus, Ramon H. Myers, and Mark R. Peattie eds. (Princeton: Princeton University Press, 1996), pp. 274–75.

2. Sugii Mitsuru, "Biruma dokuritsu undo to Minami Kikan," *Shukan Yomiuri* (8 December 1956), p. 112.
3. F. S. V. Donnison, *British Military Administration in the Far East, 1943–46* (London: HMSO, 1956), p. 345.
4. Kawashima Takenobu, "Suzuki Keiji Taisa no katsuyaku," *Rekishi to jinbutsu* (10 September 1982), p. 77; and Nagasaki, *Minami*, p. 1.
5. Suzuki, "Kaisen," p. 63; and Sugii, "Biruma," p. 112.
6. Kawashima, "Suzuki," pp. 76–77; and Hata, *Nihon Riku-Kaigun*, p. 653.
7. Nakano Koyukai, *Rikugun*, p. 354; and U Maung Maung, ed., *Aung San of Burma* (The Hague: Martinus Nijhoff, 1962), pp. 33, 34; and Sugii, "Biruma," p. 112; and Kawashima, "Suzuki," p. 77.
8. Sugii, "Biruma," p. 113.
9. Joyce Lebra, *Japanese-Trained Armies in Southeast Asia* (New York: Columbia University Press, 1977), p. 56; and Sugii, "Biruma," p. 113.
10. Nakano Koyukai, *Rikugun*, pp. 352–54.
11. Nakano Koyukai, *Rikugun*, pp. 356–57; and Izumiya Tatsuro, *The Minami Organ* (Rangoon: Universities Press, 1981), p. 27.
12. Sugii, "Biruma," p. 112.
13. Suzuki, "Kaisen," p. 66.
14. Sugii, "Biruma," p. 115; and Suzuki, "Knisen," p. 66.
15. Nakano Koyukai, *Rikugun*, p. 356.
16. Nicolas Finet. "Hainan. Du goulag à l'Eden touristique," *Le Figaro Magazine* (13 February 1999), pp. 65–66.
17. Sugii, "Biruma," p. 115.
18. Izumiya, *Minami*, p. 59.
19. U Maung Maung, ed., *Aung San*, p. 35.
20. Sugii, "Biruma," pp. 111, 115.
21. Nakano Koyukai, *Rikugun*, pp. 361, 366–67; and Izumiya, *Minami*, pp. 90–95.
22. Nakano Koyukai, *Rikugun*, pp. 368–69.
23. Sugii, "Biruma," pp. 111, 115.
24. Donnison, *British*, p. 345.
25. Izumiya, *Minami*, pp. 109, 132, 168.
26. Izumiya, *Minami*, pp. 148–49.
27. Nakano Koyukai, *Rikugun*, pp. 371–73.
28. Kawashima, "Suzuki," p. 81; and Izumiya, *Minami*, p. 172.
29. Nakano Koyukai, *Rikugun*, p. 377; and Ministry of Foreign Affairs Diplomatic Records Office and Nihon Gaikoshi Editorial Committee, eds., *Nihon*, p. 869.
30. Nakano Koyukai, *Rikugun*, pp. 377–79.
31. Izumiya, *Minami*, pp. 193–94.
32. Izumiya, *Minami*, pp. 197–98.
33. Tarora, "Nanpogun," p. 102.
34. Sugii, "Biruma," pp. 111–12, 116.

Chapter 4

1. Geoffrey Moorhouse, *India Britannica* (New York: Harper & Row, 1983), pp. 153–58.

2. P. J. Marshall, ed., *The Cambridge Illustrated History of the British Empire* (Cambridge: Cambridge University Press, 1996), pp. 46, 78–79, 87; and Moorhouse, *India*, p. 220.

3. Kato Masuo, *The Lost War: A Japanese Reporter's Inside Story* (New York: Alfred A. Knopf, 1946), p. 21.

4. Muto Tomio, *Watakushi to Manshukoku* (Tokyo: Bungei Bunshu, 1988), pp. 324–25.

5. Cordell Hull, *The Memoirs of Cordell Hull* (New York: Macmillan Co., 1948), vol. 2, p. 1003.

6. Iwakuro. "Junbi," pp. 21–23.

7. Joyce Lebra, *Jungle Alliance: Japan and the Indian National Army* (Singapore: Asia Pacific Press, 1971), p. 80.

8. Nakano Koyukai, *Rikugun*, p. 408.

9. Kunizuka, *Imparu*, pp. 121–22, 127.

10. Iwakuro Hideo, "Iwakuro Kikan shimatsuki," *Shukan Yomiuri* (8 December 1956), p. 120.

11. Nakano Koyukai, *Rikugun*, pp. 408–09; and Iwakuro, "Iwakuro Kikan," p. 119.

12. Kuwahara, *Futo*, p. 107; and Kunizuka, *Imparu*, p. 121.

13. Nakano Koyukai, *Rikugun*, pp. 409–10; and Kunizuka, *Imparu*, pp. 123–24.

14. Nakano Koyukai, *Rikugun*, pp. 411–12; and Ghosh, *Indian*, p. 104.

15. Iwakuro, "Iwakuro Kikan," p. 121.

16. Nakano Koyukai, *Rikugun*, pp. 412, 419–20.

17. Marshall, *Cambridge*, p. 86; and Moorhouse, *India*, pp. 226–28; and Iwakuro, "Iwakuro Kikan," p. 121.

18. Nakano Koyukai, *Rikugun*, p. 411; and Subhas Chandra Bose, *The Essential Writings of Netaji Subhas Chandra Bose*, Sisir K. Bose and Sugata Bose eds. (Delhi: Oxford University Press, 1997), p. 26.

19. Kuwahara, *Futo*, p. 108; and Ghosh, *Indian*, p. 118.

20. Iwakuro, "Iwakuro Kikan," pp. 119, 121.

21. Kunizuka, *Imparu*, pp. 125–26.

22. Yamaguchi, "F Kikan," p. 79.

23. Iwakuro, "Iwakuro Kikan," p. 121; and Ghosh, *Indian*, pp. 116–120; and Kuwahara, *Futo*, pp. 108–09.

24. Arisue Seizo, *Seiji to gunji to jinji: Sanbo Honbu Dainibucho no shuki* (Tokyo: Fuyo Shobo, 1982), pp. 268–69.

25. Kunizuka, *Imparu*, p. 127.

26. Nagasaki, *Minami*, pp. 41–42.

27. Kuwahara, *Futo*, p. 109; and Kunizuka, *Imparu*, p. 119.

28. Bose, *Essential Writings*, pp. 30–31, 36, 38.

29. Nirad C. Chaudhuri, *Thy Hand, Great Anarch!: India, 1921–1952* (Reading, MA: Addison-Wesley Publishing, 1987), p. 316.

30. Louis Allen, *Burma: The Longest War, 1941–1945* (New York: St. Martin's Press, 1984), pp. 167–68.

31. Yamamoto Hayashi, "Kakumeiji Umiwo wataru," *Shukan Yomiuri* (8 December 1956), pp. 122–23; and Bose, *Essential Writings*, p. 190.

32. Byron Farwell, *Armies of the Raj: From the Mutiny to Independence, 1858–1947* (New York: Norton, 1989), p. 331.

33. Yamamoto, "Kakumeiji," pp. 123–27; and United States Foreign Broadcast Intelligence Service, *Foreign Broadcast Intelligence Report on the Far East*, no. 25, 21 July 1943. Record Group 262. National Archives.

34. Aldrich, *Intelligence*, p. 159.

35. Nakano Koyukai, *Rikugun*, pp. 435–36.

36. Nakano Koyukai, *Rikugun*, p. 436; and Allen, *Burma*, p. 169.

37. Nakano Koyukai, *Rikugun*, pp. 427, 438–48.

38. Nakano Koyukai, *Rikugun*, pp. 448–54; and Kunizuka, *Indoyo*, p. 175; and Kuwahara, *Futo*, p. 113.

39. Nakano Koyukai, *Rikugun*, pp. 455–56, 466–68; and Kunizuka, *Indoyo*, p. 176.

40. Nakano Koyukai, *Rikugun*, pp. 466–71; and Ito, Nakano, pp. 200–03; and Kuwahara Takeshi, "Indo Kokumingun no yuto to zasetsu," *Rekishi to jinbutsu* (December 1985), p. 305.

Chapter 5

1. Onoda Hiroo, "Kono michi," *Tokyo Shimbun* (3 and 4 March 1995), p. 1. All dates in following references to "Kono michi" refer to articles published that day on the front page of *Tokyo Shimbun*; and Kumabe Taizo, *Himitsusen no akaki hana: Ikiteiru Nakano Gakko no tamashi* (Tokyo: Nisshin Hodo, 1973), p. 20; and Suetsugu Ichiro, "*Sengo" e no chosen* (Tokyo: Rekishi Toshosha, 1981), pp. 14–15.

2. Arisue Seizo, *Shusen hishi: Arisue Kikancho no shuki* (Tokyo: Fuyo Shobo, 1987), p. 19.

3. Tanaka Toshio, *Rikugun Nakano Gakko no Tobu Nyu Ginea yugekisen* (Tokyo: Senshi Kankokai, 1996), pp. 1–4, 7, 37–42.

4. Nakano Koyukai, *Rikugun*, pp. 602–03; and Charles A. Willoughby, ed., *Reports of General MacArthur*, vol. 2, part 1 (Washington, DC: Government Printing Office, 1966), pp. 349–52.

5. Tanaka, *Rikugun*, pp. 7–8, 37, 64; and Willoughby, ed., *Reports of General MacArthur*, vol. 2, part 1, p. 349.

6. Kumagawa, "Futamata," p. 23; and Kumabe, *Himitsusen*, p. 20.

7. Kumabe, *Himitsusen*, p. 23; and Onoda, "Kono Michi," *Tokyo Shimbun*, 6 March 1995.

8. Onoda, "Kono Michi," 4 and 6 March 1995; and Onoda Hiroo, conversation with author, 5 July 2001.

9. Onoda, "Kono Michi," 7 March 1995; and Onoda Hiroo, *No Surrender: My Thirty-Year War* (Tokyo: Kodansha International, 1974), pp. 31–32; and Yamamoto Fukuichi, "Seibugun ni funin shite," in *Mataichi Senshi* (Tokyo: Mataichikai, 1981), p. 417; and Hirakawa, *Ryukon*, p. 32; and Mainichi Shinbun Tokubetsu Hodobu Shuzaihan, ed., *Okinawa Senso*, p. 113.

10. Ronald H. Spector, *Eagle against the Sun: The American War with Japan* (New York: Free Press, 1985), pp. 440–41.

11. Nakano Koyukai, *Rikugun*, p. 522.

12. Nakajima Akifumi, "Daijuyon homengun kankei sokatsu," in *Mataichi Senshi* (Tokyo: Mataichikai, 1981), p. 170.

13. William Brand Simpson, *Special Agent in the Pacific* (New York: Rivercross Publishing, 1995), p. 60.

14. Hori, *Daihonei*, p. 151; and Nakano Koyukai, *Rikugun*, p. 524; and Nakajima Akifumi, "Nanmei Kikan to tomo ni," in *Mataichi Senshi* (Tokyo: Mataichikai, 1981), pp. 204–05.

15. Nakano Koyukai, *Rikugun*, pp. 524–26; and Onoda, "Kono Michi," 8 March 1995; and Onoda, *No Surrender*, p. 41; and Ito, *Nakano*, p. 222; and Taniguchi Yoshimi, "Onoda moto shoi ni, fukuin su," *Kaiko* (April 1974), p. 5.

16. Hori, *Daihonei*, pp. 148–49.

17. M. Hamlin Cannon, *Leyte: The Return to the Philippines* (Washington, DC: Government Printing Office, 1954), pp. 306–07; and William A. Owens, *Eye-Deep in Hell: A Memoir of the Liberation of the Philippines, 1944–45* (Dallas, TX: Southern Methodist University Press, 1989), pp. 48–49.

18. Nakano Koyukai, *Rikugun*, pp. 532–35, 544–45; and Owens, *Eye-Deep*, pp. 50–51; Cannon, *Leyte*, pp. 298–305.

19. Spector, *Eagle*, p. 518; Nakano Koyukai, *Rikugun*, pp. 526–31; and Onoda, "Kono Michi," 8 March 1995.

20. Onoda, *No Surrender*, pp. 41–44; and Onoda, "Kono Michi," 9 March 1995; and "Rikugun," *Sande Mainichi* (12 November 1972), p. 138.

21. Onoda, *No Surrender*, pp. 45, 53, 56–58; and Onoda, "Kono Michi," 11–13 March 1995.

22. Onoda Hiroo, "Rubanguto Senki," *Mataichi Senshi*, pp. 216–17; and Taniguchi, "Onoda," p. 7; and Spector, *Eagle*, p. 519; and Onoda, *No Surrender*, pp. 54–55.

23. Nakajima, "Nanmei," pp. 204–05.

24. Onoda, "Kono Michi," 14 March 1995; and Onoda, *No Surrender*, pp. 58, 68; and Onoda Hiroo, conversation with author, 5 July 2001.

25. Onoda, "Kono Michi," 16 March 1995.

26. Nakajima, "Daijuyon," *Mataichi Senshi*, pp. 171–72.

27. Nakano Koyukai, *Rikugun*, p. 522; and Ono Tadao, "Ruson Hokutan no musenhan," in *Mataichi Senshi* (Tokyo: Mataichikai, 1981), p. 174.

28. Onoda, "Kono Michi," 17–18 March 1995.

Chapter 6

1. Georges Catroux, *Deux actes du drame indochinois* (Paris: Librairie Plon, 1959), pp. 8–9.

2. Philippe Devillers, *Histoire du Viet-Nam de 1940 à 1952* (Paris: Editions du Seuil, 1952), p. 81.

3. Tachikawa Takashi, "Taiheiyo Senso (Dai Toa Senso) no kage ni nipputsu kyoryoku ari," *Securitarian* (September 2000), p. 50.

4. Kaneko Seigo, "Annam himitsu butai," *Shukan Yomiuri* (8 December 1956),

p. 161; and Claude Paillat, *Dossier secret de l'Indochine* (Paris: Presse de la Cité, 1964), p. 32; and Jean Sainteny, *Histoire d'une paix manquée: Indochine, 1945–1947* (Paris: Amiot-Dumont, 1953), p. 33.

5. Tsuchihashi Yuichi, "Furansugun o buso kaijo," *Shukan Yomiuri* (8 December 1956), p. 156; and Devillers, *Histoire*, pp. 121–23; and Paillat, *Dossier*, p. 38; and Sainteny, *Histoire*, p. 23; and Jean Decoux, *A la barre de l'Indochine* (Paris: Librairie Plon, 1949), pp. 305–24.

6. Nakano Koyukai, *Rikugun*, p. 566; and Devillers, *Histoire*, pp. 83, 88–89. The character for "akira" can also be read in Japanese as "mei."

7. Catroux, *Deux*, pp. 51–52; and Tsuchihashi, "Furansugun," p. 156.

8. Kaneko, "Annam," p. 162; and Nakano Koyukai, *Rikugun*, p. 568; and Tsuchihashi, "Furansugun," p. 156.

9. Nakano Koyukai, *Rikugun*, p. 570; and Kaneko, "Annam," p. 162; and Devillers, *Histoire*, p. 89.

10. Tsuchihashi, "Furansugun," p. 157; and Kaneko, "Annam," p. 163; and Nakano Koyukai, *Rikugun*, p. 571. Emperor Bao Dai recalled the event differently, writing in his memoirs that the Japanese had stopped him and the Empress outside the walls of Hue at around eleven o'clock the night of the attack, as they were returning from his hunting lodge. Whereas Capt. Kaneko remembered finding the royal couple at dawn, confirming their identity to a Colonel Kawai unsure of their identity, Bao Dai wrote of a colonel greeting him at close to one o'clock that night, addressing him as the emperor, and escorting him through the gate. Nor did the emperor recall meeting Capt. Kaneko or shaking his hand. Bao Dai, *Le Dragon d'Annam* (Paris: Plon, 1980), pp. 99–100.

11. Nakano Koyukai, *Rikugun*, p. 573; and Paillat, *Dossier*, pp. 39–40; and Sainteny, *Histoire*, p. 29.

12. Donnison, *British*, p. 347.

13. S. Woodburn Kirby, *The War against Japan*, vol. 4, *The Reconquest of Burma* (London: HMSO, 1965), pp. 33, 333.

14. Donnison, *British*, p. 352; and U Maung Maung, *Aung San*, p. 76; and Nagasaki, *Minami*, p. 18.

15. Farwell, *Armies*, p. 314; and Kirby, *Reconquest*, p. 386.

16. Kunizuka, *Indoyo*, p. 186; and Kuwahara, "Indo Kokumingun," p. 315.

17. Kuwahara, *Futo*, p. 125; and Kuwahara, "Indo Kokumingun," p. 315; and Farwell, *Armies*, p. 338.

18. Kuwahara, "Indo Kokumingun," p. 317.

19. Tanaka, *Rikugun*, pp. 74, 87, 100–01, 110–17, 138–43, 183–89, 196–216.

20. Nakano Koyukai, *Rikugun*, p. 214; and So Ch'un-sik et al., eds., *Pukhanhak* (Seoul: Pagyongsa, 1999), p. 23. A brief note on geographic names is due here. First, alternate spellings for Yenki (Enkitsu in Japanese) are Yanji or Yenchi. Second, the spelling for Kirin today is Jirin. Third, the Japanese and Korean readings for the Chinese characters for Chientao are both Kando. I refer to the special service agency there as the Chientao SSA rather than the Kando SSA, in line with the convention of referring to Japanese units in Manchukuo by their Chinese names.

21. Chang Ch'ang-guk, *Yuksa Cholopsaeng* (Seoul: Chungang Ilbosa, 1984), pp. 24–25; and Nakano Koyukai, *Rikugun*, p. 214; and Wan-yao Chou, "The *Kominka*

Movement in Taiwan and Korea: Comparisons and Interpretations," in *The Japanese Wartime Empire, 1931–1945*, Peter Duus, Ramon H. Myers, and Mark R. Peattie eds. (Princeton: Princeton University Press, 1996), p. 63.

22. Baba Yoshimitsu, *Shiberia kara Nagata-cho made: Joho shoko no sengoshi* (Tokyo: Tendensha, 1987), pp. 45–49.

23. Kobayashi, "Rikugun," p. 173; and Harada Tokichi, *Kaze to kumo to saigo no choko shoko* (Tokyo: Jiyu Kokuminsha, 1973), p. 8.

24. Kobayashi Hisamitsu, "'Rikugun Nakano Gakko' kaku tatakeri," *Purejidento* (December 1985), pp. 175; and Nakano Koyukai, *Rikugun*, p. 211.

25. Kobayashi, "'Rikugun,'" p. 176; and Nakano Koyukai, *Rikugun*, pp. 188–90; and Mita Kazuo, *Mukae ni kita jipu* (Tokyo: 20 Seikisha, 1955), p. 18.

26. Kinoshita, *Kesareta*, pp. 306–13.

27. Nakano Koyukai, *Rikugun*, pp. 48–51; and Kinoshita, *Kesareta*, pp. 306–13.

28. Hirakawa, *Ryukon*, p. 159; and Nakano Koyukai, *Rikugun*, pp. 49, 53–54.

Chapter 7

1. Nakano Koyukai, *Rikugun*, p. 635.

2. A. J. Barker, *Okinawa* (New York: Galahad Books, 1981), p. 11; and Okinawa Prefecture Health and Welfare Department, ed., *Heiwa e no shogen: Okinawa Kenritsu Heiwa Kinen Shiryokan gaidobukku* (Itoman, Okinawa: Okinawa-ken senbotsusha irei bosankai, August 1991), p. 6.

3. Nakano Koyukai, *Rikugun*, pp. 641–42; and United States Army Forces, Middle Pacific, Office of the Assistant Chief of Staff for Military Intelligence, "2605" (1 November 1945), pp. 54–55. On file at U.S. Army Center for Military History; and George Feifer, *Tennozan: The Battle of Okinawa and the Atomic Bomb* (New York: Ticknor & Friends, 1992), pp. 161–62; and James H. Belote and William M. Belote, *Typhoon of Steel: The Battle for Okinawa* (New York: Harper & Row, 1970), p. 188. Murakami is one of the few graduates of the Nakano School to surface in American accounts of the war. However, Feifer in *Tennozan* identifies him only as a graduate of the Military Academy and "an expert in guerrilla warfare." James and William Belote refer to him simply as the leader of "a guerrilla outfit."

4. Nakano Koyukai, *Rikugun*, pp. 663–64; and Ishihara Masaie, ed., *Mo hitotsu no Okinawa-sen: Mararia jigoku no Haterumato* (Naha, Okinawa: Hirugisha, 1983), pp. 47–48; and Miyajima Toshio, "Waga tatakawazaru no ki," in *Mataichi Senshi*, pp. 273, 275, 277, 286. Lt. Akutsu changed his name after the war to Miyajima.

5. Mainichi Shinbun Tokubetsu Hodobu Shuzaihan, *Okinawa Senso*, pp. 92, 94, 97, 113–14; and Okinawa Prefecture Health and Welfare Department, ed., *Heiwa*, pp. 10–13.

6. Uehara Masatoshi, *Okinawa-sen Toppu shikuretto* (Naha, Okinawa: Okinawa Taimususha, 1995), p. 134.

7. Barker, *Okinawa*, pp. 19, 26.

8. Barker, *Okinawa*, pp. 29–31, 33–36; and Hori, *Daihonei*, pp. 118, 156, 195–98.

9. Barker, *Okinawa*, pp. 41–43, 46.

10. Nakano Koyukai, *Rikugun*, pp. 638–39, 644, 647; and Feifer, *Tennozan*, pp. 157–62.

11. Nakano Koyukai, *Rikugun*, pp. 638, 658, 660, 663.

12. Nakano Koyukai, *Rikugun*, pp. 661–63; and Gerald Astor, *Operation Iceberg: The Invasion and Conquest of Okinawa in WWII* (New York: Donald I. Fine, 1995), pp. 319–21; and Feifer, *Tennozan*, p. 390; and Yahara Hiromichi, *The Battle for Okinawa* (New York: John Wiley & Sons, 1995), p. 62; and United States Army Forces, Middle Pacific, "2605," p. 46; and Roy E. Appleman et al., *Okinawa: The Last Battle*, in series *United States Army in World War II, The War in the Pacific* (Washington, DC: Department of the Army, 1948), pp. 361–62; and Belote and Belote, *Typhoon*, pp. 272–73.

13. Nakano Koyukai, *Rikugun*, pp. 639, 641, 646–48; Duval A. Edwards, *Spy Catchers of the U.S. Army in the War with Japan* (Gig Harbor, WA: Red Apple Publishing, 1994), p. 244.

14. Mainichi Shinbun Tokubetsu Hodobu Shuzaihan, *Mararia*, pp. 94–95, 101–02, 114; and Miyajima, "Waga tatakawazaru no ki," pp. 286–93, 296.

15. Barker, *Okinawa*, pp. 60–61; and Edward J. Drea, *In the Service of the Emperor: Essays on the Imperial Japanese Army* (Lincoln, NE: University of Nebraska Press, 1998), p. 58.

16. Okinawa Prefecture Health and Welfare Department, *Heiwa*, pp. 13–14, 18, 24–25, 139–41.

Chapter 8

1. Nakano Koyukai, *Rikugun*, p. 672–75.

2. Thomas B. Allen and Norman Polmar, *Code-Name Downfall: The Secret Plan to Invade Japan—And Why Truman Dropped the Bomb* (New York: Simon & Schuster, 1995), pp. 143, 147, 297–303.

3. Nakano Koyukai, *Rikugun*, pp. 814–17; and Walter Krueger, *From Down Under to Nippon: The Story of Sixth Army in World War II* (Washington, DC: Combat Forces Press, 1953), p. 333; and Drea, *Service of the Emperor*, pp. 149–50; and Edward J. Drea, *MacArthur's ULTRA: Codebreaking and the War against Japan, 1942–1945* (Lawrence, KS: University Press of Kansas, 1992), pp. 209–10.

4. Masuda Tomio, "Seibugun kankei sokatsu," in *Mataichi senshi*, p. 413.

5. Nakano Koyukai, *Rikugun*, pp. 706–07, 822–27; and Hirakawa, *Ryukon*, p. 182; and Masuda Tomio, "Seibugun," in *Mataichi Senshi*, p. 411; and Yamamoto Fukuichi, "Seibugun," in *Mataichi senshi*, pp. 418–20, and *Mataichi senshi*, pp. 577–78.

6. Masuda, "Seibugun," in *Mataichi Senshi*, p. 411; and Suetsugu Ichiro, "'Kirishima Butai' no omoide," in *Mataichi senshi*, pp. 441–42; and Suetsugu Ichiro, "Daini Kirishima Butai keikaku kiyu," in *Mataichi senshi*, pp. 446–47; and Nakano Koyukai, *Rikugun*, p. 824.

7. Masuda Tomio, "Kirishima Butai no ato o tazunete," in *Mataichi Senshi*, pp. 443, 445; and United States Army CCD. Testimony of Itezono Tatsuo. Record Group 331. National Archives.

8. Suetsugu Ichiro, "Daini Kirishima Butai," in *Mataichi Senshi*, pp. 446–47.

9. Testimony of Itezono Tatsuo, Record Group 331. National Archives; and United States Army. Far East Command. Trial of Japanese Army officers. Record Group 153. National Archives.

10. Nakano Koyukai, *Rikugun*, p. 775.

11. Nakano Koyukai, *Rikugun*, pp. 279–80, 777–80, 791–95.

12. Nakano Koyukai, *Rikugun*, pp. 732, 739–40.

13. Nakano Koyukai, *Rikugun*, pp. 741–77.

14. Nakano Koyukai, *Rikugun*, pp. 751–55.

15. Kato, *Rikugun* (2001), p. 217.

16. Nakano Koyukai, *Rikugun*, p. 168.

17. Nakano Koyukai, *Rikugun*, pp. 725–29; and Kato, *Rikugun* (2001), p. 217. Apart from Keijo, the Korean place names are the present-day ones, rather than their less-known Japanese renderings.

18. "Historical Testing: German and Japanese Villages," United States Army, Dugway Proving Ground, *DPG: The Nation's Chemical and Biological Defense Proving Ground*; and Hirakawa, *Ryukon*, p. 183; and William Craig, *The Fall of Japan: The Last Blazing Weeks of World War II*, 1967. Reprint (Green Farms, CT: Wildcat Publishing Company, 1997), p. 141; and *Yank*, 14 May 1943, p. 11.

19. Craig, pp. 141–43; and Stephen Harper, *Miracle of Deliverance: The Case for the Bombing of Hiroshima and Nagasaki* (New York: Stein and Day, 1985), pp. 46, 146; and War Crimes Office, United States Army Judge Advocate General's Office, "U.S. vs. Kiyoharu Tomori et al.," Record Group 153, National Archives; and United States Army, Judge Advocate General's Office, "Post-Action Review of the Case of U.S. vs. Aihara et al. 31, Docket No. 288 (Western Army Case)," Record Group 331, National Archives; and Testimony of Itezono Tatsuo at the Legal Section Office, Fukuoka, between 21 November 1946 and 10 December 1946, Record Group 331, National Archives. Nor did British aircrew escape the fate suffered by the American airmen at Aburayama. Shortly after the imperial surrender broadcast of 15 August, the Japanese executed nine fliers of the British Pacific Fleet captured after a January 1945 bombing raid against oil refineries at Palembang. In another case, a British fighter pilot shot down over Tokyo on 15 August was executed that same day several hours after the surrender announcement.

Chapter 9

1. Allen and Polmar, pp. 204–09.

2. *Mataichi Senshi*, p. 577.

3. Arisue, *Shusen hishi*, pp. 28–35; and Fujisaki Tatsumaru, "Haraguchi Shigehiko Shoi no omoide," in *Mataichi senshi*, p. 447; and John Dower, *Japan in War and Peace: Selected Essays* (New York: New Press, 1993), p. 64.

4. Allen and Polmar, pp. 263–64.

5. So et al., *Pukhanhak*, p. 25.

6. Kawahara, *Kantogun*, pp. 12, 34–35.

7. United States Army Forces Far East. *Record of Operations against Soviet Rus-*

sia: On Northern and Western Fronts of Manchuria, and in Northern Korea (Washington, DC: Department of the Army, 1954), pp. 186–87; and Stephan, Russian Fascists, pp. 351–54; and Hirakawa, Ryukon, p. 138; and Nakano Koyukai, Rikugun, p. 182.

8. Yamamoto, Four Years in Hell, pp. 33–36; and Stephan, Russian Fascists, pp. 334–35.

9. Baba, Shiberia, pp. 7, 29–33, 51.

10. Netaji Inquiry Committee Report (New Delhi: Ministry of Information and Broadcasting, 1956), p. 8.

11. Netaji Inquiry Committee Report, pp. 6–8.

12. Nihon, Iwakuro, p. 220.

13. Netaji Inquiry Committee Report, pp. 13–14; and Hugh Toye, The Springing Tiger: Study of a Revolutionary (London: Cassell, 1959), pp. 166–67.

14. Netaji Inquiry Committee, pp. 45–51. The names of Academy members are inscribed on a plaque affixed to the base of a bust of Bose at Renkoji Temple.

15. Nakano Koyukai, Rikugun, pp. 32, 144–45, 172–73, 707.

16. Hata, Showa Tenno, pp. 114–15. In another version, it was Maj. Tarora who proposed to Colonel Shiraki the plan to attack the Occupation forces in the event the imperial family was harmed. Shiraki then had the plan approved by War Minister Anami Korechika. Nakano Koyukai, Rikugun, p. 709.

17. Hirakawa, Ryukon, pp. 30–33.

18. Nakano Koyukai, Rikugun, pp. 53–54; and Hirakawa, Ryukon, p. 33.

19. Kinoshita, Kesareta, p. 380. While Unit 731 activities were hidden, authorities did reveal early during the Occupation that the Noborito Research Institute had engaged in "death ray" experiments. Nippon Times, 8 October 1945.

20. Saito Michinori, Boryakusen: Dokyumento Rikugun Noborito Kenkyujo (Tokyo: Jiji Tsushinsha, 1987), pp. 96–97.

21. Nakano Koyukai, Rikugun, p. 50.

22. Nakano Koyukai, Rikugun, p. 50.

23. Nakano Koyukai, Rikugun, pp. 707–08.

24. Christopher Thorne, Allies of a Kind: The United States, Britain and the War against Japan (London: Hamilton, 1978), p. 657.

25. Arisue, Shusen hishi, pp. 49–50.

26. Hata, Showa, p. 118.

27. Allen, End of the War in Asia, pp. 19–21.

28. Fukada, Reimei no seiki: Daitoa Kaigi to sono shuyakutachi (Tokyo: Bungei Shunju, 1994), pp. 224–27.

29. Hata, Showa, pp. 154–56; and Nakano Koyukai, Rikugun, pp. 708–09.

30. Willoughby, Reports of General MacArthur, vol. 1, p. 447; and John Toland, The Rising Sun: The Decline and Fall of the Japanese Empire, 1936–1945, vol. 2 (New York: Random House, 1970), p. 1060.

31. Nakano Koyukai, Rikugun, p. 202.

32. Willoughby, Reports of General MacArthur, vol. 1, p. 447. Willoughby obscured the intelligence coloring of the Japanese delegation, referring to Yamamoto Arata, Otake Sadao, and Takeuchi Harumi simply as officers of the Japanese Army's

general staff and to Takakura Morio as a member of the War Ministry. Then again, Willoughby referred to his own intelligence officers only as "linguist officers."

33. Willoughby, *Reports of General MacArthur*, vol. 1, p. 447.

34. Willoughby, *Reports of General MacArthur*, vol. 1, supplement, p. 117.

35. Frederick P. Munson, "Oral Reminiscences of Brigadier General Frederick P. Munson," Interview by D. Clayton James, Washington, DC, 3 July 1971, on file at MacArthur Archives, pp. 5, 13.

36. Charles Willoughby, *Shirarezaru Nihon senryo: Uirobi kaikoroku*, Yon Chong, ed. (Tokyo: Bancho Shobo, 1973), pp. 2–3.

37. Sydney Mashbir, "Oral Reminiscences of Colonel Sidney F. Mashbir," interview by D. Clayton James, Laguna Beach, California, 1 September 1971, on file at MacArthur Archives, p. 16.

38. Drea, *MacArthur's ULTRA*, p. 187.

39. Elliott Thorpe, "Oral Reminiscences of Brigadier General Elliott R. Thorpe," interview by D. Clayton James, Sarasota, FL, 29 May 1977, on file at MacArthur Archives, p. 5.

40. Faubion Bowers, "Oral Reminiscences of Major Faubion Bowers," interview by D. Clayton James, New York, NY, 18 July 1971, on file at MacArthur Archives, p. 3; and Charles Willoughby, "Oral Reminiscences of Major General Charles A. Willoughby," interview by D. Clayton James, Naples, Florida, 30 July 1971, on file at MacArthur Archives, p. 11; and Mashbir, "Oral Reminiscences," pp. 17–18.

41. William J. Sebald, *With MacArthur in Japan: A Personal History of the Occupation*, with Russell Brines (New York: W. W. Norton, 1965), p. 106; and Richard M. Nixon, *Leaders* (New York: Warner Books, 1982), p. 129.

42. United States Army Forces Far East. *Outline of Operations Prior to Termination of War and Activities Connected with the Cessation of Hostilities*, Japanese Monograph No. 119, Washington, DC: Department of the Army, pp. 16–17.

43. Willoughby, *Reports of General MacArthur*, vol. 1, p. 449.

44. Charles A. Willoughby, *Maneuver in War* (Harrisburg, PA: The Military Service Publishing Co., 1939), p. 219.

45. Yahara, *The Battle for Okinawa*, p. 232; and United States Army Forces in Korea, Headquarters, Counter Intelligence Corps, "CIC Area Study, Korea, August 1945," p. 38, in Asian Culture Research Institute, Hallim University, ed., *Migunjonggi chongbo sajip: CIC Pogoso* (1), p. 243; and Nakano Koyukai, *Rikugun*, pp. 723–27; and Military Intelligence Service, "Japanese Intelligence," *Military Research Bulletin* No. 21 (Washington, DC: Military Intelligence Division, War Department, 15 August 1945), p. 10.

46. Arisue, *Shusen hishi*, pp. 50–52, 57–58; and Kawabe Torashiro, *Kawabe Torashiro kaisoroku* (Tokyo: Mainichi Shinbunsha, 1979), pp. 184–86.

47. Willoughby, *Reports of General MacArthur*, vol. 1, p. 450.

48. United States Army Forces, Pacific, *Basic Outline Plan for 'Blacklist' Operations*, pp. 1, 11, 17. On file at the U.S. Army Center for Military History.

49. United States Army Forces, Pacific, General Headquarters, "Punitive Features of Annexes to Operations Instructions," p. 1. Memo to Chief of Staff. On file at the U.S. Army Center for Military History.

50. Willoughby, *Reports of General MacArthur*, I, p. 452; and Arisue, *Shusen hishi*, pp. 65–67, 85.

51. Hori, *Daihonei*, p. 78.

52. Arisue, *Shusen hishi*, p. 235.

53. Arisue, *Shusen hishi*, pp. 64, 67, 104–05.

54. Price, *Key to Japan*, p. 288.

55. John Gunther, *The Riddle of MacArthur* (New York: Harper & Brothers, 1950), p. 75; and Robert L. Eichelberger, with Milton MacKaye, *Our Jungle Road to Tokyo* (New York: Viking Press, 1950), pp. xii, xiii, 262, 283–84.

56. *Sankei Shimbun*, 13 August 1995; and Bowers, "Oral Reminiscences," p. 21.

57. Munson Oral Reminiscences, pp. 4, 34, 43, 53.

58. Arisue, *Shusen hishi*, pp. 122–23.

59. Willoughby, *Reports of General MacArthur*, vol. 1, pp. 447, 454; and Arisue, *Shusen hishi*, pp. 125–26; and Sugita Ichiji, *Kokka shidosha no ridashippu* (Tokyo: Hara Shobo, 1993), p. 363.

60. Hiyama Yoshiaki, *Ango o nusunda otokotachi* (Tokyo: Kojinsha, 1994), pp. 291–97; and Arisue, *Shusen hishi*, pp. 138–45, 249; and James Bamford, *The Puzzle Palace* (Boston: Houghton Mifflin, 1982), p. 159; and letter from Edward Drea, 8 August 1999.

61. Arisue, *Shusen hishi*, pp. 163–65.

62. Imperial Japanese Government, Central Liaison Office, "Erroneous Report," 30 August 1946, Record Group 331, National Archives.

63. Arisue, *Shusen hishi*, pp. 167, 169, 200–201; and Hirakawa, *Ryukon*, p. 65.

64. Reinhard Gehlen, *The Service*, trans. David Irving (New York: World Publishing, 1972), pp. 1–2.

65. Munson, "Oral Reminiscences," p. 48.

66. Arisue, *Shusen hishi*, p. 159; Kawabe, *Kawabe*, pp. 195–96; and Willoughby, *Maneuver*, pp. 196–97, 235.

67. Arisue, *Seiji to gunji to jinji*, p. 264.

68. Arisue, *Shusen hishi*, p. 191.

69. War Department. The United States Strategic Bombing Survey (Pacific), *Japanese Intelligence* (Washington, DC: Government Printing Office, 1946), pp. 72, 103.

70. Ito Takeo, *Mantetsu ni ikite* (Tokyo: Keiso Shobo, 1964), pp. 266–67; and United States Army Forces, Far East, *Small Wars and Border Problems: The Nomonhan Incident* (Washington, DC: 1956), pp. 161–62; and Hakamada Shigeki, "Japan Way Behind in Eurasian Studies, Resources" (*Daily Yomiuri On-Line*, 21 January 1999).

71. Higaki, *Matsushiro*, p. 175.

72. Hata, *Showa Tenno*, p. 169.

73. Bonner Fellers, "Oral Reminiscences of Brigadier General Bonner F. Fellers," interview by D. Clayton James, Washington, DC, 26 June 1971, on file at MacArthur Archives, Oral Reminiscences, p. 29.

74. *Nippon Times*, 23 November 1945; and Munson, "Oral Reminiscences," p. 43.

75. Arisue, *Shusen hishi*, p. 238.
76. Hata, *Showa Tenno*, p. 166.

Chapter 10

1. Kusakabe Ichiro, *Rikugun Nakano Gakko jitsuroku: Ketteiban* (Tokyo: Besuto Bukku, 1980), pp. 210–15; and Hata, *Showa Tenno*, pp. 170–71.

2. Arisue, *Shusen hishi*, pp. 236–37, 240.

3. Hata, *Showa Tenno*, pp. 174–75; and Allen, *End*, pp. 19–21; and U Ba Maw, *Breakthrough in Burma: Memoirs of a Revolution* (New Haven: Yale University Press, 1968), p. 415.

4. Willoughby, ed., *Reports of General MacArthur*, vol. 1, supplement p. 138; and Gayn, *Japan Diary*, p. 46; and Arisue, *Shusen hishi*, pp. 249–50.

5. *Nippon Times*, 24 January 1946.

6. *BCON* [newsletter of the British Commonwealth Occupation Forces], 31 August 1946.

7. *Torii*, 10 September 1998.

8. Arisue, *Shusen hishi*, pp. 250–51; and Hata, *Showa Tenno*, p. 169.

9. Tamotsu Shibutani, *Derelicts of Company K: A Sociological Study of Demoralization* (Berkeley: University of California Press, 1978), p. 364.

10. Willoughby, *Reports of General MacArthur*, vol. 1, supplement, pp. 65–66.

11. Sidney F. Mashbir, *I Was an American Spy* (New York: Vantage Press, 1953), p. 347.

12. Munson, "Oral Reminiscences," p. 48.

13. Owens, *Eye-Deep*, pp. 222–23.

14. United States Army. General Headquarters, Far East Command, *Administrative History of the 441st CIC Detachment*. On file at the U.S. Army Center for Military History, p. 15; and John Patrick Finnegan, *Military Intelligence* (Washington, DC: Center of Military History, 1998), p. 107. Finnegan noted that the numbers of CIC personnel had declined only slightly, compared to the wholesale demobilization of the U.S. military in general, but that CIC had suffered a "worrisome decline in quality" due to the elimination of the draft.

15. Faubion Bowers, "Oral Reminiscences," p. 10; and Gayn, p. 159.

16. Tad Ichinokuchi, ed., *John Aiso and the M.I.S.: Japanese American Soldiers in the Military Intelligence Service, World War II* (Los Angeles, CA: Military Intelligence Service Club of Southern California, 1988), pp. 239–44.

17. David E. Kaplan and Alec Dubro, *Yakuza: The Explosive Account of Japan's Criminal Underworld* (Reading, MA: Addison-Wesley, 1986), p. 61.

18. J. Roy Galloway, "Letter to GS," *Golden Sphinx*, vol. 50 no. 4 (Winter 1996), p. 10; and Willoughby, "Oral Reminiscences," p. 20. Willoughby proclaimed to the historian D. Clayton James that, "I forced Thorpe's transfer. Either he went or I went." Thorpe claimed he left after suffering a postwar reduction in rank. Elliott Thorpe, "Oral Reminiscences," p. 28; and Robert B. Textor, *Failure in Japan: With Keystones for a Positive Policy* (New York: The John Day Company, 1951), p. 233.

19. Mark Gayn, *Japan Diary* (Rutland, VT: Charles E. Tuttle Company, 1981), pp. 68–69; Textor, *Failure*, p. 121.

20. Tachibana Yuzuru, *Teikoku Kaigun shikan ni natta Nikkei Nisei* (Tokyo: Tsukiji Shokan, 1994), pp. 198–99.

21. Kaplan and Dubro, *Yakuza*, p. 61.

22. Arisue, *Shusen hishi*, p. 256.

23. Chalmers Johnson, *An Instance of Treason: Ozaki Hotsumi and the Sorge Spy Ring* (Rutland, VT: Charles E. Tuttle Company, 1977), pp. 65–66.

24. Hatakeyama Kiyoyuki, *Hiroku Rikugun Nakano Gakko* (Tokyo: Bancho Shobo, 1971), vol. 2, p. 308.

25. Hatakeyama, *Hiroku*, p. 315; and Nakano Koyukai, *Rikugun*, pp. 291, 293–94.

26. John Ranelagh, *The Agency: The Rise and Decline of the CIA* (New York: Simon & Schuster, 1986), pp. 70–71.

27. Oliver Caldwell, *A Secret War* (Carbondale, IL: Southern Illinois University Press, 1972), pp. 194–95; and Maochun Yu, *OSS in China: Prelude to Cold War* (Annapolis, MD: Naval Institute Press, 1996), p. 229. Donovan's remarks were paraphrased by Caldwell.

28. Sebald, *With MacArthur*, p. 22.

29. Hata, *Showa Tenno*, p. 126.

30. Kato, *Lost War*, pp. 262–63.

31. Kodama Yoshio, *I Was Defeated* (Tokyo: An Asian Publication, 1951), p. 208.

32. Harry Emerson Wildes, *Typhoon in Tokyo: The Occupation and Its Aftermath* (New York, Macmillan, 1954), p. 53.

33. Gayn, *Japan*, p. 342.

34. Theodore Cohen, *Remaking Japan: The American Occupation as New Deal* (New York: The Free Press, 1987), pp. 164–65.

35. "Letter from Nozaka, Sanzo concerning Kamata, Senichi to Mr. Marcum," 7 July 1947. Record Group 331. National Archives. The translator of the letter rendered the general's name as "Kamata," but a major guide to Japanese Army officers spells it "Kamada." See Toyama, ed., *Riku-Kaigun*, p. 404. The translator also misspelled as "Nozaka" the name of Nosaka Sanzo, leader of Japan's Communist legislators.

36. Arisue, *Shusen Hishi*, pp. 207–09.

37. Textor, *Failure*, pp. 216–17.

38. William E. Burrows, *Deep Black: Space Espionage and National Security* (New York: Random House, 1986), pp. 58–59.

39. Ariga, *Nihon*, p. 111.

40. Mita, *Mukae*, p. 16.

41. Mita, *Mukae*, p. 15.

42. "Harubin Tokumu Kikan kaimetsu su: Nokosareta hikiage e no moten," *Shukan Yomiuri*, 7 March 1954, p. 47.

43. Nakano Koyukai, *Rikugun*, p. 145.

44. Gayn, *Japan*, pp. 445–46; and Arisue Seizo, *Arisue Seizo kaikoroku* (Tokyo: Fuyo Shobo, 1989), pp. 533–34; and Arisue, *Shusen hishi*, pp. 254–55.

45. Yamamoto, *Four Years in Hell*, pp. 99, 205, 235.

46. Heinz Hohne and Hermann Zolling, *The General Was a Spy* (New York: Coward, McCann & Geoghehan, 1972), p. 83.

47. Mita, *Mukae*, p. 22–29; and Nakano Koyukai, *Rikugun*, pp. 200, 213, 723.

48. Mita, *Mukae*, p. 27; and Clifford Uyeda and Barry Saiki, eds., *The Pacific War and Peace: Americans of Japanese Ancestry in Military Intelligence Service, 1941 to 1952* (San Francisco, CA: Military Intelligence Service Association of Northern California, 1991), p. 21; In Japan, the newspaper *Yomiuri Shimbun* on 15 August 1995 marked the fiftieth anniversary of Japan's surrender announcement by breaking news of the search for atomic intelligence at Maizuru in a story on page one.

49. Mita, *Mukae*, pp. 24–25.

50. United States Army Forces Far East, ed. *Japanese Intelligence Planning against the USSR*. Distributed by Office of the Chief of Military History, Department of the Army, 1955, editor's preface.

51. Asahi Shinbunsha, ed., *Gendai Jinbutsu Jiten* (Tokyo: 1977), p. 1043.

52. United States Army Forces Far East, ed., *Strategic Study of Manchuria: Military Topography and Geography*, vol. 3, part 4 (Washington, DC, 1956), p. 1.

53. Kyodo Tsushinsha Shakaibu, ed., *Chinmoku no fairu* (Tokyo: Kyodo Tsushinsha, 1996), pp. 156–59.

54. Arisue, *Kaikoroku*, pp. 406–07.

55. Kanzankai, ed., *Gendai Chugoku jinmei jiten* (Tokyo: Kanzankai, 1978), p. 706.

56. Takayama Shinobu, *Showa meishoroku*, vol. 2 (Tokyo: Fuyo Shobo, 1980), p. 201.

57. Hata, *Showa Tenno*, pp. 169–70.

58. Oide Hisashi, *Akumateki sakusen sanbo Tsuji Masanobu* (Tokyo: Kojinsha, 1993), pp. 382–84; and Kyodo Tsushinsha Shakaibu, *Chinmoku no fairu*, pp. 225, 228–29; and John Dower, *Embracing Defeat: Japan in the Wake of World War II* (New York: W.W. Norton, 1999), p. 641.

59. Joseph C. Goulden, *Korea: The Untold Story of the War* (New York: McGraw-Hill, 1982), p. 279.

60. Nakano Koyukai, *Rikugun*, pp. 283–84, 286, 311; and Nakamura Yuetsu, *Paidan: Taiwangun o tsukutta Nihongun shokotachi* (Tokyo: Fuyo Shobo, 1995), p. 28.

61. Nakamura, *Paidan*, p. 10.

62. Nakano Koyukai, *Rikugun*, p. 340; and White, *Thunder*, pp. 145, 163–64, 184.

63. Nakano Koyukai, *Rikugun*, pp. 336–38; and Nakamura, *Paidan*, pp. 34–41.

64. Nakamura, *Paidan*, p. 28, 49. Nakamura writes of White Unit members sneaking past GHQ to reach Taiwan, but this seems unlikely. The choice for White Unit chief of Maj. Gen. Tomita, one of the Army's few officers who spent part of his career in the United States, seems hardly likely to be a coincidence. That Tatsumi was at the time Prime Minister Yoshida's advisor on rebuilding the Japanese Army and that his old acquaintance General Tang was involved with the White Unit also suggest that MacArthur and Willoughby had arranged matters with Chiang Kai-shek.

65. "Ikiteiru Nakano Gakko," *Shukan Gendai*, 2 August 1959, p. 37; and Nakamura, *Paidan*, p. 49.

66. Immanuel C.Y. Hsu, *The Rise of Modern China* (New York: Oxford University Press, 1970), p. 787; and Joseph Burkholder Smith, *Portrait of a Cold Warrior* (New York: Putnam, 1976), pp. 66–67.

67. Nakamura, *Paidan*, p. 88.

68. Nakano Koyukai, *Rikugun*, p. 338; and Nakamura, *Paidan*, p. 110. According to Nakamura, the White Unit lasted until 1968.

69. Saito, *Boryakusen*, pp. 27–28.

70. Saito, *Boryakusen*, p. 193.

71. Yamamoto Kenzo, "Giheiho kosaku no tenmatsu," *Rekishi to jinbutsu* (August 1985), p. 106; and Saito, *Boryakusen*, pp. 99–101.

72. Saito, *Boryakusen*, pp. 110–11, 116, 118–19; Imai Takeo, *Showa no boryaku* (Tokyo: Asahi Sonorama, 1985), p. 195.

73. Ban Shigeo, *Rikugun Noborito Kenkyujo no shinjutsu* (Tokyo: Fuyo Shobo Shuppan, 2001), pp. 34, 196, 203.

74. Kinoshita, *Kesareta*, pp. 385, 388.

75. *History of the Counter Intelligence Corps*, vol. 30: *CIC During the Occupation of Korea*. U.S. Army Intelligence Center, March 1959, pp. 4–8, 15–16, 111. Reproduced in *Migunjonggi chongbo saryojip: CIC pogoso*, vol. 1 (Seoul: Hallim University, 1995).

76. Counter Intelligence Corps, *Annual Progress Report for 1947*, Reproduced in *Migunjonggi chongbo saryojip: CIC pogoso*, vol. 1 (Seoul: Hallim University, 1995), p. 259.

77. Yon Chong, *Kyanon Kikan kara no shogen* (Tokyo: Bancho Shobo, 1973), pp. 191–92, 197.

78. Mainichi Shinbunsha, *Okinawa Senso mararia jiken*, p. 102.

79. Mori Ei, "Tokumu Kikan wa ima mo ikiteiru," *Gendai* (June 1977), p. 320; and Bruce Cumings, *The Origins of the Korean War. Vol. 2, The Roaring of the Cataract, 1947–1950* (Princeton: Princeton University Press, 1990), p. 808.

80. Hatakeyama, *Hiroku*, pp. 311–12.

81. Saito, *Boryakusen*, pp. 112–13; and John Toland, *In Mortal Combat: Korea, 1950–1953* (New York: Quill, 1991), pp. 183–84; and Chong Il-gwon, *Chong Il-gwon Hoegorok* (Seoul: Koryo Sojok, 1996), pp. 245–48.

82. Willoughby, *Shirarezaru*, pp. 248, 263–65.

83. "Harubin Tokumu Kikan," *Shukan Yomiuri* (7 March 1954), pp. 47–48.

84. Denis Warner and Peggy Warner, *The Tide at Sunrise: A History of the Russo-Japanese War, 1904–1905* (New York: Charterhouse, 1974), p. 81.

85. Paek Son-yop, *From Pusan to Panmunjom* (Washington, DC: Brassey's, 1992), p. 50; and Paek Son-yop, *Sillok: Chirisan* (Seoul: Koryowon, 1992), p. 40.

86. Charles A. Willoughby and John Chamberlain, *MacArthur 1941–1951* (New York: McGraw-Hill, 1954), p. 373; and Mita, *Mukae*, p. 21.

87. Kawahara, *Kantogun boryaku butai*, pp. 10, 32; and Nakano Koyukai, *Rikugun*, pp. 214–16; and Ozawa Chikamitsu, *Hishi: Manshukokugun* (Tokyo: Kashiwa Shobo, 1976), pp. 99, 100, 276.

88. Robert Scalapino and Chong-sik Lee, *Communism in Korea*, vol. 1 (Berkeley: University of California Press, 1972), p. 222. Kim claimed his force numbered 150. The Japanese estimated eighty.

89. Muto, *Watakushi*, pp. 164–74.

90. So et al., *Pukhanhak*, pp. 23–24; and Hagiwara Ryo, *Chosen to Watashi: Tabi no noto* (Tokyo: Bungei Shunju, 2000), p. 134.

91. Cumings, *Origins*, vol. 2, pp. 259–60.

92. Yang Yong-jo, "Kim Paek-il Changgun," *Kukpang Chonol* (August 1998), pp. 80, 83.

93. United States Department of State, *Foreign Relations of the United States 1952–54*, vol. 15 Korea, part I (Washington, DC: Government Printing Office, 1984), p. 254.

94. Paek, *From Panmunjom*, p. 184; and Kim Yun-gun, *Kankoku gendaishi no genten: Boku Sei-ki gunji seiken no tanjo* (Tokyo: Sairyusha, 1996), pp. 179, 182–85.

95. Paek, *From Panmunjom*, p. 183.

96. Walter G. Hermes, *Truce Tent and Fighting Front* (Washington, DC: Office of the Chief of Military History), pp. 182–83; and Paek, *From Pusan*, pp. 179–92; and Paek, *Sillok*, p. 275; and Yi T'ae, *Nambugun* (Seoul: Tule, 1988), p. 17.

Chapter 11

1. Ito, *Nakano*, pp. 201–03; and Yamamoto Fukuichi, "Senso saiban o ukete," in *Mataichi senshi*, p. 522.

2. Mainichi Shinbun Tokubetsu Hodobu Shuzaihan, *Okinawa Senso*, pp. 118–19; Mita, *Mukae*, p. 20.

3. Nakano Koyukai, *Rikugun*, pp. 168, 490, 501; and Iwakawa Takashi. *Koto no tsuchi to narutomo. BC-kyu senpan saiban* (Tokyo: Kodansha, 1995), p. 386; and Hirakawa, *Ryukon*, pp. 201–03.

4. "Post-Action Review in the Case of U.S. vs. Aihara, et 31. Docket No. 288 (Western Army Case)," Record Group 331, National Archives; and Yamamoto Fukuichi, "Senso saiban," in *Mataichi Senshi*, p. 521.

5. Lavigne, "Narazaki Sensei," p. 2.

6. Imai, *Showa no boryaku*, p. 229; and brochure to Renkoji Temple. In the temple's reckoning, the original service in 1945 was the first memorial service, which is why the fiftieth took place in 1994, rather than 1995, the fiftieth anniversary of his death.

7. Kawashima, "Suzuki," pp. 82–83.

8. Sotooka Hideyoshi, "Nakano OB ga kataru senso no naijitsu," in *AERA*, pp. 23–25; and video *Jiyu Ajia no eiko*.

9. Yanagawa, *Rikugun*, pp. 96, 260–62; and Yanagawa, "Jawa," p. 155; and John McBeth, "Secular Soldiers," *Far Eastern Economic Review*, 29 October 1998.

10. Baba, *Shiberia*, pp. 7, 29–33.

11. Nakano Koyukai, *Rikugun*, p. 184.

12. Baba, *Shiberia*, pp. 155–61; and Arisue, *Kaikoroku*, p. 407.

13. Baba, *Shiberia*, pp. 204–06; and Yuki Hiroshi and Numata Daisuke, *Uno Sosuke: Zenninsho* (Tokyo: Koken, 1988), pp. 96, 114–15.

14. Baba, *Shiberia*, pp. 204–12.

15. Taniguchi, "Onoda," *Kaiko* (April 1974), pp. 5–7; and Asaeda Shigeharu,

Taniguchi Yoshimi, and Hori Eizo, interviewed by Hando Kazutoshi, "Hito kessen o ayamaraseta mono," *Rekishi to jinbutsu* (August 1996), pp. 145–46.

16. *New York Times*, 12 March 1974; and conversation with author, 5 July 2001.

17. Taniguchi, *Kaiko*, p. 5; and Willoughby, *Reports of General MacArthur*, vol. 1, supplement, p. 169; and Takamizu Hajime, "Zanmu seiri no naka de," in *Mataichi Senshi*, pp. 537–38.

18. Takamizu Hajime, "Zanmu," pp. 537–38; and Taniguchi, "Onoda," p. 5.

19. Suetsugu Ichiro, "Rubanguto chosa made no enkaku," in *Mataichi Senshi*, pp. 461–65; and Takamizu Hajime, "Zanmu," p. 538.

20. *Tokyo Shinbun*, May 29, 1995, p. 1.

21. Terashima Fumiko, "Ah, Rubangu," in *Mataichi Senshi*, p. 460; and William Safire, "La Ronde," *New York Times*, 18 March 1974; and "The Last Dinosaur," *Far Eastern Economic Review*, 18 March 1974, p. 9; and "A Warning Bell from a Bitter Past," *Far Eastern Economic Review*, 1 April 1974, p. 29.

22. Onoda, "Kono michi," *Tokyo Shimbun*, 3 and 8 June 1995.

23. Onoda Hiroo, *Waga Burajil jinsei* (Tokyo: Kodansha, 1982), pp. 153–54; and Onoda, "Kono michi," *Tokyo Shimbun*, 7 June 1995; and Hirakawa, *Ryukon*, p. 259.

24. *Mainichi Shimbun*, 30 October 1997.

25. Suetsugu, *"Sengo,"* pp. 29–30, 88–89, 150–54, 183–85; and Nagamatsu, *Ikiteiru Uyoku*, pp. 269, 271; and Yamamoto Fukuichi, "Senso saiban," in *Mataichi Senshi*, p. 521; and Suetsugu Ichiro, "Seinen undo no ayumi," in *Mataichi senshi*, p. 527; and Takahashi Akira, "Suetsugu ani to no meguriai," in *Mataichi senshi*, p. 535; and Suetsugu Ichiro, "Irei no ji," in *Mataichi senshi*, p. 580; and "Trend of NIHON KENSEI-KAI (Japan Kensei Society) in Tokyo since its formation on August 15, 1949," Record Group 331, National Archives.

26. Yuki and Numata, *Uno*, pp. 150–51.

27. Yoshizawa Minami, *Betonamu Senso to Nihon* (Tokyo: Iwanami Shoten, 1988), pp. 24–27; and Nicholas Evan Sarantakes, *Keystone: The American Occupation of Okinawa and U.S.-Japanese Relations* (College Station, TX: Texas A&M University Press, 2000), pp. 142–43; and Robert S. Norris, William M. Arkin and William Burr, "How Much Did Japan Know?" *The Bulletin of the Atomic Scientists* January/February 2000, vol. 56, no. 1, www.bullatomsci.org/issues/issues/2000/jf00/jf00norrisarkin.html.

28. Suetsugu, "Okinawa henkan to kokumin undo," in *Kokumin koza Nihon no anzen sho bekken: Okinawa fukki e no michi* (Tokyo: Hara Shobo, 1968), pp. 194–95; and Steve Rabson, "Assimilation Policy in Okinawa; Promotion, Resistance, and 'Reconstruction,'" Occasional Paper No. 8 (Cardiff, CA: Japan Policy Research Institute, October 1996), p. 5.

29. Suetsugu, "Okinawa," p. 211.

30. Suetsugu, "Okinawa," pp. 197–98; and Suetsugu, *"Sengo,"* pp. 206, 210, 230; and Ivan I. Morris, *Nationalism and the Right Wing in Japan: A Study of Post-War Trends* (London: Oxford University Press, 1960), pp. 198, 322–24.

31. U. Alexis Johnson with Jef Olivarius McAllister, *The Right Hand of Power: The Memoirs of an American Diplomat* (Englewood Cliffs, NJ: Prentice-Hall, 1984), p. 465; and Foreign Ministry Diplomatic Record Office, *Nihon gaikoshi jiten*, p. 122; and Nixon, *Leaders*, p. 122.

32. Gilbert Rozman, *Japan's Response to the Gorbachev Era, 1985–1991: A Rising Superpower Views a Declining One* (Princeton: Princeton University Press, 1992), pp. 34–35; and *Hokkaido Shimbun*, 18 February 1998.

33. "Nakasone Shusho ga ugokasu hi 'shikaketo' no mitsumei," *Shukan Gendai*, (20 September 1986), p. 64; and "Yakoburef-shi to hisoka ni atta 'sori oniwaban' Nihon Kenseikai kaicho 67-sai no sugao," *Shukan Yomiuri* (3 December 1989), p. 178; and *Yomiuri Shimbun*, 16 November 1996.

34. *IIPS News*, vol. 9, no. 1 (Winter 1998), pp. 1–2; and ITAR-Tass, 13 September 1997.

35. Lucille Craft, "A Voice of Reason Campaigns for the Return of the Northern Territories," *Japan Times*, 3 February 2000.

36. *Asahi Shimbun*, 29 October 1997, and 17 April 1998.

37. *Hokkaido Shimbun*, 8 February 1998.

38. *Washington Post*, 31 May 1997; and *Hokkaido Shimbun*, 10 April 1998.

39. Hirakawa, *Ryukon*, p. 33; and Arisue, *Shusen hishi*, p. 239; and Kato Masao, *Rikugun Nakano Gakko no zenbo* (Tokyo: Tendensha, 1998), pp. 125–26.

40. Fujiwara Iwaichi, *Ryukonroku* (Urawa: Shingaku Shuppan, 1986), pp. 282, 290.

41. Fujiwara, *Ryukonroku*, p. 291, 296; and Kinoshita, *Kesareta*, p. 199; and Sotooka, "Nakano," p. 28.

42. Fujiwara, *Ryukonroku*, pp. 289, 296, 304, 372–77.

43. Arisue, *Shusen hishi*, p. 258.

Chapter 12

1. Paillat, *Dossier*, p. 44; and Donnison, *British*, p. 335; and Elizabeth P. McIntosh, *Sisterhood of Spies: The Women of the OSS* (New York: Dell Publishing, 1998), p. 247.

2. Catroux, *Deux actes*, pp. vi–vii.

3. Richard J. Aldrich, "Legacies of Secret Service: Renegade SOE and the Karen Struggle in Burma, 1948–50," *The Clandestine Cold War in Asia, 1945–65: Western Intelligence, Propaganda and Special Operations*, Richard J. Aldrich, Gary Rawnsley, and Ming-yeh Rawnsley, eds., special issue of *Intelligence and National Security*, vol. 14, no. 4 (Winter 1999), p. 133.

4. Chalmers Johnson, "The Three Cold Wars," Japan Policy Research Institute Occasional Paper No. 19 (December 2000), pp. 2–3.

5. Theodore H. White and Annalee Jacoby, *Thunder Out of China* (New York: William Sloane Associates, 1946), p. 152; and McIntosh, *Sisterhood*, p. 282; and "The Break-up of the Colonial Empires and Its Implications for US Security," *CIA Cold War Records: The CIA Under Harry Truman*, Michael Warner, ed. (Washington, DC: Central Intelligence Agency, 1994), pp. 222–24, 234.

6. Sotooka Hideyoshi, "Nakano," pp. 22, 24.

7. Malcolm Kennedy, *A Short History of Japan* (New American Library of World Literature, 1964), p. 199.

8. Allen, *End*, p. 262.

NOTES	297

9. Sotooka, "Nakano," pp. 23–24, 26.
10. Sankei Shimbun, 31 May 1997; and Japan Times, 31 May 1997.
11. Brochure for the Japanese movie *Pride* (undated); and Eriko Amaha, "Pride and Prejudice," *Far Eastern Economic Review*, 21 May 1998, p. 49.
12. Shiba Ryotaro, "Nomonhan jiken ni mita Nihon Rikugun no rakujitsu," in *Mikokai Koenroku Aizoban II: Shiba Ryotaro ga kataru Nihon* (Tokyo: Asahi Shimbunsha, July 10, 1997), p. 12; and Hori, *Daihonei*, p. 135.
13. Kuwahara, *Futo*, p. 97; and "Shinsetsu," p. 41; and Sotooka, "Nakano," p. 28.
14. Sotooka, "Nakano," p. 28.
15. "Shinsetsu," p. 42; and Mori, "Tokumu Kikan," p. 316.
16. Imai Takeo, "'Ajia dokuritsu' ni hatashita meishu Nihongun no kozai," *Maru* (September 1967), pp. 212–19; and Maruyama Shizuo, *Nakano Gakko*, p. 263; and Nagasaki, *Minami*, p. 35; and Sugita Ichiro, *Joho nuki senso shido*, p. 400.
17. An Myong-jin, *Kitachosen rachi kosakuin* (Tokyo: Tokuma Shoten, 1998), pp. 80–81.
18. Matsuhashi Tadamitsu, *Waga tsumi wa tsune ni waga mae ni ari* (Tokyo: Shakai Shisosha, 1994), p. 403; and Fujii Haruo, "Shinsetsu JCIA Boeicho Joho Honbu soshiki to katsudo zenchosa," *Maru* (May 1997), p. 69.
19. Kadowaki Naohira, "Teai ni miru boei jinbutsuron," *Gunji Kenkyu* (October 1996), pp. 170–71; and *Asagumo*, 23 July 1998, p. 6; and *Tokyo Shimbun*, evening edition, 1 October 1997; and Charles Pomeroy, ed., *Foreign Correspondents in Japan: Reporting a Half Century of Upheavals: From 1945 to the Present* (Rutland, VT: Charles E. Tuttle Company, 1998), p. 223.
20. Suetsugu Ichiro et al., "Tairo seisaku ni kansuru kinkyu apiru" (29 June 2001) in "Kongetsu no teigen," 1 July 2001, New Leaders' Association, http://www.ne.jp/asahi/japan/shinjukai/proposal/200107.html; and letter from the Council on National Security Problems, 30 August 2001.
21. http://www.ne.jp/asahi/japan/shinjukai/leader/leader_funeral.html; "Jinsei o ikkan shite sengo shori ni sasageta: 'Sori no goikenban' Suetsugu Ichiro shi iku," *Shukan Bunshun* (9 August 2001), pp. 170–71.

Bibliography

Books

Aldrich, Richard J. *Intelligence and the War against Japan: Britain, America and the Politics of Secret Service*. Cambridge: Cambridge University Press, 2000.

Allen, Louis. *Burma: The Longest War, 1941–1945*. New York: St. Martin's Press, 1984.

————. *The End of the War in Asia*. New York: Beekman/Esanu Publishers, 1976.

Allen, Thomas B., and Norman Polmar. *Code-Name Downfall: The Secret Plan to Invade Japan—And Why Truman Dropped the Bomb*. New York: Simon & Schuster, 1995.

An, Myong-jin. *Kitachosen rachi kosakuin* (North Korean Kidnapping Operatives). Translated from Korean into Japanese by Kim Ch'an. Tokyo: Tokuma Shoten, 2000.

Ariga, Tsutao. *Nihon Riku-Kaigun no joho kiko to sono katsudo* (Intelligence Organs and Activities of Japan's Army and Navy). Tokyo: Kindai Bungeisha, 1994.

Arisue, Seizo. *Arisue Seizo kaikoroku* (Memoirs of Arise Seizo). Tokyo: Fuyo Shobo, 1989.

————. *Shusen hishi: Arisue Kikancho no shuki* (Secret History of the War's End: Memoirs of the Chief of the Arisue Agency). Tokyo: Fuyo Shobo Shuppan, 1987.

————. *Seiji to gunji to jinji: Sanbo Honbu Daini Bucho no shuki* (Politics, Military Affairs, and Personnel: Memoirs of AGS Second Bureau Chief). Tokyo: Fuyo Shobo, 1982.

Asahi Shinbunsha, ed. *Gendai jinbutsu jiten* (Contemporary Dictionary of Who's Who). Tokyo: Asahi Shimbunsha, 1977.

Astor, Gerald. *Operation Iceberg: The Invasion and Conquest of Okinawa in World War II*. New York: Donald I. Fine, 1995.

Azuma, Teruji. *Watakushi wa Yoshida Shigeru no supai datta* (I spied on Yoshida Shingera). Hosaka Masayasu, ed. Tokyo: Kojinsha, 2001.

Ba Maw, U. *Breakthrough in Burma: Memoirs of a Revolution, 1939–1946.* New Haven: Yale University Press, 1968.

Baba, Yoshimitsu. *Shiberia kara Nagata-cho made: Joho shoko no sengoshi* (From Siberia to Nagata-cho: The Postwar History of an Intelligence Officer). Tokyo: Tendensha, 1987.

Bamford, James. *The Puzzle Palace.* Boston: Houghton Mifflin, 1982.

Ban, Shigeo. *Rikugun Noborito Kenkyujo no shinjutsu* (The Truth about the Army Noborito Research Institute). Tokyo: Fuyo Shobo Shuppan, 2001.

Bao Dai. *Le Dragon d'Annam.* Paris: Plon, 1980.

Barker, A. J. *Okinawa.* New York: Galahad Books, 1981.

Belote, James H., and William M. Belote. *Typhoon of Steel: The Battle for Okinawa.* New York: Harper & Row, 1970.

Bose, Subhas Chandra. *The Essential Writings of Netaji Subhas Chandra Bose.* Edited by Sisir K. Bose and Sugata Bose. Delhi: Oxford University Press, 1997.

Burrows, William E. *Deep Black: Space Espionage and National Security.* New York: Random House, 1986.

Caldwell, Oliver. *A Secret War: Americans in China.* Carbondale: Southern Illinois University Press, 1972.

Catroux, Georges. *Deux actes du drame indochinois: Hanoi, juin 1940; Dien Bien Phu, mars-mai 1954.* Paris: Librairie Plon, 1959.

Chang, Ch'ang-guk. *Yuksa choropsaeng* (Military Academy Graduate). Seoul: Chungang Ilbosa, 1984.

Chaudhuri, Nirad C. *Thy Hand, Great Anarch!: India, 1921–1952.* Reading, MA: Addison-Wesley Publishing, 1987.

Chong, Il-gwon. *Chong Il-gwon Hoegorok* (Memoirs of Chong Il-gwon). Seoul: Koryo Sojok, 1996.

Chou, Wan-yao. "The Kominka Movement in Taiwan and Korea: Comparisons and Interpretations," in Peter Duus, Ramon H. Myers, and Mark R. Peattie, eds. *The Japanese Wartime Empire, 1931–1945.* Princeton, NJ: Princeton University Press, 1996.

Cohen, Theodore. *Remaking Japan: The American Occupation as New Deal.* Edited by Herbert Passin. New York: The Free Press, 1987.

Craig, William. *The Fall of Japan. The Last Blazing Weeks of World War II.* 1967. Reprint. Green Farms, CT: Wildcat Publishing Company, 1997.

Craigie, Robert. *Behind the Japanese Mask.* London: Hutchinson & Co., 1945.

Cumings, Bruce. *The Origins of the Korean War.* Vol. 1, *Liberation and the Emergence of Separate Regimes, 1945–1947.* Princeton, NJ: Princeton University Press, 1981.

———. *The Origins of the Korean War.* Vol. 2, *The Roaring of the Cataract, 1947–1950.* Princeton, NJ: Princeton University Press, 1990.

Decoux, Jean. *A la barre de l'Indochine*. Paris: Librairie Plon, 1949.

Devillers, Philippe. *Histoire du Viet-Nam de 1940 à 1952*. Paris: Editions du Seuil, 1952.

Doi, Akio. *Beisosen to Nihon* (U.S.-Soviet War and Japan). Preface by Nomura Kichisaburo. Tokyo: Kodosha, 1952.

Dower, John W. *Embracing Defeat: Japan in the Wake of World War II*. New York: W.W. Norton, 1999.

———. *Japan in War and Peace: Selected Essays*. New York: New Press, 1993.

Drea, Edward J. *In the Service of the Emperor: Essays on the Imperial Japanese Army*. Lincoln, NE: University of Nebraska Press, 1998.

———. *MacArthur's ULTRA: Codebreaking and the War against Japan, 1942–1945*. Lawrence, KS: University Press of Kansas, 1992.

Duus, Peter, Ramon H. Myers, and Mark R. Peattie, eds. *The Japanese Wartime Empire, 1931–1945*. Princeton: Princeton University Press, 1996.

Edwards, Duval A. *Spy Catchers of the U.S. Army in the War with Japan: The Unfinished Story of the Counter Intelligence Corps*. Gig Harbor, WA: Red Apple Publishing, 1994.

Eichelberger, Robert L., with Milton MacKaye. *Our Jungle Road to Tokyo*. New York: Viking Press, 1950.

Farwell, Byron. *Armies of the Raj: From the Mutiny to Independence, 1858–1947*. New York: Norton, 1989.

Fay, Peter Ward. *The Forgotten Army. India's Armed Struggle for Independence, 1942–1945*. Ann Arbor: University of Michigan Press, 1995.

Feifer, George. *Tennozan: The Battle of Okinawa and the Atomic Bomb*. New York: Ticknor & Fields, 1992.

Fujioka, Nobukatsu, ed. *Kyokasho ga oshienai rekishi* (History Not Taught in Textbooks). 4 vols. Tokyo: Sankei Shinbun Nyusu Sabisu, 1996–1997.

Fujisaki, Tatsumaru. "Haraguchi Shigehiko Shoi no omoide" (Remembering Lieutenant Haraguchi Shigehiko), in Mataichi Senshi Publication Committee, ed. *Mataichi Senshi: Rikugun Nakano Gakko Futamata Bunko daiichikisei no kiroku* (War Record of the First Class, Futamata Branch, Army Nakano School). Tokyo: Mataichikai, 1981.

Fujiwara, Iwaichi. *F. Kikan: Japanese Army Operations in Southeast Asia During World War II*. Translated by Akashi Yoji. Hong Kong: Heinemann Asia, 1983. Originally published as *F Kikan* (Tokyo: Hara Shobo, 1966).

———. *Ryukonroku* (Record of the Spirit That Remains). Urawa: Shingaku Shuppan, 1986.

Fukada, Yusuke. *Reimei no seiki: Dai Toa Kaigi to sono shuyakutachi* (Century of the Dawn: The Greater East Asia Conference and Its Principle Participants). Tokyo: Bungei Shunju, 1994.

Gayn, Mark. *Japan Diary*. Rutland, VT: Charles E. Tuttle Co., 1981.

Gehlen, Reinhard. *The Service*. Translated by David Irving. New York: World Publishing, 1972.

Ghosh, Kalyan Kumar. *The Indian National Army: Second Front of the Indian Independence Movement*. Prefatory message by Fujiwara Iwaichi. Meerut, India: Meenakshi Prakashan, 1969.

Goto, Ken'ichi. "Cooperation, Submission, and Resistance of Indigenous Elites of Southeast Asia in the Wartime Empire, 1931–1945" in Peter Duus, Ramon H. Myers, and Mark R. Peattie, eds. *The Japanese Wartime Empire, 1931–1945*. Princeton, NJ: Princeton University Press, 1996.

Goulden, Joseph C. *Korea: The Untold Story of the War*. New York: McGraw-Hill, 1982.

Gunther, John. *Inside Asia*. New York: Harper & Brothers, 1939.

————. *The Riddle of MacArthur*. New York: Harper & Brothers, 1950.

Hagiwara, Ryo. *Chosen to Watashi: Tabi no noto* (Korea and I: Travel Notes). Tokyo: Bungei Shunju, 2000.

Harada, Tokichi. "Kaishu no miyroku, Onoda shoi no miryoku. Eto Jun to no taidan" (The Attraction of Kaishu, the Attraction of Lieutenant Onoda. A Conversation with Eto Jun) in *Ogoreru heiwa* (Arrogant Peace). Tokyo: Daiamondo Taimusha, 1976.

————. *Kaze to kumo to saigo no choko shoko* (Winds and Clouds and the Last Intelligence Officer). Tokyo: Jiyu Kokuminsha, 1973.

Harper, Stephen. *Miracle of Deliverance: The Case for the Bombing of Hiroshima and Nagasaki*. New York: Stein and Day, 1985.

Hata, Ikuhiko, ed. *Nihon Riku-Kaigun sogo jiten* (Comprehensive Dictionary of the Japanese Army and Navy). Tokyo: Tokyo Daigaku Shuppankai, 1991.

————. *Showa Tenno itsutsu no ketsudan* (The Emperor Showa's Five Decisions). Tokyo: Bungei Shunju, 1994.

————. *Showashi no gunjintachi* (Military Men of Showa History). Tokyo: Bungei Shunju, 1987.

Hatakeyama, Kiyoyuki. *Hiroku Rikugun Nakano Gakko* (Secret Record of the Army Nakano School), Vol. 2, Tokyo: Bancho Shobo, 1971.

Higaki, Takashi. *"Matsushiro Daihonei" no shinjitsu: Kakusareta kyodai chikago* (The Truth about "Matsushiro Imperial General Headquarters": Hidden Giant Underground Shelter). Tokyo: Kodansha, 1994.

Hirakawa, Yoshinori. *Ryukon* (The Spirit that Remains). Kagoshima: Hirakawa Yoshinori, 1992.

Hiyama, Yoshiaki. *Ango o nusunda otokotachi: Jinbutsu, Nippon Rikugun ango shi* (The Men Who Stole the Codes: A History of the Men in Japanese Army Codes). Tokyo: Kojinsha, 1994.

Hohne, Heinz, and Hermann Zolling. *The General Was a Spy*. With an introduction by Hugh Trevor-Roper and a preface to the American edition by

Andrew Tully. Translated by Richard Barry. New York: Coward, McCann & Geoghehan, 1972.

Hori, Eizo. *Daihonei sanbo no joho senki: Joho naki kokka no higeki* (Intelligence Warfare Record of an IGHQ Staff Officer: The Tragedy of a Country Without Intelligence). Tokyo: Bungei Shunju, 1989.

Howe, Russell Warren. *The Hunt for "Tokyo Rose."* Lanham, MD: Madison Books, 1990.

Hsu, Immanuel C. Y. *The Rise of Modern China.* New York: Oxford University Press, 1970.

Hull, Cordell. *The Memoirs of Cordell Hull.* 2 vols. New York: Macmillan Co., 1948.

Ichinokuchi, Tad, ed. *John Aiso and the M.I.S. Japanese-American Soldiers in the Military Intelligence Service, World War II.* Los Angeles: The Military Intelligence Service Club of Southern California, 1988.

Imai, Takeo. *Showa no boryaku* (Showa Covert Operations). Tokyo: Asahi Sonorama, 1985. First published in 1967 by Hara Shobo.

Ishibashi, Kazuya. *Rinen to genjitsu seiji* (Ideal and Reality in Politics). Tokyo: Hobokukai, 1994.

Ishihara Seminar: Senso Taiken Kiroku Kenkyukai. *Mo hitotsu no Okinawa-sen: Mararia jigoku no Haterumato* (Another Battle for Okinawa: Hateruma, Malaria Island Hell). Written under the editorial supervision of Ishihara Masaie. Naha, Okinawa: Hirugisha, 1983.

Ito, Sadatoshi. *Nakano Gakko no himitsusen: Nakano wa katarazu, saredo kataranebanaranu* (The Nakano School's Covert War: One Does Not Speak of Nakano, But I Must). Tokyo: Chuo Shorin, 1984.

Ito, Takeo. *Mantetsu ni ikite* (My Life with the South Manchuria Railway Company). New edition. Tokyo: Keiso Shobo, 1982. First published in 1964.

Iwakawa, Takashi. *Koto no tsuchi to narutomo: BC-kyu senpan saiban* (Turned to Dust on a Lonely Island: Trials of Class B and C War Criminals). Tokyo: Kodansha, 1995.

Iwakuro, Hideo. *Seiki no shingun: Shingaporu Sokogeki* (March of the Century: General Offensive on Singapore). Tokyo: Ushio Shobo, 1956.

Izumiya, Tatsuro. *The Minami Organ.* Translated by U Tun Aung Chain. Rangoon: Universities Press, 1981. Originally published as *Sono na wa Minami boryaku kikan* (Its Name Was the Minami Covert Operations Agency). Tokyo: Tokuma Shoten, 1967.

James, D. Clayton. *The Years of MacArthur.* 3 vols. Boston: Houghton Mifflin, 1970–1985.

Johnson, Chalmers. *An Instance of Treason. Ozaki Hotsumi and the Sorge Spy Ring.* Rutland, VT: Charles E. Tuttle Co., 1977. First published by Stanford University Press, 1964.

————. *Conspiracy at Matsukawa*. Berkeley: University of California Press, 1972.

Johnson, U. Alexis, with Jef Olivarius McAllister. *The Right Hand of Power. The Memoirs of an American Diplomat*. Englewood Cliffs, NJ: Prentice-Hall, 1984.

Kaplan, David E., and Alec Dubro. *Yakuza: The Explosive Account of Japan's Criminal Underworld*. Reading, MA: Addison-Wesley, 1986.

Kanzankai, ed. *Gendai Chugoku jinmei jiten* (Contemporary Dictionary of Chinese Names). Tokyo: Kanzankai, 1978.

Kato, Masao. *Rikugun Nakano Gakko no zenbo* (Portrait of the Army Nakano School). Tokyo: Tendensha, 1998.

————. *Rikugun Nakano Gakko: Himitsusenshi no jittai* (Army Nakano School: Truth about the Covert Warriors). Tokyo: Kojinsha, 2001.

Kato, Masuo. *The Lost War: A Japanese Reporter's Inside Story*. New York: Alfred A. Knopf, 1946.

Kawabe, Torashiro. *Kawabe Torashiro kaisoroku* (Memoirs of Kawabe Torashiro). Tokyo: Mainichi Shinbunsha, 1979.

Kawahara, Emon. *Kantogun boryaku butai* (Kwantung Army Covert Operation Units). Tokyo: Puresu Tokyo Shuppankyoku, 1970.

Kennedy, Malcom. *A Short History of Japan*. New York: New American Library of World Literature, 1964. First published in United Kingdom by Wiedenfeld and Nicolson.

Kim, Yun-gun. *Kankoku gendaishi no genten: Boku Sei-ki gunji seiken no tanjo* (Origin of South Korean Modern History: The Birth of the Pak Chong-hui [Park Chung-hee] Military Regime). Tokyo: Sairyusha, 1996.

Kimura, Bunpei. *Kyofu no kindai boryakusen. Rikugunsho kimitsushitsu, Nakano Gakko* (Fearsome Modern Covert Operations Warfare. The War Department's Secret Room, Nakano School). Tokyo: Tokyo Raifusha, 1957.

Kimura, Takechiyo. *Nihon gaiko no kicho: 21 seiki e no shinro* (The Basis of Japanese Diplomacy: Course for the Twenty-first Century). Tokyo: Kokusai Seikei Kenkyukai, 1981.

————. *Nihon no kiki ni tatte* (Japan in Crisis). Tokyo: Nagata Shobo, 1978.

Kinoshita, Kenzo. *Kesareta himitsusen kenkyujo* (Erased Covert Warfare Laboratory). Nagano: Shinano Mainichi Shinbunsha, 1994.

Kodama, Yoshio. *I Was Defeated*. Tokyo: An Asian Publication, 1951.

Krueger, Walter. *From Down Under to Nippon: The Story of Sixth Army in World War II*. Washington, DC: Combat Forces Press, 1953.

Kumabe, Taizo. *Himitsusen no akaki hana: Ikiteiru Nakano Gakko no tamashi* (Red Flower of Covert Warfare: The Living Spirit of the Nakano School). Tokyo: Nisshin Hodo, 1973.

Kumagawa, Mamoru. "Futamata Bunko Kaisetsu" (Overview of Futamata Branch School) in Mataichi Senshi Publication Committee, ed. *Mataichi Senshi: Rikugun Nakano Gakko Futamata Bunko daiichikisei no kiroku* (War Record of the First Class, Futamata Branch, Army Nakano School). Tokyo: Mataichikai, 1981.

Kunizuka, Kazunori. *Imparu o koete: F Kikan to Chandora Bosu* (Beyond Imphal: The F Kikan and Chandra Bose). Tokyo: Kodansha, 1995.

———. *Indoyo ni kakaru niji: Nihon heishi no eiko* (Rainbow over India: A Japanese Soldier's Story). Tokyo: Kobunsha, 1958.

Kusakabe, Ichiro. *Boryaku Taiheiyo Senso* (Covert Operations in the Pacific War). Tokyo, 1963.

———. *Rikugun Nakano Gakko jitsuroku Ketteiban* (The True Story of the Army Nakano School, Definitive Edition). Tokyo: Besuto Bukku, 1980.

Kuwahara, Takeshi. *Futo: Hito gunjin no kiseki* (Wind and Waves: A Soldier's Tracks). Yokohama: Kuwahara Takeshi, 1990.

Kyodo Tsushinsha Shakaibu, ed. *Chinmoku no fairu* (Silent Files). Tokyo: Kyodo Tsushinsha, 1996.

Lebra, Joyce. *Japanese-Trained Armies in Southeast Asia Independence and Volunteer Forces in World War II*. New York: Columbia University Press, 1977.

———. *Jungle Alliance: Japan and the Indian National Army*. Singapore: Donald Moore for Asia Pacific Press, 1971.

Mainichi Shinbun Tokubetsu Hodobu Shuzaihan. *Okinawa senso mararia jiken: Minami no shima no kyosei sokai* (Maleria Incident in the Battle for Okinawa: Forced Evacuation of a Southern Island). Tokyo: Toho Shuppan, 1994.

Marshall, P.J., ed., *The Cambridge Illustrated History of the British Empire*. Cambridge: Cambridge University Press, 1996.

Maruyama, Shizuo. *Indo Kokumingun: Mo hitotsu no Taiheiyo Senso* (The Indian National Army: Another Pacific War). Tokyo: Iwanami Shoten, 1985.

———. *Nakano Gakko: Tokumu kikanin no shuki* (The Nakano School: Notes of Special Service Agency Members). Tokyo: Heiwa Shobo, 1948.

Mashbir, Sidney F. *I Was an American Spy*. New York: Vantage Press, 1953.

Masuda, Tomio. "Kirishima Butai no ato o tazunete" (Visiting the Site of the Kirishima Unit), in Mataichi Senshi Publication Committee, ed. *Mataichi Senshi: Rikugun Nakano Gakko Futamata Bunko daiichikisei no kiroku* (War Record of the First Class, Futamata Branch, Army Nakano School). Tokyo: Mataichikai, 1981.

———. "Seibu Kankei Sokatsu" (Overview of Those Involved with Western Army), in Mataichi Senshi Publication Committee, ed. *Mataichi Senshi: Rikugun Nakano Gakko Futamata Bunko daiichikisei no kiroku* (War

Record of the First Class, Futamata Branch, Army Nakano School).
Tokyo: Mataichikai, 1981.

Mataichi Senshi Publication Committee, ed. *Mataichi Senshi: Rikugun
Nakano Gakko Futamata Bunko daiichikisei no kiroku* (War Record of
the First Class, Futamata Branch, Army Nakano School). Tokyo: Mataichikai, 1981.

Matsuhashi Tadamitsu. *Waga tsumi wa tsune ni waga mae ni ari: Kitai sareru
shin Keisatsucho Chokan e no tegami* (My Sins Are Always Before Me: A
Letter to the New Chief of the National Police Agency, in Whom I Have
Hope). Tokyo: Shakai Shisosha, 1994.

Maung Maung, U, ed. *Aung San of Burma*. Published for Yale University
Southeast Asia Studies by Martinus Nijhoff, The Hague, 1962.

McIntosh, Elizabeth P. *Sisterhood of Spies: The Women of the OSS*. Reprint.
New York: Dell Publishing, 1999.

Mita, Kazuo. *Mukae in kita jipu: Ubawareta heiwa* (The Jeep that Came for
Them: Stolen Peace). Tokyo: 20 Seikisha, 1955.

Miyajima, Toshio. "Waga tatakawazaru no ki" (My Tale of Not Fighting),
in Mataichi Senshi Publication Committee, ed. *Mataichi Senshi: Rikugun
Nakano Gakko Futamata Bunko daiichikisei no kiroku* (War Record of
the First Class, Futamata Branch, Army Nakano School). Tokyo: Mataichikai, 1981.

Moorhouse, Geoffrey. *India Britannica*. New York: Harper & Row, 1983.

Morisawa, Kikaku. *Eiwa/Waei Beigun yogo jiten* (English-Japanese/Japa-
nese-English Dictionary of U.S. Military English). Second revised edition.
Tokyo: Gakuyo Shobo, 1994.

Morris, Ivan. I. *Nationalism and the Right Wing in Japan: A Study of Post-
War Trends*. London: Oxford University Press, 1960.

Muto, Tomio. *Watakushi to Manshukoku* (Manchukuo and I). Tokyo:
Bungei Bunshu, 1988.

Nagamatsu, Asazo. *Ikiteiru uyoku* (Living Right Wing). Tokyo: Hitotsubashi
Shoten, 1954.

Nagasaki, Nobuko, ed. *Minami, F Kikan kankeisha danwa kiroku* (Record
of Discussions with Members of Minami Agency and F Agency). Discussions with Takahashi Hachiro, Sugii Mitsuru, Fujiwara Iwaichi, Ito Kei-
suke, and Nishikawa Sutesaburo. Report no. 53-6 of Research
Department, Institute for Developing Economies. First in series "Minami
Ajia no minzoku undo to Nihon" (South Asia's Popular Movements and
Japan). Tokyo: Institute for Developing Economies, March 1979.

Nakajima, Akifumi. "Daijuyon Homengun kankei sokatsu" (Overview of
Those Involved with Fourteenth Area Army), in Mataichi Senshi Publica-
tion Committee, ed. *Mataichi Senshi: Rikugun Nakano Gakko Futamata
Bunko daiichikisei no kiroku* (War Record of the First Class, Futamata
Branch, Army Nakano School). Tokyo: Mataichikai, 1981.

————. "Nanmei Kikan to tomo ni" (With the Namei Agency), in Mataichi Senshi Publication Committee, ed. *Mataichi Senshi: Rikugun Nakano Gakko Futamata Bunko daiichikisei no kiroku* (War Record of the First Class, Futamata Branch, Army Nakano School). Tokyo: Mataichikai, 1981.

Nakamura, Yuetsu. *Paidan: Taiwangun o tsukutta Nihongun shokotachi* (White Unit: The Japanese Military Officers Who Built Taiwan's Military). Tokyo: Fuyo Shobo Shuppan, 1995.

Nakano Koyukai, ed. *Rikugun Nakano Gakko* (Army Nakano School). Tokyo: Nakano Koyukai, 1978.

Nihon Kindai Shiryo Kenkyukai, ed. *Iwakuro Hideo shi danwa sokkiroku* (Shorthand Record of Conversation with Iwakuro Hideo). Tokyo: Kido Nikki Kenkyukai, 1977.

Nixon, Richard M. *Leaders*. New York: Warner Books, 1982.

Oide, Hisashi. *Akumateki sakusen sanbo Tsuji Masanobu* (Devilish Operations Staff Officer Tsuji Masanobu). Tokyo: Kojinsha, 1993. First published as *Sakusen Sanbo Tsuji Masanobu*. Tokyo: Kojinsha, 1987.

Okinawa Prefecture Health and Welfare Department, ed. *Heiwa e no shogen: Okinawa Kenritsu Heiwa Kinen Shiryokan gaidobukku* (Witness to Peace. Okinawa Prefectural Peace Prayer Materials Hall Guidebook). Revised edition. Itoman, Okinawa: Okinawa-ken Senbotsusha Irei Hosankai, August 1991. First published 25 December 1983.

Ono, Tadao. "Ruson Hokutan no musenhan" (Wireless Unit in Northern Luzon), in Mataichi Senshi Publication Committee, ed. *Mataichi Senshi: Rikugun Nakano Gakko Futamata Bunko daiichikisei no kiroku* (War Record of the First Class, Futamata Branch, Army Nakano School). Tokyo: Mataichikai, 1981.

Onoda, Hiroo. *No Surrender: My Thirty-year War*. Translated by Charles S. Terry. Tokyo: Kodansha International Ltd., 1974. Originally published as *Waga Rubanguto no 30-nen senso* (Tokyo: Kodansha International, 1974).

————. "Rubanguto Senki" (Lubang War Story), in Mataichi Senshi Publication Committee, ed. *Mataichi Senshi: Rikugun Nakano Gakko Futamata Bunko daiichikisei no kiroku* (War Record of the First Class, Futamata Branch, Army Nakano School). Tokyo: Mataichikai, 1981.

————. *Tatta hitori no 30-nen senso* (Alone in a Thirty-year War). Tokyo: Tokyo Shinbunsha, 1995.

————. *Waga Burajil jinsei* (My Life in Brazil). Tokyo: Kodansha, 1982.

————. *Waga kaiso no Rubanguto: Joho shoko no osugita kikan* (Memoirs of Lubang: An Intelligence Officer's Overly Late Return Home). Tokyo: Asahi Shinbunsha, 1988.

Owens, William A. *Eye-Deep in Hell: A Memoir of the Liberation of the Phil-

ippines, 1944–45. Dallas, TX: Southern Methodist University Press, 1989.

Ozawa, Chikamitsu. *Hishi: Manshukokugun* (Secret History: Manchukuo Army). Tokyo: Kashiwa Shobo, 1976.

Paek, Son-yop [Paik Sun Yup]. *From Pusan to Panmunjom.* Washington, DC: Brassey's, 1992.

————. *Kun-kwa na: 6.25 Hanguk Chonjaeng hoegorok* (The Army and I: Memoirs of the June 25 Korean War). Seoul: Taeryuk Yonguso, 1989.

————. *Sillok: Chirisan* (True Record: Mt. Chiri). Seoul: Koryowon, 1992.

————. *Taigerira-sen: Amerika wa naze maketa ka* (Antiguerrilla Warfare: Why Did America Lose?). Tokyo: Hara Shobo, 1993.

Paik, Sun Yup. See Paek Son-yop.

Paillat, Claude. *Dossier secret de l'Indochine.* Paris: Presses de la Cité, 1964.

Pomeroy, Charles, ed. *Foreign Correspondents in Japan: Reporting a Half Century of Upheavals From 1945 to the Present.* Rutland, VT: Charles E. Tuttle Company, 1998.

Price, Willard. *Key to Japan.* New York: The John Day Company, 1946.

Ranelagh, John. *The Agency: The Rise and Decline of the CIA.* New York: Simon & Schuster, 1986.

Rozman, Gilbert. *Japan's Response to the Gorbachev Era, 1985–1991: A Rising Superpower Views a Declining One.* Princeton: Princeton University Press, 1992.

Sainteny, Jean. *Histoire d'une paix manquée: Indochine, 1945–1947.* Paris: Amiot-Dumont, 1953.

Saito, Michinori. *Boryakusen: Dokyumento Rikugun Noborito Kenkyujo* (War of Covert Operations: Documenting the Army Noborito Research Institute). Tokyo: Jiji Tsushinsha, 1987.

Sakura, Ichiro. "Kaisetsu kara shusen made" (From Opening to the War's End) in Mataichi Senshi Publication Committee, ed. *Mataichi Senshi: Rikugun Nakano Gakko Futamata Bunko daiichikisei no kiroku* (War Record of the First Class, Futamata Branch, Army Nakano School). Tokyo: Mataichikai, 1981.

Sarantakes, Nicholas Evan. *Keystone: The American Occupation of Okinawa and U.S.-Japanese Relations.* College Station, TX: Texas A&M University Press, 2000.

Scalapino, Robert, and Chong-sik Lee. *Communism in Korea.* 2 vols. Berkeley: University of California Press, 1972.

Sebald, William J., with Russell Brines. *With MacArthur in Japan: A Personal History of the Occupation.* New York: W.W. Norton, 1965.

Shiba, Ryotaro. "Nomonhan Jiken ni mita Nippon Rikugun no rakujitsu" (The Fall of the Japanese Army Seen in the Nomonhan Incident) in Shukan Asahi, ed. *Shiba Ryotaro ga kataru Nihon: Mikokai Koenroku Aizoban*

II (The Japan of Which Shiba Ryotaro Speaks: Unpublished Recorded Speeches Treasury, Vol. 2). Special edition of *Shukan Asahi*. Asahi Shinbunsha, 10 July 1997.

Shibutani, Tamotsu. *The Derelicts of Company K: A Sociological Study of Demoralization*. Berkeley: University of California Press, 1978.

Simpson, William Brand. *Special Agent in the Pacific, WWII*. New York: Rivercross Publishing, 1995.

Smith, Joseph Burkholder. *Portrait of a Cold Warrior*. New York: Putnam, 1976.

So Ch'un-sik et al. *Pukhanhak* (The Study of North Korea). Revised edition. Edited under supervision of the Republic of Korea Military Academy. Seoul: Pagyongsa, 1999.

Spector, Ronald H. *Eagle against the Sun: The American War with Japan*. New York: Free Press, 1985.

Stephan, John J. *The Russian Fascists: Tragedy and Farce in Exile, 1925–1945*. New York: Harper & Row, 1978.

Suetsugu, Ichiro. "Daini Kirishima Butai keikaku kiyu" (Plan for Second Kirishima Unit Goes Up in Smoke), in Mataichi Senshi Publication Committee, ed. *Mataichi Senshi: Rikugun Nakano Gakko Futamata Bunko daiichikisei no kiroku* (War Record of the First Class, Futamata Branch, Army Nakano School). Tokyo: Mataichikai, 1981.

————. "Irei no ji" (Words at a Memorial Service), in Mataichi Senshi Publication Committee, ed. *Mataichi Senshi: Rikugun Nakano Gakko Futamata Bunko daiichikisei no kiroku* (War Record of the First Class, Futamata Branch, Army Nakano School). Tokyo: Mataichikai, 1981.

————. "'Kirishima Butai' no omoide" (Remembering the Kirishima Unit), in Mataichi Senshi Publication Committee, ed. *Mataichi Senshi: Rikugun Nakano Gakko Futamata Bunko daiichikisei no kiroku* (War Record of the First Class, Futamata Branch, Army Nakano School). Tokyo: Mataichikai, 1981.

————. *Mikai to hinkon e no chosen* (A Challenge to Underdevelopment and Poverty). Tokyo: Mainichi Shinbunsha, 1964.

————. "Okinawa henkan to kokumin undo" (The Return of Okinawa and the National Movement) in *Okinawa: Fukki e no michi* in Kokumin Koza Nihon no Anzen Hosho Editorial Committee, ed., *Kokumin koza, Nihon no anzen hosho bekken: Okinawa fukki e no michi* (Okinawa: The Road to Reversion). Tokyo: Hara Shobo, 1968.

————. "Rubanguto chosa made no enkaku" (The Situation Until the Search on Lubang), in Mataichi Senshi Publication Committee, ed. *Mataichi Senshi: Rikugun Nakano Gakko Futamata Bunko daiichikisei no kiroku* (War Record of the First Class, Futamata Branch, Army Nakano School). Tokyo: Mataichikai, 1981.

————. "Seinen undo no ayumi: Waga sengo no jinsei" (Steps in the Youth Movement: My Postwar Life), in Mataichi Senshi Publication Committee, ed. *Mataichi Senshi: Rikugun Nakano Gakko Futamata Bunko daiichikisei no kiroku* (War Record of the First Class, Futamata Branch, Army Nakano School). Tokyo: Mataichikai, 1981.

————, ed. *Seishonen no shakai sanka* (The Social Participation of Youth). Tokyo: Zennihon Shakai Kyoiku Rengokai, 1988.

————. *"Sengo" e no chosen* (A Challenge to the "Postwar"). Tokyo: Rekishi Toshosha, 1981.

Sugita, Ichiji. *Joho naki senso shido: Daihonei joho sanbo no kaiso* (War Leadership without Intelligence: Memoirs of an IGHQ Intelligence Staff Officer). Tokyo: Hara Shobo, 1987.

————. *Kokka shidosha no ridashippu: Seijika to sosuitachi* (Leadership of the Nation's Leaders: Politicians and Leaders). Tokyo: Hara Shobo, 1993.

Supreme Commander for the Allied Powers. *Reports of General MacArthur.* Charles A. Willoughby, editor in chief. 4 vols. Washington, DC: Center of Military History, U.S. Army, 1966.

Tachibana, Yuzuru. *Teikoku Kaigun shikan ni natta Nikkei Nisei* (A Second-Generation Japanese-American Who Became an Officer of the Imperial Japanese Navy). Tokyo: Tsukiji Shokan, 1994.

Takahashi, Akira. "Suetsugu ani no meguriai" (Chance Encounter with Elder Brother Suetsugu), in Mataichi Senshi Publication Committee, ed. *Mataichi Senshi: Rikugun Nakano Gakko Futamata Bunko daiichikisei no kiroku* (War Record of the First Class, Futamata Branch, Army Nakano School). Tokyo: Mataichikai, 1981.

Takamizu, Hajime. "Zanmu seiri no naka de" (Taking Care of Loose Ends), in Mataichi Senshi Publication Committee, ed. *Mataichi Senshi: Rikugun Nakano Gakko Futamata Bunko daiichikisei no kiroku* (War Record of the First Class, Futamata Branch, Army Nakano School). Tokyo: Mataichikai, 1981.

Takaoka, Daisuke. *Mita mama no Nanpo Ajia* (South Asia As I Saw It). Tokyo: Japan-India Association, 1939.

Takayama, Shinobu. *Showa meishoroku* (Record of Famous Generals of the Showa Era). Vol. 2. Tokyo: Fuyo Shobo, 1980.

Tanaka, Ryukichi. "Shanhai Jiken wa ko shite okosareta" (This Is How the Shanghai Incident Was Instigated) in *Bessatsu Chisei*, No. 5, *Hisomerareta Showashi* (Hidden Showa History). Tokyo: Kawade Shobo, December 1956.

Tanaka, Toshio. *Rikugun Nakano Gakko no Tobu Nyu Ginea yugekisen* (Army Nakano School's Eastern New Guinea Guerrilla Warfare). Tokyo: Senshi Kankokai, 1996.

Terashima, Fumiko. "Ah, Rubangu," in Mataichi Senshi Publication Committee, ed. *Mataichi Senshi: Rikugun Nakano Gakko Futamata Bunko daiichikisei no kiroku* (War Record of the First Class, Futamata Branch, Army Nakano School). Tokyo: Mataichikai, 1981.

Textor, Robert B. *Failure in Japan: With Keystones for a Positive Policy.* Introduction by Owen Lattimore. New York: The John Day Company, 1951.

Thorne, Christopher. *Allies of a Kind: The United States, Britain and the War against Japan.* London: Hamilton, 1978.

Toland, John. *In Mortal Combat: Korea, 1950–1953.* New York: Quill, 1991.

———. *The Rising Sun: The Decline and Fall of the Japanese Empire, 1936–1945.* 2 vols. New York: Random House, 1970.

Tomisawa, Shigeru. *Tokumu kikanin yomoyama monogatari* (Tales of Special Service Agency Officers). Tokyo: Kojinsha, 1988.

Toyama, Misao, ed. *Riku-Kaigun shokan jinji soran, rikugun hen* (Personnel Guide to Officers of the Imperial Army and Navy, Army Edition). Edited under the supervision of Joho Yoshio. Tokyo: Fuyo Shobo, 1981.

Toye, Hugh. *The Springing Tiger: A Study of A Revolutionary.* London: Cassell, 1959.

Uehara, Masatoshi. *Okinawa-sen toppu shikuretto* (Top Secret Battle for Okinawa). Naha, Okinawa: Okinawa Taimususha, 1995.

Uyeda, Clifford, and Barry Saiki, eds. *The Pacific War and Peace: Americans of Japanese Ancestry in Military Intelligence Service, 1941 to 1952.* San Francisco: Military Intelligence Service Association of Northern California, 1991.

Warner, Denis, and Peggy Warner. *The Tide at Sunrise: A History of the Russo-Japanese War, 1904–1905.* New York: Charterhouse, 1974.

White, Theodore H., and Annalee Jacoby. *Thunder Out of China.* New York: William Sloane Associates, 1946.

Wildes, Harry Emerson. *Typhoon in Tokyo: The Occupation and Its Aftermath.* New York: Macmillan, 1954.

Willmott, H.P. *Empires in the Balance: Japanese and Allied Pacific Strategies to April 1942.* Annapolis, MD: Naval Institute Press, 1982.

Willoughby, Charles A. *The Guerrilla Resistance Movement in the Philippines, 1941–1945.* New York: Vantage Press, 1972.

———. *Maneuver in War.* Harrisburg, PA: The Military Service Publishing Company, 1939.

———. *Shanghai Conspiracy: The Sorge Spy Ring.* Preface by Douglas MacArthur. New York: Dutton, 1952.

———. *Shirarezaru Nihon senryo: Uirobi kaikoroku* (Unknown Occupation of Japan. Willoughby Memoirs). Edited by Yon Chong [En Tei]. Tokyo: Bancho Shobo, 1973.

————, and John Chamberlain. *MacArthur 1941–1951*. New York: McGraw-Hill, 1954.

Yahara, Hiromichi. *The Battle for Okinawa*. Translated by Roger Pineau and Masatoshi Uehara. Introduction by Frank B. Gibney. New York: John Wiley & Sons, 1995. Originally published as *Okinawa kessen: Kokyu sanbo no shuki* (Decisive Battle for Okinawa: Memoirs of a Senior Staff Officer). Tokyo: Yomiuri Shinbunsha, 1972.

Yamamoto, Fukuichi. "Seibugun ni funin shite" (Assigned to Western District Army), in Mataichi Senshi Publication Committee, ed. *Mataichi Senshi: Rikugun Nakano Gakko Futamata Bunko daiichikisei no kiroku* (War Record of the First Class, Futamata Branch, Army Nakano School). Tokyo: Mataichikai, 1981.

————. "Senso saiban o ukete" (Tried As a War Criminal), in Mataichi Senshi Publication Committee, ed. *Mataichi Senshi: Rikugun Nakano Gakko Futamata Bunko daiichikisei no kiroku* (War Record of the First Class, Futamata Branch, Army Nakano School). Tokyo: Mataichikai, 1981.

Yamamoto, Kiyokatsu. *Jieitai 'kage no butai': Mishima Yukio o koroshita shinjitsu no kokuhaku* ('Shadow Unit' of the Self-Defense Forces: Confessing to the Truth of Killing Mishima Yukio). Tokyo: Kodansha, 2001.

Yamamoto, Tomomi. *Four Years in Hell: I Was a Prisoner Behind the Iron Curtain*. Tokyo: An Asian Publication, 1952.

Yanagawa, Motoshige. *Rikugun Chohoin Yanagawa chui* (Intelligence Officer Lieutenant Yanagawa). Tokyo: Sankei Shinbun Shuppankyoku, 1967.

Yanagawa, Munenari. See Yanagawa Motoshige.

Yi, T'ae. *Nambugun* (Southern Army). Seoul: Ture, 1988.

Yon Chong [En Tei]. *Kyanon Kikan kara no shogen* (Testimony from the Canon Agency). Tokyo: Bancho Shobo, 1973.

Yoshihara, Masami. *Nakano Gakko kyoiku: Hito kyokan no kaiso* (Nakano School Education: An Instructor's Memories). Tokyo: Shinjinbutsu Oraisha, 1974.

Yoshizawa, Minami. *Betonamu Senso to Nihon* (The Vietnam War and Japan). Tokyo: Iwanami Shoten, 1988.

Yu, Maochun. *OSS in China: Prelude to Cold War*. New Haven: Yale University Press, 1996.

Yuki, Hiroshi, and Numata Daisuke. *Uno Sosuke: Zenninsho* (Uno Sosuke: A Complete Portrait of the Man). Tokyo: Koken, 1988.

Government Documents and Publications

Appleman, Roy E. et al. *Okinawa: The Last Battle*. Washington, DC: Historical Division, Department of the Army, 1948.

BCON. Newsletter of the British Commonwealth Occupation Forces. On microfilm at the University of Maryland.

Cannon, M. Hamlin. *Leyte: The Return to the Philippines.* Washington, DC: Office of the Chief of Military History, Department of the Army, 1954.

Donnison, F.S.V. *British Military Administration in the Far East, 1943–46.* London: HMSO, 1956.

Finnegan, John Patrick. *Military Intelligence.* Washington, DC: Center of Military History, U.S. Army, 1998.

Foreign Ministry Diplomatic Records Office and Nihon Gaikoshi Jiten Editorial Committee, eds. *Nihon gaikoshi jiten* (Dictionary of Japanese Diplomatic History). Tokyo: Yamakawa Shuppansha, 1992.

Hermes, Walter G. *Truce Tent and Fighting Front.* Washington, DC: Office of the Chief of Military History, U.S. Army, 1966.

Imperial Japanese Government. Central Liaison Office. "Erroneous Report." August 30, 1946. Record Group 331, National Archives.

Kirby, S. Woodburn, et al., eds. *The War against Japan,* Vol. 4, *The Reconquest of Burma.* London: HMSO, 1965.

———. *The War against Japan.* Vol. 5, *The Surrender of Japan.* London: HMSO, 1969.

Netaji Inquiry Committee Report. New Delhi: Publications Division, Ministry of Information and Broadcasting, 1956.

United States Army. "Post-Action Review in the Case of U.S. vs. Aihara, et 31. Docket No. 288 (Western Army Case)." Record Group 331. National Archives.

United States Army. Civil Censorship Detachment. "Letter from Nozaka, Sanzo concerning Kamata, Senichi to Mr. Marcum," 7 July 1947. Record Group 331. National Archives.

———. Testimony of Itezono Tatsuo at the Legal Section Office, Fukuoka, Kyushu, Japan, between 21 November 1946 and 10 December 1946. Record Group 331. National Archives.

———. "Trend of NIHON KENSEI_KAI (Japan Kensei Society) in Tokyo since its formation on August 15, 1949." Record Group 331. National Archives.

United States Army. Counter Intelligence Corps. *Annual Progress Report for 1947,* Reproduced in *Migunjonggi chongbo saryoch'op: CIC pogoso,* vol. 1 (U.S. Military Government Records Intelligence Historical Documents Collection: CIC Reports, vol. 1). Seoul: Hallim University, 1995.

United States Army. Dugway Proving Ground. *DPG: The Nation's Chemical and Biological Defense Proving Ground.* A briefing book prepared circa 2000.

United States Army. Far East Command. *Administrative History of 441st Counter Intelligence Corps Detachment.* On file at the U.S. Army Center for Military History.

United States Army. Judge Advocate General's Office. "U.S. vs. Kiyoharu Tomomori et al." Record Group 153. National Archives.

United States Army Forces, Far East. *Outline of Operations Prior to Termination of War and Activities Connected with the Cessation of Hostilities.* Washington, DC: Distributed by the Office of the Chief of Military History, Department of the Army.

United States Army Forces, Far East. Military History Section. *Record of Operations against Soviet Russia: On Northern and Western Fronts of Manchuria, and in Northern Korea.* Washington, DC: Distributed by the Office of the Chief of Military History, Department of the Army, 1954.

————. *Strategic Study of Manchuria: Military Topography and Geography,* Vol. 3. Part 4. Washington, DC: Distributed by the Office of the Chief of Military History, Department of the Army, 1956.

United States Army Forces, Far East, and Eighth United States Army. Office of the Military History Officer, Japanese Research Division. *Japanese Intelligence Planning against the USSR.* Washington, DC: Distributed by the Office of the Chief of Military History, Department of the Army, 1955.

United States Army Forces, Far East, and Eighth United States Army (Rear). *Small Wars and Border Problems: The Nomonhan Incident.* Vol. 11, Part 3, Book B of Japanese Studies on Manchuria. Washington, DC: Distributed by the Office of the Chief of Military History, 1956.

United States Army Forces Korea. Counter Intelligence Corps. "CIC Area Study, Korea, August 1945," p. 38, in Institute of Asia Culture Studies, Hallim University, ed., *Migunjonggi chongbo sajip: CIC Pogoso,* vol. 1 (U.S. Military Government Records Intelligence Historical Documents Collection: CIC Reports, vol. 1).

United States Army Forces, Middle Pacific. *2605.* 1 November 1945. On file at U.S. Army Center for Military History.

United States Army Forces, Pacific. General Headquarters. *Basic Outline Plan for "Blacklist" Operations.* On file at U.S. Army Center for Military History.

United States Central Intelligence Agency. "The Break-up of the Colonial Empires and Its Implications for U.S. Security," *CIA Cold War Records— The CIA under Harry Truman.* Michael Warner, ed. Washington, DC: Central Intelligence Agency, Center for the Study of Intelligence, 1994.

United States Department of State. *Foreign Relations of the United States 1952–54.* Vol. 15, Korea Part I. Washington, DC: Government Printing Office, 1984.

United States Department of War. Military Intelligence Service. "Japanese Intelligence," *Military Research Bulletin* No. 21. 15 August 1945. On file at the U.S. Army Center for Military History.

————. The United States Strategic Bombing Survey (Pacific). *Japanese*

Intelligence. Washington, DC: Government Printing Office, 1946. On file at the U.S. Army Center for Military History.
United States Foreign Broadcast Intelligence Service. *Foreign Broadcast Intelligence Report on the Far East*. No. 25, 21 July 1943. Record Group 262. National Archives.

Oral Histories

Bowers, Faubion. "Oral Reminiscences of Major Faubion Bowers." Interview by D. Clayton James, New York, NY, 18 July 1971. On file at MacArthur Archives.
Fellers, Bonner F. "Oral Reminiscences of Brigadier General Bonner F. Fellers." Interview by D. Clayton James, Washington, DC, 26 June 1971. On file at MacArthur Archives.
Mashbir, Sidney F. "Oral Reminiscences of Colonel Sidney F. Mashbir." Interview by D. Clayton James, Laguna Beach, California, 1 September 1971. On file at MacArthur Archives.
Thorpe, Elliott R. "Oral Reminiscences of Brigadier General Elliott R. Thorpe." Interview by D. Clayton James, Sarasota, FL, 29 May 1977. On file at MacArthur Archives.
Munson, Frederick P. "Oral Reminiscences of Brigadier General Frederick P. Munson." Interview by D. Clayton James, Washington, DC, 3 July 1971. On file at MacArthur Archives.
Willoughby, Charles A. "Oral Reminiscences of Major General Charles A. Willoughby." Interview by D. Clayton James, Naples, FL, 30 July 1971. On file at MacArthur Archives.

Journal and Magazine Articles

"A Warning Bell from a Bitter Past." *Far Eastern Economic Review*, 1 April 1974, 29.
Aldrich, Richard J. "Legacies of Secret Service: Renegade SOE and the Karen Struggle in Burma, 1948–50." In Richard J. Aldrich, Gary Rawnsley, and Ming-yeh Rawnsley, eds. *The Clandestine Cold War in Asia, 1945–65: Western Intelligence, Propaganda and Special Operations*. Special issue of *Intelligence and National Security*, vol. 14, no. 4 (Winter 1999): 130–48.
Allen, Louis. "The Nakano School." In *Proceedings of the British Association for Japanese Studies*, Sheffield, South Yorkshire: University of Sheffield, Centre for Japanese Studies, vol. 10 (1985): 9–18.
Amaha, Eriko. "Pride and Prejudice." *Far Eastern Economic Review*, 21 May 1998, 46, 49.

Finet, Nicolas. "Hainan: Du goulag à l'Eden touristique." *Le Figaro Magazine*, 13 February 1999, 65–66.

Fujii, Haruo. "Shinsetsu JCIA Boeicho Joho Honbu soshiki to katsudo zenchosa" (Total Survey of the Organization and Activities of the New JCIA, the Defense Agency's Defense Intelligence Headquarters). *Maru*, May 1997, 63–69.

Fujiwara, Iwaichi. "Boryakuka" (Covert Operations Section). *Rekishi to jinbutsu*, August 1985, 68–71.

————. "Fujiwara kikan no katsuyaku" (Activities of the Fujiwara Agency). *Rekishi to jinbutsu*, August 1985, 106–111.

Fukumoto, Kameji. "Renin to musunda Akashi taisa" (Colonel Akashi, Who Developed Ties to Lenin). Special edition of *Shukan Yomiuri*, 8 December 1956, 22–25.

Hando, Kazutoshi. "Hito kessen wo ayamaraseta mono" (What Made Us Err in the Decisive Battle of the Philippines). Roundtable discussion with Asaeda Shigeharu, Taniguchi Yoshimi, and Hori Eizo. *Rekishi to jinbutsu*, August 1986, 132–146.

"Harubin Tokumu Kikan Kaimetsu su: Nokosareta hikiage e no moten" (The Harbin Special Service Agency Destroyed. Blind Spot to Bringing Out Those Left Behind). *Shukan Yomiuri*, 7 March 1954, 44–48.

"Hoppo Ryodo, Shiberia kaihatsu ga ugokidashita naka de Yakoburefu-shi to hisoka ni atta 'sori oniwaban' 67-sai no sugao" (Portrait of the Sixty-seven-Year-Old 'Prime Minister's Guard of the Inner Garden' Who Secretly Met Mr. Yakovlev Amidst Movement on Northern Territories, Siberian Development). *Shukan Yomiuri*, 3 December 1989, 177–181.

Hymans, Henri. "Onoda: Opening Old Wounds." *Far Eastern Economic Review*, 1 April 1974, 27, 29.

Ikeda, Masuo. "Marai no harimao (tora)" (Harimao (Tiger) of Malaya). Special edition of *Shukan Yomiuri*, 8 December 1956, 85–92.

"Iketeiru Nakano Supai Gakko" (Living Nakano Spy School). *Shukan Gendai*, 2 August 1959, 32–37.

Iwakuro, Hideo. "Iwakuro Kikan shimatsusueki" (Story of the Iwakuro Agency). Special edition of *Shukan Yomiuri*, 8 December 1956, 118–121.

————. "Junbi sareteita himitsusen" (Covert War Prepared). Special edition of *Shukan Yomiuri*, 8 December 1956, 16–26.

Kadogiwa, Naohira. "'Jinsei gogo no bu' ga kizamareta seimeisen: Moto Rikugun Shoi Onoda Hiroo-shi" (Lifeline With 'Afternoon of a Life' Carved in It: Former Army Lieutenant Onoda Hiroo). Monthly column "Teso ni miru boei jinbutsuron" (Defense Person Seen in the Lines of His Palm). *Gunji Kenkyu*, October 1996, 170–171.

Kaneko, Seigo. "Annan himitsu butai" (Annam Secret Unit). Special edition of *Shukan Yomiuri*, 8 December 1956, 161–163.

Kato, Masao. "Ajia no dokuritsu undo o enshutsu shita Rikugun Nakano Gakko no 'joho senshitachi'" (Intelligence Covert Warriors at the Army Nakano School Who Put in Play the Asian Independence Movement). *Sapio*, 11 July 2001, 14–16.

Kawashima, Takenobu. "Minami Kikancho Suzuki Keiji taisa no katsuyaku" (Minami Agency Chief Colonel Suzuki Keiji's Activity). *Rekishi to jinbutsu*, September 1982, 76–83.

Kobayashi, Hisamitsu. "'Rikugun Nakano Gakko' kaku tatakaeri" (This Is How the "Army Nakano School" Fought). *Purejidento*, December 1985, 166–176.

Kuwahara, Takeshi. "Biruma sensen: Indo Kokumingun no yuto to zasetsu" (Burmese Battlefront: Ambition and Failure of the Indian National Army). *Rekishi to jinbutsu*, December 1985, 300–317.

"The Last Dinosaur." Editorial, *Far Eastern Economic Review*, 18 March 1974, 9.

Sugii, Mitsuru. "Biruma dokuritsu undo to Minami Kikan" (Burma's Independence Movement and the Minami Agency). Special edition of *Shukan Yomiuri*, 8 December 1956, 111–117.

Mori, Ei. "Tokumu kikan wa ima mo ikiteiru" (The Special Service Agencies Are Alive Even Now). *Gendai*, June 1977, 314–323.

"Nakasone shusho ga ugokasu hi 'shikaketo' no mitsumei" (The Secret Orders of the Secret "Piece" That Prime Minister Nakasone Put Into Play). *Shukan Gendai*, 20 September 1986, 62–65.

"Okay, Tojo, You Asked for It." *Yank*, 14 May 1943, 11. Collected in *Yank: The Army Weekly*, 1942–1945. Vol. II, 7 May 1943 through 31 March 1944. New York: Arm Press, 1967.

Onoda, Hiroo. "Heisei Nihonjin ni oshietai: Sabaibaru no kihon" (What I Would Like to Teach People of Heisei Japan: The Basics of Survival). *Chuo Koron*, August 1992, 232–239.

———. "Kono Michi" (This Path). Series of 100 articles published in *Tokyo Shinbun*, 13 February–14 June 1995.

"Onoda Shoi to tomo ni Firipin ni senko shita: Rikugun Nakano gakko Futamata Ikki 10-nin no unmei" (I Went Underground in the Philippines with Lieutenant Onoda: The Fate of Ten Men of the First Class of Futamata Branch, Army Nakano School). *Sande Mainichi*, 12 November 1972, 138–141.

Safire, William. "La Ronde," *New York Times*, 18 March 1974, 29.

"Shinsetsu: Rikugun Nakano Gakko" (The Truth: Army Nakano School), *Shukan Sankei*, separate issue, 1 February 1960, 35–43.

Sotooka, Hidetoshi. "Nakano OB ga kataru senso no naijitsu" (The True Story of the War Told by Nakano Old Boys). *AERA*, 10 October 1995, 22–28.

Suetsugu, Ichiro. "Gorubi rainichi de mo Hoppo Ryodo wa rakkan dekinu" (Even If Gorby Comes to Japan, I Cannot Be Optimistic about the Northern Territories). Interview by Uruma Kazumoto, editorial staff. *AERA*, 9 April 1991, 14.

Suzuki, Taisuke. "Kaisen zenya: Fuun no Bankokku" (Eve of War: The Situation in Bangkok). Special edition of *Shukan Yomiuri*, 8 December 1956, 63–69.

Tachikawa, Kyo. "Taiheiyo Senso (Daitoa Senso) no kage ni Nipputsu kyoryoku ari" (In the Shadows of the Pacific War (Great East Asia War), There Was Japanese-French Cooperation). *Securitarian*, September 2000, 50–51.

Taniguchi, Yoshimi. "Onoda moto shoi koko ni, fukuin su" (Former Lieutenant Onoda, You Are Hereby Discharged). *Kaiko*, April 1974, 5–8.

Tarora, Sadao. "Nanpogun kimitsushitsu" (Southern Army Secret Room). Special edition of *Shukan Yomiuri*, 8 December 1956, 98–102.

"The Torturing and Killing of American Prisoners in the Philippines." *Yank*, 18 February 1944. Collected in *Yank: The Army Weekly, 1942–1945*. Vol. II, 7 May 1943 through 31 March 1944. New York: Arm Press, 1967.

Tsuchihashi,Yuichi. "Furansugun wo buso kaijo" (Disarming the French Army). Special edition of *Shukan Yomiuri*, 8 December 1956, 156–160.

Yamaguchi, Hitoshi. "F Kikan Senkoki" (Record of the F Agency's Travel in Disguise). Special edition of *Shukan Yomiuri*, 8 December 1956, 70–80.

Yamamoto, Hayashi. "Kakumeiji umi wo wataru" (Child of Revolution Crosses the Sea). Special edition of *Shukan Yomiuri*, 8 December 1956, 122–127.

Yamamoto, Kenzo. "Gihohei kosaku no tenmatsu" (Circumstances of the Counterfeit Chinese Currency Operations). *Rekishi to jinbutsu*, August 1985, 103–106.

Yanagawa, Motoshige. "Jawa no beppan" (Java Annex). Special edition of *Shukan Yomiuri*, 8 December 1956, 149–155.

Yang Yong-jo. "Kim Paek-il Changgun" (General Kim Paek-il). *Kukpang Chonol*, August 1998, 79–83.

Internet Sources

Craft, Lucille. "A Voice of Reason Campaigns for the Return of Japan's Northern Territories," *Japan Times*, 3 February 2000, www.japantimes. co.jp/cgi-bin/getarticle.p15?eo20000203a1.htm.

Hakamada, Shigeki. "Japan Way Behind in Eurasian Studies, Resources." *Daily Yomiuri On-Line*, 21 January 1999, www.yomiuri.co.jp/newse/ 0121cu17.htm.

Lavigne, J.J. "Décès de Narazaki Sensei." Translated excerpt from Japanese monthly magazine *Kendo Nippon*. All Belgium Kendo Federation. http://www.bkr.be/BKR/nouvelles/Narazaki.htm.

Norris, Robert S., William M. Arkin, and William Burr. "How Much Did Japan Know?" *The Bulletin of the Atomic Scientists*, vol. 56, no. 1 (January/February 2000), www.bullatomsci.org/issues/issues/2000/jf00/jf00norrisarkin.html.

Onoda Shizenjuku (Onoda Nature Camp) www.andec.com/onoda/.

"Shinjukai Daihyo Kanji Suetsugu Ichiro kankei dantai godoso" (Joint Funeral for Organizations Related to New Leaders' Association Leader Suetsugu Ichiro), http://www.ne.jp/asahi/japan/shinjukai/leader/leader_funeral.html.

Suetsugu, Ichiro, et al. "Tairo seisaku ni kansuru kinkyu apiru" (Urgent Appeal on Russian Policy), 29 June 2001, in Kongetsu no teigen (This Month's Proposal) of the New Leaders' Association, http://www.ne.jp/asahi/japan/shinjukai/proposal/200107.html.

Video Materials

Shusen goju shunen kokumin iinkai (People's Committee on the Fiftieth Anniversary of the War's Termination). *Jiyu Ajia no eiko: Indo/Myanma dokuritsushi* (The Glory of Free Asia: History of Indian, Burmese Independence). Tokyo: Kyodo Television, 1995. Video.

Tanaka Tokuzo, director. *Rikugun Nakano Gakko: Ryusango shirei* (Army Nakano School: Order Ryu-Three). Tokyo: Daiei, 1967. Issued as one of a series in the Ichikawa Raizo special collection in Daihonei Video Museum series.

Miscellaneous Documents

Johnson, Chalmers. "The Three Cold Wars." Japan Policy Research Institute (JPRI) Occasional Paper No. 19, December 2000.

Rabson, Steve. "Assimilation Policy in Okinawa: Promotion, Resistance, and 'Reconstruction.'" JPRI Occasional Paper No. 8, October 1996.

Renkoji. *Nichi renshu Chokosan Renkoji/Renkoji Temple*. Brochure to Renkoji Temple published in Japanese and English in Japan, March 1996.

Index

About the Author

Stephen C. Mercado has written more than a dozen articles and book reviews on issues in intelligence and national security history. His writings have appeared in several publications, including *Intelligence and National Security, International Journal of Intelligence and CounterIntelligence,* and *Studies in Intelligence.* For one of his articles, he received the CIA's Studies in Intelligence Award in 2001. An Asian expert and former CIA analyst, he graduated from the University of Virginia, then earned a master's degree in international affairs from Columbia University's School of International and Public Affairs and a certificate from the university's East Asian Institute. He lives in the Washington, D.C., area.